Teach Yourself Java™ for Macintosh® in 21 Days

Laura Lemay and Charles L. Perkins

with Timothy Webster

Hayden
Books

Hayden Books

Publisher
Lyn Blake

Publishing Manager
Laurie Petrycki

Managing Editor
Lisa Wilson

Acquisitions Editors
Brian Gill, Mark Taber

Development Editor
Steve Mulder

Copy/Production Editor
Bront Davis

Technical Editor
Kevin Shay, Natural
Intelligence, Inc.

Publishing Coordinator
Rosemary Lewis

Cover Designer
Karen Ruggles

Book Designer
Sandra Schroeder

Production Team Supervisor
Laurie Casey

Production Team
Heather Butler,
Angela Calvert,
Kim Cofer,
Tricia Flodder,
Jason Hand,
Aleata Howard,
Joe Millay,
Erika Millen,
Regina Rexrode,
Erich J. Richter,
Bobbi Satterfield

Indexers
Tom Dinse
Cheryl Dietsch

Teach Yourself Java™ for Macintosh® in 21 Days

Library of Congress Catalog Number: 96-07586
ISBN: 1-56830-280-0

Warning and Disclaimer

About the Authors

Laura Lemay is a technical writer and a nerd. After spending six years writing software documentation for various computer companies in Silicon Valley, she decided writing books would be much more fun (but has still not yet made up her mind). In her spare time she collects computers, email addresses, interesting hair colors, and nonrunning motorcycles. She is also the perpetrator of *Teach Yourself Web Publishing with HTML in 14 Days* by Sams.net.

You can reach her by email at lemay@lne.com, or visit her home page at http://www.lne.com/lemay/.

Charles L. Perkins is the founder of Virtual Rendezvous, a company building a Java-based service that will foster socially focused, computer-mediated, real-time filtered interactions between people's personas in the virtual environments of the near future. In previous lives, he has evangelized NeXTSTEP, SmallTalk, and Unix, and has degrees in both physics and computer science. Before attempting this book, he was an amateur columnist and author. He's done research in speech recognition, neural nets, gestural user interfaces, computer graphics, and language theory, but had the most fun working at Thinking Machines and Xerox PARC's SmallTalk group. In his spare time, he reads textbooks for fun.

You can reach him via email at virtual@rendezvous.com, or visit his Java page at http://rendezvous.com/java.

Tim Webster is *still* employed (to everyone's continued surprise) in the demilitarized zone between design and prepress. He enjoys food and noise, and lives with his wife, Chris Corcoran, on the south side of Chicago—the baddest part of town. Tim climbed on the Mac wagon ten years ago to make posters for his band, the late, great Angry Young Men. He has been riding it for fun and profit ever since, most recently as the coauthor (with Greg Holden) of *Mastering Netscape Navigator 2.0 for Macintosh*.

Trademark Acknowledgments

Acknowledgments

From Laura Lemay:

To Sun's Java team, for all their hard work on Java the language and on the browser, and particularly to Jim Graham, who demonstrated Java and HotJava to me on very short notice in May and planted the idea for this book.

To everyone who bought my previous books, and liked them. Buy this one too.

From Charles L. Perkins:

To Patrick Naughton, who first showed me the power and the promise of OAK (Java) in early 1993.

To Mark Taber, who shepherded this lost sheep through his first book.

From Timothy Webster:

To John Dhabolt, Kevin Shay, and Roland Tokumi at Natural Intelligence, for their friendly and expert advise; to my supervisors, Julie Robinson and Roberta Baranowski, for their leadership and for the impromptu vacation; to the Hayden team, who never once complained about my whining; and to my wife, Chris Corcoran, who kept things together, as she always does.

Hayden Books

The staff of Hayden Books is committed to bringing you the best computer books. What our readers think of Hayden is important to our ability to serve our customers. If you have any comments, no matter how great or how small, we'd appreciate your taking the time to send us a note.

You can reach Hayden Books at the following:

Hayden Books
201 West 103rd Street
Indianapolis, IN 46290
(317) 581-3833

Email addresses:

| America Online: | Hayden Bks |
| Internet: | hayden@hayden.com |

Visit the Hayden Books Web site at http://www.hayden.com

Contents at a Glance

Table of Contents

Week 1

14 Windows, Networking, and Other Tidbits   327

Week 3

FOREWORD

"May you live in interesting times."

As developers, we are indeed living in interesting times. The world of computing is changing rapidly around us, and it is often difficult for hobbyists and even professionals to stay abreast of the latest technology. Books such as the one you are currently holding can go a long way toward giving you that technological edge.

Java is one of those rapidly emerging technologies that is introduced and quickly accepted, leaving many of us wondering, "What happened?" and scrambling to catch up. Fortunately, by buying this book with our Roaster CD, you have acquired two of the tools that will greatly assist you in your quest to learn Java.

Java is the first tool that programmers like yourself can use to create truly interactive, cross-platform Web content. We are all just beginning to realize the power that comes in this small package. With Java, the World Wide Web and distributed computing will never be the same!

In the summer of 1995, Natural Intelligence realized that Java was going to be a big force in the Internet industry. We also realized that a large piece of that Internet industry, the Macintosh, was being slated as nearly last priority in terms of porting plans. Natural Intelligence took advantage of that fact, and worked fast to create what we feel is the best tool out there for developing in Java: Roaster, the development environment for Java.

Roaster makes it much easier to organize, compile, and test your code. We have tried to design this product to make coding in Java as enjoyable an experience as possible. As Java developers ourselves, we intend to keep pushing the envelope with Roaster, further improving the tool and exercising the language to the full extent of its possibilities. Note that we're also developing Roaster Professional, a programming environment for developing stand-alone Java applications. We look forward to hearing suggestions from you, our users, as to how we can continue to make Java development easier and more productive. Please visit our Web site at http://www.roaster.com/ to take a look at some of our plans for Roaster and the Roaster product line.

Our users, who range in experience from C/C++ developers and HTML Web page designers to people who just want to know what all the hype is about, have been clamoring for resources for learning Java. We've evaluated all the current resources for our users, and have found that *Teach Yourself Java for Macintosh in 21 Days* is the best place for them to find all of the information they need to evaluate whether Java is for them, and if so, how to get the most out of the language. Incorporating Roaster's intuitive development environment with this excellent book was a natural fit for us, and we hope it will be the same for you.

This is truly an interesting and exciting time to be a developer.

Welcome.

The Roaster Product Team

INTRODUCTION

The World Wide Web, for much of its existence, has been a method for distributing passive information to a widely distributed number of people. The Web has, indeed, been exceptionally good for that purpose. With the addition of forms and image-maps, Web pages began to become interactive—but the interaction was often simply a new way to get at the same information. The limitations of Web distribution were all too apparent when designers began to stretch the boundaries of what the Web can do. Even other innovations, such as Netscape Navigator's server push to create dynamic animation, were merely clever tricks layered on top of a framework that wasn't built to support much other than static documents with images and text.

Enter Java, and the capability for Web pages to contain Java applets. Applets are small programs that create animation, multimedia presentations, real-time (video) games, multi-user networked games, and real interactivity—in fact, most anything a small program can do, Java applets can. Downloaded over the Net and executed inside a Web page by a browser that supports Java, applets are an enormous step beyond standard Web design.

The disadvantage of Java is that to create Java applets right now, you need to write them in the Java language. Java is a programming language, and as such, creating Java applets is more difficult than creating a Web page or a form using HTML.

That's where *Teach Yourself Java for Macintosh in 21 Days* comes in. This book teaches you all about the Java language and how to use it to create applets and stand-alone applications using Natural Intelligence's powerful Roaster Integrated Development Environment. Roaster is the product that brought Java to the Macintosh, and we think you'll find that Roaster's thoughtful, programmer-friendly features make writing in Java especially easy. By the time you get through with this book, you'll know enough about Java and Roaster to do just about anything, inside an applet or out.

Soon there will be tools and programs that will make creating Java applets even easier. Natural Intelligence's forthcoming Roaster Pro, for example, will bring Macintosh drag-and-drop simplicity to Java application development. For now, however, the only way to delve into Java is to learn the language and start playing with the raw Java code. To get the best performance from special development tools, you'll a basic foundation knowledge the Java language. This book and the Roaster IDE can give you that knowledge.

Who Should Read This Book

Teach Yourself Java for Macintosh in 21 Days is intended for people with at least some basic programming background—which includes people with years of programming experience and people with only a small amount of experience. If you understand what variables, loops, and functions are, you'll be just fine for this book. The sorts of people who might want to read this book include you, if one or more of the following is true:

☐ You're a real whiz at HTML, understand CGI programming (in MacPerl, AppleScript, Aretha/Frontier, or some other popular CGI language) pretty well, and want to move onto the next level in Web page design.

☐ You had some Basic or Pascal in school, or you've got a basic grasp of what programming is, and you've heard that Java is easy to learn, really powerful, and very cool.

☐ You've programmed C and C++ for many years, you've heard this Java thing is becoming really popular, and you're wondering what all the fuss is all about.

☐ You've heard that Java is really good for Web-based applets, and you're curious about how good it is for creating more general applications.

What if you know programming, but you don't know object-oriented programming? Fear not. *Teach Yourself Java for Macintosh in 21 Days* assumes no background in object-oriented design. If you know object-oriented programming, the first couple of days will be easy for you.

What if you're a rank beginner? This book might move a little fast for you. Java is a good language to start with, though, and if you take it slow and work through all the examples, you will be able to pick up Java and start creating your own applets.

How This Book Is Organized

Teach Yourself Java for Macintosh in 21 Days describes Java primarily in its current state—Version 1.0 API (Application Programming Interface). This is the version of Java that versions of Netscape Navigator and other browsers, such as Spyglass's Mosaic, support. A previous version of Java, the alpha API, was significantly different from the version described in this book, and the two versions are not compatible with each other.

Teach Yourself Java for Macintosh in 21 Days covers the Java language and its class libraries in 21 days, organized as three separate weeks. Each week covers a different broad area of developing Java applets and applications.

In the first week, you'll learn about the Java language itself:

☐ Day 1 is the basic introduction: what Java is and how to use the Roaster tools. You'll also create your first Java applications and applets.

☐ On Day 2, you'll explore basic object-oriented programming concepts as they apply to Java.

☐ On Day 3, you start getting down to details with the basic Java building blocks: data types, variables, and expressions such as arithmetic and comparisons.

☐ Day 4 goes into detail about how to deal with objects in Java: how to create them, how to access their variables and call their methods, and how to compare and copy them. You'll also get your first glance at the Java class libraries.

☐ On Day 5, you'll learn more about Java with arrays, conditional statements, and loops.

☐ Day 6 is the best one yet. You'll learn how to create classes, the basic building blocks of any Java program, as well as how to put together a Java application (an application being a Java program that can run on its own without a Web browser).

☐ Day 7 builds on what you learned on Day 6. On Day 7, you'll learn more about how to create and use methods, including overriding and overloading methods and creating constructors.

Week 2 is dedicated to applets and the Java class libraries:

☐ Day 8 provides the basics of applets—how they're different from applications, how to create them, and the most important parts of an applet's life cycle. You'll also learn how to create HTML pages that contain Java applets.

☐ On Day 9, you'll learn about the Java classes for drawing shapes and characters to the screen—in black, white, or any other color.

☐ On Day 10, you'll start animating those shapes you learned about on Day 9, including learning what threads and their uses are.

☐ Day 11 covers more detail about animation, adding bitmap images and audio to the soup.

☐ Day 12 delves into interactivity—handling mouse and keyboard clicks from the user in your Java applets.

☐ Day 13 is ambitious; on that day you'll learn about using Java's Abstract Window Toolkit to create a user interface in your applet including menus, buttons, checkboxes, and other elements.

☐ On Day 14, you explore the last of the main Java class libraries for creating applets: windows and dialogs, networking, and a few other tidbits.

Week 3 finishes up with advanced topics, for when you start doing larger and more complex Java programs, or when you want to learn more:

☐ On Day 15, you'll learn more about the Java language's modifiers—for abstract and final methods and classes as well as for protecting a class's private information from the prying eyes of other classes.

☐ Day 16 covers interfaces and packages, useful for abstracting protocols of methods to aid reuse and for the grouping and categorization of classes.

☐ Day 17 covers exceptions: errors and warnings and other abnormal conditions, generated either by the system or by you in your programs.

☐ Day 18 builds on the thread basics you learned on Day 10 to give a broad overview of multithreading and how to use it to enable different parts of your Java programs to run in parallel.

☐ On Day 19, you'll learn all about the input and output streams in Java's I/O library.

☐ On Day 20, we'll stop to catch our breath, and look at some advanced Roaster secrets, like debugging, auto-documenting programs, and Roaster's spiffy new HTML tools.

☐ Finally, on Day 21, you'll get an overview of some of the "behind-the-scenes" technical details of how Java works: the bytecode compiler and interpreter, the techniques Java uses to ensure the integrity and security of your programs, and the Java garbage collector.

Conventions Used in This Book

Text that you type and text that should appear on your screen is presented in `mono-space type`:

```
It will look like this.
```

to mimic the way text looks on your screen. Variables and placeholders will appear in `monospace italic`.

NOTE   A Note box presents interesting pieces of information related to the surrounding discussion, including technical details and tips.

WARNING   A Warning box advises you about potential problems and helps you steer clear of disaster.

NEW TERM   New terms are introduced in New Term boxes, with the term in italics.

 A Roaster IDE icon identifies text that pays particular attention to the Roaster environment.

The end of each chapter offers common questions asked about that day's subject matter with answers from the authors.

Web Sites for Further Information

Before, while, and after you read this book, there are a few Web sites that may be of interest to you as a Macintosh Java developer.

The official Java Web site is at http://java.sun.com/. At this site, you'll find the Java development software, the HotJava Web browser, and online documentation for all aspects of the Java language. It has several mirror sites that it lists online, and you should probably use the site "closest" to you on the Internet for your downloading and Java Web browsing. There is also a site for developer resources, called Gamelan, at http://www.gamelan.com/.

The official Roaster site is at http://www.Roaster.com/. Here you'll find news about Roaster upgrades, information about other products from Natural Intelligence, and technical support, and you'll be able to give feedback about Roaster to its developers.

Before You Begin

An Introduction to Roaster™

by Timothy Webster

We are about to embark upon a three-week journey through the basics of the Java language. We'll need some tools for our trip, so let's first prepare for our trip with a look at the Swiss army knife of Java development on the Mac: Natural Intelligence's Roaster™.

Roaster is an Integrated Development Environment, tailored for the special needs of the Java programmer. The Roaster package includes:

- ☐ A source editor—a specialized text editor with tools to handle code-specific issues, such as complicated indentation, embedded parentheses, and frequent batch-searching

- ☐ A project manager—to organize information about all the files that comprise a programming project into a single project database

- ☐ A compiler—to translate your Java source code into Java applications and applets

- ☐ A run-time environment—to run your Java programs (or sample programs from the CD-ROM or that you've downloaded from the Internet)

You can access most of Roaster's features through the Roaster IDE application. Most of the action takes place in the source code editor: Let's start our tour by launching the Roaster application and choosing File > New > New Document (Command-N). Roaster presents an empty editor window, like the one in Figure 0.1.

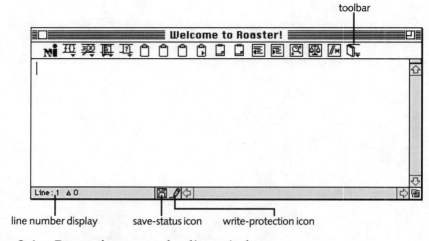

Figure 0.1 *Roaster's source code editor window.*

We'll take a closer look at the toolbar later in this introduction. Take note of the line number display at the bottom of the editor's window. You can jump to any line you like by clicking on the display and entering the desired line number.

The write-protection icon (the little pen at the bottom of the window) simply shows if the file that contains the code is locked. In this case, the file is *not* write-protected—if it were, the icon would be barred.

The save-status icon (the little disk at the bottom of the window) shows at a glance whether there are unsaved changes in a file. If you type a few characters into the editor's window, you'll see a bar appear across the icon to indicate that there are changes to the file that have not been saved to disk.

Let's run through Roaster's menus and preferences, focusing on the elements that are unique to Roaster. Then, we'll take a look at the source code editor's special toolbar.

Special Menu Features

Many of Roaster's menu commands will be familiar to Mac users—commands like Save, Undo, and Cut and Paste work in the same way they do in all Mac applications. We'll focus our attention on features that may be new to you, rather than Macintosh basics.

NOTE   Roaster supports Balloon Help. We know, some of you find balloons hokey, but Roaster's balloon comments are actually pretty helpful and well thought-out. It will be our little secret if you use it.

File Menu

We'll introduce the File > New > Class Browser and File > New > Class Tree commands later, when they'll make more sense. The File > New > Project command also appears in the Project menu, and we'll look at it in that context, later in this section.

Edit Menu

Shift Left/Shift Right: Indenting your Java code isn't strictly necessary, but using indentation to set off blocks of code makes your code easier to read. The Shift Left (Command-[) and Shift Right (Command-]) commands are easy ways to move blocks around, and they do pretty much what you'd expect: move all of the code in the selected line or lines.

Balance: It's important that things like brackets and parentheses come in pairs: Every left bracket must have a right bracket somewhere, although not necessarily on the same line. This sounds easy enough, but when you're confronted with code like

```
x = ((Math.abs(y)) + ((Math.abs(z)-1))
```

it's hard to tell at a glance if the parentheses are correct. (In the example above, they're not: There are six left parentheses and five right parentheses.) The Balance (Command-B) command highlights everything between the innermost pair of brackets or parentheses that contain the cursor, making it a little easier to see that you've grouped expressions the way you intended. This kind of feature is really nice, especially if you spent a lot of time counting parentheses through bleary eyes in the Bad Old Days of the 70s and 80s. (Please, no cranky email about punch-card readers.)

Search Menu

Roaster offers powerful (and fast) search tools. Writing code requires industrial-strength searching commands that aren't usually found in word processors. For instance, you might decide that you need to change a variable's name throughout several files. You might want to find every use of a variable or method (function) at once. You might to find instances of variables with names like x_coordinate and y_coordinate without stopping to look at things like z_coordinate. Roaster's search tools make these kinds of searches easy.

The Find Dialog Box

Take a look at Figure 0.2, which shows the Find dialog box. You can summon the Find box by choosing Find (Command-F) or Replace (Command-=) commands from the Search menu. (You'll get a smaller version of the box when you first call it; click the little outline-triangle at the bottom left side to expand the box to its full size.)

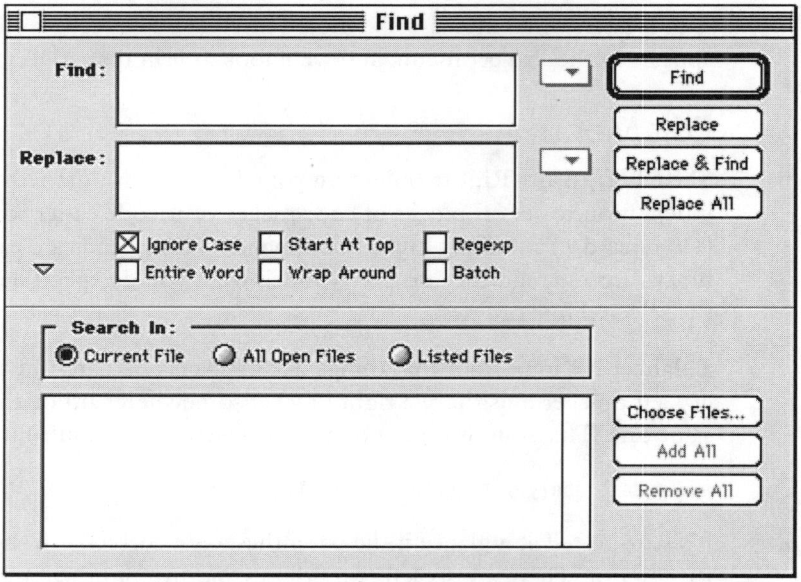

Figure 0.2   *Roaster's Find dialog box.*

Pay special attention to the Regexp and Batch checkboxes, because this is where Roaster is special. Here's how they work:

Regexp is short for "regular expression," and if you guessed that this is a term invented by Unix weenies, you're right. Basically, regular expressions use a special syntax to specify patterns, rather than strings, as the search item. For example, when the Regexp box is checked, you could search for both "thread" and "the end" by entering the "th.+d" into the search field. The "." acts as a wild card that matches any character, and the "+" indicates that any number of wild cards can appear between "th" and "d." See Appendix E, "Roaster and Regular Expressions," for a tutorial on regular expressions.

Batch searching enables you to find every instance of the search item, presenting its finding in a Messages window like the one shown in Figure 0.3, which shows the results of a search for the string "thread" in one of the demo files that comes bundled with Roaster. Each instance of "thread" is shown in the context in which it appears, and you can jump to each instance by double-clicking its icon in the Messages window.

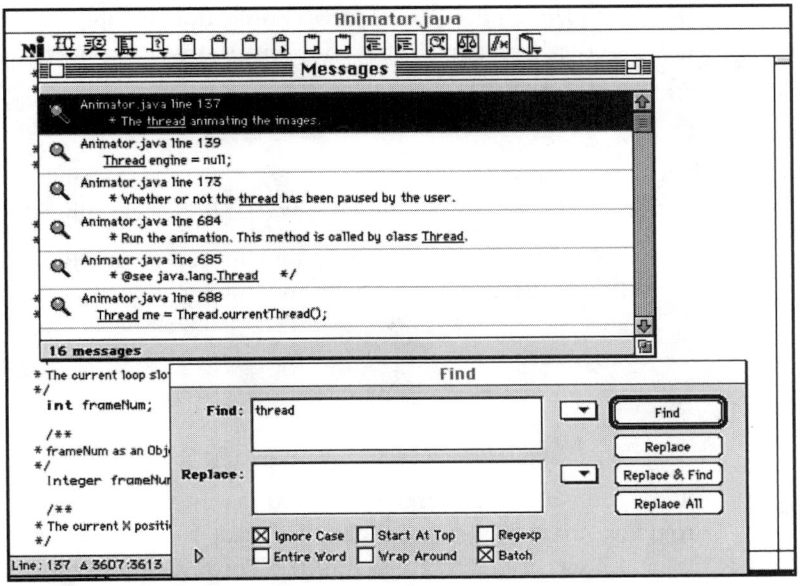

Figure 0.3   *Results of a batch search.*

The bottom half of the search box in the Find dialog box is used to specify the files to be searched. By default, Roaster searches the file in the current source editor window, but you may add as many files as you like by checking the Listed Files radio button and clicking the Choose Files button to get a standard "add" file dialog box. Clicking the All Open Files radio button adds all the open source code files to the seach list, and clicking Add All adds all of the files in the current project. You may also select files by dragging their Finder icons into the file-selection field.

Finding Class Definitions and Method Definitions

We'll explain exactly what classes and methods are in the first week of the book. Basically, these commands search for classes and methods *in the current project*. If it's not in the current project, Roaster can't find it.

Class Documentation

The Find Class Documentation (Command-Shift-') command launches your Web browser and looks up a class's documentation in HTML format in the Documentation folder in the Roaster folder hierarchy, and if it can't find it there, on Sun's Web site. Naturally, you must have a Web browser installed for this command to be useful. (Be sure to launch the Peter Lewis's public domain application Internet Config [included in the Roaster package] to specify the Web browser, such as Netscape Navigator, that you want to use.)

NOTE

If Roaster can't find a class that you know is in the Documentation folder, try typing the class's full name: for example, java.awt.Rectangle rather than just Rectangle.

You didn't hear it from your Uncle Tim, but you can use ResEdit to change the URL that Roaster uses to look for the API documentation. It's in the STR# resource with ID 128. If you don't know what ResEdit is, you probably shoudn't make this your first ResEdit project.

Project Menu

Often, you will need to create several different files when you are working on a Java program. Roaster uses special databases called *projects* to help you keep track of these files and how they relate to each other. Throughout the book, we'll show you nice little features of the project system, as we introduce new concepts, like methods and packages, that projects are designed to handle.

NOTE

Many of the commands in this section may be applied only to projects—that's why they're in the Project menu. For example, you might think that you could compile source code directly in the Editor window; in fact, you must add the code to a project before it can be compiled.

Creating New Project Files

You can create new projects by choosing Project > New Project (Command-Shift-N) or File > New > New Project (also Command-Shift-N). Roaster will prompt you to name the project immediately when you create it; by convention, project file names are suffixed with a . (Option-P) extension. Figur e 0.4 shows a newly made project window.

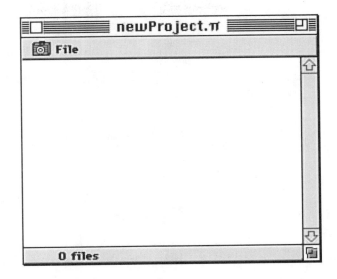

Figure 0.4   *A new, empty project window.*

You can add whatever files you like to a project, but it's really meant for source files, class (compiled source code) files, and HTML files. Once a file has been entered into a project, Roaster can compile and run it, and link it to other code in the project.

File Management

To add a file to a project, simply choose Project > Add Files, and use the dialog box provided to pick the desired files. Alternatively, you may drag the files' Finder icons into the project window, or drag files from one project window to another. Once a file has been added to a project, you may open the file in the source code editor by double-clicking the file's name.

Normally, files will appear under the <default> subhead in the Project window. As we'll see on Day 16, Java code can be organized into "packages" to organize extensive code libraries: if a source file contains the Package keyword, the package appears as a subhead, and the file appears beneath the package subhead (see Figure 0.5). You may hide the contents of a subhead by clicking the outline rectangle next to the subhead.

NOTE   You can quickly navigate a long list of projects by typing the first few letters of a project's name. Roaster will highlight the first file in the Project window whose name begins with those letters—just as in the Finder or a File dialog box.

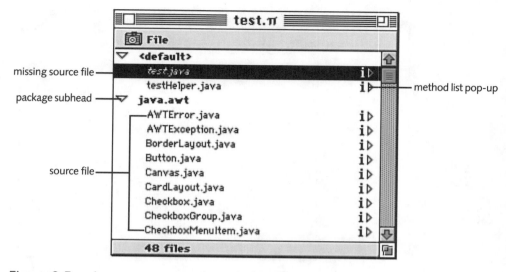

missing source file — *test.java*

package subhead — java.awt

method list pop-up

source file — Canvas.java

Figure 0.5 *A not-so-empty project window.*

If Roaster can't find a file, the file's name is listed in italic (see Figure 0.5). Roaster is pretty savvy about finding files that have been moved and renamed, but it won't update its records until the project has been closed and reopened, or until you have chosen Project > Update File Paths.

To remove a file from the project window, click it and choose Project > Remove Files or Edit > Clear.

Startup Files

When Roaster runs a project, the Applet Runner must find a subroutine called main() *somewhere*. (We'll talk about exactly what main() is on Day 2.) By default, the Runner assumes that your project is an applet, and looks for main() in the file AppletViewer.class, even if the file hasn't been added to your project. If, however, a project includes a code segment with its own main() method, and you want to run your application using your own main(), you must specify your code as the startup file. Do so by picking Projects > Set Startup File; a large arrow appears to the left of the file that you've specified as startup.

As an experiment, open the project Roaster:java:demo:ArcTest:ArcTest. and choose Project > Run. ArcTest will run as an Applet, with an Applet menu in the menu bar. Close the ArcTest applet, and in the ArcTest project window, highlight ArcTest.java and pick Projects > Set Startup File. Now run ArcTest again: you'll notice that the

ArcTest's window is of a different size, and there's no Applet menu in the menu bar. ArcTest is using its own `main()` method, rather than the one built into the Applet Runner.

(Confused? This will seem much clearer after Days 2 and 6.)

Method

You've probably noticed the little pop-up menus that appear in the project window. These pop-ups provide an easy shortcut to locations in the source files. Specifically, they point to methods definitions—what this means will become clear on Day 2. The method-list commands in this menu manage the pop-up list; you can make sure Roaster displays an up-to-date pop-up with Project > Update Method List and remove the pop-up altogether with Project > Clear Method List.

Compile and Make

The Compile and Make commands translate Java source code into Virtual Machine-readable bytecodes. Both commands act upon the file that's highlighted in the project window. We'll explain this further (and you'll compile some code) on Day 1.

Enable Debugger

The Debugger is a special tool that you'll use to find problems with your Java code; we'll explain the Debugger on Day 20. Roaster's Debugger is still under development, and the Enable Debugger command is grayed out in the DR2 release of Roaster. A future version of Roaster will support full debugging.

Run

The Run command runs the current project. If any files haven't been compiled and the "Make all before run" preference is turned on, Roaster will compile them before running the project.

You may also run files by dragging the project file's icon onto the Applet Runner, or, if the project includes an HTML file, by dragging the HTML file onto the Runner.

Go ahead and try out the demo files that you'll find in the Roaster:java:demo folder (I'm especially fond of GraphLayout).

Debug Menu

As we mentioned in the discussion of the Project menu, the Debugger has been disabled in Roaster DR2. We'll give you a preview of the Debugger on Day 20.

Windows Menu

The commands in the Windows menu are fairly self-explanatory, and very handy. Every window that's open in Roaster will appear in the Windows menu, and if you have several windows open and on top of each other, it's often easiest to find the window you want by selecting it from the menu.

If you prefer to look at the windows one by one without taking your hands from the keyboard, you can choose Windows > Next Window and Windows > Previous Window with Command-Tab and Command-Shift-Tab respectively.

Scripts Menu

NOTE   If you're interested in learning more about how to program in AppleScript and Frontier/Aretha, you might check out *The Tao of AppleScript,* by Derrick Schneider (Hayden Books) and *Applied Mac Scripting,* by Tom Trinko (M & T Books). You might find Aretha/Frontier's syntax more similar to that of Java, but you'll probably be able to find more documentation on how to use AppleScript.

Roaster's IDE is fully scriptable, and if you're familiar with AppleScript or Frontier, you can automate many common procedures in the development process. Even if you don't script, you'll probably find the ready-made scripts included with Roaster useful.

The Roaster folder hierarchy contains a Scripts folder; any AppleScript or Frontier script that you drop into this folder will appear in Roaster's Scripts menu. To run the script, simply choose it from the menu.

As an experiment, open the Roaster:java:demo:Animator:Animator. pr oject file and choose Scripts > Run with Netscape Navigator™ (assuming, of course, that you have a Java-capable version of Navigator installed on your Mac). Roaster launches Navigator for you, and loads the applet into Navigator.

You may also execute AppleScript code directly in the source code editor window. For example, enter

```
//    display dialog "Hello, World."
```

in the source code editor window and select it, excluding the comment characters (//) from the selection. Choose Scripts > Run Selection in AppleScript (Command-Return). Voilà. AppleScript presents a dialog box containing your message, as seen in Figure 0.6.

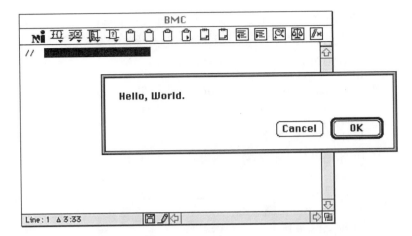

Figure 0.6   *Executing an AppleScript from within the source code editor.*

Preferences

Many of Roaster's preferences will seem a little cryptic until you've spent some time working with Roaster and Java. We'll discuss some of these settings as they become relevant—especially the project preferences—but you might want to check back at the end of Week 2, when most of the preference options will seem self-apparent.

Editor

Most of the editor preferences don't need explanation, but there are a few options that may be unfamiliar to you.

If you've played around with the source code editor, you might have noticed that when you type a right parenthesis or bracket, the matching left-parenthesis is briefy highlighted. If you type a right parenthesis or bracket that has no mate, the editor beeps at you. This is called "kissing," and it drives some people crazy, so you can turn it off, if you like.

Because it's standard practice to organize blocks of code by indentation, Roaster automatically indents a new line to match the indentation of the previous line. If, for some reason, auto-indentation is counterproductive for a particular task, you may turn this feature off.

Text Styles

One of the very nice features of Roaster is support for text styles, which give you visual feedback about the correctness of your Java code. The source code editor "knows" the reserved keywords in the Java language, and after you've typed one, Java bolds the word in blue automatically. For example, if you type

```
final static int MY_CONSTANT = new int;
```

the Roaster source code editor will bold the reserve words `final`, `static`, `int`, and `new` for you, thus:

```
final static int MY_CONSTANT = new int;
```

(This assumes that you've saved your file with the .java extension to its name—if the file is unsaved, Roaster won't mark it.) Java is case-sensitive, and it's quite easy to type "Final" for "final," which is wrong. Because Roaster won't mark "Final," you'll have an instant clue that something is wrong. After you've worked with Roaster for a while, you'll pick up on these kinds of subtle signals immediately.

If you prefer to mark reserved words in some other way—by displaying them in a different color, or with underlined type, or whatever you like—you may do so in the Text Styles Preferences. Simply click the word "keyword" in the scrolling list at the top of the box, and choose the text effect you want.

Another common typing mistake is to leave strings unterminated. In a statement like

```
g.drawString("Hello, World",100,100);
```

(which means "draw the string "Hello, World" at screen coordinates 100,100"), it's vitally important to distinguish the string from coordinates. If you forget to close the string with the " (straight, or dumb, quote) character, like this

```
g.drawString("Hello, World, 100,100);
```

the compiler will interpret the whole line, and all of the subsequent lines of the program (up to the next " character), as one giant string that begins "Hello World..." It's not hard to see why this is a Bad Thing.

To help solve this problem, the source code editor marks unterminated strings by displaying them in red. Once you've terminated the string with a second " character, the string turns gray. As with reserved words, you can specify how Roaster signifies unterminated and terminated strings in the Text Styles Preferences dialog box.

User Keywords

You may also specify your own keywords to be marked by the source code editor. Most likely, you will choose things like names of variables and classes that you use in several programming projects, but you can be as arbitrary as you like: It's perfectly legal to make, say, "Charles" or "weasel" user keywords, even if you don't use them to name parts of your programs. To specify your own keywords, simply type them into the field in the User Keywords dialog box.

By default, user keywords are marked with bold blue type. You can have the editor mark them any way you like, by changing the Text Styles (*not* User Keyword) preferences.

File Types

Actually, Roaster is subtle enough to mark different files in different ways: It bolds Java keywords in Java files, C/C++ keywords in C/C++ files, and HTML keywords in HTML files. Roaster determines the type of the file by looking at the extension on the file's name, and looking up the extension in the table in File Types preferences dialog. If the file has no extension, Roaster assumes it's a plain text file.

Figure 0.7 shows how this system works: Each of three files shown contains the same code, but each file is named with a different extension. As you can see, the editor marks only the keywords appropriate to the language: #include, which is a keyword in C but not Java, is bolded in only the c-syntax.c window.

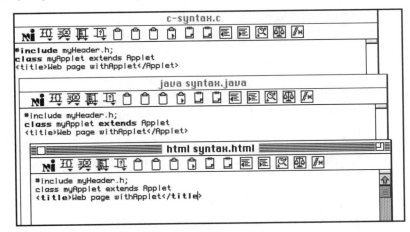

Figure 0.7 *Roaster can mark a file using Java, C/C++, or HTML syntax.*

Compiler

Roaster actually ships with *two* compilers: an implementation of Sun's javac compiler, and Natural Intelligence's own Roaster compiler. Early implementations of the Roaster compiler aren't quite perfect; it's best to use javac, especially if you plan to distribute your Java applications and applets to users on other platforms. The Roaster compiler has been included with early releases of the package to show you how wicked-fast it is: You might want to try compiling something like the Neko applet on Day 11 with both compilers to see just how dramatic the difference really is.

Project

The Startup File field shows the name of the file that contains the `main()` method—see the discussion of the Project menu in the previous section for an explanation of what this means. You can type in a name here, if you like, but it's easier to avoid typos if you use the Project > Set Startup File command instead.

We'll cover the Arguments for `main()` field on Day 6, when it will make a great deal more sense.

The Application Name and Application Creator fields are really placeholders for functionality that will be implemented in the future. They specify the attributes of stand-alone Mac applications, which cannot be created with the current Roaster package.

Class Paths

The Class Paths preferences enable you to let Roaster know about Java files that you have stored, for whatever reason, outside the Roaster folder hierarchy.

Roaster (and Netscape Navigator) can read class libraries that have been stored in ZIP archives (the DOS/Windows equivalent of StuffIt or Compact Pro archives) *without* unZIPping the archive. This is a really convenient feature, especially when you're dealing with libraries that contain dozens or even hundreds of files. You may add such archives to Roaster's "collection" with the Add Library button or by dragging the archive from the Finder into the Class Paths field. Likewise, you can add a folder full of files with the Add Folder button or by dragging the folder into the Class Paths field.

The Source Code Editor Toolbar

Some of the items in the source code editor toolbar provide an alternate path to commands available through Roaster's menus; some items are unique to the toolbar. The toolbar is completely configurable, as we'll see below; you can add and remove icons to suit your needs.

NOTE   If you've forgotten what a particular icon means, hold the cursor over it—after a second or two, a mnemonic label appears over the icon.

NI

The NI icon enables you to configure the toolbar and to set up hot-key shortcuts for other toolbar commands. Let's add the QuickFormat icon to your icon bar, since it may not be there already, and then set up a keyboard shortcut for it.

Choose Configure Toolbar from the NI icon menu. You'll see a scrolling list of icon names. Scroll down to QuickFormat, and drag the name into the icon bar. Naturally, it becomes an icon.

Now choose Configure HotKeys from the NI icon menu. Click the QuickFormat icon, and it the word "Format" appears in the Commands column of the HotKeys table. Click "Format" to select it, and press the key combination of your choice (say, Command-F1) to designate your shortcut. (Make sure you don't use a shortcut that's already built into Roaster, like Command-S.)

 ## Methods

The Methods icon provides a quick shortcut to the methods defined in the source code in the current window. What's a method, you ask? We'll cover that on Day 2.

 ## Zip Find

The Zip Find icon is similar to the batch search option provided by Search > Find. To use Zip Find, choose Configure Zip Find from the icon's menu, and enter the search string. If you'd like to search for a regular expression (as mentioned in the section above and detailed in Appendix E), check the Use Zip Grep box.

Now, take another look at the Zip Find icon's menu: All of the instances of the search term now appear in the menu, along with the context in which they appear. Neat, eh?

 ## Macros

The Macros icon enables you to store commonly used expressions and quickly insert them into your code. We'll take a detailed look at macros on Day 20.

File Formats

The File Formats icon enables you to quickly change the format of your source code from Mac text to Windows or Unix text, so you can distribute your files to users on other platforms. The main difference between text file formats on these platforms is the character used to indicate the ends of lines: Macs use a carriage return, DOS/Windows uses linefeeds, and Unix uses both.

You don't really need to change your source code's format; text editors on other platforms can read it whether you convert it or not, and as we'll see on Day 1, Java compilers ignore things like carriage returns and linefeeds anyway. You change the source code's file format for the benefit of humans, so your intricately structured indentation isn't lost when your file is opened on another platform.

NOTE

> Actually, if your file is commented, and it probably should be, parts of your Java code may become comments (or vice versa) if the line breaks get weird. It's a good idea not to change file formats, just to be absolutely safe.

 ## Clipboards

Roaster's clipboards are a really convenient feature. They act in almost exactly the same way as the Mac's system clipboard, but you can have as many clipboards as you like. This makes it easy to grab several parts of one file and move them into a second file, without moving back and forth between files several times.

Roaster's clipboards add an *append* command to basic Mac clipboard functionality. If you choose Append from the clipboard's menu, the contents of the current selection are appended to the end of the contents of the clipboard. You can also move material back and forth between the Mac's system clipboard and Roaster clipboards—naturally, the Mac clipboard can hold only one Roaster clipboard at a time.

 ## Bookmarks

Bookmarks enable you to save your place in a source code file. When you click a bookmark, it stores the current location, and a paperclip figure is added to the bookmark icon. Clicking a stored bookmark returns to the saved location. To clear a bookmark, Option-click it.

Shift Left/Shift Right

The Shift Left and Shift Right icons provide exactly the same functionality as the Edit > Shift Left (Command-[) and Edit > Shift Right (Command-]) commands.

 ## Quick Search

The Quick Search tool finds the next occurrence of the highlighted text. (It won't do anything if no text is selected.) If you hold down the the Option key when you click the icon, Quick Search will find the previous occurrence of the highlighted text. In either case, if Quick Search can't find a match for the selection, it will beep.

Balance

The Balance command provides exactly the same functionality as the Edit > Balance (Command-B) menu command. (It will even balance HTML tag pairs like <STRONG></STRONG> if you're working on a file named with an .html extension.)

 ## Comment

Java enables you to mark your comments with special characters so that the compiler doesn't interpret them as part of the Java code. (You've already seen a comment—the AppleScript that we ran from inside the source code editor field was "commented out.")

You can always use the basic comment characters by manually typing them into the editor, like this:

```
y += x;   // add x to y
```

where y += x; is actual code, and add x to y is a comment, or

```
/*
 *    ...it is a book too mad to read
 *    before one merely reads to pass the time.
 */
```

where all four lines are comments. (You'll notice that the source code editor marks all comments in red.)

The Comment icon is a shortcut to adding comment characters by hand. When you click it, all the selected text is commented out.

NOTE Sometimes when you're working on a project, it's helpful to comment out lines to see what happens when they're gone. You can uncomment lines that you've commented this purpose by highlighting the lines and Command-clicking the Comment icon.

QuickFormat

One click of the QuickFormat icon formats your text with a standard form of notation, indenting and separating the blocks of code to make your program read more easily. Note that the QuickFormat uses a slightly different convention than we do in this book—it will break brackets onto the next line, like this:

```
if (myCondition)
    {
```

where we usually keep brackets on the line before, like this:

```
if (myCondition) {
```

This is purely a matter of taste and habit.

Other Toolbar Tools

The real beauty of the toolbar is in its extensibility. You don't need to wait for a new release of Roaster to add useful new features; new tools can be added to the framework of the Roaster environment as soon as the tool is developed.

For example, as this book went to press, Natural Intelligence released a new "Wizard" tool that creates templates for object and method code. If you'd like to try it (you might want to wait a few days, when you'll know what objects and methods are), simply add it to the toolbar.

(While you're looking around, you may notice that Roaster has a full complement of HTML processing tools. These "plug-ins" make Roaster a formidable HTML editor, as we'll see on Day 20. In the meantime, feel free to play around with these HTML gadgets.)

Summary

As you work through this book, you'll quickly become accustomed to the Roaster environment. We think you'll find that Roaster's special features make the Java learning curve much less steep, and the process of programming more enjoyable. Keep an eye out for the Roaster icon in the margins, which we've used to mark passages of special interest to Roaster users.

Now that we've had a look at the Roaster IDE, we're ready to start our tour of the Java language. On Day 1, we'll look at the basic principles behind Java, and you'll use the tools you learned about in this section to create your own working applets and applications. In subsequent chapters, we'll learn more about the building blocks of the Java language.

Week 1

☐ **An Introduction to Java Programming**
Platform-independence
The Roaster IDE

☐ **Object-Oriented Programming and Java**
Objects and classes
Encapsulation
Modularity

☐ **Java Basics**
Java statements and expressions
Variables and data types
Comparisons and logical operators

☐ **Working with Objects**
Testing and modifying instance variables
Converting objects

☐ **Arrays, Conditionals, and Loops**
Conditional tests
Iteration
Block statements

☐ **Creating Classes and Applications in Java**
Defining constants, instance and class variables, and methods

☐ **More About Methods**
Overloading methods
Constructor methods
Overriding methods

An Introduction to Java Programming

by Laura Lemay with Timothy Webster

 Hello and welcome to *Teach Yourself Java for Macintosh in 21 Days*! Starting today and for the next three weeks you'll learn all about the Java language and how to use it to create Web-ready applets and stand-alone applications that anyone with Roaster can run with Natural Intellience, Inc.'s Roaster Integrated Development Environment. When Natural Intelligence releases Roaster Pro in mid-1996, you'll be able to create truly stand-alone programs with Java—programs just like any other Macintosh applications.

NEW TERM

An *applet* is a dynamic and interactive program that can run inside a Web page displayed by a Java-capable browser such as HotJava or Netscape Navigator.

The *HotJava browser* is a World Wide Web browser used to view Web pages, follow links, and submit forms. It can also download and play applets on the reader's system.

Learning to create applets is the overall goal for the next three weeks. Today, the goals are somewhat more modest, and you'll learn about the following:

- [ ] What exactly Java and Roaster are, and their current status

- [ ] Why you should learn Java—its various features and advantages over other programming languages

- [ ] Getting started programming in Java—what you'll need in terms of software and background, as well as some basic terminology

- [ ] How to create your first Java programs—to close this day, you'll create an application and a simple Java applet with Roaster!

What Is Java?

Java is an object-oriented programming language developed by Sun Microsystems, a company best known for its high-end Unix workstations. Modeled after C++, the Java language was designed to be small, simple, and portable across platforms and operating systems, both at the source and at the binary level (more about this later).

 The Roaster Integrated Development Environment is a set of tools, including a compiler, a programming-savvy text editor, a debugger, and an applet player, designed to help you create applets on your Macintosh. The version of Roaster on the CD included with this book has all the functionality you will need in order to learn Java, work with the examples in this book, and experiment with writing your own programs.

To create an applet, you write it in the Java language, compile it using Roaster's compiler tool, and refer to that applet in your HTML Web pages. You put the resulting HTML and Java files on a Web site much in the same way that you make ordinary HTML and image files available. Then, when someone using a Java-aware browser views your page with the embedded applet, the browser downloads the applet to the local system and executes it. The reader can view and interact with your applet in all its glory (readers using non-Java browsers won't see the applet). You'll learn more about how applets, browsers, and the World Wide Web work together later on in this book.

The important thing to understand about Java is that you can do so much more with it besides create applets. Java was written as a full-fledged programming language, and when a complete set of tools have been developed for the MacOS platform, you will be able to accomplish the same sorts of tasks and solve the same sorts of problems that you can in other programming languages, such as C or C++. (Roaster Professional is Natural Intelligence's forthcoming software product that will enable you to create stand-alone Java applications; take a look at the Roaster home page at http://www.Roaster.com/ for more information about its release.)

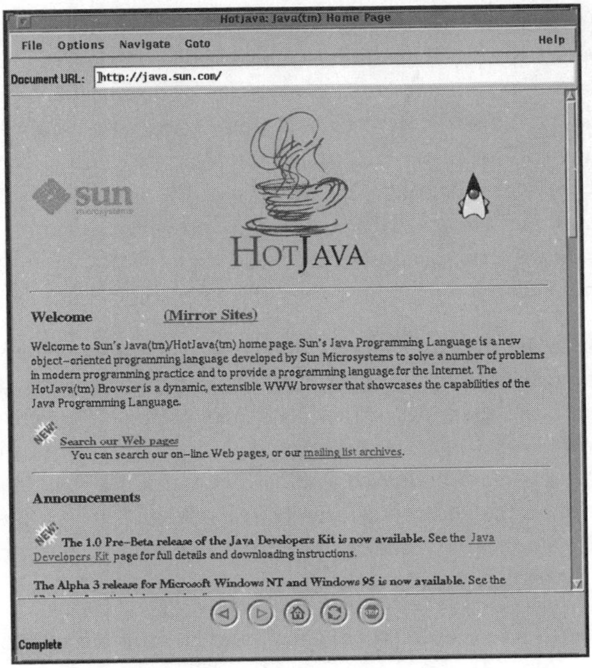

Figure 1.1   *The HotJava browser.*

Java's Past, Present, and Future

The Java language was developed at Sun Microsystems in 1991 as part of a research project to develop software for consumer electronics devices—television sets, VCRs, toasters, and the other sorts of machines you can buy at any department store. Java's goals at that time were to be small, fast, efficient, and easily portable to a wide range of hardware devices. It is those same goals that made Java an ideal language for distributing executable programs via the World Wide Web, and also a general-purpose programming language for developing programs that are easily usable and portable across different platforms.

The Java language was used in several projects within Sun, but did not get very much commercial attention until it was paired with HotJava. HotJava was written in 1994 in a matter of months, both as a vehicle for downloading and running applets and also as an example of the sort of complex application that can be written in Java.

At the time this book is being written, Sun has released version 1.0 of the Java Developer's Kit (JDK), which includes tools for developing Java applets and applications on Sun systems running Solaris 2.3 or higher for Windows NT and for Windows 95. *Just* as the book went to press, Sun released a beta version of the JDK for Mac—the Sun JDK does not include a version of HotJava or any development tools, just a compiler and applet viewer. Natural Intelligence developed Roaster as a third-party implementation of the Java Virtual Machine, along with a full-featured development environment, Java, using the language specification that Sun has freely distributed on the Net.

Note that the Java specification is still in a state of development and subject to changes between releases. Applets and applications that you write using the JDK and using the examples in this book may require some changes to work with future versions of and Java-savvy browsers. However, because the Java language has been around for several years and has been used for several projects, the language itself is quite stable and robust and most likely will not change excessively. However, keep Java's provisional status in mind as you read through this book and as you develop your own Java programs.

Until very recently, the Applet Runner program included with the Roaster package and Sun's Applet Viewer were the only ways to view applets on the Mac. However, just as this book was going to press, Netscape Communications released a public beta of a Java-capable Macintosh version of their popular Navigator 2.0 browser (which already supported Java on other platforms). You can download the Java-capable beta of Navigator from Netscape's site at http://home.netscape.com. Microsoft has licensed Java and will most likely support applets in a future release of its Internet Explorer browser. It's a safe bet that before long, no self-respecting Web browser will be without Java capability. Roaster's Applet Runner is also a perfectly adequate tool for previewing how your applets will behave inside a browser window. Take a peek at Duke, Java's mascot in the Applet Runner window in Figure 1.2.

Figure 1.2   *Greetings from Sun Microsystems, Inc.*

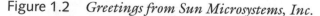

Why Learn Java?

At the moment, probably the most compelling reason to learn Java—and probably the reason you bought this book—is that applets for the World Wide Web are written in Java. Even if that were not the case, Java as a language has significant advantages over other languages and other programming environments that make it suitable for just about any programming task. This section describes some of those advantages.

Java Is Platform-Independent

Platform-independence is one of the most significant advantages that Java has over other programming languages, particularly for systems that need to work on many different platforms. Java is platform-independent at both the source and the binary level.

NEW TERM
> *Platform-independence* is a program's capability of moving easily from one computer system to another.

At the source level, Java's primitive data types have consistent sizes across all development platforms. Java's foundation class libraries make it easy to write code that can be moved from platform to platform without the need to rewrite it to work with that platform.

Platform-independence doesn't stop at the source level, however. Java binary files are also platform-independent and can run on multiple platforms without the need to recompile the source. How does this work? Java binary files are actually in a form called bytecodes.

NEW TERM
> *Bytecodes* are a set of instructions that looks a lot like some machine codes, but that is not specific to any one processor

Normally, when you compile a program written in C or in most other languages, the compiler translates your program into machine codes or processor instructions. Those instructions are specific to the processor your computer is running—so, for example, if you compile your code on a Macintosh, the resulting program will run only on other Macintoshes. If you want to use the same program on a Windows machine, you have to go back to your original source code, get a compiler for that particular version of Windows, and recompile your code. Figure 1.3 shows the result of this system: multiple executable programs for multiple systems.

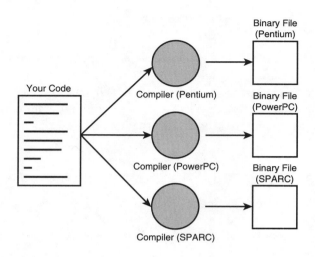

Figure 1.3   *Traditional compiled programs.*

Things are different when you write code in Java. The Java development environment has two parts: a Java compiler and a Java interpreter. The Java compiler takes your Java program and instead of generating machine codes from your source files, it generates bytecodes.

To run a Java program, you run a program called a bytecode interpreter, which in turn executes your Java program (see Figure 1.4). You can either run the interpreter by itself, or—for applets—use the bytecode interpreter built into Java-capable browsers to run the applet for you.

Why go through all the trouble of adding this extra layer of the bytecode interpreter? Having your Java programs in bytecode form means that instead of being specific to any one system, your programs can run on any platform and any operating or window system as long as the Java interpreter is available. This capability of a single binary file to be executable across platforms is crucial to what enables applets to work, because the Web itself is also platform-independent. Just as HTML files can be read on any platform, so applets can be executed on any platform that is a Java-capable browser.

The disadvantage of using bytecodes is in execution speed. Because system-specific programs run directly on the hardware for which they are compiled, they run significantly faster than Java bytecodes, which must be processed by the interpreter. For most Java programs, the speed will not be an issue—they'll still be faster than the user.

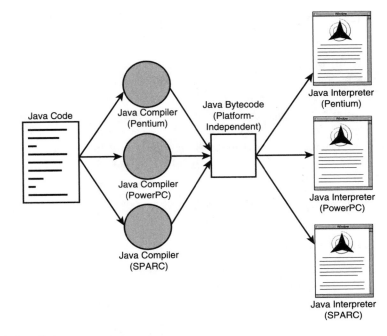

Figure 1.4   *Java programs.*

If you write programs that *do* require more execution speed than the Java interpreter can provide, you will (eventually) have two solutions available to you.

☐ You can write parts of your program in native code and incorporate these fast native routines into your Java program (this option, called "linking to native methods," will not be supported by the first commercial version of Roaster or Sun's JDK for the Mac). Future implementations of Roaster will support linking to native methods.

☐ You can use the Natural Intelligence's forthcoming Roaster Pro application to save your entire Java application as compiled native code for MacOS or Windows.

Note that by using either of these solutions, you lose the portability that Java byte-codes provide. See the Roaster Web site at http://www.Roaster.com for information about support for native methods and Roaster Pro release information.

Java Is Object-Oriented

To some, object-oriented programming (OOP) technique is merely a way of orga-nizing programs, and it can be accomplished using any language. Working with a real object-oriented language and programming environment, however, enables you to take full advantage of object-oriented methodology and its capabilities of creating flexible, modular programs and reusing code.

Many of Java's object-oriented concepts are inherited from C++, the language on which it is based, but it borrows many concepts from other object-oriented languages as well. Like most object-oriented programming languages, Java includes a set of class libraries that provide basic data types, system input and output capabilities, and other utility functions. These basic classes are part of the Java development kit, which also has classes to support networking, common Internet protocols, and user interface toolkit functions. Because these class libraries are written in Java, they are portable across platforms as all Java applications are.

You'll learn more about object-oriented programming and Java tomorrow.

Java Is Easy to Learn

In addition to its portability and object-orientation, one of Java's initial design goals was to be small and simple, and therefore easier to write, easier to compile, easier to debug, and, best of all, easy to learn. Keeping the language small also makes it more robust because there are fewer chances for programmers to make difficult-to-find mistakes. Despite its size and simple design, however, Java still has a great deal of power and flexibility.

Java is modelled after C and C++, and much of the syntax and object-oriented structure is borrowed from C++. If you are familiar with C++, learning Java will be particularly easy for you, because you have most of the foundation already.

Although Java looks similar to C and C++, most of the more complex parts of those languages have been excluded from Java, making the language simpler without sacrificing much of its power. There are no pointers in Java, nor is there pointer arithmetic. Strings and arrays are real objects in Java. Memory management is automatic. To an experienced programmer, these omissions may be difficult to get used to, but to beginners or programmers who have worked in other languages, they make the Java language far easier to learn.

Getting Started with Programming in Java

Enough background! Let's finish off this day by using Roaster to create a genuine Java applet, "HelloWorld," and a stand-alone Java application. Both these programs are extremely simple, but the procedure will give you an idea of what an applet looks like and how to compile and run it.

Applets and Applications

Java programs fall into two main groups: applets and applications.

Applets, as you have learned, are Java programs that are downloaded over the World Wide Web and executed by a Web browser on the reader's machine. Applets depend on a Java-capable browser or Roaster's Applet Runner in order to run. Java applications are more general programs written in the Java language. Java applications don't require a browser to run, but they do require a Java run-time system—in this case, Roaster's Applet Runner. Different platforms and packages may implement Java differently; the point is, "stand-alone" applications won't run on computers that do not have the Java virtual machine installed.

Installing the Software

Ready? It's *very* simple:

1. Make sure that there's at least 35 MB free on your hard drive.

2. Boot up the Roaster CD-ROM and drag the Roaster™ folder onto your hard drive. Go get a cup of coffee—no pun intended—it will take 10 to 15 minutes for all the files to transfer.

3. Restart your Mac to load the new extension. Because you just added hundreds of new files to your directory, you might as well rebuild your desktop by holding down ⌘-Option as your Mac reboots.

4. Start Roaster by double-clicking the Roaster IDE icon.

NOTE   We've included copies of all the examples in this book on the CD-ROM. The CD-ROM also contains a project called TestFile.java, which you can play around with all you like, experimenting with writing your own applets or testing smaller code examples scattered throughout this book.

Creating Your First Applet

HelloWorld isn't exactly Adobe Photoshop.... The idea behind the exercise is to give you an opportunity to practice using the Roaster tools, not illustrate exactly what's going on in the applet. You'll use several different tools and create several different files, and these parts will work together to print the message "Hello, World!" in the Applet Runner window.

Part One: The Project File

The central repository for all the code that comprises your applet is called a project file. It's important that the part of the project file's name before the extension matches the names of the source file (described below) and the name of the applet, as it's defined in the code; Roaster uses this information to find all the necessary files when it loads a project. By convention, project files' names are appended with the .π (Option-P) suffix. We've included finished project files for all the exercises in the book, because you won't be able to create and modify project files with the limited version of Roaster.

Part Two: The Source Code

Source code for all the examples in this book are included on the CD-ROM. If you really want to learn how to program in Java, however, it's a good idea to type out lots of code, so that you can take a good look at it and how it's constructed. We *strongly* suggest that you enter the text of examples into TestFile.java. You'll need to substitute "TestFile" the name of your Java classes—we'll remind you the first few times.

If you're working with the full version of Roaster, create a new source file by choosing New (⌘-N) from the File menu. Remember, it's important to save this file with the same name as your project file and your program. By convention, source code file names are appended with the .java suffix.

Start typing. Here's the source for HelloWorld:

```
 1:  import java.applet.*;
 2:  import java.awt.*;
 3:
 4:  public class HelloWorld extends Applet {
 5:
 6:    public void paint(Graphics g) {
 7:      g.drawString("Hello World!",100,100);
 8:      System.out.println("Hello again.");
 9:    }
10:  }
```

If you're working in TestFile.java, line 4 should be:

```
 4:  public class TestFile extends Applet {
```

WARNING   The numbers before each line are part of the listing and not part of the program; they're there so I can refer to specific line numbers when I explain what's
going on in the program. Do not include them in your own file.

Java is, sadly, case-sensitive and picky about punctuation. Be sure to type in the
code (without the line numbers) exactly as it is listed above. Indentation and line
breaks are more flexible—the Java compiler simply ignores spaces and returns.

If you're working with TestFile.java, the source file has already been added to
the TestFile project. If you're working with the full version of Roaster, choose
Add File (⌘-A) from the Project folder, or drag-and-drop the source file into
the project window. Figure 1.5 shows what your project window should look
like when you're done.

Figure 1.5   *The project window, with all the parts in place.*

Part Three: The HTML File

Applet Runner isn't an HTML browser, but you'll need to feed it an HTML file
anyway. Why? Some applets—in fact, many applets—take information (called "parameters," which we'll discuss on Day 6) from the HTML file. The essential HTML
you'll need to give to Applet Runner is:

```
<title>HelloWorld</title>
<applet code=HelloWorld.class width=200 height=400></applet>
```

That's it, gentle reader. If you poke around in the demo files in the Java folder that
came with Roaster, you'll notice that there's significantly more HTML; you'll also
notice that Applet Runner ignores everything but these tags, anyway. (The demo files

originated with the Sun JDK.) We've already created the HTML files for all the applets described in this book, and included them in the folders along with the projects and source code.

You'll note that all the HTML files that go along with the projects on the CD are called example1.html; with the current release of Roaster, you need to use this filename if you want to run your applet from within the Roaster IDE. However, by dragging an HTML file onto the Applet Runner's icon in the Finder, or by launching the Applet Runner directly, you can use an HTML file with any name (as long as it contains the <APPLET> tag as described above, and the Java class file it refers to is in the correct location). If you try to run your applet from within the IDE and there is no file called example1.html in the project's folder, the Applet Runner will quit immediately after it launches.

Part Four: The Compiler

There are several ways to compile your files. You may do so from the project window or the source file window, but in either case, the project file window must be open.

You can ask the compiler to compile only those files in your project that have been changed since the last time you compiled the project; do this by choosing Make (⌘-M) from the Project menu. If you want the compiler to compile the files that are selected in the Project menu, choose Compile (⌘-K) from the Project menu. Even the best compilers can be stupid about these kinds of things, and it might not realize you've changed a file... in which case, Make won't do anything. Just choose Compile.

If you've made any typing mistakes—and it's easy to do—the compiler will provide you with some sort of terse little error message. Figure 1.6 shows what happens if you forget the right parenthesis in line 6 and the semicolon in line 7.

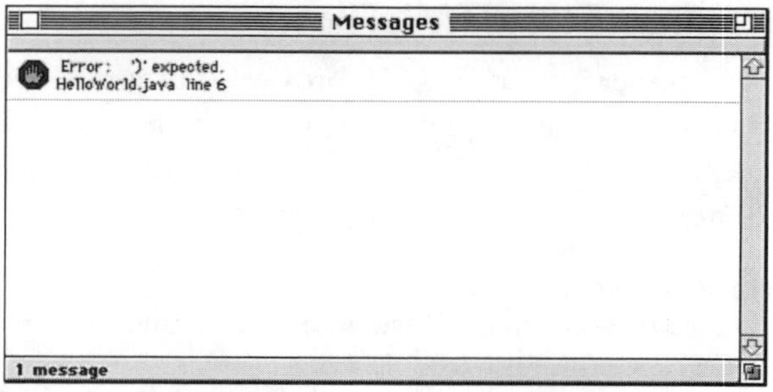

Figure 1.6   *Compiler error messages.*

The compiler hasn't noticed yet that the semicolon is missing. It will find the problem on the next pass, once you've fixed the parenthesis. Sometimes, a single mistake on the order of a missing parenthesis will generate four or five error messages. Welcome to the world of programming!

Roaster makes this process slightly more bearable. If you double-click an error message, Roaster will take you to the place in the source file where it thinks it has found the problem. Sometimes it's wrong about the location, but the problem code is usually nearby.

You can probably track down any mistakes that you've made in HelloWorld... there's not much code there. When the code is perfect, the compiler window will simply disappear. (You will learn to appreciate this moment.)

Take a look in the folder that contains the project and source file. You'll find a new file called HelloWorld.class. Open it if you like—it contains the famous Java bytecodes—we'll explain them in agonizing detail on Day 21.

Part Five: The Applet Runner

After you have all the pieces in place, it's time to run your applet. There are three easy ways to do so:

☐ Choose Run from the Project menu.

☐ Drag the project's HTML file onto the Applet Runner icon.

☐ Drag the project's project file onto the Applet Runner icon.

There's no comparative advantage to any of these approaches. Figure 1.7 shows the resulting applet.

Figure 1.7   *HelloWorld in all its glory.*

Part Six: The AppletViewer.log

"Hey!" you're probably asking yourself, "what happened to the following line?"

```
8:      System.out.println("Hello again.");
```

As you've probably guessed from the subtitle, it's in the AppletViewer.log file. (No, I don't know why it's not called the AppletRunner.log file, either.) You'll use `System.out.println` on every day of this fantastic voyage; plan to spend a lot of time reading AppletViewer.log files. (Your friends in the world of Unix and Windows 95 have the option of outputting this information to screen as the applet runs, at the price of a command-line interface.... unfortunately, Applet Runner won't start if AppletViewer.log is open.)

For the record, here are the contents of the entire log file:

```
status: applet loaded
status: applet initialized
status: applet started
Hello again.
```

Looking at the Java Code

Let's take another look at the code of the HelloWorld applet.

```
 1: import java.applet.*;
 2: import java.awt.*;
 3:
 4: public class HelloWorld extends Applet {
 5:
 6:     public void paint(Graphics g) {
 7:         g.drawString("Hello World!",100,100);
 8:         System.out.println("Hello again.");
 9:     }
10: }
```

☐ The `import` statements in lines 1 and 2 are somewhat analogous to an `#include` statement in C; they enable this applet to interact with the JDK classes for creating applets and for drawing graphics on the screen.

☐ The `paint()` method (line 6) displays the content of the applet onto the screen. Here, the string `Hello World` is drawn. Applets use several standard methods to take the place of `main()`, which include `init()` to initialize the applet, `start()` to start it running, and `paint()` to display it to the screen. You'll learn about all of these in Week 2.

Creating a Stand-Alone Java Application

If you don't plan to distribute your programs on the Web, you can create them as stand-alone applications that will run on any machine with a Java run-time system isnstalled. It's a little bit simpler to create a stand-alone application.

Part One: The Project File

A stand-alone application also uses a project file. The project file needn't contain AppletViewer.class or an HTML file. In fact, all it needs is your source code.

Part Two: The Source Code

The source code for a stand-alone application is similar, but a little simpler, than the code for an applet:

```
1: class HelloAgain{
2:     public static void main (String args[]) {
3:         System.out.println("Hello World!");
4:     }
5: }
```

If you're working with testFile.java, line 1 should read:

```
1: class testFile {
```

After your source code is ready, go to the project window and click the name of the source code file. Choose Set Startup File (⌘-Shift-F) from the Project menu.

A Java application starts by executing a class's `main()` method. The Set Startup File command tells the Applet Runner program where to look for the `main()` method to execute when it runs a project. You may recall that your applet didn't have a `main()` method—that's why you did not use the set startup File command for your applet. Because you did not specify a startup file for the project, Roaster assumed you wanted to run the project as an applet, and told the Applet Runner to run the AppletViewer.class file. Technically speaking, Applet Runner didn't run your applet—it ran the compiled Java application Applet Viewer, *which in turn ran the applet*. Pretty cool, eh? This kind of resourceful sneakiness pervades the world of Java. Thus, in an applet's project, you set startup to the `main()` method in Applet Viewer; in a stand-alone project, Roaster automatically sets startup to your own `main()` method.

(For the stand-alone applications on the CD, the startup file for each project has already been set to the correct file.)

Part Three: The Compiler

Next, compile your source code by choosing Make (⌘-M) or Compile (⌘-K) from the Project menu. The compiler treats applications and applets in exactly the same way.

Part Four: The Applet Runner

The Applet Runner is also the tool you'll use to run your stand-alone Java programs. (I know, it sounds paradoxical.) In fact, the Applet Runner is *really* a Mac application for running Java applications. Because it's usually running the Java application Applet Viewer, which runs applets, it seems (almost) sensible to call this application-runner "Applet Runner," and that's how we'll refer to it.

Applets automatically create their own windows. A stand-alone application doesn't create its own window—it must be coded into the application. We haven't coded one into HelloAgain, so it won't create one.

However, Applet Runner can create windows for the system output of stand-alone applications, even if the application doesn't make a window of its own. When we call `System.out.println()` in line 3, Applet Runner provides a window called Applet Runner.out that displays the message "Hello World." (See Figure 1.6.)

NOTE

You've probably asked yourself why an Applet can't send to the AppletRunner.out window. It's a good question. In a future version of Roaster, Applets will be able to use AppletRunner.out, too.

You may have looked for the AppletViewer.log file for NewHello. There isn't one. This file is created by the AppletViewer Java application that we talked about in the section on source code—not by the Applet Runner application. If you think about it for a moment, you'll realize that that's why applets don't write to AppletRunner.out—Applet Viewer redirects this output from the screen to a file.

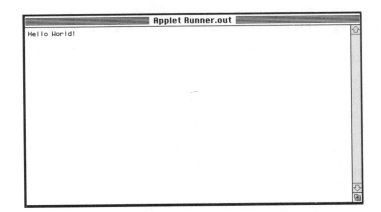

Figure 1.8   *The Hello Java application, which displays its output in the System.out window.*

Summary

Today, you got a basic introduction to the Java language and its goals and features. Java is a programming language, similar to C or C++, in which you can develop a wide range of applets, and eventually stand-alone applications. The most common use of Java at the moment is in creating applets that can be downloaded and run from a Web page. Applets add animations, games, interactive programs, and other multimedia effects to the Web.

Java's strengths lie in its portability—both at the source and at the binary level—in its object-oriented design, and in its simplicity. Each of these features helps make applets possible, but also makes Java an excellent language for writing more general-purpose programs that do not require Java-capable browser to run. These general-purpose Java programs are called applications.

To end this day, you experimented with a sample applet, getting a feel for the Roaster environment. From here, you now have the foundation to create more complex and useful applets.

Questions and Answers

Q I know a lot about HTML, but not much about computer programming. Can I still write Java programs?

A If you have no programming experience whatsoever, you most likely will find programming Java significantly more difficult than HTML, but easier than income taxes. However, Java is an excellent language to learn programming with, and if you patiently work through the examples and the exercises in this book, you should be able to learn enough to get started with Java.

Q According to today's lesson, Java applets are downloaded via Web browsers and run on the reader's system. Isn't that an enormous security hole? What stops someone from writing an applet that compromises the security of my system—or worse, that damages my system?

A Sun's Java team has thought a great deal about the security of applets within Java-capable browsers and has implemented several checks to make sure applets cannot do nasty things:

- ☐ Java applets cannot read or write to the disk on the local system.

- ☐ Java applets cannot execute any programs on the local system.

- ☐ Java applets cannot connect to any machines on the Web except for the server from which they are originally downloaded.

In addition, the Java compiler and interpreter check both the Java source code and the Java bytecodes to make sure that the Java programmer has not tried any sneaky tricks (for example, overrunning buffers or stack frames).

These checks obviously cannot stop every potential security hole, but they can significantly reduce the potential for hostile applets. You'll learn more about security issues later in this book.

Q Where can I find information about Java and Roaster on the Internet?

A There are dozens of Web sites devoted to Java. Sun's site at http://java.sun.com/ is a good place to start. Natural Intelligence maintains a page of links to Java-related sites at http://www.roaster.com/javalinks.html. A great repository of Java applets of all descriptions can be found at http://www.gamelan.com/. On Usenet, try the comp.lang.java newsgroup (which is likely to break into several subgroups before long).

NI's home page for Roaster is located at http://WWW.roaster.com/. From here, you can subscribe to the java-mac mailing list and/or the java-win mailing list, two unmoderated lists for the discussion of topics related to using Java on the Macintosh and Windows platforms, respectively. There is also a mailing list devoted exclusively to announcing the latest Roaster news.

Object-Oriented Programming and Java

by Laura Lemay with Timothy Webster

Object-oriented programming (OOP) is one of the bigger programming buzzwords of recent years, and you can spend years learning all about object-oriented programming methodologies and how they can make your life easier than The Old Way of programming. It all comes down to organizing your programs in ways that echo how things are put together in the real world.

Today, you'll get an overview of object-oriented programming concepts in Java and how they relate to how you structure your own programs:

- ☐ What classes and objects are, and how they relate to each other
- ☐ The two main parts of a class or object: its behaviors and its attributes
- ☐ Class inheritance and how inheritance affects the way you design your programs
- ☐ Some information about packages and interfaces

If you're already familiar with object-oriented programming, much of today's lesson will be old hat to you. You may want to skim it and go to a movie today instead. Tomorrow, you'll get into more specific details.

Thinking in Objects: An Analogy

Consider, if you will, Legos. Legos, for those who do not spend much time with children, are small plastic building blocks in various colors and sizes. They have small round bits on one side that fit into small round holes on other Legos, so that they fit together snugly to create larger shapes. With different Lego bits (Lego wheels, Lego engines, Lego hinges, Lego pulleys), you can put together castles, automobiles, giant robots that swallow cities, or just about anything else you can imagine. Each Lego bit is a small object that fits together with other small objects in predefined ways to create other larger objects.

Here's another example. You can walk into a computer store and, with a little background knowledge and some help, assemble an entire Macintosh system from various components: a base machine, a monitor, an external storage device, a keyboard, and so on. When you finish assembling all the various self-contained units, you have a system in which all the units work together to create a larger system that can solve the problems you bought the computer for in the first place.

Internally, each component may be vastly complicated and engineered by different companies with different methods of design. But you don't need to know how the component works, what every chip on the board does, or how, when you press the A key, an "A" gets sent to your computer. As the assembler of the overall system, each component you use is a self-contained unit, and all you are interested in is how the units interact with each other. Will this video card fit into the slots on the motherboard and will this monitor work with this video card? Will each particular component speak the right commands to the other components it interacts with so that each part of the computer is understood by every other part? When you know what the interactions are between the components and can match the interactions, putting together the overall system is easy.

What does this have to do with programming? Everything. Object-oriented programming works in exactly this same way. Using object-oriented programming, your overall program is made up of lots of different self-contained components (objects), each of which has a specific role in the program and all of which can talk to each other in predefined ways.

Objects and Classes

Object-oriented programming is modeled on how, in the real world, objects are often made up of many kinds of smaller objects. This capability of combining objects, however, is only one very general aspect of object-oriented programming. Object-oriented programming provides several other concepts and features to make creating and using objects easier and more flexible, and the most important of these features is that of classes.

NEW TERM A *class* is a template for multiple objects with similar features. Classes embody all the features of a particular set of objects.

When you write a program in an object-oriented language, you don't define actual objects. You define classes of objects.

For example, you might have a `Tree` class that describes the features of all trees (has leaves and roots, grows, creates chlorophyll). The `Tree` class serves as an abstract model for the concept of a tree—to reach out and grab, or interact with, or cut down a tree you have to have a concrete instance of that tree. Of course, after you have a tree class, you can create lots of different instances of that tree, and each different tree instance can have different features (short, tall, bushy, drops leaves in autumn), while still behaving like and being immediately recognizable as a tree (see Figure 2.1).

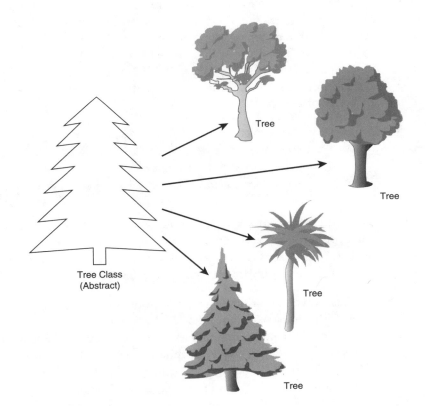

Figure 2.1   *The tree class and tree instances.*

NEW TERM   An *instance* of a class is another word for an actual object. If classes are an abstract representation of an object, an instance is its concrete representation.

So what, precisely, is the difference between an instance and an object? Nothing, really. Object is the more general term, but both instances and objects are the concrete representation of a class. In fact, the terms instance and object are often used interchangeably in OOP language. An instance of a tree and a tree object are both the same thing.

In an example closer to the sorts of things you might want to do in Java programming, you might create a class for the user interface element called a button. The Button class defines the features of a button (its label, its size, its appearance) and how it behaves (does it need a single-click or a double-click to activate it, does it change color when it's clicked, what does it do when it's activated?). After you define the Button class, you can then easily create instances of that button—that is, button objects—that all take on the basic features of the button as defined by the class, but may have different appearances and behavior based on what you want that particular button to do. By creating a Button class, you don't have to keep rewriting the code for each individual button you want to use in your program, and you can reuse the Button class to create different kinds of buttons as you need them in this program and in other programs.

NOTE

If you're used to programming in C, you can think of a class as creating a new composite data type by using struct and typedef. Classes, however, can provide much more than just a collection of data, as you'll discover in the rest of today's lesson.

When you write a Java program, you design and construct a set of classes. Then, when your program runs, instances of those classes are created and discarded as needed. Your task, as a Java programmer, is to create the right set of classes to accomplish what your program needs to accomplish.

Fortunately, you don't have to start from the very beginning: the Java environment comes with a library of classes that implement a lot of the basic behavior you need—not only for basic programming tasks (classes to provide basic math functions, arrays, strings, and so on), but also for graphics and networking behavior. In many cases, the Java class libraries may be enough, so that all you have to do in your Java program is create a single class that uses the standard class libraries. For complicated Java programs, you may have to create a whole set of classes with defined interactions between them.

NEW TERM

A *class library* is a set of classes.

Behavior and Attributes

Every class you write in Java is generally made up of two components: attributes and behavior. In this section, you'll learn about each one as it applies to a theoretical class called Motorcycle. To finish up this section, you'll create the Java code to implement a representation of a motorcycle.

Attributes

Attributes are the individual things that differentiate one object from another and determine the appearance, state, or other qualities of that object. Let's create a theoretical class called Motorcycle. The attributes of a motorcycle might include the following:

- ☐ *Color:* red, green, silver, brown
- ☐ *Style:* cruiser, sport bike, standard
- ☐ *Make:* Honda, BMW, Bultaco

Attributes of an object can also include information about its state; for example, you could have features for engine condition (off or on) or current gear selected.

Attributes are defined by variables; in fact, you can consider them analogous to global variables for the entire object. Because each instance of a class can have different values for its variables, each variable is called an instance variable.

NEW TERM
> *Instance variables* define the attributes of an object. The class defines the kind of attribute, and each instance stores its own value for that attribute.

Each attribute, as the term is used here, has a single corresponding instance variable. Changing the value of a variable changes the attribute of that object. Instance variables may be set when an object is created and stay constant throughout the life of the object, or they may be able to change as the program runs.

In addition to instance variables, there are also class variables, which apply to the class itself and to all its instances. Unlike instance variables, whose values are stored in the instance, class variables' values are stored in the class itself. You'll learn about class variables later this week. You'll learn more specifics about instance variables tomorrow.

Behavior

A class's behavior determines what instances of that class do when their internal state changes or when that instance is asked to do something by another class or object. Behavior is the way objects do something to themselves or have something done to them. For example, to go back to the theoretical Motorcycle class, here are some behaviors that the Motorcycle class might have:

- ☐ Start the engine
- ☐ Stop the engine
- ☐ Speed up
- ☐ Change gear
- ☐ Stall

To define an object's behavior, you create methods, which look and behave just like functions in other languages, but are defined inside a class. Java does not have functions defined outside classes (as C++ does).

NEW TERM   *Methods* are functions defined inside classes that operate on instances of those classes.

Methods don't always affect only a single object; objects communicate with each other using methods as well. A class or object can call methods in another class or object to communicate changes in the environment or to ask that object to change its state.

Just as there are instance and class variables, there are also instance and class methods. Instance methods (which are so common they're usually just called methods) apply and operate on instances; class methods apply and operate on classes (or on other objects). You'll learn more about class methods later this week.

Creating a Class

Up to this point, today's lesson has been pretty theoretical. In this section, you'll create a working example of the Motorcycle class so that you can see how instance variables and methods are defined in a class. You'll also create a Java application that creates a new instance of the Motorcycle class and shows its instance variables.

NOTE I'm not going to go into a lot of detail about the actual syntax of this example. Don't worry too much about it if you're not really sure what's going on; it will become clear to you later this week. All you really need to worry about in this example is understanding the basic parts of this class definition.

Ready? Let's start with a basic class definition. Open the Motorcycle.π project, which is inside the Examples folder in the Roaster™ folder you copied to your hard drive on Day 1. Double-click "Motorcycle.java" in the project window to open the file (which is blank). Enter the following:

```
class Motorcycle {

}
```

Congratulations! You've now created a class. Of course, it doesn't do very much at the moment, but that's a Java class at its very simplest.

First, let's create some instance variables for this class—three of them, to be specific. Just below the first line, add the following three lines:

```
String make;
String color;
boolean engineState;
```

Here, you've created three instance variables: make and color can contain String objects (String is part of that standard class library mentioned earlier), and engineState is a boolean that refers to whether the engine is off or on.

NOTE boolean in Java is a real data type that can have the value true or false. Unlike C, booleans are not numbers. You'll hear about this again tomorrow so you won't forget.

Now let's add some behavior (methods) to the class. There are all kinds of things a motorcycle can do, but to keep things short, let's add just one method—a method that starts the engine. Add the following lines below the instance variables in your class definition:

```
void startEngine() {
    if (engineState == true)
        System.out.println("The engine is already on.");
    else {
        engineState = true;
        System.out.println("The engine is now on.");
    }
}
```

The startEngine method tests to see whether the engine is already running (in the line engineState == true) and, if it is, merely prints a message to that effect. If the engine isn't already running, it changes the state of the engine to true and then prints a message.

```java
class Motorcycle {

    String make;
    String color;
    boolean engineState;

    void startEngine() {
        if (engineState == true)
            System.out.println("The engine is already on.");
        else {
            engineState = true;
            System.out.println("The engine is now on.");
        }
    }
}
```

NOTE The indentation of each part of the class isn't important to the Java compiler. Using some form of indentation, however, makes your class definition easier for you and for other people to read. The indentation used here, with instance variables and methods indented from the class definition, is the style used throughout this book. The Java class libraries use a similar indentation. You can choose any indentation style that you like. In Roaster, unlike in many code editors, hitting the Tab key does not simply add several spaces; it creates an actual tab, as in a word processing program. This, combined with the "Shift Left" and "Shift Right" tools on the Roaster toolbar, makes it much easier to indent your code neatly and consistently.

Before you compile this class, let's add one more method. The showAtts method prints the current values of the instance variables in an instance of your Motorcycle class. Here's what it looks like:

```java
void showAtts() {
    System.out.println("This motorcycle is a "
        + color + " " + make);
    if (engineState == true)
        System.out.println("The engine is on.");
    else System.out.println("The engine is off.");
}
```

The showAtts method prints two lines to the screen: the make and color of the motorcycle object, and whether the engine is on or off.

Here's a reminder on how to get an application ready for compiling. (From now on, I'll assume you know how to compile your applications.)

1. Make sure that you rename your class TestFile if you're using the TestFile.java source file from the CD-ROM. In this case, you're not, but keep this in mind if you use the TestFile project and TestFile.java file to work with some of the examples you'll encounter later in the book.

2. Select .java in the project window, and choose Set Start-up File (⌘-Shift-F) from the Project menu.

3. Choose Make (⌘-M) from the Project menu.

 Here's a nice feature of Roaster: after you've compiled Motorcycle.java, a popup menu appears to the right of the file's name in the project menu. Try clicking it—it's a list of shortcuts to each of Motorcycle's methods! (See Figure 2.2.) There's a similar popup menu at the top of the the source code editor window—it's under the icon second from the left. (If you hold the cursor over the icon for a moment, the "method" label will magically appear.)

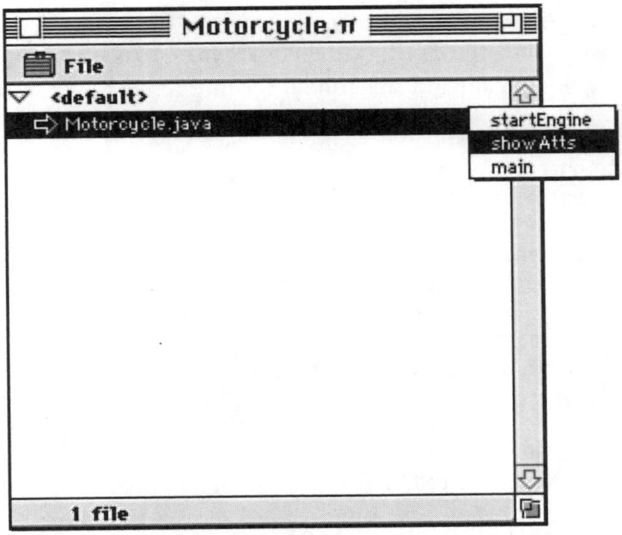

Figure 2.2   *The method popup menu in the project window.*

What happens if you now run this compiled class? Nothing. The Applet Runner assumes that this class is an application and looks for a main method. This is just a class, however, so it doesn't have a main method. When Applet Runner can't find what it needs, it won't even open a Runner.out window. To do something with the

`Motorcycle` class—for example, to create instances of that class and play with them—you're going to need to create a Java application that uses this class or add a `main` method to this one. For simplicity's sake, let's do the latter. The following code shows the `main()` method you'll add to the `Motorcycle` class (you'll go over what this does in a bit).

```
 1:    public static void main (String args[]) {
 2:    Motorcycle m = new Motorcycle();
 3:    m.make = "Yamaha RZ350";
 4:    m.color = "yellow";
 5:    System.out.println("Calling showAtts...");
 6:    m.showAtts();
 7:    System.out.println("--------");
 8:    System.out.println("Starting engine...");
 9:    m.startEngine();
10:    System.out.println("--------");
11:    System.out.println("Calling showAtts...");
12:    m.showAtts();
13:    System.out.println("--------");
14:    System.out.println("Starting engine...");
15:    m.startEngine();
16:    }
```

With the `main()` method, the `Motorcycle` class is now an application, and you can compile it again and this time it'll run. Here's how the output should look:

```
Calling showAtts...
This motorcycle is a yellow Yamaha RZ350
The engine is off.
--------
Starting engine...
The engine is now on.
--------
Calling showAtts...
This motorcycle is a yellow Yamaha RZ350
The engine is on.
--------
Starting engine...
The engine is already on.
```

The content of the `main()` method is all going to look very new to you, so let's go through it line by line so that you at least have a basic idea of what it does (you'll get details about the specifics of all of this tomorrow and the day after).

The first line declares the `main()` method. The `main()` method always looks like this; you'll learn the specifics of each part later this week.

Line 2, `Motorcycle m = new Motorcycle()`, creates a new instance of the `Motorcycle` class and stores a reference to it in the variable `m`. Remember, you don't usually operate directly on classes in your Java programs; instead, you create objects from those classes and then modify and call methods in those objects.

Lines 3 and 4 set the instance variables for this motorcycle object: the make is now a `Yamaha RZ350` (a very pretty motorcycle from the mid-1980s), and the color is `yellow`.

Lines 5 and 6 call the `showAtts()` method, defined in your motorcycle object. (Actually, only 6 does; 5 just prints a message that you're about to call this method.) The new motorcycle object then prints out the values of its instance variables—the `make` and `color` as you set in the previous lines—and shows that the engine is off.

Line 7 prints a divider line to the screen; this is just for prettier output.

Line 9 calls the `startEngine()` method in the motorcycle object to start the engine. The engine should now be on.

Line 12 prints the values of the instance variables again. This time, the report should say the engine is now on.

Line 15 tries to start the engine again, just for fun. Because the engine is already on, this should print the error message.

Inheritance, Interfaces, and Packages

Now that you have a basic grasp of classes, objects, methods, variables, and how to put it all together in a Java program, it's time to confuse you again. Inheritance, interfaces, and packages are all mechanisms for organizing classes and class behaviors. The Java class libraries use all these concepts, and the best class libraries you write for your own programs will also use these concepts.

Inheritance

Inheritance is one of the most crucial concepts in object-oriented programming, and it has a very direct effect on how you design and write your Java classes. Inheritance is a powerful mechanism that means when you write a class you have to specify only how that class is different from some other class, while also giving you dynamic access to the information contained in those other classes.

NEW TERM
With *inheritance*, all classes—those you write, those from other class libraries that you use, and those from the standard utility classes as well—are arranged in a strict hierachy (see Figure 2.3).

Each class has a *superclass* (the class above it in the hierarchy), and each class can have one or more *subclasses* (classes below that class in the hierarchy). Classes farther down in the hierarchy are said to *inherit* from classes farther up in the hierarchy.

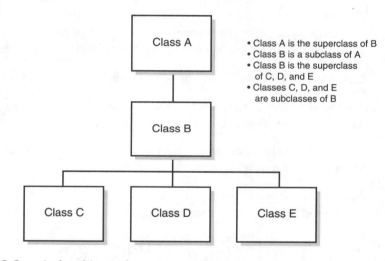

Figure 2.3   *A class hierarchy.*

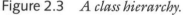

Subclasses inherit all the methods and variables from their superclasses—that is, in any particular class, if the superclass defines behavior that your class needs, you don't have to redefine it or copy that code from some other class. Your class automatically gets that behavior from its superclass, that superclass gets behavior from its superclass, and so on all the way up the hierarchy. Your class becomes a combination of all the features of the classes above it in the hierarchy.

At the top of the Java class hierarchy is the class Object; all classes inherit from this one superclass. Object is the most general class in the hierarchy; it defines behavior specific to all objects in the Java class hierarchy. Each class farther down in the hierarchy adds more information and becomes more tailored to a specific purpose. In this way, you can think of a class hierarchy as defining very abstract concepts at the top of the hierarchy that become more concrete the farther down the chain of superclasses you go.

Most of the time when you write new Java classes, you'll want to create a class that has all the information some other class has, plus some extra information. For example, you may want a version of a Button with its own built-in label. To get all the Button information, all you have to do is define your class to inherit from Button. Your class will automatically get all the behavior defined in Button (and in Button's superclasses), so all you have to worry about are the things that make your class different from Button itself. This mechanism for defining new classes as the differences between them and their superclasses is called *subclassing*.

NEW TERM

Subclassing involves creating a new class that inherits from some other class in the class hierarchy. Using subclassing, you need to define only the differences between your class and its parent; the additional behavior is all available to your class through inheritance.

What if your class defines entirely new behavior, and isn't really a subclass of another class? Your class can also inherit directly from Object, which still allows it to fit neatly into the Java class hierarchy. In fact, if you create a class definition that doesn't indicate its superclass in the first line, Java automatically assumes you're inheriting from Object. The Motorcycle class you created in the previous section inherited from Object.

Creating a Class Hierarchy

If you're creating a larger set of classes, it makes sense for your classes not only to inherit from the existing class hierarchy, but also to make up a hierarchy themselves. This may take some planning beforehand when you're trying to figure out how to organize your Java code, but the advantages are significant:

☐ When you develop your classes in a hierarchy, you can factor out information common to multiple classes in superclasses, and then reuse that superclass's information over and over again. Each subclass gets that common information from its superclass.

☐ Changing (or inserting) a class farther up in the hierarchy automatically changes the behavior of the lower classes—no need to change or recompile any of the lower classes, because they get the new information through inheritance and not by copying any of the code.

For example, let's go back to that Motorcycle class, and pretend you created a Java program to implement all the features of a motorcycle. It's done, it works, and everything is fine. Now, your next task is to create a Java class called Car.

`Car` and `Motorcycle` have many similar features—both are vehicles driven by engines. Both have transmissions and headlamps and speedometers. So, your first impulse may be to open up your `Motorcycle` class file and copy over a lot of the information you already defined into the new class `Car`.

A far better plan is to factor out the common information for `Car` and `Motorcycle` into a more general class hierarchy. This may be a lot of work just for the classes `Motorcycle` and `Car`, but after you add `Bicycle`, `Scooter`, `Truck`, and so on, having common behavior in a reuseable superclass significantly reduces the amount of work you have to do overall.

Let's design a class hierarchy that might serve this purpose. Starting at the top is the class `Object`, which is the root of all Java classes. The most general class to which motorcycle and car both belong might be called `Vehicle`. A vehicle, generally, is defined as a thing that propels someone from one place to another. In the `Vehicle` class, you define only the behavior that enables someone to be propelled from point a to point b, and nothing more.

Below `Vehicle`? How about two classes: `PersonPoweredVehicle` and `EnginePowered-Vehicle`? `EnginePoweredVehicle` is different from `Vehicle` because is has an engine, and the behaviors might include stopping and starting the engine, having certain amounts of gasoline and oil, and perhaps the speed or gear in which the engine is running. Personpowered vehicles have some kind of mechanism for translating people motion into vehicle motion—pedals, for example. Figure 2.4 shows what you have so far.

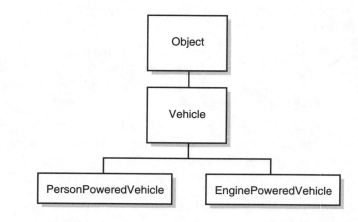

Figure 2.4   *The basic vehicle hierarchy.*

Now, let's become even more specific. With `EnginePoweredVehicle`, you might have several classes: `Motorcycle`, `Car`, `Truck`, and so on. Or you can factor out still more behavior and have intermediate classes for `TwoWheeled` and `FourWheeled` vehicles, with different behaviors for each (see Figure 2.5).

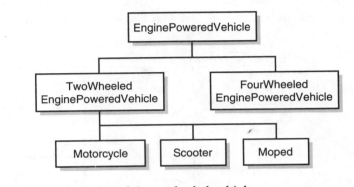

Figure 2.5   *Two-wheeled and four-wheeled vehicles.*

Finally, with a subclass for the two-wheeled engine-powered vehicles you can finally have a class for motorcycles. Alternatively, you could define scooters and mopeds, both of which are two-wheeled engine-powered vehicles but have different qualities from motorcycles.

Where do qualities such as make or color come in? Wherever you want them to go—or, more usually, where they fit most naturally in the class hierarchy. You can define the make and color on `Vehicle`, and all the subclasses will have those variables as well. The point to remember is that you have to define a feature or a behavior only once in the hierarchy; it's automatically reused by each subclass.

Roaster's Class Tree Tool

Roaster provides a class tree tool that enables you to look at your code in a way that's very similar to the charts that we've created here by hand. The code that follows is the skeleton of a program based on our class hierarchy. As you can see, each class is defined by an empty pair of brackets. At this stage, we want to make sure that we have the inheritance correct—we can worry about the specifics of the implementation later.

```
1:  class EnginePoweredVehicle{}
2:  class TwoWheeledEnginePoweredVehicle extends EnginePoweredVehicle {}
3:  class FourWheeledEnginePoweredVehicle extends EnginePoweredVehicle {}
4:  class Motorcycle extends TwoWheeledEnginePoweredVehicle {}
```

```
5:  class Scooter extends TwoWheeledEnginePoweredVehicle {}
6:  class Moped extends TwoWheeledEnginePoweredVehicle {}
```

We've stored this snippet of code in the file VehicleTree.java, and added it to the VehicleTree. pr oject in the VehicleTree folder on the CD-ROM. Open Vehicle-Tree. , and choose File > New > Class T ree (Command-Shift-C). Roaster will open a new window with a graphic display like the one shown in Figure 2.6.

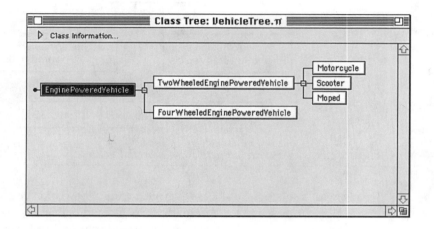

Figure 2.6   *Roaster's class tree tool in action.*

Notice that Roaster has added a new menu, called Tree. I've clicked the `EnginePoweredVehicle` node and chosen Tree > Make Root to focus attention on the hierarchy we've just created. Changing the root this way alters only the way that the tree is represented, *not* the code that establishes the hierarchy.

At the top of the class tree window, you'll see an outline-triangle next to the label Class Information. If you click the triangle, Roaster shows a three-panel display of information about the classes in the tree. Because our classes have no methods and no instance variables, these panels are empty.

NOTE   What's that Implements panel all about? The Implements panel shows the interfaces that each class uses. What's an interface? We'll explain in detail on Day 16.

Let's add a method and an instance variable to one of our classes to see how the class tree tool displays this information. For line 1 in the previous code, we'll substitute all of the following lines:

```
1:  class EnginePoweredVehicle{
2:     public int fuel;
3:     public void revEngine() {}
4:  }
```

Now, choose Project > Update Method List (Command-Shift-U) so that Roaster knows to incorporate the new information into the tree. As we can see in Figure 2.7, Roaster has added our method and instance variable to the panels at the top of the window, and the EnginePoweredVehicle node in the tree diagram has become a pop-up menu that points to each of the methods defined in the class.

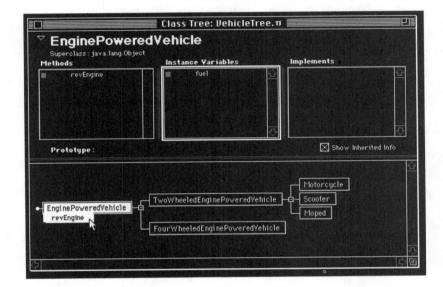

Figure 2.7   *The class tree tool shows information about each of the classes contained in the tree.*

If we check the Show Inherited Info checkbox and click the TwoWheeledEnginePowered-Vehicle node, we see that RevEngine and Fuel still appear, but in italics, to show that they are inherited from the EnginePoweredVehicle class. If we uncheck Show Inherited Info, these items disappear from the panels.

While you're designing your project's basic class structure, you can use the class tree tool to visualize changes by "pruning." To hide a class's subclasses, click the connector box between the class and subclass(es). As with the Make Root command, hiding classes doesn't affect your code at all; it's merely a visualization tool.

How Inheritance Works

How does inheritance work? How is it that instances of one class can automatically get variables and methods from the classes farther up in the hierarchy?

For instance variables, when you create a new instance of a class, you get a "slot" for each variable defined in the current class and for each variable defined in all its superclasses. In this way, all the classes combine to form a template for the current object and then each object fills in the information appropriate to its situation.

Methods operate similarly: new objects have access to all the method names of their class and its superclasses, but method definitions are chosen dynamically when a method is called. That is, if you call a method on a particular object, Java first checks the object's class for the definition of that method. If it's not defined in the object's class, it looks in that class's superclass, and so on up the chain until the method definition is found (see Figure 2.8).

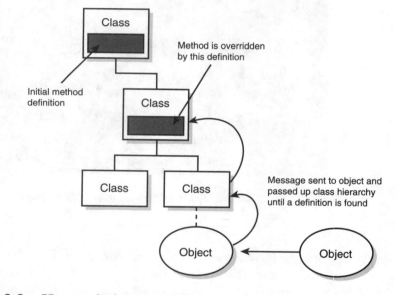

Figure 2.8   *How methods are located.*

Things get complicated when a subclass defines a method that has the same signature (name and number and type of arguments) as a method defined in a superclass. In this case, the method definition that is found first (starting at the bottom and working upward toward the top of the hierarchy) is the one that is actually executed. Because of this, you can purposefully define a method in a subclass that has the same signature as a method in a superclass, which then "hides" the superclass's method. This is called *overriding* a method. You'll learn all about methods on Day 7.

NEW TERM

Overriding a method creates a method in a subclass that has the same signature (name, number, and type of arguments) as a method in a superclass. That new method then hides the superclass's method (see Figure 2.9).

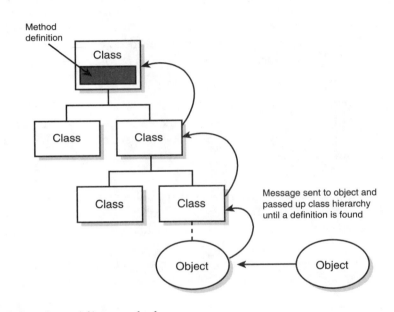

Figure 2.9 *Overriding methods.*

Single and Multiple Inheritance

Java's form of inheritance, as you learned in the previous sections, is called single inheritance. Single inheritance means that each Java class can have only one superclass (although any given superclass can have multiple subclasses).

In other object-oriented programming languages, such as C++, classes can have more than one superclass, and they inherit combined variables and methods from all those classes. This is called multiple inheritance. Multiple inheritance can provide enormous power in terms of being able to create classes that factor just about all imaginable behavior, but it can also significantly complicate class definitions and the code to produce them. Java makes inheritance simpler by being only singly inherited.

Interfaces and Packages

Java has two remaining concepts to discuss here: packages and interfaces. Both are advanced topics for implementing and designing groups of classes and class behavior. You'll learn about both interfaces and packages on Day 16, but they are worth at least introducing here.

Recall that Java classes have only a single superclass, and they inherit variables and methods from that superclass and all its superclasses. Although single inheritance makes the relationship between classes and the functionality those classes implement easy to understand and to design, it can also be somewhat restricting—in particular, when you have similar behavior that needs to be duplicated across different "branches" of the class hierarchy. Java solves this problem of shared behavior by using the concept of interfaces.

NEW TERM   An *interface* is a collection of method names, without actual definitions, that indicate that a class has a set of behaviors in addition to the behaviors the class gets from its superclasses.

Although a single Java class can have only one superclass (due to single inheritance), that class can also implement any number of interfaces. By implementing an interface, a class provides method implementations (definitions) for the method names defined by the interface. If two very disparate classes implement the same interface, they can both respond to the same method calls (as defined by that interface), although what each class actually does in response to those method calls may be very different.

You don't need to know very much about interfaces right now. You'll learn more as the book progresses, so if all this is very confusing, don't panic!

The final new Java concept for today is that of packages.

NEW TERM   *Packages* in Java are a way of grouping together related classes and interfaces. Packages enable modular groups of classes to be available only if they are needed and eliminate potential conflicts between class names in different groups of classes.

You'll learn all about packages, including how to create and use them, in Week 3. For now, there are only a few things you need to know:

□ The class libraries in the Java Developer's Kit are contained in a package called `java`. The classes in the `java` package are guaranteed to be available in any Java implementation, and are the *only* classes guaranteed to be available across different implementations. The `java` package itself contains other packages for classes that define the language itself, the input and output classes, some basic networking, and the window toolkit functions. Classes in other packages (for example, classes in the Sun or Netscape packages) may be available only in specific implementations.

□ By default, your Java classes have access to only the classes in `java.lang` (the base language package inside the `java` package). To use classes from any other package, you have to either refer to them explicitly by package name or import them in your source file.

□ To refer to a class within a package, list all the packages that class is contained in and the class name, all separated by periods (`.`). For example, take the `Color` class, which is contained in the `awt` package (awt stands for Abstract Window Toolkit). The `awt` package, in turn, is inside the `java` package. To refer to the `Color` class in your program, you use the notation `java.awt.Color`.

Creating a Subclass

To finish up today, let's create a class that is a subclass of another class and override some methods. You'll also get a basic feel for how packages work in this example.

Probably the most typical instance of creating a subclass, at least when you first start programming in Java, is in creating an applet. All applets are subclasses of the class `Applet` (which is part of the `java.applet` package). By creating a subclass of `Applet`, you automatically get all the behavior from the window toolkit and the layout classes that enables your applet to be drawn in the right place on the page and to interact with system operations, such as keypresses and mouse clicks.

In this example, you'll create an applet similar to the HelloWorld applet from yesterday, but one that draws the `Hello` string in a larger font and a different color. To start this example, let's first construct the class definition itself. Open the `HelloAgainApplet.π` project, which is inside the `Examples` folder in the `Roaster`™ folder you copied to your hard drive on Day 1. Double-click "`HelloAgainApplet.java`" in the project window to open the file (which is blank). Now enter the following class definition:

```
public class HelloAgainApplet extends java.applet.Applet {
}
```

Here, you're creating a class called `HelloAgainApplet`. Note the part that says `extends java.applet.Applet`—that's the part that says your applet class is a subclass of the `Applet` class. Note that because the `Applet` class is contained in the `java.applet` package, you don't have automatic access to that class, and you have to refer to it explicitly by package and class name.

The other part of this class definition is the `public` keyword. Public means that your class is available to the Java system at large once it is loaded. Most of the time you need to make a class `public` only if you want it to be visible to all the other classes in your Java program; but applets, in particular, must be declared to be `public`. You'll learn more about `public` classes in Week 3.

A class definition with nothing in it doesn't really have much of a point; without adding or overriding any of its superclasses' variables or methods, there's no point to creating a subclass at all. Let's add some information to this class to make it different from its superclass.

First, add an instance variable to contain a `Font` object:

```
Font f = new Font("TimesRoman",Font.BOLD,36);
```

The `f` instance variable now contains a new instance of the class `Font`, part of the `java.awt` package. This particular `Font` object is a Times Roman font, boldface, 36 points high. In the previous HelloWorld applet, the font used for the text was the default font: 12 point Times Roman. Using a `Font` object, you can change the font of the text you draw in your applet.

By creating an instance variable to hold this `Font` object, you make it available to all the methods in your class. Now let's create a method that uses it.

When you write applets, there are several "standard" methods defined in the applet superclasses that you will commonly override in your applet class. These include methods to initialize the applet, to start it running, to handle operations such as mouse movements or mouse clicks, or to clean up when the applet stops running. One of those standard methods is the `paint()` method, which actually displays your applet on screen. The default definition of `paint()` doesn't do anything—it's an empty method. By overriding `paint()`, you tell the applet just what to draw on the screen. Here's a definition of `paint()`:

```
public void paint(Graphics g) {
    g.setFont(f);
    g.setColor(Color.red);
    g.drawString("Hello again!", 5, 25);
}
```

There are two things to know about the paint() method. First, note that this method is declared public, just as the applet itself was. The paint() method is actually public for a different reason—because the method it's overriding is also public. If you try to override a method in your own class that's public in a superclass, you get a compiler error if your override method is not public, so the public is required.

Secondly, note that the paint() method takes a single argument: an instance of the Graphics class. The Graphics class provides platform-independent behavior for rendering fonts, colors, and basic drawing operations. You'll learn a lot more about the Graphics class in Week 2, when you create more extensive applets.

Inside your paint() method, you've done three things:

☐ You've told the graphics object that the default drawing font will be the one contained in the instance variable f.

☐ You've told the graphics object that the default color is an instance of the Color class for the color red.

☐ Finally, you've drawn your "Hello Again!" string onto the screen itself, at the x and y positions of 5 and 25. The string will be rendered in the default font and color.

For an applet this simple, this is all you need to do. Here's what the applet looks like so far:

```
public class HelloAgainApplet extends java.applet.Applet {

  Font f = new Font("TimesRoman",Font.BOLD,36);

  public void paint(Graphics g) {
    g.setFont(f);
    g.setColor(Color.red);
    g.drawString("Hello again!", 5, 50);
  }
}
```

If you've been paying attention, you'll notice something is wrong with this example up to this point. If you don't know what it is, try compiling the file.

You should get a bunch of errors similar to this one:

```
HelloAgainApplet.java:7: Class Graphics not found in type declaration.
```

Why are you getting these errors? Because the classes you're referring to are part of a package. Remember that the only package you have access to automatically is `java.lang`. You referred to the `Applet` class in the first line of the class definition by referring to its full package name (`java.applet.Applet`). Further on in the program, however, you referred to all kinds of other classes as if they were already available.

There are two ways to solve this problem: refer to all external classes by full package name or import the appropriate class or package at the beginning of your class file. Which one you choose to do is mostly a matter of choice, although if you find yourself referring to a class in another package lots of times, you may want to import it to cut down on the amount of typing.

In this example, you'll import the classes you need. There are three of them: `Graphics`, `Font`, and `Color`. All three are part of the `java.awt` package. Here are the lines to import these classes. These lines go at the top of your program, before the actual class definition:

```
import java.awt.Graphics;
import java.awt.Font;
import java.awt.Color;
```

NOTE

You also can import an entire package of (`public`) classes by using an asterisk (`*`) in place of a specific class name. For example, to import all the classes in the awt package, you can use this line:

```
import java.awt.*;
```

Now, with the proper classes imported into your program, Hello-AgainApplet should compile cleanly to a class file. To test it, create an HTML file with the <APPLET> tag as you did yesterday. Here's an HTML file to use:

```
<TITLE>Another Applet</TITLE>
<APPLET CODE="HelloAgainApplet.class" WIDTH=200 HEIGHT=50>
</APPLET>
```

Save this HTML file as `example1.html` in the same folder as the HelloAgainApplet project. To see the applet in action, choose Run from the Project menu or drag the HTML file or the project file onto the Appet Runner icon.

Figure 2.10 *The Hello Again applet.*

Summary

If this is your first encounter with object-oriented programming, a lot of the information today is going to seem really theoretical and overwhelming. Fear not—the further along in this book you get, and the more Java applications you create, the easier it is to understand.

One of the biggest hurdles of object-oriented programming is not necessarily the concepts, it's their names. OOP has lots of jargon surrounding it. To summarize today's material, here's a glossary of terms and concepts you learned today:

☐ *Class:* A template for an object that contains variables and methods representing behavior and attributes. Classes can inherit variables and methods from other classes.

☐ *Object:* A concrete instance of a class. Multiple objects that are instances of the same class have access to the same methods, but often have different values for their instance variables.

☐ *Instance:* The same thing as an object; each object is an instance of some class.

☐ *Superclass:* A class farther up in the inheritance hierarchy than its child, the subclass.

☐ *Subclass:* A class lower in the inheritance hierarchy than its parent, the superclass. When you create a new class, that's often called *subclassing*.

- ☐ *Instance method:* A method defined in a class that operates on an instance of that class. Instance methods are usually called just *methods.*

- ☐ *Class method:* A method defined in a class that can operate on the class itself.

- ☐ *Instance variable:* A variable that is owned by an individual instance and whose value is stored in the instance.

- ☐ *Class variable:* A variable that is owned by the class and all its instances as a whole, and is stored in the class.

- ☐ *Interface:* A collection of abstract behavior specifications that individual classes can then implement.

- ☐ *Package:* A collection of classes and interfaces. Classes from packages other than java.lang must be explicitly imported or referred to by full package name.

Questions and Answers

Q **Methods are effectively functions that are defined inside classes. If they look like functions and act like functions, why aren't they called functions?**

A Some object-oriented programming languages do call them functions (C++ calls them member functions). Other object-oriented languages differentiate between functions inside and outside a body of a class or object, where having separate terms is important to understanding how each works. Because the difference is relevant in other languages, and because the term method is now in such common use in object-oriented technology, Java uses the word as well.

Q **I understand instance variables and methods, but not class variables and methods.**

A Almost everything you do in a Java program will be with objects. Some behaviors and attributes, however, make more sense if they are stored in the class itself rather than in the object. For example, to create a new instance of a class, you need a method that is defined for the class itself, not for an object. (Otherwise, how can you create an instance of a class? You need an object to call the new method in, but you don't have an object yet.) Class variables, on the other hand, are often used when you have an attribute whose value you want to share with the instances of a class.

Most of the time, you'll use instance variables and methods. You'll learn more about class variables and methods later on this week.

Java Basics

by Laura Lemay with Timothy Webster

On Days 1 and 2, you learned about Java programming in very broad terms—what a Java program and an executable look like, and how to create simple classes. For the remainder of this week, you're going to get down to details and deal with the specifics of what the Java language looks like.

Today, you won't define any classes or objects or worry about how any of them communicate inside a Java program. Rather, you'll draw closer and examine simple Java statements—the basic things you can do in Java within a method definition such as `main()`.

Today you'll learn about the following:

☐ Java statements and expressions

☐ Variables and data types

☐ Comments

☐ Literals

☐ Arithmetic

☐ Comparisons

☐ Logical operators

NOTE   Java looks a lot like C++, and—by extension—like C. Much of the syntax will be very familiar to you if you are used to working in these languages. If you are an experienced C or C++ programmer, you may want to pay special attention to the Notes (such as this one), because they will provide information about the specific differences between these and other traditional languages and Java.

Statements and Expressions

A statement is the simplest thing you can do in Java; a statement forms a single Java operation. All the following are simple Java statements:

```
int i = 1;
import java.awt.Font;
System.out.println("This motorcycle is a "
    + color + " " + make);

m.engineState = true;
```

Statements sometimes return values—for example, when you add two numbers together or test to see whether one value is equal to another. These kind of statements are called *expressions*. We'll discuss these later today.

The most important thing to remember about Java statements is that each one ends with a semicolon. Forget the semicolon and your Java program won't compile.

Java also has compound statements, or blocks, which can be placed wherever a single statement can. Block statements are surrounded by braces ({}). You'll learn more about blocks on Day 5, "Arrays, Conditionals, and Loops."

Variables and Data Types

Variables are locations in memory in which values can be stored. Each variable has a name, a type, and a value. Before you can use a variable, you have to declare it. After it is declared, you can then assign a value to it.

Java actually has three kinds of variables: instance variables, class variables, and local variables.

Instance variables, as you learned yesterday, are used to define attributes or the state for a particular object. Class variables are similar to instance variables, except their values apply to all that class's instances (and to the class itself) rather than having different values for each object.

Local variables are declared and used inside method definitions—for example, for index counters in loops, as temporary variables, or to hold values that you need only inside the method definition itself. They can also be used inside blocks ({}), which you'll learn about later this week. Once the method (or block) finishes executing, the variable definition and its value cease to exist. Use local variables to store information needed by a single method and instance variables to store information needed by multiple methods in the object.

Although all three kinds of variables are declared in much the same ways, class and instance variables are accessed and assigned in slightly different ways than are local variables. Today, you'll focus on variables as used within method definitions; tomorrow, you'll learn how to deal with instance and class variables.

NOTE

> Unlike other languages, Java does not have global variables—that is, variables that are global to all parts of a program. Instance and class variables can be used to communicate global information between and among objects. Remember, Java is an object-oriented language, so you should think in terms of objects and how they interact, rather than in terms of programs.

Declaring Variables

To use any variable in a Java program, you must first declare it. Variable declarations consist of a type and a variable name:

```
int myAge;
String myName;
boolean isTired;
```

Variable definitions can go anywhere in a method definition (that is, anywhere a regular Java statement can go), although they are most commonly declared at the beginning of the definition before they are used:

```
public static void main (String args[]) {
    int count;
    String title;
    boolean isAsleep;
...
}
```

You can string together variable names with the same type:

```
int x, y, z;
String firstName, LastName;
```

You can also give each variable an initial value when you declare it:

```
int myAge, mySize, numShoes = 28;
String myName = "Laura";
boolean isTired = true;
int a = 4, b = 5, c = 6;
```

If there are multiple variables on the same line with only one initializer (as in the first of the previous examples), the initial value applies to only the last variable in a declaration. You can also group individual variables and initializers on the same line using commas, as with the last example.

Local variables must be given values before they can be used (your Java program will not compile if you try to use an unassigned local variable). For this reason, it's a good idea always to give local variables initial values. Instance and class variable definitions do not have this restriction (their initial value depends on the type of the variable: `null` for instances of classes, `0` for numeric variables, `'\0'` for characters, and `false` for boolean).

Notes on Variable Names

Variable names in Java can start with a letter, an underscore (_), or a dollar sign ($). They cannot start with a number. After the first character, your variable names can include any letter or number. Symbols, such as `%`, `*`, `@`, and so on, are often reserved for operators in Java, so be careful when using symbols in variable names.

In addition, the Java language uses the Unicode character set. Unicode is a character set definition that offers not only characters in the standard ASCII character set, but also several million other characters for representing most international alphabets. This means that you can use accented characters and other glyphs as legal characters in variable names, as long as they have a Unicode character number above `00C0`.

WARNING

> The Unicode specification is a two-volume set of lists of thousands of characters. If you don't understand Unicode, or don't think you have a use for it, it's safest just to use plain numbers and letters in your variable names. You'll learn a little more about Unicode later on.

Finally, note that the Java language is case-sensitive, which means that uppercase letters are different from lowercase letters. This means that the variable `X` is different from the variable `x`, and a `rose` is not a `Rose` is not a `ROSE`. Keep this in mind as you write your own Java programs and as you read Java code that other people have written.

By convention, Java variables have meaningful names, often made up of several words combined. The first word is lowercase, but all following words have an initial uppercase letter:

```
Button theButton;
long reallyBigNumber;
boolean currentWeatherStateOfPlanetXShortVersion;
```

Variable Types

In addition to the variable name, each variable declaration must have a type, which defines what values that variable can hold. The variable type can be one of three things:

☐ One of the eight basic primitive data types

☐ The name of a class or interface

☐ An array

You'll learn about how to declare and use array variables on Day 5.

 The eight primitive data types handle common types for integers, floating-point numbers, characters, and boolean values (true or false). They're called primitive because they're built into the system and are not actual objects, which makes them more efficient to use. Note that these data types are machine-independent, which means that you can rely on their sizes and characteristics to be consistent across your Java programs. (You'll notice that Roaster bolds the reserved words for these types automatically in your code.)

There are four Java integer types, each with different ranges of values (as listed in Table 3.1). All are signed, which means they can hold either positive or negative numbers. Which type you choose for your variables depends on the range of values you expect that variable to hold; if a value becomes too big for the variable type, it is truncated. (See the Questions and Answers at the end of this chapter for more on what actually happens in this case.)

Table 3.1 *Integer Types*

Type	Size	Range
byte	8 bits	–128 to 127
short	16 bits	–32,768 to 32,767
int	32 bits	–2,147,483,648 to 2,147,483,647
long	64 bits	–9,223,372,036,854,775,808 to 9,223,372,036,854,775,807

Floating-point numbers are used for numbers with a decimal part. Java floating-point numbers are compliant with IEEE 754 (an international standard for defining floating-point numbers and arithmetic). There are two floating-point types: float (32 bits, single-precision) and double (64 bits, double-precision).

The char type is used for individual characters. Because Java uses the Unicode character set, the char type has 16 bits of precision, unsigned.

Finally, the boolean type can have one of two values, true or false. Note that unlike in other C-like languages, boolean is not a number, nor can it be treated as one. All tests of boolean variables should test for true or false.

In addition to the eight basic data types, variables in Java can also be declared to hold an instance of a particular class:

```
String LastName;
Font basicFont;
OvalShape myOval;
```

Each of these variables can then hold only instances of the given class. As you create new classes, you can declare variables to hold instances of those classes (and their subclasses) as well.

NOTE Java does not have a typedef statement (as in C and C++). To declare new types in Java, you declare a new class; then variables can be declared to be of that class's type.

Assigning Values to Variables

After a variable has been declared, you can assign a value to that variable by using the assignment operator =:

```
size = 14;
tooMuchCaffeine = true;
```

Comments

Java has three kinds of comments. /* and */ surround multiline comments, as in C or C++. All text between the two delimiters is ignored:

```
/* I don't know how I wrote this next part; I was working
    really late one night and it just sort of appeared. I
    suspect the code elves did it for me. It might be wise
    not to try to change it.
*/
```

Comments cannot be nested; that is, you cannot have a comment inside a comment.

Double-slashes (//) can be used for a single line of comment. All the text up to the end of the line is ignored:

```
int vices = 7; // are there really only 7 vices?
```

The final type of comment begins with /** and ends with */. These special comments are used by the javadoc compiler (included in the Roaster package) to compile HTML documentation from your Java code—automatically! We'll take a closer look at javadoc on Day 20.

You may have noticed the Comment button in the toolbar at the top of Roaster's editor window. When you click this button, Roaster "comments out" the selected text. If you hold down the Command key as you click the Comment button, it will "uncomment" previously commented text. (It's common practice to try to isolate troublesome code by hiding different parts of your program in comment blocks and recompiling.)

Literals

Literals are used to indicate simple values in your Java programs.

NEW TERM

Literal is a programming language term, which essentially means that what you type is what you get. For example, if you type 4 in a Java program, you automatically get an integer with the value 4. If you type a, you get a character with the value a.

Literals may seem intuitive most of the time, but there are some special cases of literals in Java for different kinds of numbers, characters, strings, and boolean values.

Number Literals

There are several integer literals. 4, for example, is a decimal integer literal of type int (although you can assign it to a variable of type byte or short, because it's small enough to fit into those types). A decimal integer literal larger than an int is automatically of type long. You also can force a smaller number to a long by appending an L or l to that number (for example, 4L is a long integer of value 4). Negative integers are preceded by a minus sign—for example, -45.

Integers can also be expressed as octal or hexadecimal: a leading 0 indicates that a number is octal—for example, 0777 or 0004. A leading 0x (or 0X) means that it is in hex (0xFF, 0XAF45). Hexadecimal numbers can contain regular digits (0–9) or upper- or lowercase hex digits (a–f or A–F).

Floating-point literals usually have two parts: the integer part and the decimal part—for example, 5.677777. Floating-point literals result in a floating-point number of type double, regardless of the precision of that number. You can force the number to the type float by appending the letter f (or F) to that number—for example, 2.56F.

You can use exponents in floating-point literals using the letter e or E followed by the exponent (which can be a negative number): 10e45 or .36E-2.

Boolean Literals

Boolean literals consist of the keywords true and false. These keywords can be used anywhere you need a test or as the only possible values for boolean variables.

Character Literals

Character literals are expressed by a single character surrounded by single quotes: 'a', '#', '3', and so on. Characters are stored as 16-bit Unicode characters. Table 3.2 lists the special codes that can represent nonprintable characters, as well as characters from the Unicode character set. The letter d in the octal, hex, and Unicode escapes represents a number or a hexadecimal digit (a–f or A–F).

Table 3.2   *Character Escape Codes*

Escape	Meaning
\n	Newline
\t	Tab
\b	Backspace
\r	Carriage return
\f	Formfeed
\\	Backslash
\'	Single quote
\"	Double quote
\ddd	Octal
\xdd	Hexadecimal
\udddd	Unicode character

NOTE   C and C++ programmers should note that Java does not include character codes for \a (bell) or \v (vertical tab).

String Literals

 A combination of characters is a string. (You may recall from Day 1 that Roaster's editor shows strings in green type.) Strings in Java are instances of the class String. Strings are not simple arrays of characters as they are in C or C++, although they do have many array-like characteristics (for example, you can test their length and add and delete individual characters). Because String objects are real objects in Java, they have methods that enable you to combine, test, and modify strings very easily.

String literals consist of a series of characters inside double quotes:

```
"Hi, I'm a string literal."
"" //an empty string
```

When you type a string literal in Roaster's code-editing window, it appears in a different color (and font and style, if you want) from the rest of your code. There is also a special style (italic by default) for unterminated strings (strings that have an opening quotation mark but not a closing one). This gives you a visual cue to keep you from forgetting to close your quotation.

Strings can contain character constants such as newline, tab, and Unicode characters:

```
"A string with a \t tab in it"
"Nested strings are \"strings inside of\" other strings"
"This string brought to you by Java\u2122"
```

In the last example, the Unicode code sequence for \u2122 produces a trademark symbol (™).

NOTE

Just because you can represent a character using a Unicode escape does not mean your computer can display that character—the computer or operating system you are running may not support Unicode, or the font you're using may not have a glyph (picture) for that character. All that Unicode escapes in Java provide is a way to encode special characters for systems that support Unicode.

When you use a string literal in your Java program, Java automatically creates an instance of the class String for you with the value you give it. Strings are unusual in this respect; the other literals do not behave in this way (none of the primitive base types are actual objects), and creating a new object usually involves explicitly creating a new instance of a class. You'll learn more about strings, the String class, and the things you can do with strings later today and tomorrow.

Expressions and Operators

Expressions are the simplest form of Java statements that actually accomplish something.

NEW TERM   *Expressions* are statements that return a value. *Operators* are special symbols that are commonly used in expressions.

Arithmetic and tests for equality and magnitude are common examples of expressions. Because they return a value, you can assign that result to a variable or test that value in other Java statements.

Operators in Java include arithmetic, various forms of assignment, increment and decrement, and logical operations. This section describes all of these operators.

Arithmetic

Java has five operators for basic arithmetic (see Table 3.3).

Table 3.3   *Arithmetic Operators*

Operator	Meaning	Example
+	Addition	3 + 4
−	Subtraction	5 − 7
*	Multiplication	5 * 5
/	Division	14 / 7
%	Modulus	20 % 7

Each operator takes two operands, one on either side of the operand. The subtraction operator (-) also can be used to negate a single operand.

Integer division results in an integer. Because integers don't have decimal fractions, any remainder is ignored. The expression 31 / 9, for example, results in 3 (9 goes into 31 only 3 times).

Modulus (%) gives the remainder after the operands have been evenly divided. For example, 31 % 9 results in 4 because 9 goes into 31 three times, with 4 left over.

Note that, for integers, the result type of most operations is an int or a long, regardless of the original type of the operands. Large results are of type long; all others are int. Arithmetic wherein one operand is an integer and another is a floating point results in a floating-point result. (If you're interested in the details of how Java promotes and converts numeric types from one type to another, you may want to check out the Java Language Specification; that's more detail than I want to cover here.)

Here is an example of simple arithmetic.

```
 1: class ArithmeticTest {
 2: public static void main (String args[]) {
 3:      short x = 6;
 4:      int y = 4;
 5:      float a = 12.5f;
 6:      float b = 7f;
 7:
 8:      System.out.println("x is " + x + ", y is " + y);
 9:      System.out.println("x + y = " + (x + y));
10:      System.out.println("x - y = " + (x - y));
11:      System.out.println("x / y = " + (x / y));
12:      System.out.println("x % y = " + (x % y));
13:
14:      System.out.println("a is " + a + ", b is " + b;
15:      System.out.println("a / b = " + (a / b));
16: }
17:
18: }
```

Here's the output:

```
x is 6, y is 4

x + y = 10
x - y = 2
x / y = 1
x % y = 2
a is 12.5000000, b is 7.000000
a / b = 1.785714
```

In this simple Java application (note the main() method), you initially define four variables in lines 3 through 6: x and y, which are integers (type int), and a and b, which are floating-point numbers (type float). Keep in mind that the default type for floating-point literals (such as 12.5) is double, so to make sure these are numbers of type float, you have to use an f after each one (lines 5 and 6).

The remainder of the program merely does some math with integers and floating-point numbers and prints out the results.

There is one other thing to mention about this program: the method `System.out.println()`. You've seen this method on previous days, but you haven't really learned exactly what it does. The `System.out.println()` method merely prints a message to the window Applet Runner.out (in the case of applications) or the file AppletView.log (in the case of Applets). The `System.out.println()` method takes a single argument—a string—but you can use + to concatenate values into a string, as you'll learn later today.

More About Assignment

Variable assignment is a form of expression; in fact, because one assignment expression results in a value, you can string them together like this:

```
x = y = z = 0;
```

In this example, all three variables now have the value 0.

The right side of an assignment expression is always evaluated before the assignment takes place. This assures that expressions such as x = x + 2 do the right thing; 2 is added to the value of x, and then that new value is reassigned to x. In fact, this sort of operation is so common that Java has several operators, borrowed from C and C++, to do a shorthand version of this. Table 3.4 shows these shorthand assignment operators.

Table 3.4   *Assignment Operators*

Expression	Meaning
x += y	x = x + y
x -= y	x = x − y
x *= y	x = x * y
x /= y	x = x / y

NOTE

If you rely on complicated side effects of subexpressions on either side of these assignments, the shorthand expressions may not be entirely equivalent to their longhand equivalents. For more information about very complicated expressions, evaluation order, and side effects, you might want to consult the Java Language Specification.

Incrementing and Decrementing

As in C and C++, the ++ and -- operators are used to increment or decrement a value by 1. For example, x++ increments the value of x by 1 just as if you had used the expression x = x + 1. Similarly x-- decrements the value of x by 1. (Unlike C and C++, Java enables you to use these operators with floating-point numbers.)

These increment and decrement operators can be prefixed or postfixed; that is, the ++ or -- can appear before or after the value it increments or decrements. For simple increment or decrement expressions, which one you use isn't overly important. In complex assignments, in which you are assigning the result of an increment or decrement expression, which one you use makes a difference.

Take, for example, the following two expressions:

```
y = x++;
y = ++x;
```

These two expressions give very different results because of the difference between prefix and postfix. When you use postfix operators (x++ or x--), y gets the value of x *before* x is incremented; using prefix operators, the value of x is assigned to y *after* the increment has occurred. The following is a Java example of how all this works.

```
 1: class PrePostFixTest {
 2:
 3: public static void main (String args[]) {
 4:     int x = 0;
 5:     int y = 0;
 6:
 7:     System.out.println("x and y are " + x + " and " + y );
 8:     x++;
 9:     System.out.println("x++ results in " + x);
10:     ++x;
11:     System.out.println("++x results in " + x);
12:     System.out.println("Resetting x back to 0.");
13:     x = 0;
14:     System.out.println("-------------");
15:     y = x++;
16:     System.out.println("y = x++ (postfix) results in:");
17:     System.out.println("x is " + x);
18:     System.out.println("y is " + y);
19:     System.out.println("-------------");
20:
21:     y = ++x;
22:     System.out.println("y = ++x (prefix) results in:");
23:     System.out.println("x is " + x);
24:     System.out.println("y is " + y);
```

```
25:        System.out.println("------------");
26:
27: }
28:
29: }
```

Here's the output: x and y are 0 and 0

```
x++ results in 1
++x results in 2
Resetting x back to 0.
------------
y = x++ (postfix) results in:
x is 1
y is 0
------------
y = ++x (prefix) results in:
x is 2
y is 2
------------
```

In the first part of this example, you increment x alone using both prefix and postfix increment operators. In each, x is incremented by 1 each time. In this simple form, using either prefix or postfix works the same way.

In the second part of this example, you use the expression y = x++, in which the postfix increment operator is used. The value of x is incremented *after* that value is assigned to y. Hence the result: y is assigned the original value of x (0), and then x is incremented by 1.

In the third part, you use the prefix expression y = ++x. Here, the reverse occurs: x is incremented before its value is assigned to y. Because x is 1 from the previous step, its value is incremented (to 2), and then that value is assigned to y. Both x and y end up being 2.

NOTE
Technically, this description is not entirely correct. In reality, Java *always* completely evaluates all expressions on the right of an expression before assigning that value to a variable, so the concept of "assigning x to y before x is incremented" isn't precisely right. Instead, Java takes the value of x and "remembers" it, evaluates (increments) x, and *then* assigns the original value of x to y. Although in most simple cases this distinction may not be important, for more complex expressions with side effects it may change the overall behavior of the expression. See the Language Specification for many more details about expression evaluation in Java.

Comparisons

Java has several expressions for testing equality and magnitude. All of these expressions return a boolean value (that is, true or `false`). Table 3.5 shows the comparison operators.

Table 3.5 *Comparison Operators*

Operator	Meaning	Example
==	Equal	x == 3
!=	Not equal	x != 3
<	Less than	x < 3
>	Greater than	x > 3
≤	Less than or equal to	x ≤ 3
≥	Greater than or equal to	x ≥ 3

Logical Operators

Expressions that result in boolean values (for example, the comparison operators) can be combined by using logical operators that represent the logical combinations AND, OR, XOR, and logical NOT.

For AND combinations, use either the & or &&. The expression will be true only if both expressions are also true; if either expression is false, the entire expression is false. The difference between the two operators is in expression evaluation. Using &, both sides of the expression are evaluated regardless of the outcome. Using &&, if the left side of the expression is false, the entire expression returns `false`, and the right side of the expression is never evaluated.

For OR expressions, use either ¦ or ¦¦. OR expressions result in true if either or both of the operands is also true; if both operands are false, the expression is false. As with & and &&, the single ¦ evaluates both sides of the expression regardless of the outcome; with ¦¦, if the left expression is true, the expression returns `true` and the right side is never evaluated.

In addition, there is the XOR operator ^, which returns `true` only if its operands are different (one true and one false, or vice versa) and `false` otherwise (even if both are true).

In general, only the && and ¦¦ are commonly used as actual logical conbinations. &, ¦, and ^ are more commonly used for bitwise logical operations.

For NOT, use the ! operator with a single expression argument. The value of the NOT expression is the negation of the expression; if x is true, !x is false.

Bitwise Operators

Finally, here's a short summary of the bitwise operators in Java. These are all inherited from C and C++ and are used to perform operations on individual bits in integers. This book does not go into bitwise operations; it's an advanced topic covered in books on C or C++. Table 3.6 summarizes the bitwise operators.

Table 3.6 *Bitwise Operators*

Operator	Meaning
&	Bitwise AND
¦	Bitwise OR
^	Bitwise XOR
<<	Left shift
>>	Right shift
>>>	Zero fill right shift
~	Bitwise complement
<<=	Left shift assignment (x = x << y)
>>=	Right shift assignment (x = x >> y)
>>>=	Zero fill right shift assignment (x = x >>> y)
x&=y	AND assignment (x = x & y)
x¦=y	OR assignment (x + x ¦ y)
x^=y	XOR assignment (x = x ^ y)

Operator Precedence

Operator precedence determines the order in which expressions are evaluated. This, in some cases, can determine the overall value of the expression. For example, take the following expression:

```
y = 6 + 4 / 2
```

Depending on whether the 6 + 4 expression or the 4 / 2 expression is evaluated first, the value of y can end up being 5 or 8. Operator precedence determines the order in which expressions are evaluated, so you can predict the outcome of an expression. In general, increment and decrement are evaluated before arithmetic, arithmetic expressions are evaluated before comparisons, and comparisons are evaluated before logical expressions. Assignment expressions are evaluated last.

Table 3.7 shows the specific precedence of the various operators in Java. Operators further up in the table are evaluated first; operators on the same line have the same precedence and are evaluated left to right based on how they appear in the expression itself. For example, give that same expression y = 6 + 4 / 2, you now know, according to this table, that division is evaluated before addition, so the value of y will be 8.

Table 3.7   *Operator Precedence*

Operator	Notes
. [] ()	Parentheses () group expressions; dot (.) is used for access to methods and variables within objects and classes (discussed tomorrow); [] is used for arrays (discussed later on in the week)
++ -- ! ~ instanceof	Returns true or false based on whether the object is an instance of the named class or any of that class's superclasses (discussed tomorrow)
new (type)expression	The new operator is used for creating new instances of classes; () in this case is for casting a value to another type (you'll learn about both of these tomorrow)
* / %	Multiplication, division, modulus
+ -	Addition, subtraction
<< >> >>>	Bitwise left and right shift
< > ≤ ≥	Relational comparison tests
== !=	Equality
&	AND
^	XOR
¦	OR
&&	Logical AND
¦¦	Logical OR
? :	Shorthand for if...then...else (discussed on Day 5)
= += -= *= /= %= ^= ➥&= ¦= <<= >>= >>>=	Various assignments

You can always change the order in which expressions are evaluated by using parentheses around the expressions you want to evaluate first. You can nest parentheses to

make sure expressions evaluate in the order you want them to (the innermost parenthetical expression is evaluated first). The following expression results in a value of 5,
because the 6 + 4 expression is evaluated first, and then the result of that expression
(10) is divided by 2:

```
y = (6 + 4) / 2
```

Parentheses also can be useful in cases in which the precedence of an expression isn't
immediately clear—in other words, they can make your code easier to read. Adding
parentheses doesn't hurt, so if they help you figure out how expressions are evaluated, go ahead and use them.

String Arithmetic

One special expression in Java is the use of the addition operator (+) to create and
concatenate strings. In most of the previous examples shown today and in earlier
lessons, you've seen lots of lines that looked something like this:

```
System.out.println(name + " is a " + color " beetle");
```

The output of that line (to the standard output) is a single string, with the values of
the variables (here, name and color) inserted in the appropriate spots in the string. So
what's going on here?

The + operator, when used with strings and other objects, creates a single string that
contains the concatenation of all its operands. If any of the operands in string concatenation is not a string, it is automatically converted to a string, making it easy to
create these sorts of output lines.

NOTE An object or type can be converted to a string if you implement the method
`toString()`. All objects have a default string representation, but most classes override
`toString()` to provide a more meaningful printable representation.

String concatenation makes lines, such as the previous one, especially easy to construct. To create a string, just add all the parts together—the descriptions plus the
variables—and output it to the standard output, to the screen, to an applet, or anywhere.

The += operator, which you learned about earlier, also works for strings. For example,
take the following expression:

```
myName += " Jr.";
```

This expression is equivalent to this:

```
myName = myName + " Jr.";
```

... just as it would be for numbers. In this case, it changes the value of myName (which might be something like John Smith to have a Jr. at the end (John Smith Jr.).

Summary

As you learned in the last two lessons, a Java program is made up primarily of classes and objects. Classes and objects, in turn, are made up of methods and variables, and methods are made up of statements and expressions. These are the basic building blocks that enable you to create classes and methods and build them up to a full-fledged Java program.

Today, you learned about variables, how to declare them and assign values to them; literals for easily creating numbers, characters, and strings; and operators for arithmetic, tests, and other simple operations. With this basic syntax, you can move on tomorrow to learning about working with objects and building simple, useful Java programs.

To finish up this summary, Table 3.8 is a list of all the operators you learned about today so that you can refer back to them.

Table 3.8   *Operator Summary*

Operator	Meaning
+	Addition
-	Subtraction
*	Multiplication
/	Division
%	Modulus
<	Less than
>	Greater than
≤	Less than or equal to
≥	Greater than or equal to
==	Equal
!=	Not equal

continues

Table 3.8 *Continued*

Operator	Meaning
&&	Logical AND
¦¦	Logical OR
!	Logical NOT
&	AND
¦	OR
^	XOR
<<	Left shift
>>	Right shift
>>>	Zero fill right shift
~	Complement
=	Assignment
++	Increment
--	Decrement
+=	Add and assign
-=	Subtract and assign
*=	Multiply and assign
/=	Divide and assign
%=	Modulus and assign
&=	AND and assign
¦=	OR and assign
^=	XOR and assign
<<=	Left shift and assign
>>=	Right shift and assign
>>>=	Zero fill right shift and assign

Questions and Answers

Q I didn't see a way to define constants.

A You can't create local constants in Java; you can create only constant instance and class variables. You'll learn how to do this tomorrow.

Q **What happens if you declare a variable to be some integer type, and then give it a number outside the range of values that that variable can hold?**

A Logically, you would think that the variable is just converted to the next larger type, but this isn't what happens. What does happen is called *overflow*. This means that if a number becomes too big for its variable, that number wraps around to the smallest possible negative number for that type and starts counting upward toward zero again.

Because this can result in some very confusing (and wrong) results, make sure that you declare the right integer type for all your numbers. If there's a chance a number will overflow its type, use the next larger type instead.

Q **How can you find out the type of a given variable?**

A If you're using the base types (int, float, boolean), and so on, you can't. If you care about the type, you can convert the value to some other type by using casting (you'll learn about this tomorrow).

If you're using class types, you can use the instanceof operator, which you'll learn more about tomorrow.

Q **Why does Java have all these shorthand operators for arithmetic and assignment? It's really hard to read that way.**

A The syntax of Java is based on C++, and therefore on C. One of C's implicit goals is the capability of doing very powerful things with a minimum of typing. Because of this, shorthand operators, such as the wide array of assignments, are common.

There's no rule, however, that says you have to use these operators in your own programs. If you find your code to be more readable using the long form, no one will come to your house and make you change it.

Working with Objects

by Laura Lemay with Timothy Webster

Let's start today's lesson with an obvious statement: Because Java is an object-oriented language, you're going to be dealing with a lot of objects. You'll create them, modify them, move them around, change their variables, call their methods, combine them with other objects—and, of course, develop classes and use your own objects in the mix.

Today, therefore, you'll learn all about the Java object in its natural habitat. Today's topics include:

- ☐ Creating instances of classes
- ☐ Testing and modifying class and instance variables in your new instance
- ☐ Calling methods in that object
- ☐ Casting (converting) objects and other data types from one class to another
- ☐ Learning other odds and ends about working with objects
- ☐ Getting an overview of the Java class libraries

Creating New Objects

When you write a Java program, you define a set of classes. As you learned on Day 2, classes are templates for objects. For the most part, you merely use the class to create instances and then work with those instances. In this section, therefore, you'll learn how to create a new object from any given class.

Remember strings from yesterday? You learned that using a string literal—a series of characters enclosed in double quotes—creates a new instance of the class String with the value of that string.

The String class is unusual in that respect—although it's a class, there's an easy way to create instances of that class using a literal. The other classes don't have that shortcut; to create instances of those classes you have to do so explicitly by using the new operator.

NOTE

> What about the literals for numbers and characters? Don't they create objects, too? Actually, they don't. The primitive data types for numbers and characters create numbers and characters, but for efficiency, they aren't actually objects. You can put object-wrappers around them if you need to treat them like objects (you'll learn how to do this later).

Using new

To create a new object, you use new with the name of the class you want to create an instance of, then parentheses after that:

```
String str = new String();

Random r = new Random();

Motorcycle m2 = new Motorcycle();
```

The parentheses are important; don't leave them off. The parentheses can be empty, in which case the most simple, basic object is created, or the parentheses can contain arguments that determine the initial values of instance variables or other initial qualities of that object. The number and type of arguments you can use with new are defined by the class itself by using a special method called a *constructor*; you'll learn about how to create constructors in your own classes later this week.

WARNING

> Some classes may not enable you to create instances without any arguments. Check the class to make sure.

For example, take the Date class, which creates Date objects. Here is a Java program that shows three different ways of creating a Date object using new:

```
1: import java.util.Date;
2:
3: class CreateDates {
4:
5:     public static void main (String args[]) {
6:         Date d1, d2, d3;
7:
```

```
 8:          d1 = new Date();
 9:          System.out.println("Date 1: " + d1);
10:
11:          d2 = new Date(71, 8, 1, 7, 30);
12:          System.out.println("Date 2: " + d2);
13:
14:          d3 = new Date("April 3 1993 3:24 PM");
15:          System.out.println("Date 3: " + d3);
16:      }
17: }
```

And the output:

```
Date 1: Sun Feb 25 19:10:56 PST 1996
Date 2: Sun Aug 01 07:30:00 PDT 1971
Date 3: Sat Apr 03 15:24:00 PST 1993
```

In this example, three different dates are created by using different arguments to new. The first instance (line 8) uses new with no arguments, which creates a Date object for today's date (as the first line of the output shows).

The second Date object you create in this example has five integer arguments. The arguments represent a date: year, month, day, hours, and seconds. And, as the output shows, this creates a Date object for that particular date: Sunday, August first, 1971, at 7:30 AM.

The third version of Date takes one argument, a string, representing the date as a text string. When the Date object is created, that string is parsed, and a Date object with that date and time is created (see the third line of output). The date string can take many different formats; see the API documentation for the Date class (part of the java.util package) for information about what strings you can use.

What new Does

What does new do? When you use the new operator, several things happen: first, the new instance of the given class is created, and memory is allocated for it. In addition (and most importantly), when the new object is created, a special method defined in the given class is called. This special method is called a constructor.

NEW TERM *Constructors* are special methods for creating and initializing new instances of classes. Constructors initialize the new object and its variables, create any other objects that object needs, and generally perform any other operations the object needs to run.

Multiple constructor definitions in a class can each have a different number or type of arguments—then, when you use new, you can specify different arguments in the argument list, and the right constructor for those arguments will be called. That's how each of those different versions of new that were listed previously can create different things.

When you create your own classes, you can define as many constructors as you need to implement that class's behavior. You'll learn how to create constructors on Day 7.

A Note on Memory Management

Memory management in Java is dynamic and automatic. When you create a new object in Java, Java automatically allocates the right amount of memory for that object in the heap. You don't have to allocate any memory for any objects explicitly; Java does it for you.

What happens when you're finished with that object? How do you deallocate the memory that object uses? The answer is again: memory management is automatic. When you finish with an object, that object no longer has any live references to it (it won't be assigned to any variables you're still using or stored in any arrays). Java has a garbage collector that looks for unused objects and reclaims the memory that those objects are using. You don't have to do any explicit freeing of memory; you just have to make sure you're not still holding onto an object you want to get rid of. You'll learn more specific details about the Java garbage collector and how it works on Day 21.

Accessing and Setting Class and Instance Variables

Now you have your very own object, and that object may have class or instance variables defined in it. How do you work with those variables? Easy! Class and instance variables behave in exactly the same ways as the local variables you learned about yesterday; you just refer to them slightly differently than you do regular variables in your code.

Getting Values

To get at the value of an instance variable, you use dot notation.

NEW TERM   With *dot notation*, an instance or class variable name has two parts: the object on the left side of the dot, and the variable on the right side of the dot.

For example, if you have an object assigned to the variable myObject, and that object has a variable called var, you refer to that variable's value like this:

```
myObject.var
```

This form for accessing variables is an expression (it returns a value), and both sides of the dot are also expressions. This means that you can nest instance variable access. If that var instance variable itself holds an object, and that object has its own instance variable called state, you can refer to it like this:

```
myObject.var.state
```

Dot expressions are evaluated left to right, so you start with myObject's variable var, which points to another object with the variable state. You end up with the value of that state variable.

Changing Values

Assigning a value to that variable is equally easy—just tack an assignment operator on the right side of the expression:

```
myObject.var.state = true;
```

The following is an example of a program that tests and modifies the instance variables in a Point object. Point is part of the java.awt package and refers to a coordinate point with an x and a y value.

```
 1: import java.awt.Point;
 2:
 3: class TestPoint {
 4:
 5:     public static void main (String args[]) {
 6:         Point thePoint = new Point(10,10);
 7:
 8:         System.out.println("x is " + thePoint.x);
 9:         System.out.println("y is " + thePoint.y);
10:
11:         System.out.println("Setting x to 5.");
12:         thePoint.x = 5;
13:         System.out.println("Setting y to 15.");
14:         thePoint.y = 15;
15:
16:         System.out.println("x is " + thePoint.x);
17:         System.out.println("y is " + thePoint.y);
```

```
18:
19:     }
20: }
```

The output looks like this:

```
x is 10
y is 10
Setting x to 5.
Setting y to 15.
x is 5
y is 15
```

In this example, you first create an instance of `Point` where x and y are both `10` (line 6). Lines 8 and 9 print out those individual values, and you can see dot notation at work there. Lines 11 through 14 change the values of those variables to `5` and `15`, respectively. Finally, lines 16 and 17 print out the values of x and y again to show how they've changed.

Class Variables

Class variables, as you learned before, are variables that are defined and stored in the class itself. Their values, therefore, apply to the class and to all its instances.

With instance variables, each new instance of the class gets a new copy of the instance variables that class defines. Each instance can then change the values of those instance variables without affecting any other instances. With class variables, there is only one copy of that variable. Every instance of the class has access to that variable, but there is only one value. Changing the value of that variable changes it for all the instances of that class.

You define class variables by including the `static` keyword before the variable itself. You'll learn more about this on Day 6. For example, take the following partial class definition:

```
class FamilyMember {
    static String surname = "Johnson";
    String name;
    int age;
    ...
}
```

Instances of the class `FamilyMember` have their own values for name and age. But the class variable `surname` has only one value for all family members. When you change `surname`, all the instances of `FamilyMember` are affected.

To access class variables, you use the same dot notation as you do with instance variables. To get or change the value of the class variable, you can use either the instance or the name of the class on the left side of the dot. Both the lines of output in this example print the same value:

```
FamilyMember dad = new FamilyMember();
System.out.println("Family's surname is: " + dad.surname);
System.out.println("Family's surname is: " + FamilyMember.surname);
```

Because you can use an instance to change the value of a class variable, it's easy to become confused about class variables and where their values are coming from (remember, the value of a class variable affects all the instances). For this reason, it's a good idea to use the name of the class when you refer to a class variable—it makes your code easier to read and strange results easier to debug.

Calling Methods

Calling a method in objects is similar to referring to its instance variables: method calls also use dot notation. The object whose method you're calling is on the left side of the dot; the name of the method and its arguments are on the right side of the dot:

```
myObject.methodOne(arg1, arg2, arg3);
```

Note that all methods must have parentheses after them, even if that method takes no arguments:

```
myObject.methodNoArgs();
```

If the method you've called results in an object that has methods, you can nest methods as you would variables:

```
myObject.getClass().getName();
```

You can combine nested method calls and instance variable references as well:

```
myObject.var.methodTwo(arg1, arg2);
```

`System.out.println()`, the method you've been using through the book this far, is a great example of nesting variables and methods. The `System` class (part of the `java.lang` package) describes system-specific behavior. `System.out` is a class variable that contains an instance of the class `PrintStream` that points to the standard output of the system. `PrintStream` instances have a `println()` method that prints a string to that output stream.

The following code shows an example of calling methods defined in the `String` class. Strings include methods for string tests and modification, similar to what you would expect in a string library in other languages.

```
 1: class TestString {
 2:
 3:     public static void main (String args[]) {
 4:         String str = "Now is the winter of our discontent";
 5:
 6:         System.out.println("The string is: " + str);
 7:         System.out.println("Length of this string: "
 8:                 + str.length());
 9:         System.out.println("The character at position 5: "
10:                 + str.charAt(5));
11:         System.out.println("The substring from 11 to 18: "
12:                 + str.substring(11, 18));
13:         System.out.println("The index of the character d: "
14:                 + str.indexOf('d'));
15:         System.out.print("The index of the beginning of the ");
16:         System.out.println("substring \"winter\":"
17:                 + str.indexOf("winter"));
18:         System.out.println("The string in uppercase: "
19:                 + str.toUpperCase());
20:     }
21: }
```

And the output:

```
The string is: Now is the winter of our discontent
Length of this string: 35
The character at position 5: s
The substring from positions 11 to 18: winter
The index of the character d: 25
The index of the beginning of the substring "winter": 11
The string in uppercase: NOW IS THE WINTER OF OUR DISCONTENT
```

In line 4, you create a new instance of `String` by using a string literal (it's easier that way than using `new` and then putting the characters in individually). The remainder of the program simply calls different string methods to do different operations on that string:

☐ Line 6 prints the value of the string we created in line 4:
   `"Now is the winter of our discontent"`.

☐ Lines 7–8 call the length() method in the new String object. This string has 35 characters.

☐ Lines 9–10 call the charAt() method, which returns the character at the given position in the string. Note that string positions start at 0, so the character at position 5 is s.

☐ Lines 11–12 call the substring() method, which takes two integers indicating a range and returns the substring at those starting and ending points. The substring() method can also be called with only one argument, which returns the substring from that position to the end of the string.

☐ Lines 13–14 call the indexOf() method, which returns the position of the first instance of the given character (here, 'd').

☐ Line 15 shows a different use of the indexOf() method, which takes a string argument and returns the index of the beginning of that string.

☐ Finally, lines 18–19 use the toUpperCase() method to return a copy of the string in all uppercase.

Class Methods

Class methods, like class variables, apply to the class as a whole and not to its instances. Class methods are commonly used for general utility methods that may not operate directly on an instance of that class, but fit with that class conceptually. For example, the String class contains a class method called valueOf(), which can take one of many different types of arguments (integers, booleans, other objects, and so on). The valueOf() method then returns a new instance of String containing the string value of the argument it was given. This method doesn't operate directly on an existing instance of String, but getting a string from another object or data type is definitely a String-like operation, and it makes sense to define it in the String class.

Class methods can also be useful for gathering general methods together in one place (the class). For example, the Math class, defined in the java.lang package, contains a large set of mathematical operations as class methods—there are no instances of the class Math, but you can still use its methods with numeric or boolean arguments.

To call a class method, use dot notation as you do with instance methods. As with class variables, you can use either an instance of the class or the class itself on the left site of the dot. However, for the same reasons noted in the discussion on class variables, using the name of the class for class methods makes your code easier to read. The last two lines in this example produce the same result:

```
String s, s2;
s = "foo";
s2 = s.valueOf(5);
s2 = String.valueOf(5);
```

References to Objects

As you work with objects, one important thing going on behind the scenes is the use of references to those objects. When you assign objects to variables or pass objects as arguments to methods, you are passing references to those objects, not the objects themselves or copies of those objects.

An example should make this clearer. Examine the following snippet of code:

```
import java.awt.Point;

class ReferencesTest {

    public static void main (String args[]) {
        Point pt1, pt2;
        pt1 = new Point(100, 100);
        pt2 = pt1;

        pt1.x = 200;
        pt1.y = 200;
        System.out.println("Point1: " + pt1.x + ", " + pt1.y);
        System.out.println("Point2: " + pt2.x + ", " + pt2.y);
    }
}
```

In this program, you declare two variables of type Point, and assign a new Point object to pt1. Then you assign the value of pt1 to pt2.

Now, here's the challenge. After changing pt1's x and y instance variables, what will pt2 look like?

Here's the output of that program:

```
Point1: 200, 200
Point2: 200, 200
```

As you can see, pt2 was also changed. When you assign the value of pt1 to pt2, you actually create a reference from pt2 to the same object to which pt1 refers. When you change the object that pt2 refers to, you also change the object that pt1 points to, because both are references to the same object.

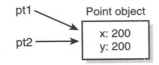

Figure 4.1 *References.*

Java references become particularly important when you pass arguments to methods. You'll learn more about this later on today, but keep these references in mind.

There are no explicit pointers or pointer arithmetic in Java—just references. However, because of Java references, you have most of the capabilities that you have with pointers without the confusion and lurking bugs that explicit pointers can create.

Casting and Converting Objects and Primitive Types

Sometimes in your Java programs you may have a value stored somewhere that is the wrong type. Maybe it's an instance of the wrong class, or perhaps it's a `float` and you want it to be an `int`, or it's an integer and you want it to be a string. To convert the value of one type to another, you use a mechanism called casting.

NEW TERM

Casting is a mechanism of converting the value of an object or primitive type into another type. The result of a cast is a new object reference or value; casting does not affect the original object or value.

Although the concept of casting is a simple one, the rules for what types in Java can be converted to what other types are complicated by the fact that Java has both primitive types (`int`, `float`, `boolean`) and object types (`String`, `Point`, `Window`, and so on). There are three forms of casts and conversions to talk about in this section:

☐ Casting between primitive types: `int` to `float` to `boolean`

☐ Casting between object types: an instance of a class to an instance of another class

☐ Converting primitive types to objects and then extracting primitive values back out of those objects

Casting Primitive Types

Casting between primitive types enables you to "convert" the value of one type to another primitive type—for example, to assign a number of one type to a variable of another type. Casting between primitive types most commonly occurs with the numeric types; boolean values cannot be cast to any other primitive type. You can, however, cast 1 or 0 to boolean values.

Often, if the type you are casting to is "larger" than the type of the value you're converting, you may not have to use an explicit cast. You can often automatically treat a byte or a character as an int, for example, or an int as a long, an int as a float, or anything as a double automatically. In this case, because the larger type provides more precision than the smaller, no loss of information occurs when the value is cast.

To convert a large value to a smaller type, you must use an explicit cast, because converting that value may result in a loss of precision. Explicit casts look like this:

```
(typename) value
```

In this form, *typename* is the name of the type you're converting to (for example: short, int, float, boolean) and *value* is an expression that results in the value you want to convert. This expression divides the values of x by the value of y and casts the result to an int:

```
(int) (x / y);
```

Note that because the precedence of casting is higher than that of arithmetic, you have to use parentheses so that the result of the division is what gets cast to an int.

Casting Objects

Instances of classes can also be cast to instances of other classes, with one restriction: the class of the object you're casting and the class you're casting it to must be related by inheritance; that is, you can cast an object only to an instance of its class's sub- or superclass—not to any random class.

Analogous to converting a primitive value to a larger type, some objects may not need to be cast explicitly. In particular, because instances' subclasses usually contain all the information that instances' superclasses do, you can use an instance of a subclass anywhere a superclass is expected. Suppose you have a method that takes two arguments: one of type Object, and one of type Number. You don't have to pass instances of those particular classes to that method. For the Object argument, you can pass any subclass of Object (any object, in other words), and for the Number argument you can pass in any instance of any subclass of Number (Integer, Boolean, Float, and so on).

Casting an object to an instance of one of that object's superclasses loses the information the original subclass provided and requires a specific cast. To cast an object to another class, you use the same casting operation that you used for base types:

```
(classname) object
```

In this case, *classname* is the name of the class you want to cast the object to, and object is a reference to the object you're casting. Note that casting creates a reference to the old object, of the type classname; the old object still continues to exist as it did before.

Here's a fictitious example of a cast of an instance of the class GreenApple to an instance of the class Apple (where GreenApple is theoretically a subclass of Apple):

```
GreenApple a;
Apple a2;
a = new GreenApple();
a2 = (Apple) a;
```

In addition to casting objects to classes, you can also cast objects to interfaces—but only if that object's class or one of its superclasses actually implements that interface. Casting an object to an interface then enables you to call one of that interface's methods even if that object's class does not directly implement that interface. You'll learn more about interfaces in Week 3.

Converting Primitive Types to Objects and Vice Versa

Now that you know how to cast a primitive type to another primitive type and how to cast between classes, how can you cast one to the other?

The answer is you can't. Primitive types and objects are very different things in Java and you can't automatically cast or convert between the two. However, the java.lang package includes several special classes that correspond to each primitive data type: Integer for ints, Float for floats, Boolean for booleans, and so on.

Using class methods defined in these classes, you can create an object-equivalent for all the primitive types using new. The following line of code creates an instance of the Integer class with the value 35:

```
Integer intObject = new Integer(35);
```

When you have actual objects, you can treat those values as objects. Then, when you want the primitive values back again, there are methods for that as well—for example, the intValue() method extracts an int primitive value from an Integer object:

```
int theInt = intObject.intValue();  // returns 35
```

See the Java API documentation for these special classes for specifics on the methods for converting primitives to and from objects.

Odds and Ends

This section is a catchall for other information about working with objects, in particular:

☐ Comparing objects

☐ Copying objects

☐ Finding out the class of any given object

☐ Testing to see whether an object is an instance of a given class

Comparing Objects

Yesterday, you learned about operators for comparing values: equal, not equal, less than, and so on. Most of these operators work only on primitive types, not on objects. If you try to use other values as operands, the Java compiler produces errors.

The exception to this rule is with the operators for equality: == (equal) and != (not equal). These operators, when used with objects, test whether the two operands refer to exactly the same object.

What should you do if you want to compare instances of your class and have meaningful results? You have to implement special methods in your class, and you have to call those methods using those method names.

NOTE
> Java does not have the concept of operator overloading—that is, the capability of defining the behavior of the built-in operators by defining methods in your own classes. The built-in operators remain defined only for numbers.

A good example of this is the String class. It is possible to have two strings and two independent objects in memory with the same values—that is, the same characters in the same order. According to the == operator, however, those two String objects will not be equal, because, although their contents are the same, they are not the same object.

The String class, therefore, defines a method called equals() that tests each character in the string and returns true if the two strings have the same values. The following code illustrates this.

```
 1: class EqualsTest {
 2:
 3:     public static void main (String args[]) {
 4:         String str1, str2;
 5:         str1 = "she sells sea shells by the sea shore.";
 6:         str2 = str1;
 7:
 8:         System.out.println("String1: " + str1);
 9:         System.out.println("String2: " + str2);
10:         System.out.println("Same object? " + (str1 == str2));
11:
12:         str2 = new String(str1);
13:
14:         System.out.println("String1: " + str1);
15:         System.out.println("String2: " + str2);
16:         System.out.println("Same object? " + (str1 == str2));
17:         System.out.println("Same value? " + str1.equals(str2));
18:     }
19: }
```

Here's the output:

```
String1: she sells sea shells by the sea shore.
String2: she sells sea shells by the sea shore.
Same object? true
String1: she sells sea shells by the sea shore.
String2: she sells sea shells by the sea shore.
Same object? false
Same value? true
```

The first part of this program (lines 4 through 6) declares two variables, str1 and str2, assigns the literal she sells sea shells by the sea shore. to str1, and then assigns that value to str2. As you know from object references, now str1 and str2 point to the same object, and the test at line 10 proves that.

In the second part, you create a new String object with the value of str1. Now you have two different String objects with the same value. Testing them to see whether they're the same object by using the == operator (line 16) returns the expected answer, as does testing them using the equals() method (line 17) to compare their values.

NOTE   Why can't you just use another literal when you change str2, rather than using new? String literals are optimized in Java—if you create a string using a literal and then use another literal with the same characters, Java knows enough merely to give you the first String object back. Both strings are the same objects—to create two separate objects you have to go out of your way.

Copying Objects

Recall from the section on object references that assigning variables and passing objects as arguments to methods affect only the object's reference and don't create copies of those objects. How do you create copies of objects? There are two ways: the copy() method and the clone() method.

The copy() method (defined in Object, and available to all objects), takes a single argument—another instance of the same class—and copies the values of all the argument's instance variables into the instance variables of the current object (the one in which you're calling the method). Note that if those instance variables in turn hold references to objects, only the references are copied, not the objects.

```
Point pt1, pt2, pt3;
pt1 = new Point(0,0);
pt2 = new Point(100,100);

pt2.copy(pt1); // pt1's values are copied into pt2; both now are (0,0).
```

The clone() method is similar to copy(), except that clone() takes no arguments. The clone() method creates a new instance of the same class as the source object and then copies the values of the instance variables (either primitive types or references to other objects). clone() returns an instance of the class Object; to use it as an instance of the original class you have to cast it. Here's an example that clones the Point object in pt2 and stores the result in pt3:

```
pt3 = (Point) pt2.clone();
```

Determining the Class of an Object

Want to find out the class of an object? Here's the way to do it for an object assigned to the variable obj:

```
String name = obj.getClass().getName();
```

What does this do? The getClass() method is defined in the Object class and is available for all objects. The result of that method is a Class object (where Class is itself a class), which has a method called getName(). getName() returns a string representing the name of the class.

Another test that might be useful to you is the instanceof operator. instanceof has two operands: an object on the left and the name of a class on the right. The expression returns true or false based on whether the object is an instance of the named class or any of that class's superclasses:

```
"foo" instanceof String // true
Point pt = new Point(10,10);
pt instanceof String // false
```

The `instanceof` operator can also be used for interfaces; if an object implements an interface, the `instanceof` operator with that interface name on the right side returns `true`. You'll learn all about interfaces in Week 3.

The Java Class Libraries

To finish up today, let's look at the some of the Java class libraries. Actually, you've had some experience with them already, so they shouldn't seem that strange.

 The Java class libraries provide the set of classes that are guaranteed to be available in any commercial Java environment. (You can find the source code for the libraries that came with Roaster in the folder Roaster DR1:Roaster:java:src:java. Those classes are in the `java` package and include all the classes you've seen so far in this book, plus a whole lot more classes you'll learn about later on in this book (and more you may not learn about at all).)

The Java Developer's Kit comes with documentation for all the Java class libraries, including descriptions of each class's instance variables, methods, constructors, interfaces, and so on. A shorter summary of the Java API is in Appendix B as well. Exploring the Java class libraries and their methods and instance variables is a great way to figure out what Java can and cannot do, as well as a starting point for your own development.

Here are the class packages that are part of the Java class libraries:

- [ ] `java.lang`: Classes that apply to the language itself, including the `Object` class, the `String` class, and the `System` class. It also contains the special classes for the primitive types (`Integer`, `Character`, `Float`, and so on).

- [ ] `java.util`: Utility classes, such as `Date`, as well as simple collection classes, such as `Vector` and `Hashtable`.

- [ ] `java.io`: Input and output classes for writing to and reading from streams (such as standard input and output) and for handling files.

- [ ] `java.net`: Classes for networking support, including `Socket` and `URL` (a class to represent references to documents on the World Wide Web).

- [ ] `java.awt` *(the Abstract Window Toolkit):* Classes to implement a graphical user interface, including classes for `Window`, `Menu`, `Button`, `Font`, `CheckBox`, and so on.

This package also includes classes for processing images (the `java.awt.Image` package).

☐ `java.applet`: Classes to implement Java applets, including the `Applet` class itself, as well as the `AudioClip` class.

Summary

Objects, objects everywhere. Today, you learned all about how to deal with objects: how to create them, how to find out and change the values of their variables, and how to call their methods. You also learned how to copy and compare them, and how to convert them into other objects. Finally, you learned a bit about the Java class libraries—which give you a whole slew of classes to play with in your own programs.

You now have the fundamentals of how to deal with most simple things in the Java language. All you have left are arrays, conditionals, and loops, which you'll learn about tomorrow. You'll learn how to define and use classes in Java applications on Day 6, and launch directly into applets next week. With just about everything you do in your Java programs, you'll always come back to objects.

Questions and Answers

Q I'm confused about the differences between objects and the primitive data types, such as `int` and `boolean`.

A The primitive types in the language (`byte`, `short`, `int`, `long`, `float`, `double`, and `char`) represent the smallest things in the language. They are not objects, although in many ways they can be handled like objects—they can be assigned to variables and passed in and out of methods. Most of the operations that work exclusively on objects, however, will not.

Objects usually represent instances of classes and, as such, are much more complex data types than simple numbers and characters. Objects often contain numbers and characters as instance or class variables.

Q In the section on calling methods, you had examples of calling a method with a different number of arguments each time—and it gave a different kind of result. How is that possible?

A That's called *method overloading*. Overloading enables the same function name to have different behavior based on the arguments it's called with—and the number and type of arguments can vary. When you define methods in your own classes, you define separate method signatures with different sets or arguments and different definitions. When that method is called, Java figures out which definition to execute based on the number and type of arguments with which you called it.

You'll learn all about this on Day 6.

Q No operator overloading in Java? Why not? I thought Java was based on C++, and C++ has operator overloading.

A Java was indeed based on C++, but it was also designed to be simple, so many of C++'s features have been removed. The argument against operator overloading is that because the operator can be defined to mean anything, it makes it very difficult to figure out what any given operator is doing at any one time. This can result in entirely unreadable code. Given the potential for abuse, the designers of Java felt it was one of the C++ features that was best left out.

Arrays, Conditionals, and Loops

by Laura Lemay with Timothy Webster

Although you could write Java programs using what you've learned so far, those programs would be pretty dull. Much of the good stuff in Java or in any programming language results when you have arrays to store values in and control flow constructs (loops and conditionals) to execute different bits of a program based on tests. Today, you'll find out about the following:

- [ ] Arrays, one of the most useful objects in Java, which enable you to collect objects into an easy-to-manage list

- [ ] Block statements, for grouping together related statements

- [ ] `if` and `switch`, for conditional tests

- [ ] `for` and `while` loops, for iteration or repeating a statement or statements multiple times

Arrays

Arrays in Java are different than they are in other languages. Arrays in Java are actual objects that can be passed around and treated just like other objects.

NEW TERM
> *Arrays* are a way to store a list of items. Each element of the array holds an individual item, and you can place items into and remove items from those slots as you need to.

Arrays can contain any type of value (base types or objects), but you can't store different types in a single array. You can have an array of integers, or an array of strings, or an array of arrays, but you can't have an array that contains, for example, both strings and integers.

To create an array in Java, use three steps:

1. Declare a variable to hold the array.

2. Create a new array object and assign it to the array variable.

3. Store things in that array.

Declaring Array Variables

The first step to creating an array is creating a variable that will hold the array, just as you would any other variable. Array variables indicate the type of object the array will hold (just as they do for any variable) and the name of the array, followed by empty brackets ([]). The following are all typical array variable declarations:

```
String difficultWords[];
Point hits[];
int temps[];
```

An alternative method of defining an array variable is to put the brackets after the type instead of after the variable. They are equivalent, but this latter form is often much more readable. So, for example, these three declarations could be written like this:

```
String[] difficultWords;
Point[] hits;
int[] temps;
```

Creating Array Objects

The second step is to create an array object and assign it to that variable. There are two ways to do this:

☐ Using new

☐ Directly initializing the contents of that array

The first way is to use the new operator to create a new instance of an array:

```
String[] names = new String[10];
```

That line creates a new array of Strings with ten *slots*, or elements. When you create the new array object using new, you must indicate how many elements that array will hold.

Array objects can contain primitive types such as integers or booleans, just as they can contain objects:

```
int[] temps = new int[99];
```

When you create an array object using `new`, all its elements are initialized for you (`0` for numeric arrays, `false` for boolean, `'\0'` for character arrays, and `null` for everything else). You can also create and initialize an array of primitives at the same time. Instead of using `new` to create the new array object, enclose the elements of the array inside braces, separated by commas:

```
String[] chiles = { "jalapeno", "anaheim", "serrano",
    "habanero", "thai" };
```

Each of the elements inside the braces must be a primitive of the same type and must be the same type as the variable that holds that array. An array the size of the number of elements you've included will be automatically created for you. This example creates an array of String objects named `chiles` that contains five elements.

Accessing Array Elements

Once you have an array with initial values, you can test and change the values in each slot of that array. To get at a value stored within an array, use the array `subscript` expression:

```
myArray[subscript];
```

The `myArray` part of this expression is a variable holding an array object, although it can also be an expression that results in an array. The `subscript` is the slot within the array to access, which can also be an expression. Array subscripts start with `0`, as they do in C and C++. So, an array with ten elements has array values from subscript `0` to `9`.

Note that all array subscripts are checked to make sure that they are inside the boundaries of the array (greater than 0 but less than the array's length) either when your Java program is compiled or when it is run. It is impossible in Java to access or assign a value to an array element outside of the boundaries of the array. Note the following two statements, for example:

```
String[] arr = new String[10];
arr[10] = "eggplant";
```

A program with that last statement in it produces a compiler error at that line when you try to compile it. The array stored in `arr` has only ten elements numbered from 0, the element at subscript `10` doesn't exist, and the Java compiler will check for that.

If the array subscript is calculated at run time (for example, as part of a loop) and ends up outside the boundaries of the array, the Java interpreter also produces an error (actually, to be technically correct, it throws an exception. You'll learn more about exceptions later on next week and on Day 17).

How can you keep from overrunning the end of an array accidentally in your own programs? You can test for the length of the array in your programs using the `length` instance variable—it's available for all array objects, regardless of type:

```
int len = arr.length // returns 10
```

Changing Array Elements

To assign a value to a particular array slot, merely put an assignment statement after the array access expression:

```
myarray[1] = 15;
sentence[0] = "The";
sentence[10] = sentence[0];
```

An important thing to note is that an array of objects in Java is an array of references to those objects (similar in some ways to an array of pointers in C or C++). When you assign a value to a slot in an array, you're creating a reference to that object, just as you do for a plain variable. When you move values around inside arrays (as in that last line), you just reassign the reference; you don't copy the value from one slot to another. Arrays of primitive types such as `ints` or `floats` do copy the values from one slot to another.

Arrays of references to objects, as opposed to the objects themselves, are particularly useful because it means you can have multiple references to the same objects both inside and outside arrays—for example, you can assign an object contained in an array to a variable and refer to that same object by using either the variable or the array position.

Multidimensional Arrays

Java does not support multidimensional arrays. However, you can declare and create an array of arrays (and those arrays can contain arrays, and so on, for however many dimensions you need), and access them as you would C-style multidimensional arrays:

```
int coords[][] = new int[12][12];
coords[0][0] = 1;
coords[0][1] = 2;
```

Block Statements

A block statement is a group of other statements surrounded by braces ({}). You can use a block anywhere a single statement would go, and the new block creates a new local scope for the statements inside it. This means that you can declare and use local variables inside a block, and those variables will cease to exist after the block is finished executing. For example, here's a block inside a method definition that declares a new variable y. You cannot use y outside the block in which it's declared:

```
void testblock() {
    int x = 10;
    { // start of block
      int y = 50;
      System.out.println("inside the block:");
      System.out.println("x:" + x);
      System.out.println("y:" + y);
    } // end of block
}
```

Blocks are not usually used in this way—alone in a method definition. You've mostly seen blocks up to this point surrounding class and method definitions, but another very common use of block statements is in the control flow constructs you'll learn about in the remainder of today's lesson.

if Conditionals

The if conditional, which enables you to execute different bits of code based on a simple test in Java, is nearly identical to if statements in C. if conditionals contain the keyword if, followed by a boolean test, followed by a statement (often a block statement) to execute if the test is true:

```
if (x < y)
    System.out.println("x is smaller than y");
```

An optional else keyword provides the statement to execute if the test is false:

```
if (x < y)
    System.out.println("x is smaller than y");
else System.out.println("y is bigger.");
```

NOTE	The difference between if conditionals in Java and in C or C++ is that the test must return a boolean value (true or false). Unlike in C, the test cannot return an integer.

```
if (engineState == true )
    System.out.println("Engine is already on.");
else {
    System.out.println("Now starting Engine");
    if (gasLevel >= 1)
```

```
        engineState = true;
    else System.out.println("Low on gas! Can't start engine.");
}
```

This example uses the test (engineState == true). For boolean tests of this type, a common shortcut is merely to include the first part of the expression, rather than explicitly testing its value against true or false:

```
if (engineState)
    System.out.println("Engine is on.");
else System.out.println("Engine is off");
```

The Conditional Operator

An alternative to using the if and else keywords in a conditional statement is to use the conditional operator, sometimes called the ternary operator.

NEW TERM   A *conditional operator* is a ternary operator because it has three terms.

The conditional operator is an expression, meaning that it returns a value (unlike the more general if, which can result in any statement or block being executed). The conditional operator is most useful for very short or simple conditionals, and looks like this:

```
test ? trueresult : falseresult
```

The *test* is an expression that returns true or false, just like the test in the if statement. If the test is true, the conditional operator returns the value of *trueresult*; if it's false, it returns the value of *falseresult*. For example, the following conditional tests the values of x and y, returns the smaller of the two, and assigns that value to the variable smaller:

```
int smaller = x < y ? x : y;
```

The conditional operator has a very low precedence; that is, it's usually evaluated only after all its subexpressions are evaluated. The only operators lower in precedence are the assignment operators. See the precedence chart on Day 3 for a refresher on precedence of all the operators.

NOTE   The source code editor will automatically add an if conditional construct around selected text when you choose If() from the Control Structure icon's menu.

`switch` Conditionals

A common practice in programming in any language is to test a variable against some value, and if it doesn't match that value, to test it again against a different value, and if it doesn't match that one to make yet another test, and so on. Using only `if` statements, this can become unwieldy, depending on how it's formatted and how many different options you have to test. For example, you might end up with a set of `if` statements something like this or longer:

```
if (oper == '+')
  addargs(arg1,arg2);
else if (oper == '-')
    subargs(arg1,arg2);
else if (oper == '*')
    multargs(arg1,arg2);
else if (oper == '/')
    divargs(arg1,arg2);
```

This form of `if` statement is called a nested `if`, because each `else` statement in turn contains yet another `if`, and so on, until all possible tests have been made.

A common shorthand mechanism for nested `ifs` that you can use in some cases enables you to group tests and actions together in a single statement. This is the `switch` or case statement; in Java it's `switch` and behaves as it does in C:

```
switch (test) {
    case valueOne:
    resultOne;
      break;
    case valueTwo:
    resultTwo;
      break;
    case valueThree:
    resultThree;
      break;
    ...
    default: defaultresult;
}
```

In the `switch` statement, the test (a primitive type of `byte`, `char`, `short`, or `int`) is compared with each of the case values in turn. If a match is found, the statement or statements after the test are executed. If no match is found, the `default` statement is executed. The `default` is optional, so if there isn't a match in any of the cases and `default` doesn't exist, the `switch` statement completes without doing anything.

Note that the significant limitation of the `switch` in Java is that the tests and values can be only simple primitive types (and then only primitive types that are castable to `int`).

You cannot use larger primitive types (`long`, `float`) or objects within a `switch`, nor can you test for any relationship other than equality. This limits the usefulness of `switch` to all but the simplest cases; nested `if`s can work for any kind of test on any type.

Here's a simple example of a `switch` statement similar to the nested `if` shown earlier:

```
switch (oper) {
    case '+':
        addargs(arg1,arg2);
        break;
    case '*':
        subargs(arg1,arg2);
        break;
    case '-':
        multargs(arg1,arg2);
        break;
    case '/':
        divargs(arg1,arg2);
        break;
}
```

Note the `break` statement included in every line. Without the explicit break, once a match is made, the statements for that match and also all the statements further down in the `switch` are executed until a `break` or the end of the `switch` is found (and then execution continues after the end of the `switch`). In some cases, this may be exactly what you want to do, but in most cases, you'll want to make sure to include the `break` so that only the statements you want to be executed are executed.

One handy use of falling through occurs when you want multiple values to execute the same statements. In this instance, you can use multiple case lines with no result, and the `switch` will execute the first statements it finds. For example, in the following `switch` statement, the string `"x is an even number."` is printed if x has values of 2, 4, 6, or 8. All other values of x print the string `"x is an odd number."`

```
switch (x) {
    case 2:
    case 4:
    case 6:
    case 8:
        System.out.println("x is an even number.");
        break;
    default: System.out.println("x is an odd number.");
}
```

for Loops

The `for` loop, as in C, repeats a statement or block of statements some number of times until a condition is matched. `for` loops are frequently used for simple iteration in which you repeat a block of statements a certain number of times and then stop, but you can use `for` loops for just about any kind of loop.

The `for` loop in Java looks roughly like this:

```
for (initialization; test; increment) {
    statements;
}
```

The start of the `for` loop has three parts:

☐ *initialization* is an expression that initializes the start of the loop. If you have a loop index, this expression might declare and initialize it—for example, `int i = 0`. Variables that you declare in this part of the `for` loop are local to the loop itself; they cease existing after the loop is finished executing.

☐ *test* is the test that occurs after each pass of the loop. The test must be a boolean expression or function that returns a boolean value, for example, `i < 10`. If the test is true, the loop executes. Once the test is false, the loop stops executing.

☐ *increment* is any expression or function call. Commonly, the increment is used to change the value of the loop index to bring the state of the loop closer to returning `false` and completing.

The statement part of the `for` loop is the statement that is executed each time the loop iterates. Just as with `if`, you can include either a single statement here or a block; the previous example used a block because that is more common. Here's an example of a `for` loop that initializes all the values of a `String` array to null strings:

```
String strArray[] = new String[10];
int i; // loop index

for (i = 0; i < strArray.length; i++)
    strArray[i] = "";
```

Any of the parts of the `for` loop can be empty statements, that is, you can simply include a semicolon with no expression or statement, and that part of the `for` loop will be ignored. Note that if you do use a null statement in your `for` loop, you may have to initialize or increment any loop variables or loop indices yourself elsewhere in the program.

You can also have an empty statement for the body of your `for` loop, if everything you want to do is in the first line of that loop. For example, here's one that finds the first prime number higher than 4000:

```
for (i = 4001; notPrime(i); i += 2)
    ;
```

Note that a common mistake in C that also occurs in Java is accidentally to put a semicolon after the first line of the for loop:

```
for (i = 0; i < 10; i++);
    System.out.println("Loop!");
```

Because the first semicolon ends the loop with an empty statement, the loop doesn't actually do anything. The println function will be printed only once, because it's actually outside the for loop entirely. Be careful not to make this mistake in your own Java programs.

NOTE   The source code editor will automatically build a for loop construct around the selected text when you choose For() from the Control Structure's icon's menu.

while and do Loops

Finally, there are while and do loops. while and do loops, like for loops, enable a block of Java code to be executed repeatedly until a specific condition is met. Whether you use a for loop, a while, or a do is mostly a matter of your programming style.

while and do loops, like for, are exactly the same as those same constructions in C and C++.

while Loops

The while loop is used to repeat a statement or block of statements as long as a particular condition is true. while loops look like this:

```
while (condition) {
    bodyOfLoop;
}
```

The condition is a boolean expression. If it returns true, the while loop executes the statements in bodyOfLoop and then tests the condition again, repeating until the condition is false. I've shown the while loop here with a block statement, because it's most commonly used, although you can use a single statement in place of the block.

Here's an example of a while loop that copies the elements of an array of integers (in array1) to an array of floats (in array2), casting each element to a float as it goes. The one catch is that if any of the elements in the first array is 0, the loop will immediately exit at that point. To cover both the cases wherein all the elements have been copied and an element is 0, you can use a compound test with the && operator:

```
int i = 0;
while ((i < array1.length) && (array1[i] != 0)) {
    array2[i] = (float) array1[i];
    i++;
}
```

Note that if the condition is initially false the first time it is tested (for example, if the first element in that first array is 0), the body of the while loop will never be executed. If you need to execute the loop at least once, you can do one of two things:

☐ Duplicate the body of the loop outside the while loop

☐ Use a do loop (described below)

The do loop is considered the better solution of the two.

do...while Loops

The do loop is just like a while loop, except that do executes a given statement or block until a condition is false. The main difference is that while loops test the condition before looping, making it possible that the body of the loop will never execute if the condition is false the first time it's tested. do loops run the body of the loop at least once before testing the condition. do loops look like this:

```
do {
    bodyOfLoop;
} while (condition);
```

Here, the bodyOfLoop part is the statements that are executed with each iteration. It's shown here with a block statement because it's most commonly used that way, but you can substitute the braces for a single statement as you can with the other control flow constructs. The condition is a boolean test. If it returns true, the loop is run again. If it returns false, the loop exits. Keep in mind that with do loops, the body of the loop executes at least once.

Here's a simple example of a do loop that prints a message each time the loop iterates:

```
int x = 1;
do {
    System.out.println("Looping, round " + x);
    x++;
} while (x <= 10);
```

Here's the output of these statements (saved on the CD-ROM as DoTest):

```
Looping, round 1
Looping, round 2
Looping, round 3
Looping, round 4
Looping, round 5
Looping, round 6
Looping, round 7
Looping, round 8
Looping, round 9
Looping, round 10
```

Breaking Out of Loops

In all the loops (for, while, and do), the loop ends when the condition you're testing for is met. What happens if something odd occurs within the body of the loop and you want to exit the loop early? For that, you can use the break and continue keywords.

You've already seen break as part of the switch statement; it stops execution of the switch, and the program continues. The break keyword, when used with a loop, does the same thing—it immediately halts execution of the current loop. If you've nested loops within loops, execution picks up in the next outer loop; otherwise, the program merely continues executing the next statement after the loop.

For example, suppose you have a while loop that copies elements from one array into another. Each element in the array should be copied until the end of the array is reached or if an element contains 0. You can test for that latter case inside the body of the while and then use a break to exit the loop:

```
while (count < array1.length) {
    if (array1[count] == 0) {
        break;
    }
    array2[count] = array1[count];
    count++;
    }

}
```

continue is similar to break except that instead of halting execution of the loop entirely, the loop starts over at the next iteration. For do and while loops, this means the execution of the block starts over again; for for loops, the increment expression is evaluated and then block is executed. continue is useful when you want to special-case elements within a loop. With the previous example of copying one array to another, you can test for whether the current element is 0 and restart the loop if you find it so that the resulting array will never contain zero. Note that because you're skipping elements in the first array, you now have to keep track of two different array counters:

```
while (count < array1.length) {
    if (array1[count] == 0)
        continue;

    array2[count2++] = (float)array1[count++];
}
```

Labeled Loops

Both break and continue can have an optional label that tells Java where to break to. Without a label, break jumps outside the nearest loop (to an enclosing loop or to the next statement outside the loop), and continue restarts the enclosing loop. Using labeled breaks and continues enables you to break outside nested loops or to continue a loop outside the current loop.

To use a labeled loop, add the label before the initial part of the loop, with a colon between them. Then, when you use break or continue, add the name of the label after the keyword itself:

```
out:
    for (int i = 0; i <10; i++) {
        while (x < 50) {
            if (i * x == 400)
                break out;
            ...
        }
        ...
    }
```

In this snippet of code, the label out labels the outer for loop. Then, inside both the for and the while loop, if a particular condition is met inside both loops, a break causes the execution to break out of both loops and restart back at the label (out).

Here's another example. The following program contains a nested for loop. Inside the innermost loop, if the sum of the values of the two counters is greater than four, both loops exit at once:

```
foo:
    for (int i = 1; i <= 5; i++)
        for (int j = 1; j <= 3; j++) {
            System.out.println("i is " + i + ", j is " + j);
            if ((i + j) > 4)
                break foo;
        }
System.out.println("end of loops");
```

Here's the output from this program (saved on the CD-ROM as LabelTest):

```
i is 1, j is 1
i is 1, j is 2
i is 1, j is 3
i is 2, j is 1
i is 2, j is 2
i is 2, j is 3
end of loops
```

As you can see, the loop iterated until the sum of i and j was greater than 4, and then both loops exited back to the outer block and the final message was printed.

Summary

Today, you learned about three main topics that you'll most likely use quite often in your own Java programs: arrays, conditionals, and loops.

You learned how to declare an array variable, create and assign an array object to that variable, and access and change elements within that array.

Conditionals include the if and switch statements, with which you can branch to different parts of your program based on a boolean test.

Finally, you learned about the for, while, and do loops, each of which enable you to execute a portion of your program repeatedly until a given condition is met.

Now that you've learned the small stuff, all that's left is to go over the bigger issues of declaring classes and creating methods within which instances of those classes can communicate with each other by calling methods. Get to bed early tonight, because tomorrow is going to be a wild ride.

Questions and Answers

Q **If arrays are objects, and you use new to create them, and they have an instance variable length, where is the Array class? I didn't see it in the Java class libraries.**

A Arrays are implemented weirdly in Java. The Array class is constructed automatically when your Java program runs; Array provides the basic framework for arrays, including the length variable. Additionally, each primitive type and object has an implicit subclass of Array that represents an array of that class or object. When you create a new array object, it may not have an actual class, but it behaves as if it does.

Q Does Java have gotos?

A The Java language defines the keyword goto, but it is not currently used for anything. In other words, no, Java does not have gotos.

Q I declared a variable inside a block statement for an if. When the if was done, the definition of that variable vanished. Where did it go?

A In technical terms, block statements inside braces form a new lexical scope. What this means is that if you declare a variable inside a block, it's visible and usable only inside that block. Once the block finishes executing, all the variables you declared go away.

It's a good idea to declare most of your variables in the outermost block in which they'll be needed—usually at the top of a block statement. The exception might be very simple variables, such as index counters in for loops, where declaring them in the first line of the for loop is an easy shortcut.

You'll learn more about variables and scope tomorrow.

Q Why can't you use switch with strings?

A Strings are objects, and switch in Java works only for the primitive types that can be cast to integers (byte, char, short, and int). To compare strings, you have to use nested ifs, which enable more general expression tests, including string comparison.

Q It seems to me that a lot of for loops could be written as while loops, and vice versa, couldn't they?

A True. The for loop is actually a special case of while that enables you to iterate a loop a specific number of times. You could just as easily do this with a while and then increment a counter inside the loop. Either works equally well. This is mostly just a question of programming style and personal choice.

Creating Classes and Applications in Java

by Laura Lemay with Timothy Webster

In just about every lesson up to this point, you've been creating Java applications—writing classes, creating instance variables and methods, and running those applications to perform simple tasks. Also up to this point, you've focused either on the very broad (general object-oriented theory) or the very minute (arithmetic and other expressions). Today, you pull it all together and learn how and why to create classes by using the following basics:

☐ Learning the parts of a class definition

☐ Declaring and using instance variables

☐ Defining and using methods

☐ Creating Java applications, including the main() method and how to pass arguments to a Java program from a command line

Defining Classes

Defining classes is pretty easy; you've seen how to do it a bunch of times in previous lessons. To define a class, use the class keyword and the name of the class:

```
class MyClassName {
...
}
```

If this class is a subclass of another class, use extends to indicate the superclass of this class:

```
class myClassName extends mySuperClassName {
...
}
```

If this class implements a specific interface, use `implements` to refer to that interface:

```
class MyRunnableClassName implements Runnable {
...
}
```

Both `extends` and `implements` are optional. You'll learn about using and defining interfaces in Week 3.

Creating Instance and Class Variables

A class definition with nothing in it is pretty dull; usually, when you create a class, you have something you want to add to make that class different from its superclasses. Inside each class definition are declarations and definitions for variables or methods or both—for the class *and* for each instance. In this section, you'll learn all about instance and class variables; the next section talks about methods.

Defining Instance Variables

On Day 3, you learned how to declare and initialize local variables—that is, variables inside method definitions. Instance variables, fortunately, are declared and defined in exactly the same way as local variables; the only difference is their location in the class definition. Instance variables are considered instance variables if they are declared outside a method definition. Customarily, however, most instance variables are defined just after the first line of the class definition. For example, the following code shows a simple class definition for the class `Bicycle`, which inherits from the class `PersonPoweredVehicle`. This class definition contains four instance variables:

☐ `bikeType`: the kind of bicycle this bicycle is—for example, `Mountain` or `Street`

☐ `chainGear`: the number of gears in the front

☐ `rearCogs`: the number of minor gears on the rear axle

☐ `currentGearFront` and `currentGearRear`: the gears the bike is currently in, both front and rear

```
1: class Bicycle extends PersonPoweredVehicle {
2:     String bikeType;
3:     int chainGear;
4:     int rearCogs;
5:     int currentGearFront;
6:     int currentGearRear;
7: }
```

Constants

Constants are useful for setting global states in a method or object, or for giving meaningful names to object-wide values that will never change. In Java, you can create constants only for instance or class variables, not for local variables.

A *constant variable* or *constant* is a variable whose value never changes (which may seem strange given the meaning of the word "variable").

To declare a constant, use the `final` keyword before the variable declaration and include an initial value for that variable:

```
final float pi = 3.141592;
final boolean debug = false;
final int maxsize = 40000;
```

NOTE The only way to define constants in Java is by using the `final` keyword. Neither the C and C++ constructs for `#define` nor `const` are available in Java.

Constants can be useful for naming various states of an object and then testing for those states. For example, suppose you have a test label that can be aligned left, right, or center. You can define those values as constant integers:

```
final int LEFT = 0;
final int RIGHT = 1;
final int CENTER = 2;
```

The variable alignment is then also declared as an `int`:

```
int alignment;
```

Then, later on in the body of a method definition, you can either set the alignment:

```
this.alignment = CENTER;
```

... or test for a given alignment:

```
switch (this.alignment) {
    case LEFT: // deal with left alignment
            ...
            break;
    case RIGHT: // deal with right alignment
            ...
            break;
```

```
        case CENTER: // deal with center alignment
                ...
                break;
}
```

Class Variables

As you learned in previous lessons, class variables are global to a class and to all that class's instances. You can think of class variables as being even more global than instance variables. Class variables are good for communicating between different objects with the same class, or for keeping track of global states among a set of objects.

To declare a class variable, use the `static` keyword in the class declaration:

```
static int sum;
static final int maxObjects = 10;
```

Creating Methods

Methods, as you learned on Day 2, define an object's behavior—this is, what happens when that object is created and the various operations that object can perform during its lifetime. In this section, you'll get a basic introduction to method definition and how methods work; tomorrow, you'll go into more detail about advanced things you can do with methods.

Defining Methods

Method definitions have four basic parts:

☐ The name of the method

☐ The type of object or primitive type this method returns

☐ A list of parameters

☐ The body of the method

NEW TERM   The method's *signature* is a combination of the name of the method, the type of object or base type this method returns, and a list of parameters.

To keep things simple today, I've left off two optional parts of the method definition: an access qualifier such as `public` or `private`, and the `throws` keyword, which indicates the exceptions a method can throw. You'll learn about these parts of a method definition in Week 3.

In other languages, the name of the method (or function, subroutine, or procedure) is enough to distinguish it from other methods in the program. In Java, you can have different methods that have the same name but a different return type or argument list. This is called method overloading, and you'll learn more about it tomorrow.

Here's what a basic method definition looks like:

```
returntype methodname (type1 arg1, type2 arg2, type3 arg3..) {
    ...
}
```

The `returntype` is the primitive type or class of the value this method returns. It can be one of the primitive types, a class name, or `void` if the method does not return a value at all.

Note that if this method returns an array object, the array brackets can go either after the return type or after the parameter list; because the former way is considerably easier to read, it is used in the examples today (and throughout this book):

```
int[] makeRange (int lower, int upper) {...}
```

NOTE   Roaster provides several shortcuts that enable you to manage methods:

- ☐ Each source file in a project window has a pop-up menu of the source's methods.

- ☐ The method list icon in the source code toolbar provides a list of the methods in the current source code.

- ☐ Search > Find Method Definition finds the method anywhere in the current project.

- ☐ The class tree tool, covered on Day 2, and the class browser, which we'll look at on Day 20, each schematically displays the project's methods.

In short, there's almost always a quick and easy way to find the method you're looking for.

The method's parameter list is a set of variable declarations, separated by commas, inside parentheses. These parameters become local variables in the body of the method, whose values are the objects or values of primitives passed in when the method is called.

Inside the body of the method you can have statements, expressions, method calls to other objects, conditionals, loops, and so on—everything you've learned about in the previous lessons.

If your method has a real return type (that is, it has not been declared to return void), somewhere inside the body of the method you need to return a value. Use the return keyword to do this. The following code shows an example of a class that defines a makeRange() method. makeRange() takes two integers—a lower bound and an upper bound—and creates an array that contains all the integers between those two boundaries (inclusive).

```
1: class RangeClass {
2:     int[] makeRange (int lower, int upper) {
3:         int arr[] = new int[ (upper - lower) + 1 ];
4:
5:         for (int i = 0; i < arr.length; i++) {
6:             arr[i] = lower++;
7:         }
8:         return arr;
9:     }
10:
11:     public static void main (String arg[]) {
12:         int theArray[];
13:         RangeClass theRange = new RangeClass();
14:
15:         theArray = theRange.makeRange(1,10);
16:         System.out.print("The array: [ ");
17:         for (int i = 0; i < theArray.length; i++) {
18:             System.out.print(theArray[i] + " ");
19:         }
20:         System.out.println("]");
21:     }
22:
23: }
```

Here's the output of this program:

```
The array: [ 1 2 3 4 5 6 7 8 9 10 ]
```

The main() method in this class tests the makeRange() method by creating a range where the lower and upper boundaries of the range are 1 and 10, respectively (see line 6), and then uses a for loop to print the values of the new array.

The `this` Keyword

Sometimes, in the body of a method definition, you may want to refer to the current object—for example, to refer to that object's instance variables or to pass the current object as an argument to another method. To refer to the current object in these cases, you can use the `this` keyword. `this` refers to the current object, and you can use it anywhere that object might appear—in dot notation to refer to the object's instance variables, as an argument to a method, as the return value for the current method, and so on. Here's an example:

```
t = this.x          // the x instance variable for this object
this.myMethod(this) // call the myMethod method, defined in
                    // this class, and pass it the current
                    // object
return this;        // return the current object
```

In many cases, however, you may be able to omit the `this` keyword. You can refer to both instance variables and method calls defined in the current class simply by name; the `this` is implicit in those references. So, the first two examples could be written like this:

```
t = x            // the x instance variable for this object
myMethod(this) // call the myMethod method, defined in this
                 // class
```

NOTE

Omitting the `this` keyword for instance variables depends on whether there are no variables of the same name declared in the local scope. See the next section for details.

Keep in mind that because `this` is a reference to the current instance of a class, it makes sense to use it only inside the body of an instance method definition. Class methods, that is, methods declared with the `static` keyword, cannot use `this`.

Variable Scope and Method Definitions

When you refer to a variable within your method definitions, Java checks for a definition of that variable first in the current scope (which may be a block), then in the outer scopes up to the current method definition. If that variable is not a local variable, Java then checks for a definition of that variable as an instance variable in the current class, and then, finally, in each superclass in turn.

Because of the way Java checks for the scope of a given variable, it is possible for you to create a variable in a lower scope such that a definition of that same variable "hides" the original value of that variable. This can introduce subtle and confusing bugs into your code.

For example, note this small Java program:

```
class ScopeTest {
    int test = 10;

    void printTest () {
        int test = 20;
        System.out.println("test = " + test);
    }
}
```

In this class, you have two variables with the same name and definition: the first, an instance variable, has the name `test` and is initialized to the value `10`. The second is a local variable with the same name, but with the value `20`. Because the local variable hides the instance variable, the `println()` method will print that `test` is `20`.

You can get around this particular instance by using `this.test` to refer to the instance variable, and just `test` to refer to the local variable.

A more insidious example of this occurs when you redefine a variable in a subclass that already occurs in a superclass. This can create very insidious bugs in your code—for example, you may call methods that are intended to change the value of an instance variable, but that change the wrong one. Another bug might occur when you cast an object from one class to another—the value of your instance variable may mysteriously change (because it was getting that value from the superclass instead of from your class). The best way to avoid this behavior is to make sure that, when you define variables in a subclass, you're aware of the variables in each of that class's superclasses and you don't duplicate what is already there.

Passing Arguments to Methods

When you call a method with object parameters, the variables you pass into the body of the method are passed by reference, which means that whatever you do to those objects inside the method affects the original objects as well. This includes arrays and all the objects that arrays contain; when you pass an array into a method and modify its contents, the original array is affected. (Note that primitive types are passed by value.)

Here's an example to demonstrate how this works. First, you have a simple class definition, which includes a single method called `OnetoZero()`:

```
1: class PassByReference {
2:     int OnetoZero (int arg[]) {
3:         int count = 0;
4:
5:         for (int i = 0; i < arg.length; i++) {
```

```
6:              if (arg[i] == 1) {
7:                  count++;
8:                  arg[i] = 0;
9:              }
10:        }
11:        return count;
12:    }
13: }
```

The OnetoZero() method does two things:

- [ ] It counts the number of 1s in the array and returns that value.

- [ ] If it finds a 1, it substitutes a 0 in its place in the array.

The following code shows the main() method for the PassByReference class, which tests the OnetoZero() method:

```
1: public static void main (String arg[]) {
2:     int arr[] = { 1, 3, 4, 5, 1, 1, 7 };
3:     PassByReference test = new PassByReference();
4:     int numOnes;
5:
6:     System.out.print("Values of the array: [ ");
7:     for (int i = 0; i < arr.length; i++) {
8:         System.out.print(arr[i] + " ");
9:     }
10:    System.out.println("]");
11:
12:    numOnes = test.OnetoZero(arr);
13:    System.out.println("Number of Ones = " + numOnes);
14:    System.out.print("New values of the array: [ ");
15:    for (int i = 0; i < arr.length; i++) {
16:        System.out.print(arr[i] + " ");
17:    }
18:    System.out.println("]");
19: }
```

Here is the output of this program:

```
Values of the array: [ 1 3 4 5 1 1 7 ]
Number of Ones = 3
New values of the array: [ 0 3 4 5 0 0 7 ]
```

Let's go over the main() method line by line so that you can see what is going on.

Lines 2 through 4 set up the initial variables for this example. The first one is an array of integers; the second one is an instance of the class PassByReference, which is stored in the variable test. The third is a simple integer to hold the number of 1s in the array.

Lines 6 through 11 print out the initial values of the array; you can see the output of these lines in the first line of the output.

Line 12 is where the real work takes place; this is where you call the OnetoZero() method, defined in the object test, and pass it the array stored in arr. This method returns the number of 1s in the array, which you'll then assign to the variable numOnes.

Got it so far? Line 13 prints out the number of 1s, that is, the value you got back from the OnetoZero() method. It returns 3, as you would expect.

The last bunch of lines prints out the array values. Because a reference to the array object is passed to the method, changing the array inside that method changes that original copy of the array. Printing out the values in lines 14 through 18 proves this—that last line of output shows that all the 1s in the array have been changed to 0s.

Class Methods

Just as you have class and instance variables, you also have class and instance methods, and the difference between the two types of methods are analogous. Class methods are global to the class itself and available to any other classes or objects. Therefore, class methods can be used anywhere regardless of whether an instance of the class exists.

For example, the Java class libraries include a class called Math. The Math class defines a whole set of math operations that can be used in any program with the various number types:

```
float root = Math.sqrt(453.0);
System.out.print("The larger of x and y is" + Math.max(x,y));
```

To define class methods, use the static keyword in front of the method definition, just as you would create a class variable. For example, that max class method might have a signature like this:

```
static int max (int arg1, int arg2) { ... }
```

In a similar example, Java supplies "wrapper" classes for each of the base types—for example, classes for Integer, Float, and Boolean. Using class methods defined in those classes, you can convert to and from objects and base types. For example, the parseInt() class method in the Integer class takes a string and a radix (base) and returns the value of that string as an integer:

```
int count = Integer.parseInt("42", 10); // returns 42
```

Most methods that operate on a particular object, or that affect that object, should be defined as instance methods. Methods that provide some general utility but do not directly affect an instance of that class are better declared as class methods.

Creating Java Applications

Now that you know how to create classes, objects, and class and instance variables and methods, all that's left is to put it together into something that can actually run—in other words, to create a Java application.

Applications, to refresh your memory, are Java programs that run on their own outside the Applet Runner's window. Applications are different from applets, which must play inside the Applet Runner's window or inside a Java-capable browser, like Netscape Navigator's Java beta or the Atlas preview of Navigator 3.0. Much of what you've been using up to this point have been Java applications; next week you'll dive into how to create applets. (Applets require a bit more background in order to get them to interact with the browser and draw and update with the graphics system. You'll learn all of this next week.)

A Java application consists of one or more classes and can be as large or as small as you want it to be. HotJava is an example of a Java application. The only thing you need to make a Java application run is one class that serves as the "jumping-off" point for the rest of your Java program. If your program is small enough, it may need only the one class.

The jumping-off class for your program needs one thing: a `main()` method. When you run your compiled Java class (using the Java interpreter), the `main()` method is the first thing that gets called. None of this should be much of a surprise to you at this point; you've been creating Java applications with `main()` methods all along.

The signature for the `main()` method always looks like this:

```
public static void main (String arg[]) {...}
```

Here's a run-down of the parts of the `main()` method:

- [ ] `public` means that this method is available to other classes and objects. The `main()` method must be declared `public`. You'll learn more about `public` and `private` methods in Week 3.

- [ ] `static` means that this is a class method.

- [ ] `void` means the `main()` method doesn't return anything.

- [ ] `main()` takes one parameter: an array of strings. These arguments are passed to `main()` in an unusual way when you're working on the MacOS; we'll talk about it in the next section.

The body of the `main()` method contains any code you need to get your application started: initializing variables or creating instances of any classes you may have declared.

When Java executes the main() method, keep in mind that main() is a class method—the class that holds it is not automatically instantiated when your program runs. If you want to treat that class as an object, you have to instantiate it in the main() method yourself (all the examples up to this point have done this).

Java Applications and "Command-Line" Arguments

Because Java applications are stand-alone programs, it's useful to be able to pass arguments or options to that program to determine how the program is going to run, or to enable a generic program to operate on many different kinds of input. Our friends in the worlds of Unix and Windows are able to communicate with an application by typing data directly into the operating system. You've probably seen the command-line prompt on a PC before.It looks something like this:

```
C:>
```

... and PC users can run a program and feed the program an argument in one fell swoop:

```
C:> java Myprogram argumentOne 2 three
```

Don't feel like a second-class citizen here—you bought a Mac so you wouldn't have to mess around with those wonky, typo-sensitive, ugly command lines, didn't you? You, too, can feed your Java application arguments, without a command line.

These arguments can be used for many different purposes—for example, to indicate a filename to read or write from, or for any other information that you might want your Java program to know.

Passing Arguments to Java Programs

To pass arguments to a Java program:

1. Choose Preferences (⌘-;) from the Edit menu.
2. Click on the project in the left-hand column.
3. Type your argument into the Arguments for Main() field. Don't include the word "Java" or the name of your program as I did in the PC command lines demonstration—all you need is the argument.

Figure 6.1 shows how the Preferences dialog box should look when you're done.

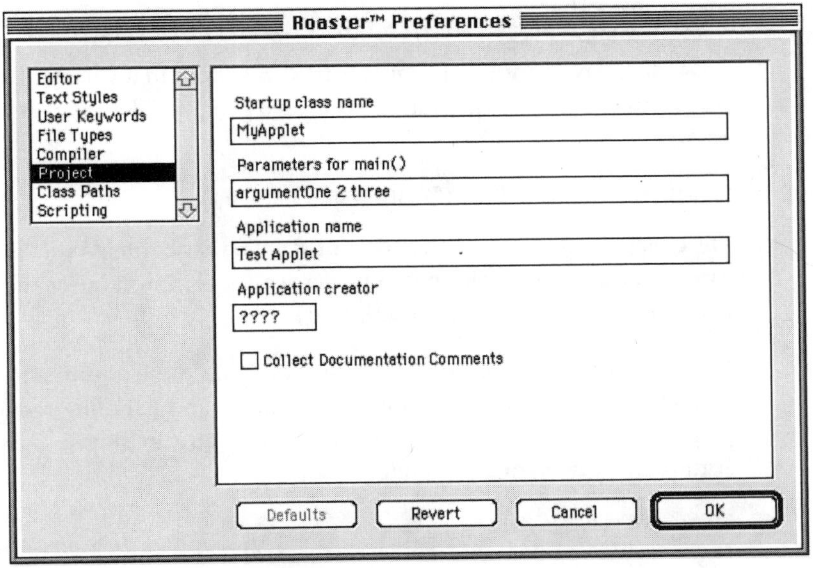

![Roaster Preferences dialog box]

Figure 6.1   *Passing an argument to Roaster's* main() *method.*

Formatting Your Argument

argumentOne 2 three

In the example above, you have three arguments: argumentOne, the number 2, and three.

Java is cool

Note that a space separates arguments, so the example above produces three arguments:

"Roaster is cool"

To group arguments, surround them with double quotes. The example above produces one argument: The double quotes are stripped off before the argument gets to your Java program.

WARNING

Actually, that's the way it should work in future implementations of Roaster to be consistent with the way Java works on other platforms—in the current version, Roaster collects the whole line into one string, quotes and all, rather than as separate strings. If you've got a newer version of Roaster, you'll have to experiment to find out how it handles argument formats.

Handling Arguments in Your Java Program

How does Java handle arguments? It stores them in an array of strings, which is passed to the main() method in your Java program. Remember the signature for main():

```
public static void main (String arg[]) {...}
```

Here, arg is the name of the array of strings that contains the list of arguments. You can actually call it anything you want; argv is common (after the array of the same name from C and Unix shell scripting).

Inside your main() method, you can then handle the arguments your program was given by iterating over the array of arguments and handling those arguments any way you want. For example, the following code is a really simple class that prints out the arguments it gets, one per line.

```
1: class EchoArgs {
2:     public static void main(String args[]) {
3:         for (int i = 0; i < args.length; i++) {
4:             System.out.println("Argument " + i + ": " + args[i]);
5:         }
6:     }
7: }
```

NOTE

The array of arguments in Java is not analogous to argv in C and Unix. In particular, arg[0], the first element in the array of arguments, is the first command-line argument after the name of the class—*not* the name of the program as it would be in C. Be careful of this as you write your Java programs.

An important thing to note about the arguments you pass into a Java program is that those arguments will be stored in an array of strings. This means that any arguments you pass to your Java program will be converted to strings so they can be stored in the argument array. To treat them as non-strings, you'll have to convert them to whatever type you want them to be.

For example, suppose you have a very simple Java program called SumAverage that takes any number of numeric arguments and returns the sum and the average of those arguments. Here is a first pass at this program:

```
1: class SumAverage {
2:     public static void main (String args[]) {
3:         int sum = 0;
4:
```

```
 5:          for (int i = 0; i < args.length; i++) {
 6:              sum += args[i];
 7:          }
 8:
 9:          System.out.println("Sum is: " + sum);
10:          System.out.println("Average is: " +
11:              (float)sum / (float)args.length);
12:      }
13: }
```

At first glance, this program seems rather straightforward—a for loop iterates over the array of arguments, summing them, and then the sum and the average are printed out as the last step.

What happens when you try to compile this? You get the following error:

```
SumAverage.java:9: Incompatible type for +=. Can't convert java.lang.String to int.
    sum += args[i];
```

You get this error because the argument array is an array of strings. Even though you passed integers into the program from the command line, those integers were converted to strings before they were stored in the array. To be able to sum those integers, you have to convert them back from strings to integers. There's a class method for the Integer class, called parseInt, that does just this. If you change line 7 to use that method, everything works just fine:

```
sum += Integer.parseInt(args[i]);
```

Now, compiling the program produces no errors and running it with various arguments returns the expected results. For example, setting the parameters to 1 2 3 in Roaster's Preferences dialog would produce the following output (although this example will not run correctly in Roaster DR1.1):

```
Sum is: 6
Average is: 2
```

Summary

Today, you put together everything you've come across in the preceding days of this week about how to create Java classes and use them in Java applications. This included the following:

- ☐ Instance and class variables, which hold the attributes of the class and its instances. You learned how to declare them, how they are different from regular local variables, and how to declare constants.

☐ Instance and class methods, which define a class's behavior. You learned how to define methods, including the parts of a method's signature, how to return values from a method, how arguments are passed in and out of methods, and the `this` keyword to refer to the current object.

☐ Java applications—all about the `main()` method and how it works as well as how to pass arguments into a Java application with Roaster.

Questions and Answers

Q I tried creating a constant variable inside a method, and I got a compiler error when I tried it. What was I doing wrong?

A You can create only constant (`final`) class or instance variables; local variables cannot be constant.

Q `static` and `final` are not exactly the most descriptive words for creating class variables, class methods, and constants. Why not use `class` and `const`?

A `static` comes from Java's C++ heritage; C++ uses the `static` keyword to retain memory for class variables and methods (and, in fact, they aren't called class methods and variables in C++: `static` member functions and variables are more common terms).

`final`, however, is new. `final` is used in a more general way for classes and methods to indicate that those things cannot be subclassed or overridden. Using the `final` keyword for variables is consistent with that behavior. `final` variables are not quite the same as constant variables in C++, which is why the `const` keyword is not used.

Q In my class, I have an instance variable called `name`. I also have a local variable called `name` in a method, which, because of variable scope, gets hidden by the local variable. Is there any way to get hold of the instance variable's value?

A The easiest way is not to name your local variables the same names as your instance variables. If you feel you must, you can use `this.name` to refer to the instance variable and `name` to refer to the local variable.

Q I want to pass arguments to an applet. How do I do this?

A You're writing applets already? Been skipping ahead, have you? The answer is that you use HTML attributes to pass arguments to an applet, not Roaster's Preferences dialog. You'll learn how to do this next week.

Q I wrote a program to take four arguments, but if I give it too few arguments, it crashes with a run-time error.

A Testing for the number and type of arguments your program expects is up to you in your Java program; Java won't do it for you. If your program requires four arguments, test that you have indeed been given four arguments, and return an error message if you haven't.

More About Methods

by Laura Lemay with Timothy Webster

Methods are arguably the most important part of any object-oriented language. Whereas classes and objects provide the framework, and class and instance variables provide a way of holding that class or object's attributes and state, it is the methods that actually provide an object's behavior and define how that object interacts with other objects in the system.

Yesterday, you learned a little about defining methods. With what you learned yesterday, you could create lots of Java programs, but you'd be missing some of the features of methods that make them really powerful, and that make your objects and classes more efficient and easier to understand. Today, you'll learn about these additional features, including the following:

- ☐ Overloading methods—that is, creating methods with multiple signatures and definitions but with the same name

- ☐ Creating constructor methods—methods that enable you to initialize objects to set up an initial state in the system when an object is created

- ☐ Overriding methods—creating a different definition for a method that has been defined in a superclass

- ☐ Finalizer methods—a way for an object to clean up after itself before it is removed from the system

Creating Methods with the Same Name, Different Arguments

Yesterday, you learned how to create methods with a single name and a single signature. Methods in Java can also be overloaded—that is, you can create methods that have the same name, but different signatures and different definitions. Method overloading enables instances of your class to have a simpler interface to other objects (no need for entirely different methods that do essentially the same thing) and to behave differently based on the input to that method.

When you call a method in an object, Java matches up the method name and the number and type of arguments to choose which method definition to execute.

To create an overloaded method, all you need to do is create several different method definitions in your class, all with the same name, but with different parameter lists (either in number or type of arguments) and with different bodies. Java can understand method overloading as long as each parameter list is unique for each method name.

Note that Java differentiates overloaded methods with the same name, based on the number and type of parameters to that method, not on its return type. That is, if you try to create two methods with the same name, same parameter list, but different return types, you'll get a compiler error. The variable names you choose for each parameter to the method are irrelevant—all that matters is the number and the type.

Here's an example of creating an overloaded method. The following code shows a simple class definition for a class called MyRect, which defines a rectangular shape. The MyRect class has four instance variables to define the upper left and lower right corners of the rectangle: x1, y1, x2, and y2.

NOTE Why did I call it MyRect? Java's awt package has a class called Rectangle that implements much of this same behavior. I called this class MyRect to prevent confusion between the two classes.

```
class MyRect {
    int x1 = 0;
    int y1 = 0;
    int x2 = 0;
    int y2 = 0;
}
```

When a new instance of the myRect class is initially created, all its instance variables are initialized to 0. Let's define a buildRect() method that takes four integer arguments and "resizes" the rectangle to have the appropriate values for its corners, returning the resulting rectangle object (note that because the arguments have the same names as the instance variables, you have to make sure to use this to refer to them):

```
MyRect buildRect(int x1, int y1, int x2, int y2) {
    this.x1 = x1;
    this.y1 = y1;
```

```
        this.x2 = x2;
        this.y2 = y2;
        return this;
}
```

What if you want to define a rectangle's dimensions in a different way—for example, by using Point objects rather than individual coordinates? You can overload build-Rect() so that its parameter list takes two Point objects (note that you'll need to import the Point class at the top of your source file so Java can find it):

```
MyRect buildRect(Point topLeft, Point bottomRight) {
    x1 = topLeft.x;
    y1 = topLeft.y;
    x2 = bottomRight.x;
    y2 = bottomRight.y;
    return this;
}
```

Perhaps you want to define the rectangle using a top corner and a width and height. Just create a different definition for buildRect():

```
MyRect buildRect(Point topLeft, int w, int h) {
    x1 = topLeft.x;
    y1 = topLeft.y;
    x2 = (x1 + w);
    y2 = (y1 + h);
    return this;
}
```

To finish up this example, let's create a method to print out the rectangle's coordinates, and a main() method to test it all (just to prove that this does indeed work). Here is the completed class definition with all its methods:

```
import java.awt.Point;

class MyRect {
    int x1 = 0;
    int y1 = 0;
    int x2 = 0;
    int y2 = 0;

    MyRect buildRect(int x1, int y1, int x2, int y2) {
        this.x1 = x1;
        this.y1 = y1;
        this.x2 = x2;
        this.y2 = y2;
        return this;
    }
```

```
MyRect buildRect(Point topLeft, Point bottomRight) {
    x1 = topLeft.x;
    y1 = topLeft.y;
    x2 = bottomRight.x;
    y2 = bottomRight.y;
    return this;
}

MyRect buildRect(Point topLeft, int w, int h) {
    x1 = topLeft.x;
    y1 = topLeft.y;
    x2 = (x1 + w);
    y2 = (y1 + h);
    return this;
}

void printRect(){
    System.out.print("MyRect: <" + x1 + ", " + y1);
    System.out.println(", " + x2 + ", " + y2 + ">");
}

public static void main (String args[]) {
    MyRect rect = new MyRect();

    System.out.println("Calling buildRect with coordinates 25,25 50,50:");
    rect.buildRect(25, 25, 50, 50);
    rect.printRect();
    System.out.println("----------");

    System.out.println("Calling buildRect w/points (10,10), (20,20):");
    rect.buildRect(new Point(10,10), new Point(20,20));
    rect.printRect();
    System.out.println("----------");

    System.out.print("Calling buildRect w/1 point (10,10),");
    System.out.println(" width (50) and height (50)");

    rect.buildRect(new Point(10,10), 50, 50);
    rect.printRect();
    System.out.println("----------");

    }
}
```

Here's the output of this Java program:

```
Calling buildRect with coordinates 25,25 50,50:
MyRect: <25, 25, 50, 50>
----------
Calling buildRect w/points (10,10), (20,20):
MyRect: <10, 10, 20, 20>
```

```
- - - - - - - - - -
Calling buildRect w/1 point (10,10), width (50) and height (50)
MyRect: <10, 10, 60, 60>
- - - - - - - - - -
```

As you can see from this example, all the buildRect() methods work based on the arguments with which they are called. You can define as many versions of a method as you need in your own classes to implement the behavior you need for that class.

Constructor Methods

In addition to regular methods, you can also define constructor methods in your class definition.

NEW TERM

A *constructor* method is a special kind of method that determines how an object is initialized when it's created.

Unlike regular methods, you can't call a constructor method by calling it directly; instead, constructor methods are called by Java automatically. Here's how it works: when you use new to create a new instance of a class, Java does three things:

☐ Allocates memory for the object

☐ Initializes that object's instance variables, either to their initial values or to a default (0 for numbers, null for objects, false for booleans, '10' for characters)

☐ Calls the class's constructor method (which may be one of several methods)

If a class doesn't have any special constructor methods defined, you'll still end up with an object, but you'll have to set its instance variables or call other methods that object needs to initialize itself on that object afterward. All the examples you've created up to this point have behaved like this.

By defining constructor methods in your own classes, you can set initial values of instance variables, call methods based on those variables or call methods on other objects, or calculate initial properties of your object. You can also overload constructors, as you would regular methods, to create an object that has specific properties based on the arguments you give to new.

Basic Constructors

Constructors look a lot like regular methods, with two basic differences:

☐ Constructors always have the same name as the class.

☐ Constructors don't have a return type.

For example, the following code shows a simple class called Person, with a constructor that initializes its instance variables based on the arguments to new. The class also includes a method for the object to introduce itself, and a main() method to test each of these things.

```
class Person {
    String name;
    int age;

    Person(String n, int a) {
        name = n;
        age = a;
    }

    void printPerson() {
        System.out.print("Hi, my name is " + name);
        System.out.println(". I am " + age + " years old.");
    }

    public static void main (String args[]) {
        Person p;

        p = new Person("Laura", 20);
        p.printPerson();
        System.out.println("--------");
        p = new Person("Tommy", 3);
        p.printPerson();
        System.out.println("--------");
    }
}
```

Here's the output for this example program:

```
Hi, my name is Laura. I am 20 years old.
--------
Hi, my name is Tommy. I am 3 years old.
--------
```

Calling Another Constructor

Some constructors you write may be a superset of another constructor defined in your class; that is, they might have the same behavior plus a little bit more. Rather than duplicating identical behavior in multiple constructor methods in your class, it makes sense to be able to just call that first constructor from inside the body of the second constructor. Java provides a special syntax for doing this. To call a constructor defined on the current class, use this form:

```
this(arg1, arg2, arg3...);
```

The arguments to this are, of course, the arguments to the constructor.

Overloading Constructors

Like regular methods, constructors can also take varying numbers and types of parameters, enabling you to create your objects with exactly the properties you want, or to be able to calculate properties from different kinds of input.

For example, the buildRect() methods you defined in the MyRect class earlier today would make excellent constructors, because what they're doing is initializing an object's instance variables to the appropriate values. So, instead of the original buildRect() method you had defined (which took four parameters for the coordinates of the corners), you can create a constructor instead. This code shows a new class, called MyRect2, that has all the same functionality of the original MyRect, except with overloaded constructor methods instead of the buildRect() method:

```java
import java.awt.Point;

class MyRect2 {
    int x1 = 0;
    int y1 = 0;
    int x2 = 0;
    int y2 = 0;

    MyRect2(int x1, int y1, int x2, int y2) {
        this.x1 = x1;
        this.y1 = y1;
        this.x2 = x2;
        this.y2 = y2;
    }

    MyRect2(Point topLeft, Point bottomRight) {
        x1 = topLeft.x;
        y1 = topLeft.y;
        x2 = bottomRight.x;
        y2 = bottomRight.y;
    }

    MyRect2(Point topLeft, int w, int h) {
        x1 = topLeft.x;
        y1 = topLeft.y;
        x2 = (x1 + w);
        y2 = (y1 + h);
    }
```

```
    void printRect(){
        System.out.print("MyRect: <" + x1 + ", " + y1);
        System.out.println(", " + x2 + ", " + y2 + ">");
    }

    public static void main (String args[]) {
        MyRect2 rect;

        System.out.println("Calling MyRect2 with coordinates 25,25 50,50:");
        rect = new MyRect2(25, 25, 50,50);
        rect.printRect();
        System.out.println("--------");

        System.out.println("Calling MyRect2 w/points (10,10), (20,20):");
        rect= new MyRect2(new Point(10,10), new Point(20,20));
        rect.printRect();
        System.out.println("--------");

        System.out.print("Calling MyRect2 w/1 point (10,10),");
        System.out.println(" width (50) and height (50)");
        rect = new MyRect2(new Point(10,10), 50, 50);
        rect.printRect();
        System.out.println("--------");

    }
}
```

Here's the output for this sample program (it's the same output from the previous example; only the code to produce it has changed):

```
Calling MyRect2 with coordinates 25,25 50,50:
MyRect: <25, 25, 50, 50>
--------
Calling MyRect2 w/points (10,10), (20,20):
MyRect: <10, 10, 20, 20>
--------
Calling MyRect2 w/1 point (10,10), width (50) and height (50)
MyRect: <10, 10, 60, 60>
--------
```

Overriding Methods

When you call a method on an object, Java looks for that method definition in the class of that object, and if it doesn't find one, it passes the method call up the class hierarchy until a method definition is found. Method inheritance enables you to define and use methods repeatedly in subclasses without having to duplicate the code itself.

However, there may be times when you want an object to respond to the same methods but have different behavior when that method is called. In this case, you can override that method. Overriding a method involves defining a method in a subclass that has the same signature as a method in a superclass. Then, when that method is called, the method in the subclass is found and executed instead of the one in the superclass.

Creating Methods that Override Existing Methods

To override a method, all you have to do is create a method in your superclass that has the same signature (name, return type, and parameter list) as a method defined by one of your class's superclasses. Because Java executes the first method definition it finds that matches the signature, this effectively "hides" the original method definition. Here's a simple example that shows a simple class with a method called print-Me(), which prints out the name of the class and the values of its instance variables:

```
class PrintClass {
    int x = 0;
    int y = 1;

    void printMe() {
        System.out.println("X is " + x + ", Y is " + y);
        System.out.println("I am an instance of the class " +
        this.getClass().getName());
    }
}
```

This next one shows a class called PrintSubClass that is a subclass of (extends) PrintClass. The only difference between PrintClass and PrintSubClass is that the latter has a z instance variable.

```
class PrintSubClass extends PrintClass {
    int z = 3;

    public static void main (String args[]) {
        PrintSubClass obj = new PrintSubClass();
        obj.printMe();
    }
}
```

Here's the output from PrintSubClass:

```
X is 0, Y is 1
I am an instance of the class PrintSubClass
```

In the main() method of PrintSubClass, you create a PrintSubClass object and call the printMe() method. Note that PrintSubClass doesn't define this method, so Java looks for it in each of PrintSubClass's superclasses—and finds it, in this case, in PrintClass. Unfortunately, because printMe() is still defined in PrintClass, it doesn't print the z instance variable.

Now, let's create a third class. PrintSubClass2 is nearly identical to PrintSubClass, but you override the printMe() method to include the z variable. The following code shows this class.

```
class PrintSubClass2 extends PrintClass {
    int z = 3;

    void printMe() {
        System.out.println("x is " + x + ", y is " + y +
                ", z is " + z);
        System.out.println("I am an instance of the class " +
                this.getClass().getName());
    }

    public static void main (String args[]) {
        PrintSubClass2 obj = new PrintSubClass2();
        obj.printMe();
    }
}
```

Now, when you instantiate this class and call the printMe() method, the version of printMe() you defined for this class is called instead of the one in the superclass PrintClass, as you can see in this output:

```
x is 0, y is 1, z is 3
I am an instance of the class PrintSubClass2
```

Calling the Original Method

Usually, there are two reasons why you want to override a method that a superclass has already implemented:

☐ To replace the definition of that original method completely

☐ To augment the original method with additional behavior

You've already learned about the first one; by overriding a method and giving that method a new definition, you've hidden the original method definition. But sometimes you may just want to add behavior to the original definition rather than erase it altogether. This is particularly useful where you end up duplicating behavior in both the original method and the method that overrides it; by being able to call the original method in the body of the overridden method, you can add only what you need.

To call the original method from inside a method definition, use the super keyword to pass the method call up the hierarchy:

```
void myMethod (String a, String b) {
    // do stuff here
    super.myMethod(a, b);
    // maybe do more stuff here
}
```

The super keyword, like the this keyword, is a placeholder for this class's superclass. You can use it anywhere you want to refer to your superclass rather than to the current class.

For example, here are those printMe() methods used in the previous example.

```
// from PrintClass
void printMe() {
        System.out.println("X is " + x + ", Y is " + y);
        System.out.println("I am an instance of the class" +
                this.getClass().getName());
    }
}
```

```
//from PrintSubClass2
    void printMe() {
        System.out.println("X is " + x + ", Y is " + y + ", Z is " + z);
        System.out.println("I am an instance of the class " +
                this.getClass().getName());
    }
```

Rather than duplicating most of the behavior of the superclass's method in the subclass, you can rearrange the superclass's method so that additional behavior can easily be added:

```
// from PrintClass
void printMe() {
    System.out.println("I am an instance of the class" +
                this.getClass().getName());
    System.out.println("X is " + x);
    System.out.println("Y is " + y);
    }
}
```

Then, in the superclass, when you override printMe, you can merely call the original method and then add the extra stuff:

```
// From PrintSubClass2
void printMe() {
    super.printMe();
```

```
    System.out.println("Z is " + z);
    }
}
```

Here's the output of calling `printMe()` on an instance of the superclass:

```
I am an instance of the class PrintSubClass2
X is 0
Y is 1
Z is 3
```

Overriding Constructors

Constructors technically cannot be overridden. Because they always have the same name as the current class, you're always creating new constructors instead of inheriting the ones you've got. Much of the time, this is fine, because when your class's constructor is called, the constructor with the same signature for all your superclass is also called, so initialization of all the parts of a class you inherit can happen.

However, when you're defining constructors for your own class, you may want to change how your object is initialized, not only by initializing the information your class adds, but also to change the information that is already there. You can do this by explicitly calling your superclass's constructors.

To call a regular method in a superclass, you use `super.methodname(arguments)`. With constructors you don't have a method name to call, however; you have to use a different form:

```
super(arg1, arg2, ...);
```

Similar to using `this(...)` in a constructor, `super(...)` calls the constructor method for the immediate superclass (which may, in turn, call the constructor of its superclass, and so on).

For example, the following shows a class called `NamedPoint`, which extends the class `Point` from Java's awt package. The `Point` class has only one constructor, which takes an x and a y argument and returns a `Point` object. `NamedPoint` has an additional instance variable (a string for the name) and defines a constructor to initialize x, y, and the name.

```
1: import java.awt.Point;
2: class NamedPoint extends Point {
3:     String name;
4:
5:     NamedPoint(int x, int y, String name) {
6:         super(x,y);
```

```
7:          this.name = name;
8:      }
9: }
```

The constructor defined here for NamedPoint (lines 6 through 8) calls Point's constructor method to initialize Point's instance variables (x and y). Although you can just as easily initialize x and y yourself, you may not know what other things Point is doing to initialize itself, so it's always a good idea to pass constructors up the hierarchy to make sure everything is set up correctly.

Finalizer Methods

Finalizer methods are like the opposite of constructor methods; whereas a constructor method is used to initialize an object, finalizer methods are called just before the object is garbage-collected and its memory reclaimed.

To create a finalizer method, include a method with the following signature in your class definition:

```
void finalize() {
    ...
}
```

Inside the body of that finalize() method, include any cleaning up you want to do for that object.

Before you start using finalizer methods extensively in your Java programs, however, be aware that finalizer methods have several very important restrictions. First of all, the finalizer method is not guaranteed to be called until the object's memory is actually reclaimed, which may be some time after you've removed all references to that object.

You can always call the finalize() method yourself at any time; it's just a plain method like any other. However, calling finalize() does not trigger an object to be garbage-collected. Only removing all references to an object will cause it to be marked for deleting, and even then, Java may or may not call the finalize() method itself—regardless of whether or not you've already called it.

Finalizer methods are best used for optimizing the removal of an object—for example, by removing references to other objects, by cleaning up things that object may have touched, or for other optional behaviors that may make it easier for that object to be removed. In most cases, you may not need to use finalize() at all.

Summary

Today, you learned all kinds of techniques for using, reusing, defining, and redefining methods. You learned how to overload a method name so that the same method can have different behaviors based on the arguments with which it's called. You learned about constructor methods, which are used to initialize a new object when it's created. You learned about method inheritance and how to override methods that have been defined in a class's superclasses. Finally, you learned about finalizer methods, that can be used to clean up after an object just before that object is garbage-collected and its memory reclaimed.

Congratulations on completing your first week of *Teach Yourself Java for Macintosh in 21 Days*! Starting next week, you'll apply everything you've learned this week to writing Java applets and to working with more advanced concepts in putting together Java programs and working with the standard Java class libraries.

Questions and Answers

Q I created two methods with the following signatures:

```
int total(int arg1, int arg2, int arg3) {...}
float total(int arg1, int arg2, int arg3) {...}
```

Roaster's compiler complains when I try to compile the class with these method definitions. But their signatures are different—what have I done wrong?

A Method overloading in Java works only if the parameter lists are different—either in number or type of arguments. Return type is not relevant for method overloading. Think about it—if you had two methods with exactly the same parameter list, how would Java know which one to call?

Q You described using the `this()` method (`this(arg, arg, ...)`) to call a constructor from inside another constructor. Are you limited to using the `this()` method call inside constructors?

A No, you can use that method anywhere to refer to the current object's constructor. On an existing object, calling a constructor is an easy way to reinitialize that object back to its default state (or to change it to have the state that you want it to have).

Q Can I overload overridden methods (that is, can I create methods that have the same name as an inherited method, but a different parameter list)?

A   Sure! As long as a parameter lists vary, it doesn't matter whether you've defined a new method name or one that you've inherited from a superclass.

Q   **I created a finalizer method to decrement a class variable and print a message when my object gets garbage-collected. This way I can keep track of how many objects of this class are running at any given time. But sometimes `finalize()` gets called and sometimes it doesn't. How can I guarantee that `finalize()` will be called and my program will operate correctly?**

A   `finalize()` is provided as a convenience, to give an object a chance to clean up after itself. `finalize()` may or may not be called on any given object before it is garbage-collected, so you should not depend on its existence; you should be using `finalize()` only to provide program optimizations.

If you absolutely require that an object perform some operation before that object gets garbage-collected, you should create a specific method other than `finalize()` and explicitly call that method before discarding references to that object.

Week 2

- ☐ **Java Applet Basics**
  Including an applet on a Web page
  Passing parameters

- ☐ **Graphics, Fonts, and Color**
  Graphics primitives
  The `Color` class

- ☐ **Simple Animation and Threads**
  `paint()` and `repaint()`
  Reducing animation flicker
  `stop()` and `start()`

- ☐ **More Animation, Images, and Sound**
  Scaling options, executing sound effectively
  Double-buffering

- ☐ **Managing Simple Events and Interactivity**
  `MouseDown()` and `MouseUp()`
  The Java event handler

- ☐ **The Java Abstract Window Toolkit**
  Canvases, text components, widgets, and window construction
  components

- ☐ **Windows, Networking, and Other Tidbits**
  Programming menus and creating links inside applets

Java Applet Basics

by Laura Lemay with Timothy Webster

Much of Java's current popularity has come about because of Java-capable World Wide Web browsers and their support for applets: small programs that run inside a Web page and can be used to create dynamic, interactive Web designs. Applets, as I noted at the beginning of this book, are written in the Java language, and can be viewed in any browser that supports Java, including Sun's HotJava and Netscape's Navigator 2.0. Learning how to create applets is most likely the reason you bought this book, so let's waste no more time.

Last week, you focused on learning about the Java language itself, and most of the little programs you created were Java applications. This week, now that you have the basics down, you move on to creating and using applets, which includes a discussion of many of the classes in the standard Java class library.

Today, you'll start with the basics:

☐ A small review of differences between Java applets and applications

☐ Getting started with applets: the basics of how an applet works and how to create your own simple applets

☐ Including an applet on a Web page by using the <APPLET> tag, including the various features of that tag

☐ Passing parameters to applets

How Applets and Applications Are Different

Although you explored the differences between Java applications and Java applets in the early part of this book, let's review them.

In short, Java applications are standalone Java programs that can be run by using just the Java interpreter built into Roaster's Applet Runner. (Only users with a Java run-time package can use these "stand-alone" applications; to create applications for

people who don't have Roaster or Sun's run-time system, you'll have to wait for Roaster Pro.) Most everything you've been working with up to this point in the book have been Java applications, albeit simple ones.

Java applets, however, are run from inside a World Wide Web browser. A reference to an applet is embedded in a Web page using a special HTML tag. When a reader, using a Java-aware browser, loads a Web page with an applet in it, the browser downloads that applet from a Web server and executes it on the local system (the one the browser is running on).

Because Java applets run inside the Java browser, they have access to the same capabilities that the browser has: sophisticated graphics, drawing, and image processing packages; user interface elements; networking; and event handling. Java applications can also take advantage of these features, but they don't require them (you'll learn how to create Java applications that use applet-like graphics and UI features on Day 14).

The advantages applets have over applications in terms of graphics and UI capabilities, however, are hampered by restrictions on what applets can do. Given the fact that Java applets can be downloaded from anywhere and run on a client's system, restrictions are necessary to prevent an applet from causing system damage or security breaches. Without these restrictions in place, Java applets could be written to contain viruses or trojan horses (programs that seem friendly but do some sort of damage to the system), or be used to compromise the security of the system that runs them. The restrictions on what an applet can do include the following:

☐ Applets can't read from or write to the reader's file system, except in specific directories (which are defined by the user through an access control list that, by default, is empty). Some browsers may not even allow an applet to read from or write to the file system at all.

☐ Applets can't usually communicate with a server other than the one that had originally stored the applet. (This may be configurable by the browser; however, you should not depend on having this behavior available.)

☐ Applets can't run any programs on the reader's system. For Unix systems, this includes forking a process.

☐ Applets can't load programs native to the local platform, including shared libraries such as DLLs.

In addition, Java itself includes various forms of security and consistency checking in the Java compiler and interpreter to prevent unorthodox use of the language (you'll learn more about this on Day 21). This combination of restrictions and security features makes it more difficult for a rogue Java applet to do damage to the client's system.

NOTE
> The most important words in the last sentence are "more difficult." These restrictions can prevent most of the more obvious ways of trying to cause damage to a client's system, but it's impossible to be absolutely sure that a clever programmer cannot somehow work around those restrictions. Sun has asked the Net at large to try to break Java's security and to create an applet that can work around the restrictions imposed on it. If a hole is found, Sun will patch it. You'll learn about more issues in Java security on Day 21.
>
> One such flaw has been found in Netscape Navigator's implementation of Java—not in Java itself. This flaw, discovered in March 1996, will have been fixed by the time you read this.

Creating Applets

For the most part, all the Java programs you've created up to this point have been Java applications—simple programs with a single `main()` method that created objects, set instance variables, and ran methods. Today and in the days following, you'll be creating applets exclusively, so you should have a good grasp of how an applet works, what sorts of features an applet has, and where to start when you first create your own applets. Without further ado, let's get on with it.

To create an applet, you create a subclass of the class `Applet` in the `java.applet` package. The `Applet` class provides behavior to enable your applet not only to work within the browser itself, but also to take advantage of the capabilities of AWT to include UI elements, to handle mouse and keyword events, and to draw to the screen. Although your applet can have as many "helper" classes as it needs, it's the main applet class that triggers the execution of the applet. That initial applet class always has a signature like this:

```
public class myClass extends java.applet.Applet {
    ...
}
```

Note the `public` keyword. Java requires that your applet subclass be declared `public`. Again, this is true only of your main applet class; any helper classes you create can be `public` or `private` as you want. Public, private, and other forms of access control are described on Day 15.

When Java encounters your applet in a Web page, it loads your initial applet class over the network, as well as any other helper classes that first class uses. Unlike with applications, where Java calls the `main()` method directly on your initial class, when your applet is loaded, the interpreter creates an instance of that class, and all the system-based methods are sent to that instance. Different applets on the same page, or on different pages that use the same class, use different instances, so each one can behave differently from other applets running on the same system.

Major Applet Activities

To create a basic Java application, your class has to have one method, `main()`, with a specific signature. Then, when your application starts up, `main()` is executed, and from `main()` you can set up the behavior that your programs need. Applets are similar, but more complicated. Applets have many different activities that correspond to various major events in the life cycle of the applet—for example, initialization, painting, or mouse events. Each activity has a corresponding method, so when an event occurs, the browser or other Java-capable tool calls those specific methods.

By default, none of those activity methods have any definitions; to provide behavior for those events you must override the appropriate method in your applet's subclass. You don't have to override all of them, of course; different applet behavior requires different methods to be overridden.

You'll learn about the various important methods to override as the week progresses, but, for a general overview, here are five of the more important methods in an applet's execution: initialization, starting, stopping, destroying, and painting.

Initialization

Initialization occurs when the applet is first loaded (or reloaded). Initialization can include creating the objects it needs, setting up an initial state, loading images or fonts, or setting parameters. To provide behavior for the initialization of your applet, override the `init()` method:

```
public void init() {
    ...
}
```

Starting

After an applet is initialized, it is started. Starting can also occur if the applet was previously stopped. For example, an applet is stopped if the reader follows a link to a different page, and it is started again when the reader returns to this page. Note that starting can occur several times during an applet's life cycle, whereas initialization happens only once. To provide startup behavior for your applet, override the `start()` method:

```
public void start() {
    ...
}
```

Functionality that you put in the start() method might include starting up a thread to control the applet, sending the appropriate messages to helper objects, or in some way telling the applet to begin running. You'll learn more about starting applets on Day 10.

Stopping

Stopping and starting go hand in hand. Stopping occurs when the reader leaves the page that contains a currently running applet. By default, when the reader leaves a page, the applet continues running, using up system resources. By overriding stop(), you can suspend execution of the applet and then restart it if the applet is viewed again. To stop an applet's execution, use the stop() method:

```
public void stop() {
   ...
}
```

Destroying

Destroying sounds more violent than it is. Destroying enables the applet to clean up after itself just before it or the browser exits; for example, to kill any running threads or to release any other running objects. Generally, you won't want to override destroy() unless you have specific resources that need to be released; for example, threads that the applet has created. To provide clean-up behavior for your applet, override the destroy() method:

```
public void destroy() {
   ...
}
```

NOTE
How is destroy() different from finalize(), which was described on Day 7? First, destroy() applies only to applets. finalize() is a more general-purpose way for a single object of any type to clean up after itself.

The other difference is that destroy() is always called when the applet has finished executing, either because the browser is exiting or because the applet is being reloaded. finalize() is not guaranteed to be executed.

Painting

Painting is how an applet actually draws something on the screen, be it text, a line, a colored background, or an image. Painting can occur many hundreds of times during an applet's life cycle; for example, once after the applet is initialized, if the browser is placed behind another window on the screen and then brought forward again, if the browser window is moved to a different position on the screen, or perhaps repeatedly in the case of animations. You override the `paint()` method for your applet to have an actual appearance on the screen. The `paint()` method looks like this:

```
public void paint(Graphics g) {
    ...
}
```

Note that unlike the other major methods in this section, `paint()` takes an argument, an instance of the class `Graphics`. This object is created and passed to `paint()` by the browser, so you don't have to worry about it. However, you will have to make sure that the `Graphics` class (part of the `java.awt` package) gets imported into your applet code, usually through an `import` statement at the top of your Java file:

```
import java.awt.Graphics;
```

A Simple Applet

On Day 2, you created a simple applet called HelloAgainApplet (this was the one with the big red `Hello Again`). There, you created and used that applet as an example of creating a subclass. Let's go over the code for that applet again, this time looking at it slightly differently in light of the things you just learned about applets. Here's the code for that applet.

```
 1: import java.awt.Graphics;
 2: import java.awt.Font;
 3: import java.awt.Color;
 4:
 5: public class HelloAgainApplet extends java.applet.Applet {
 6:
 7:     Font f = new Font("TimesRoman",Font.BOLD,36);
 8:
 9:     public void paint(Graphics g) {
10:         g.setFont(f);
11:         g.setColor(Color.red);
12:         g.drawString("Hello again!", 5, 50);
13:     }
14: }
```

This applet overrides `paint()`, one of the major methods described in the previous section. Because the applet doesn't actually do much (all it does is print a couple of words to the screen), and there's not really anything to initialize, you don't need a start() or a stop() or an init() method.

The paint() method is where the real work of this applet (what little work goes on) really occurs. The Graphics object passed into the paint() method holds that graphics state—that is, the current features of the drawing surface. Lines 10 and 11 set up the default font and color for this graphics state (here, the font object in the f instance variable, and an object representing the color red that's stored in the Color class's variable red).

Line 12 then draws the string "Hello Again!" by using the current font and color at the position 5, 50. Note that the 0 point for y is at the top left of the applet's drawing surface, with positive y moving downward, so 50 is actually at the bottom of the applet. Figure 8.1 shows how the applet's bounding box and the string are drawn on the page.

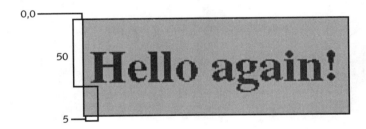

Figure 8.1   *Drawing the applet.*

Including an Applet on a Web Page

After you create a class or classes that contain your applet and compile them into class files as you would any other Java program, you have to create a Web page that will hold that applet by using the HTML language. There is a special HTML tag for including applets in Web pages; Java-capable browsers use the information contained in that tag to locate the compiled class files and execute the applet itself. In this section, you'll learn about how to put Java applets in a Web page and how to serve those files to the Web at large.

NOTE   The following section assumes you have at least a passing understanding of writing HTML pages. If you need help in this area, you may find Greg Holden's book, *Publishing on the World Wide Web for Macintosh,* also from Hayden, useful.

The <APPLET> Tag

To include an applet on a Web page, use the <APPLET> tag. <APPLET> is a special extension to HTML for including applets in Web pages. Here is a very simple example of a Web page with an applet included in it.

```
 1: <HTML>
 2: <HEAD>
 3: <TITLE>This page has an applet on it</TITLE>
 4: </HEAD>
 5: <BODY>
 6: <P>My second Java applet says:
 7: <BR>
 8: <APPLET CODE="HelloAgainApplet.class" WIDTH=200 HEIGHT=50>
 9: There would be an applet here if your browser
10: supported Java.
11: </APPLET>
12: </BODY>
13: </HTML>
```

There are three things to note about the <APPLET> tag in this page:

☐ The CODE attribute indicates the name of the class file that contains this applet, including the .class extension. In this case, the class file must be in the same directory as this HTML file. To indicate applets are in a different directory, use CODEBASE, described later today.

☐ WIDTH and HEIGHT are required and used to indicate the bounding box of the applet—that is, how big a box to draw for the applet on the Web page. Be sure you set WIDTH and HEIGHT to be an appropriate size for the applet; depending on the browser, if your applet draws outside the boundaries of the space you've given it, you may not be able to see or get to those parts of the applet outside the bounding box.

☐ The text between the <APPLET> and </APPLET> tags is displayed by browsers that do not understand the <APPLET> tag (which includes most browsers that are not Java-capable). Because your page may be viewed in many different kinds of browsers, it is a very good idea to include alternate text here so that readers of your page who don't have Java will see something other than a blank line. Here, you include a simple statement that says, "There would be an applet here if your browser supported Java" (or if you're feeling snazzy, you could add a GIF snapshot of your Applet rather than a text disclaimer).

Note that the <APPLET> tag, like the <IMG> tag, is not itself a paragraph, so it should be enclosed inside a more general text tag, such as <P> or one of the heading tags (<H1>, <H2>, and so on).

Testing the Result

Now with a class file and an HTML file that refers to your applet, you should be able to load that HTML file into your Java-capable browser (using either the Open Local... dialog item or a file URL, or by indicating the filename on a command line). The browser loads and parses your HTML file, and then loads and executes your applet class.

If you've got access to a Java-savvy version, drag your HTML file onto the Navigator's icon. The browser will load and parse your HTML file, and then load and execute your applet class.

Otherwise, drag your HTML file onto Roaster's Applet Runner icon. Applet Runner will ignore all the HTML outside the <APPLET> tag, but it will parse those important Applet parameters, and then load and execute your applet class.

Figure 8.2 shows the HelloAgain applet, in case you've forgotten what it looks like.

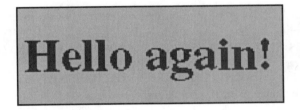

Figure 8.2 *The HelloAgain applet.*

Making Java Applets Available to the Web

Once you have an applet and an HTML file, and you've verified that everything is working correctly on your local system, the last step is making that applet available to the World Wide Web at large so that anyone with a Java-capable browser can view that applet. *Even if you don't have a Java-savvy browser, you can still serve your applet to the world with any old Mac HTTP server software, like WebSTAR or MacHTTP.*

Java applets are served by a Web server the same way that HTML files, images, and other media are. You don't even need to configure your server to handle Java files. If you have a Web server up and running, or space on a Web server available to you, all you have to do is move your HTML and compiled class files to that server, as you would any other file.

If you don't have a Web server, you have to rent space on one or set one up yourself. (Web server setup and administration, as well as other facets of Web publishing in general, are outside the scope of this book.) See Stewart Buskirk's *Web Server Construction Kit for Macintosh*, also from Hayden books, for more information about setting up a complete Web server on the MacOS.

More About the <APPLET> Tag

In its simplest form, by using CODE, WIDTH, and HEIGHT, the <APPLET> tag merely creates a space of the appropriate size and then loads and plays the applet in that space. The <APPLET> tag, however, does include several attributes that can help you better integrate your applet into the overall design of your Web page.

NOTE   The attributes available for the <APPLET> tag are almost identical to those for the HTML <IMG> tag.

ALIGN

The ALIGN attribute defines how the applet will be aligned on the page. This attribute can have one of nine values: LEFT, RIGHT, TOP, TEXTTOP, MIDDLE, ABSMIDDLE, BASELINE, BOTTOM, and ABSBOTTOM.

In the case of ALIGN=LEFT and ALIGN=RIGHT, the applet is placed at the left or right margins of the page, respectively, and all text following that applet flows in the space to the right or left of that applet. The text will continue to flow in that space until the end of the applet, or you can use a line break tag (<BR>) with the CLEAR attribute to start the left line of text below that applet. The CLEAR attribute can have one of three values: CLEAR=LEFT starts the text at the next clear left margin, CLEAR=RIGHT does the same for the right margin, and CLEAR=ALL starts the text at the next line where both margins are clear.

For example, here's a snippet of HTML code that aligns an applet against the left margin, has some text flowing alongside it, and then breaks at the end of the paragraph so that the next bit of text starts below the applet:

```
<P><APPLET CODE="HelloAgainApplet" WIDTH=300 HEIGHT=200
ALIGN=LEFT>Hello Again!</APPLET>
To the left of this paragraph is an applet. It's an
unassuming applet, in which a small string is printed
in red type, set in 36 point Times bold.
<BR CLEAR=ALL>
```

```
<P>In the next part of the page, we demonstrate how
under certain conditions, styrofoam peanuts can be
used as a healthy snack.
```

Figure 8.3 shows how this applet and the text surrounding it might appear in a Java-capable browser.

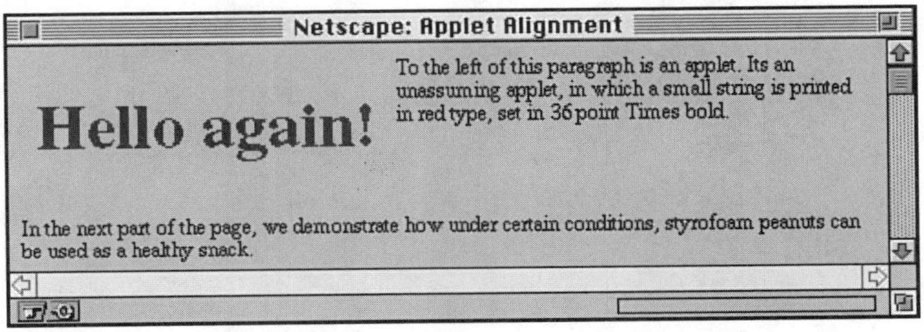

Figure 8.3 *An applet aligned left.*

For smaller applets, you may want to include your applet within a single line of text. To do this, there are seven values for ALIGN that determine how the applet is vertically aligned with the text:

- ☐ ALIGN=TEXTTOP aligns the top of the applet with the top of the tallest text in the line.

- ☐ ALIGN=TOP aligns the applet with the topmost item in the line (which may be another applet, or an image, or the top of the text).

- ☐ ALIGN=ABSMIDDLE aligns the middle of the applet with the middle of the largest item in the line.

- ☐ ALIGN=MIDDLE aligns the middle of the applet with the middle of the baseline of the text.

- ☐ ALIGN=BASELINE aligns the bottom of the applet with the baseline of the text. ALIGN=BASELINE is the same as ALIGN=BOTTOM, but ALIGN=BASELINE is a more descriptive name.

- ☐ ALIGN=ABSBOTTOM aligns the bottom of the applet with the lowest item in the line (which may be the baseline of the text or another applet or image).

Figure 8.4 shows the various alignment options, where the line is an image and the arrow is a small applet.

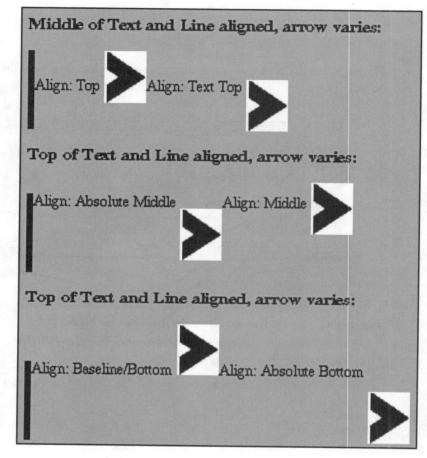

Figure 8.4 *Applet alignment options.*

HSPACE and VSPACE

The HSPACE and VSPACE attributes are used to set the amount of space, in pixels, between an applet and its surrounding text. HSPACE controls the horizontal space (the space to the left and right of the applet). VSPACE controls the vertical space (the space above and below). For example, here's that sample snippet of HTML with vertical space of 50 and horizontal space of 10:

```
<P><APPLET CODE="HelloAgainApplet" WIDTH=300 HEIGHT=200
ALIGN=LEFT VSPACE=50 HSPACE=10>Hello Again!</APPLET>
To the left of this paragraph is an applet. It's an
unassuming applet, in which a small string is
printed in red type, set in 36 point Times bold.
<BR CLEAR=ALL>
```

```
<P>In the next part of the page, we demonstrate how
under certain conditions, styrofoam peanuts can be
used as a healthy snack.
```

The result in a typical Java browser might look like that in Figure 8.5.

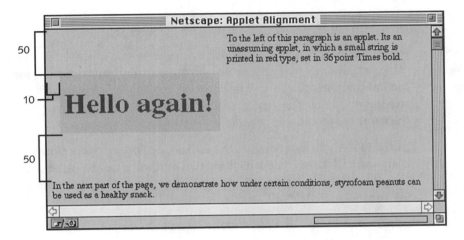

Figure 8.5 *Vertical and horizontal space.*

CODE and CODEBASE

CODE is used to indicate the name of the class file that holds the current applet. If CODE is used alone in the <APPLET> tag, the class file is searched for in the same folder as the HTML file that references it.

If you want to store your class files in a different folder than that of your HTML files, you have to tell the client's browser where to find those class files. To do this, you use CODEBASE. CODE contains only the name of the class file; CODEBASE contains an alternate pathname where classes are contained. For example, if you store your class files in a folder called "classes," and this folder is in the same folder as your HTML files, the CODEBASE parameter would be as follows:

```
<APPLET CODE="myclass.class" CODEBASE="classes"
    WIDTH=100 HEIGHT=100>
```

Passing Parameters to Applets

With Java applications, you can pass parameters to your main() routine by using Roaster's Preferences dialog. You can then parse those arguments inside the body of your class, and the application acts accordingly based on the arguments it is given.

Applets, however, don't have a `main()` method. How do you pass in different arguments to an applet? Applets can get different input from the HTML file that contains the <APPLET> tag through the use of applet parameters. To set up and handle parameters in an applet, you need two things:

☐ A special parameter tag in the HTML file

☐ Code in your applet to parse those parameters

Applet parameters come in two parts: a name, which is simply a name you pick, and a value, which determines the value of that particular parameter. So, for example, you can indicate the color of text in an applet by using a parameter with the name `color` and the value `red`. You can determine an animation's speed using a parameter with the name `speed` and the value `5`.

In the HTML fie that contains the embedded applet, you indicate each parameter using the <PARAM> tag, which has two attributes for the name and the value called (surprisingly enough) NAME and VALUE. The <PARAM> tag goes inside the opening and closing <APPLET> tags:

```
<APPLET CODE="MyApplet.class" WIDTH=100 HEIGHT=100>
<PARAM NAME=font VALUE="TimesRoman">
<PARAM NAME=size VALUE="36">
A Java applet appears here.</APPLET>
```

This particular example defines two parameters to the MyApplet applet: one whose name is `font` and whose value is `TimesRoman`, and one whose name is `size` and whose value is `36`.

NOTE

> There is an easy way to get all the <APPLET> tag parameters exactly right: use the source code editor's built-in HTML tools. See Day 20 for details.

Those parameters are passed to your applet when it is loaded. In the `init()` method for your applet, you can then get hold of those parameters by using the `getParameter()` method. `getParameter()` takes one argument—a string representing the name of the parameter you're looking for—and returns a string containing the corresponding value of that parameter. (Like arguments in Java applications, all the parameter values are converted to strings.) To get the value of the `font` parameter from the HTML file, you might have a line such as this in your `init()` method:

```
String theFontName = getParameter("font");
```

NOTE The names of the parameters as specified in <PARAM> and the names of the parameters in getParameter() must match identically, including having the same upperand lowercase. In other words, <PARAM NAME="name"> is different from <PARAM NAME="Name">. If your parameters are not being properly passed to your applet, make sure the parameter names match.

Note that if a parameter you expect has not been specified in the HTML file, getParameter(), returns null. Most often, you will want to test for a null parameter and supply a reasonable default:

```
if (theFontName == null)
    theFontName = "Courier";
```

Keep in mind also that because getParameter() returns strings, if you want a parameter to be some other object or type, you have to convert it yourself. To parse the size parameter from that same HTML file and assign it to an integer variable called theSize, you might use the following lines:

```
int theSize;
String s = getParameter("size");
if (s == null)
    theSize = 12;
else theSize = Integer.parseInt(s);
```

Get it? Not yet? Let's create an example of an applet that uses this technique. You'll modify the HelloAgainApplet so that it says hello to a specific name, for example "Hello Bill" or "Hello Alice". The name is passed into the applet through an HTML parameter.

Let's start with the original HelloAgainApplet class:

```
import java.awt.Graphics;
import java.awt.Font;
import java.awt.Color;

public class MoreHelloApplet extends java.applet.Applet {

    Font f = new Font("TimesRoman",Font.BOLD,36);

    public void paint(Graphics g) {
        g.setFont(f);
        g.setColor(Color.red);
        g.drawString("Hello Again!", 5, 50);
    }
}
```

The first thing you need to add in this class is a place for the name. Because you'll need that name throughout the applet, let's add an instance variable for the name, just after the variable for the font:

```
String name;
```

To set a value for the name, you have to get the parameter. The best place to handle parameters to an applet is inside an `init()` method. The `init()` method is defined similarly to `paint()` (`public`, with no arguments, and a return type of void). Make sure when you test for a parameter that you test for a value of `null`. The default, in this case, if a name isn't indicated, is to say hello to `"Laura"`:

```
public void init() {
this.name = getParameter("name");
    if (this.name == null)
        this.name = "Laura";
    }
```

One last thing to do now that you have the name from the HTML parameters is to modify the name so that it's a complete string—that is, to tack `"Hello "` onto the beginning, and an explanation point onto the end. You could do this in the `paint()` method just before printing the string to the screen. Here it's done only once, however, whereas in `paint()` it's done every time the screen is repainted—in other words, it's slightly more efficient to do it inside `init()` instead:

```
this.name = "Hello " + this.name + "!";
```

And now, all that's left is to modify the `paint()` method. The original `drawString` method looked like this:

```
g.drawString("Hello Again!", 5, 50);
```

To draw the new string you have stored in the `name` instance variable, all you need to do is substitute that variable for the literal string:

```
g.drawString(this.name, 5, 50);
```

The following code shows the final result of the `MoreHelloApplet` class. Compile it so that you have a class file ready.

```
1:  import java.awt.Graphics;
2:  import java.awt.Font;
3:  import java.awt.Color;
4:
5:  public class MoreHelloApplet extends java.applet.Applet {
6:
7:      Font f = new Font("TimesRoman",Font.BOLD,36);
8:      String name;
```

```
 9:
10:     public void init() {
11:         this.name = getParameter("name");
12:         if (this.name == null)
13:             this.name = "Laura";
14:
15:         this.name = "Hello " + this.name + "!";
16:     }
17:
18:     public void paint(Graphics g) {
19:         g.setFont(f);
20:         g.setColor(Color.red);
21:         g.drawString(this.name, 5, 50);
22:     }
23: }
```

Now, let's look at the HTML file that contains this applet. Here's a new Web page for the MoreHelloApplet applet.

```
 1:  <HTML>
 2:  <HEAD>
 3:  <TITLE>Hello!</TITLE>
 4:  </HEAD>
 5:  <BODY>
 6:  <P>
 7:  <APPLET CODE="MoreHelloApplet.class" WIDTH=300 HEIGHT=50>
 8:  <PARAM NAME=name VALUE="Bonzo">
 9:  Hello to whoever you are!
10:  </APPLET>
11:  </BODY>
12:  </HTML>
```

Note the <APPLET> tag, which points to the class file for the applet with the appropriate width and height (300 and 50). Just below it (line 8) is the <PARAM> tag, which you use to pass in the name. Here, the NAME parameter is simply name, and the value is the string "Bonzo".

Loading up this HTML file produces the result shown in Figure 8.6.

Figure 8.6   *The result of MoreHelloApplet, first try.*

Let's try a second example. Remember that in the code for MoreHelloApplet, if no name is specified, the default is the name "Laura". The following shows an HTML file with no parameter tag for name.

```
 1:  <HTML>
 2:  <HEAD>
 3:  <TITLE>Hello!</TITLE>
 4:  </HEAD>
 5:  <BODY>
 6:  <P>
 7:  <APPLET CODE="MoreHelloApplet.class" WIDTH=300 HEIGHT=50>
 8:  Hello to whoever you are!
 9:  </APPLET>
10:  </BODY>
11:  </HTML>
```

Here, because no name was supplied, the applet uses the default, and the result is what you might expect (see Figure 8.7).

Figure 8.7 *The result of MoreHelloApplet, second try.*

Summary

Applets are probably the most common use of the Java language today. Applets are more complicated than many Java applications because they are executed and drawn inline with a Web page. Applets can provide easy access to the graphics, user interface, and events systems in the Web browser itself. Today, you learned the basics of creating applets, including the following things:

☐ All applets you develop using Java inherit from the Applet class, part of the java.applet package. The Applet class provides basic behavior for how the applet will be integrated with and react to the browser and various forms of input from that browser and the person running it. By subclassing Applet, you have access to all that behavior.

☐ Applets have five main methods, which are used for the basic activities an applet performs during its life cycle: init(), start(), stop(), destroy(), and paint().

Although you don't need to override all these methods, these are the most common methods you'll see repeated in many of the applets you'll create in this book and in other sample programs.

☐ To run a compiled applet class file, you include it in an HTML Web page by using the <APPLET> tag. When a Java-capable browser comes across <APPLET>, it loads and plays the applet described in that tag. Note that to publish Java applets on the World Wide Web alongside HTML files you do not need special server software; any Web server will do just fine.

☐ Unlike applications, applets do not have a main() method on which to pass arguments, so those arguments must be passed into the applet through the HTML file that contains it. You indicate parameters in an HTML file by using the <PARAM> tag inside the opening and closing <APPLET> tags. <PARAM> has two attributes: NAME for the name of the parameter, and VALUE for its value. Inside the body of your applet (usually in init()) you can then gain access to those parameters using the getParameter() method.

Questions and Answers

Q **In the first part of today's lesson, you say that applets are downloaded from random Web servers and run on the client's system. What's to stop an applet developer from creating an applet that deletes all the files on that system, or in some other way compromises the security of the system?**

A Recall that Java applets have several restrictions that make it difficult for most of the more obvious malicious behavior to take place. For example, because Java applets cannot read or write files on the client system, they cannot delete files or read system files that might contain private information. Because they cannot run programs on the client's system, they cannot, for example, use the system's mail system to mail files to someone elsewhere on the network.

In addition, Java's very architecture makes it difficult to circumvent these restrictions. The language itself, the Java compiler, and the Java interpreter all have checks to make sure that no one has tried to sneak in bogus code or play games with the system itself. You'll learn more about these checks at the end of this book.

Of course, no system can claim to be entirely secure, and the fact that Java applets are run on the client's system makes them especially ripe for suspicion.

Q **Wait a minute. If I can't read or write files or run programs on the system the applet is running on, doesn't that mean I basically can't do anything other than simple animations and flashy graphics? How can I save state in** an applet? How can I create, say, a word processor or a spreadsheet as a Java applet?

A For everyone who doesn't believe that Java is secure enough, there is someone who believes that Java's security restrictions are too severe for just these reasons. Yes, Java applets are limited because of the security restrictions. But given the possibility for abuse, I believe that it's better to err on the side of being more conservative as far as security is concerned. Consider it a challenge.

Keep in mind, also, that Java applications have none of the restrictions that Java applets do, but because they are also compiled to bytecode, they are portable across platforms. It may be that the thing you want to create would make a much better application than an applet.

Q **I have an older version of HotJava. I followed all the examples in this section, but HotJava cannot read my applets (it seems to ignore that they exist). What's going on?**

A You most likely have an alpha version of HotJava. Recall that significant changes were made to the Java API and how Java applets are written between alpha and beta. The results of these changes are that browsers that support alpha applets cannot read beta applets, and vice versa. The HTML tags are even different, so an older browser just skips over newer applets, and vice versa.

By the time you read this, there may be a new version of HotJava with support for beta. If not, you can use Netscape 2.0 or the JDK's applet viewer to view applets written to the beta specification.

Q **I noticed in a page about the <APPLET> tag that there's also a NAME attribute. You didn't discuss it here.**

A NAME is used when you have multiple applets on a page that need to communicate with each other. You'll learn about this on Day 12.

Q **I have an applet that takes parameters and an HTML file that passes it those parameters. But when my applet runs, all I get are null values. What's going on here?**

A Do the names of your parameters (in the NAME attribute) match exactly with the names you're testing for in `getParameter()`? They must be exact, including case, for the match to be made. Make sure also that your <PARAM> tags are inside the opening and closing <APPLET> tags, and that you haven't misspelled anything.

Graphics, Fonts, and Color

by Laura Lemay with Timothy Webster

Now you have a basic understanding of how applets work. For the remainder of this week you'll cover the sorts of things you can do with applets with the built-in Java class libraries, and how you can combine them to produce interesting effects. You'll start today with how to draw to the screen—that is, how to produce lines and shapes with the built-in graphics primitives, how to print text using fonts, and how to use and modify color in your applets. Today you'll learn, specifically:

- ☐ How the graphics system works in Java: the Graphics class, the coordinate system used to draw to the screen, and the way applets paint and repaint

- ☐ Using the Java graphics primitives, including drawing and filling lines, rectangles, ovals, and arcs

- ☐ Creating and using fonts, including how to draw characters and strings and how to find out the metrics of a given font for better layout

- ☐ All about color in Java, including the Color class and how to set the foreground (drawing) and background color for your applet

NOTE Today's lesson discusses many of the basic operations available to you with the Java class libraries regarding graphics, fonts, and color. However, today's lesson, as well as all of this book, also is intended to be more of an introduction and an overview than an exhaustive description of all the features available to you. Be sure to check out the Java API documentation for more information on the classes described today.

The Graphics Class

With Java's graphics capabilities, you can draw lines, shapes, characters, and images to the screen inside your applet. Most of the graphics operations in Java are methods defined in the Graphics class. You don't have to create an instance of Graphics in order to draw something in your applet; in your applet's `paint()` method (which you learned about yesterday), you are given a `Graphics` object. By drawing on that object, you draw onto your applet and the results appear onscreen.

The `Graphics` class is part of the `java.awt` package, so if your applet does any painting (as it usually will), make sure you import that class at the beginning of your Java file:

```
import java.awt.Graphics;

public class MyClass extends java.applet.Applet {
...
}
```

The Graphics Coordinate System

To draw an object onscreen, you call one of the drawing methods available in the `Graphics` class. All the drawing methods have arguments representing endpoints, corners, or starting locations of the object as values in the applet's coordinate system—for example, a line starts at the point `10,10` and ends at the point `20,20`.

Java's coordinate system has the origin (`0,0`) in the top left corner. Positive x values are to the right, and positive y values are down. All pixel values are integers; there are no partial or fractional pixels. Figure 9.1 shows how you might draw a simple square by using this coordinate system.

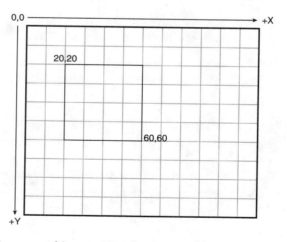

Figure 9.1   *The Java graphics coordinate system.*

Java's coordinate system is different from many painting and layout programs that have their x and y in the bottom left. If you're not used to working with this upside-down graphics system, it may take some practice to get familiar with it.

Drawing and Filling

The Graphics class provides a set of simple built-in graphics primitives for drawing, including lines, rectangles, polygons, ovals, and arcs.

NOTE   Bitmap images, such as GIF files, can also be drawn by using the Graphics class. You'll learn about this tomorrow.

Lines

To draw straight lines, use the drawLine() method. drawLine() takes four arguments: the x and y coordinates of the starting point and the x and y coordinates of the ending point.

```
public void paint(Graphics g) {
    g.drawLine(25,25,75,75);
}
```

Figure 9.2 shows the result of this snippet of code.

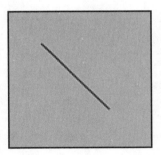

Figure 9.2   *Drawing lines.*

Rectangles

The Java graphics primitives provide not just one, but three kinds of rectangles:

☐ Plain rectangles

☐ Rounded rectangles, which are rectangles with rounded corners

☐ Three-dimensional rectangles, which are drawn with a shaded border

For each of these rectangles, you have two methods to choose from: one that draws the rectangle in outline form, and one that draws the rectangle filled with color.

To draw a plain rectangle, use either the `drawRect()` or `fillRect()` methods. Both take four arguments: the x and y coordinates of the top left corner of the rectangle and the width and height of the rectangle to draw. For example, the following `paint()` method draws two squares: the left one is an outline and the right one is filled (Figure 9.3 shows the result):

```
public void paint(Graphics g) {
    g.drawRect(20,20,60,60);
    g.fillRect(120,20,60,60);
}
```

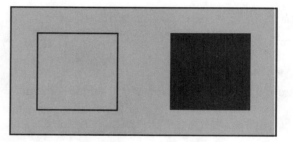

Figure 9.3   *Rectangles.*

Rounded rectangles are, as you might expect, rectangles with rounded edges. The `drawRoundRect()` and `fillRoundRect()` methods to draw rounded rectangles are similar to regular rectangles except that rounded rectangles have two extra arguments for the width and height of the angle of the corners. Those two arguments determine how far along the edges of the rectangle the arc for the corner will start—the first for the angle along the horizontal plane, the second for the vertical. Larger values for the angle width and height make the overall rectangle more rounded; values equal to the width and height of the rectangle itself produce a circle. Figure 9.4 shows some examples of rounded corners.

Here's a `paint()` method that draws two rounded rectangles: one as an outline with a rounded corner 10 pixels square; the other filled, with a rounded corner 20 pixels square (Figure 9.5 shows the resulting squares):

```
public void paint(Graphics g) {
    g.drawRoundRect(20,20,60,60,10,10);
    g.fillRoundRect(120,20,60,60,20,20);
}
```

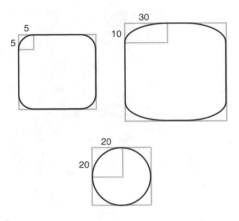

Figure 9.4   *Rounded corners.*

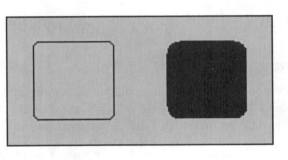

Figure 9.5   *Rounded rectangles.*

Finally, there are three-dimensional rectangles. These rectangles aren't really 3D; instead, they have a shadow effect that makes them appear either raised or indented from the surface of the applet. Three-dimensional rectangles have four arguments for the x and y of the start position and the width and height of the rectangle. The fifth argument is a boolean indicating whether the 3D effect is to raise the rectangle (true) or indent it (false). As with the other rectangles, there are also different methods for drawing and filling: draw3DRect() and fill3DRect(). Here's code to produce two of them—the left one indented, the right one raised (Figure 9.6 shows the result):

```
public void paint(Graphics g) {
    g.draw3DRect(20,20,60,60,true);
    g.draw3DRect(120,20,60,60,false);
}
```

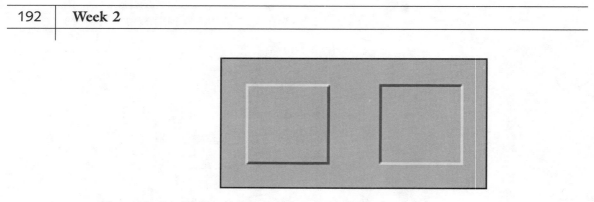

Figure 9.6   *Three-dimensional rectangles.*

NOTE

In the current beta version of the Java developer's kit, it is very difficult to see the 3D effect on 3D rectangles, due to a very small line width. (In fact, I enhanced Figure 9.6 to better show the effect.) If you are having troubles with 3D rectangles, this may be why. Drawing 3D rectangles in any color other than black is also easier to see.

Polygons

Polygons are shapes with an unlimited number of sides. To draw a polygon, you need a set of x and y coordinates, and the drawing method then starts at one, draws a line to the second, then a line to the third, and so on.

As with rectangles, you can draw an outline or a filled polygon (the drawPolygon() and fillPolygon() methods, respectively). You also have a choice of how you want to indicate the list of coordinates—either as arrays of x and y coordinates or as an instance of the Polygon class.

Using the first method, the drawPolygon() and fillPolygon() methods take three arguments:

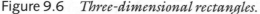

☐ An array of integers representing x coordinates

☐ An array of integers representing y coordinates

☐ An integer for the total number of points

The x and y arrays should, of course, have the same number of elements.

Here's an example of drawing a polygon's outline by using this method (Figure 9.7 shows the result):

```
public void paint(Graphics g) {
    int exes[] = { 39,94,97,142,53,58,26 };
    int whys[] = { 33,74,36,70,108,80,106 };
    int pts = exes.length;

    g.drawPolygon(exes,whys,pts);
}
```

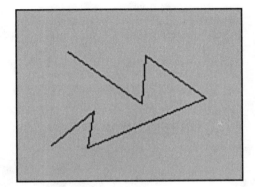

Figure 9.7   *A polygon.*

Note that Java does not automatically close the polygon; if you want to complete the shape, you have to include the starting point of the polygon at the end of the array. Drawing a filled polygon, however, joins the starting and ending points.

The second way of calling `drawPolygon()` and `fillPolygon()` is to use a `Polygon` object. The `Polygon` class is useful if you intend to add points to the polygon or if you're building the polygon on the fly. The `Polygon` class enables you to treat the polygon as an object rather than having to deal with individual arrays.

To create a `Polygon` object you can either create an empty polygon:

```
Polygon poly = new Polygon();
```

… or create a polygon from a set of points using integer arrays, as in the previous example:

```
int exes[] = { 39,94,97,142,53,58,26 };
int whys[] = { 33,74,36,70,108,80,106 };
int pts = exes.length;
Polygon poly = new Polygon(exes,whys,pts);
```

Once you have a `Polygon` object, you can append points to the polygon as you need to:

```
poly.addPoint(20,35);
```

Then, to draw the polygon, just use the `Polygon` object as an argument to `drawPolygon()` or `fillPolygon()`. Here's that previous example, rewritten this time with a `Polygon` object. You'll also fill this polygon rather than just drawing its outline (Figure 9.8 shows the output):

```
public void paint(Graphics g) {
    int exes[] = { 39,94,97,142,53,58,26 };
    int whys[] = { 33,74,36,70,108,80,106 };
    int pts = exes.length;
    Polygon poly = new Polygon(exes,whys,pts);
    g.fillPolygon(poly);
}
```

Figure 9.8   *Another polygon.*

Ovals

Use ovals to draw ellipses or circles. Ovals are just like rectangles with overly rounded corners. In fact, you draw them using the same four arguments: the x and y of the top corner and the width and height of the oval itself. Note that because you're drawing an oval, the starting point is some distance to the left and up from the actual outline of the oval itself. Again, if you think of it as a rectangle, it's easier to place.

As with the other drawing operations, the `drawOval()` method draws an outline of an oval, and the `fillOval()` method draws a filled oval.

Here's an example of two ovals: a circle and an ellipse (Figure 9.9 shows how these two ovals appear onscreen):

```
public void paint(Graphics g) {
    g.drawOval(20,20,60,60);
    g.fillOval(120,20,100,60);
}
```

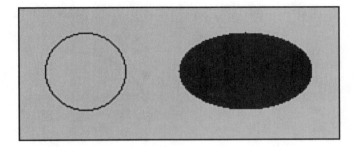

Figure 9.9 *Ovals.*

Arcs

Of the drawing operations, arcs are the most complex to construct, which is why I saved them for last. An arc is a part of a oval; in fact, the easiest way to think of an arc is as a section of a complete oval. Figure 9.10 shows some arcs.

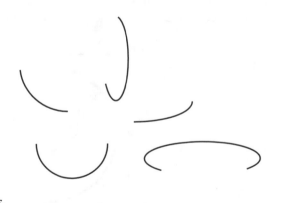

Figure 9.10 *Arcs.*

The drawArc() method takes six arguments: the starting corner, the width and height, the angle at which to start the arc, and the degrees to draw it before stopping. Once again, there is a drawArc() method to draw the arc's outline and the fillArc() to fill the arc. Filled arcs are drawn as if they were sections of a pie; instead of joining the two endpoints, both endpoints are joined to the center of the circle.

The important thing to understand about arcs is that you're actually formulating the arc as an oval and then drawing only some of that. The starting corner and width and height are not the starting point and width and height of the actual arc as drawn on the screen; they're the width and height of the full ellipse of which the arc is a part. Those first points determine the size and shape of the arc; the last two arguments (for the degrees) determine the starting and ending points.

Let's start with a simple arc, a C shape on a circle as shown in Figure 9.11.

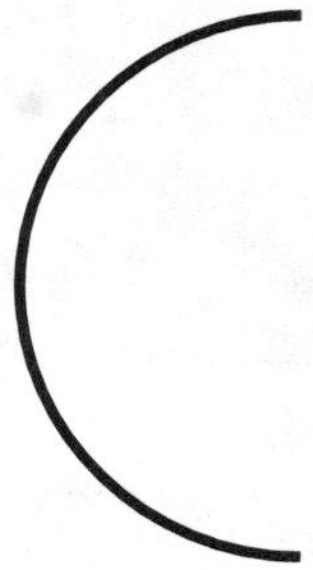

Figure 9.11   *A C arc.*

To construct the method to draw this arc, the first thing you do is think of it as a complete circle. Then you find the x and y coordinates and the width and height of that circle. Those four values are the first four arguments to the drawArc() or fillArc() methods. Figure 9.12 shows how to get those values from the arc.

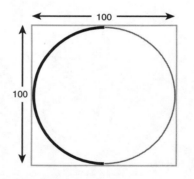

Figure 9.12   *Constructing a circular arc.*

To get the last two arguments, think in degrees around the circle. Zero degrees is at 3 o'clock, 90 degrees is at 12 o'clock, 180 is at 9 o'clock, and 270 is at 6 o'clock. The start of the arc is the degree value of the start of the arc. In this example, the starting point is the top of the C at 90 degrees; 90 is the fifth argument.

The sixth and last argument is another degree value indicating how far around the circle to sweep and the direction to go in (it's *not* the ending degree angle, as you might think). In this case, because you're going halfway around the circle, you're sweeping 180 degrees—and 180 is therefore the last argument in the arc. The important part is that you're sweeping 180 degrees counterclockwise, which is in the positive direction in Java. If you are drawing a backward C, you sweep 180 degrees in the negative direction, and the last argument is -180. See Figure 9.13 for the final illustration of how this works.

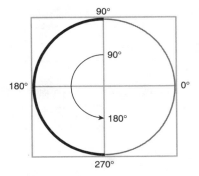

Figure 9.13   *Arcs on circles.*

It doesn't matter which side of the arc you start with; because the shape of the arc has already been determined by the complete oval it's a section of, starting at either endpoint will work.

Here's the code for this example; you'll draw an outline of the C and a filled C to its right, as shown in Figure 9.14:

```
public void paint(Graphics g) {
    g.drawArc(20,20,60,60,90,180);
    g.fillArc(120,20,60,60,90,180);
}
```

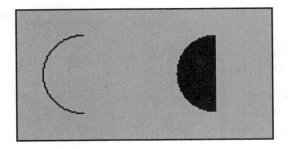

Figure 9.14   *Two circular arcs.*

Circles are an easy way to visualize arcs; arcs on ellipses are slightly more difficult. Let's go through this same process to draw the arc shown in Figure 9.15.

Figure 9.15   *An elliptical arc.*

Like the arc on the circle, this arc is a piece of a complete oval, in this case, an elliptical oval. By completing the oval that this arc is a part of, you can get the starting points and the width and height arguments for the drawArc() or fillArc() method (see Figure 9.16).

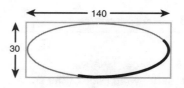

Figure 9.16   *Arcs on ellipses.*

Then, all you need is to figure out the starting angle and the angle to sweep. This arc doesn't start on a nice boundary, such as 90 or 180 degrees, so you'll need some trial and error. This arc starts somewhere around 25 degrees, and then sweeps clockwise about 130 degrees (see Figure 9.17).

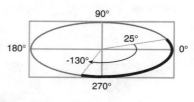

Figure 9.17   *Starting and ending points.*

With all portions of the arc in place, you can write the code. Here's the Java code for this arc, both drawn and filled (note in the filled case how filled arcs are drawn as if they were pie sections):

```
public void paint(Graphics g) {
    g.drawArc(10,20,150,50,25,-130);
    g.fillArc(10,80,150,50,25,-130);
}
```

Figure 9.18 shows the two elliptical arcs.

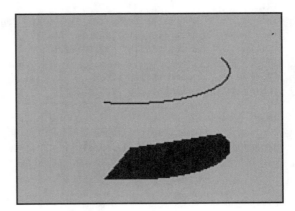

Figure 9.18   *Two elliptical arcs.*

To summarize, here are the steps to construct arcs in Java:

- ☐ Think of the arc as a slice of a complete oval.

- ☐ Construct the full oval with the starting point and the width and height (it often helps to draw the full oval on the screen to get an idea of the right positioning).

- ☐ Determine the starting angle for the beginning of the arc.

- ☐ Determine how far to sweep the arc and in which direction (counterclockwise indicates positive values, clockwise indicates negatives).

A Simple Graphics Example

Here's an example of an applet that uses many of the built-in graphics primitives to draw a rudimentary shape. In this case, it's a lamp with a spotted shade (or a sort of cubist mushroom, depending on your point of view). Here is the complete code for the lamp; Figure 9.19 shows the resulting applet.

```
1: import java.awt.*;
2:
3: public class Lamp extends java.applet.Applet {
4:
```

```
5:    public void paint(Graphics g) {
6:        // the lamp platform
7:        g.fillRect(0,250,290,290);
8:
9:        // the base of the lamp
10:        g.drawLine(125,250,125,160);
11:        g.drawLine(175,250,175,160);
12:
13:        // the lamp shade, top and bottom edges
14:         g.drawArc(85,157,130,50,-65,312);
15:         g.drawArc(85,87,130,50,62,58);
16:
17:         // lamp shade, sides
18:         g.drawLine(85,177,119,89);
19:         g.drawLine(215,177,181,89);
20:
21:         // dots on the shade
22:         g.fillArc(78,120,40,40,63,-174);
23:         g.fillOval(120,96,40,40);
24:         g.fillArc(173,100,40,40,110,180);
25:    }
26: }
```

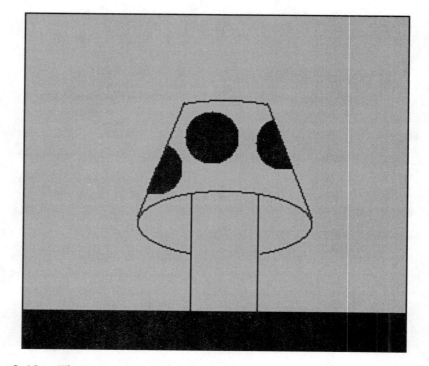

Figure 9.19   *The Lamp applet.*

Copying and Clearing

After you've drawn a few things on the screen, you may want to move them around or clear the entire applet. The Graphics class provides methods for doing both these things.

The copyArea() method copies a rectangular area of the screen to another area of the screen. copyArea() takes six arguments: the x and y of the top corner of the rectangle to copy, the width and the height of that rectangle, and the distance in the x and y directions to which to copy it. For example, this line copies a square area 100 pixels on a side 100 pixels directly to its right:

```
g.copyArea(0,0,100,100,100,0);
```

To clear a rectangular area, use the clearRect() method. clearRect(), which takes the same four arguments as the drawRect() and fillRect() methods, fills the given rectangle with the current background color of the applet (you'll learn how to set the current background color later on today).

To clear the entire applet, you can use the size() method, which returns a Dimension object representing the width and height of the applet. You can then get to the actual values for width and height by using the width and height instance variables:

```
g.clearRect(0,0,this.size().width,this.height());
```

Text and Fonts

The Graphics class also enables you to print text on the screen, in conjunction with the Font class and, sometimes, the Fontmetrics class. The Font class represents a given font—its name, style, and point size—and Fontmetrics gives you information about that font (for example, the actual height or width of a given character) so that you can precisely lay out text in your applet.

Note that the text here is static text, drawn to the screen once and intended to stay there. You'll learn about entering text from the keyboard later this week.

Creating Font Objects

To draw text to the screen, first you need to create an instance of the Font class. Font objects represent an individual font—that is, its name, style (bold, italic), and point size. Font names are strings representing the family of the font, for example, "Times-Roman", "Courier", or "Helvetica". Font styles are constants defined by the Font class; you can get to them using class variables—for example, Font.PLAIN, Font.BOLD, or Font.ITALIC. Finally, the point size is the size of the font, as defined by the font itself; the point size may or may not be the height of the characters.

To create an individual Font object, use these three arguments to the Font class's new constructor:

```
Font f = new Font("TimesRoman", Font.BOLD, 24);
```

This example creates a Font object for the TimesRoman BOLD font, in 24 points. Note that like most Java classes, you have to import this class before you can use it.

Font styles are actually integer constants that can be added to create combined styles; for example, Font.BOLD + Font.ITALIC produces a font that is both bold and italic.

The fonts you have available to you in your applet depend on the system on which the applet is running. List fonts in the current system with the getfontlist() method in the java.awt.Toolkit class and make choices based on that list. To make sure your applet is completely compatible across systems, it's a good idea to limit the fonts you use in your applets to TimesRoman, Helvetica, and Courier. If Java can't find a font you want to use, it will substitute some default font. Applet Runner substitutes the Mac system font Geneva, but your type may appear in some other font—usually Courier—on other systems or browsers.

Drawing Characters and Strings

With a Font object in hand, you can draw text on the screen using the methods drawChars() and drawString(). First, though, you need to set the current font to your Font object using the setFont() method.

The current font is part of the graphics state that is kept track of by the Graphics object on which you're drawing. Each time you draw a character or a string to the screen, that text is drawn by using the current font. To change the font of the text, first change the current font. Here's a paint() method that creates a new font, sets the current font to that font, and draws the string "This is a big font", starting from the point 10,100.

```
public void paint(Graphics g) {
    Font f = new Font("TimesRoman", Font.PLAIN,72);
    g.setFont(f);
    g.drawString("This is a big font.",10,100);
}
```

This should all look familiar to you; this is how the Hello applets throughout this book were produced.

The latter two arguments to drawString() determine the point where the string will start. The x value is the start of the leftmost edge of the text; y is the baseline for the entire string.

Similar to drawString() is the drawChars() method that, instead of taking a string as an argument, takes an array of characters. drawChars() has five arguments: the array of characters, an n integer representing the first character in the array to draw, another integer for the last character in the array to draw (all characters between the first and last are drawn), and the x and y for the starting point. Most of the time, drawString() is more useful than drawChars().

The following code shows an applet that draws several lines of text in different fonts; Figure 9.20 shows the result.

```
 1: import java.awt.Font;
 2: import java.awt.Graphics;
 3:
 4: public class ManyFonts extends java.applet.Applet {
 5:
 6:     public void paint(Graphics g) {
 7:         Font f = new Font("TimesRoman", Font.PLAIN, 18);
 8:         Font fb = new Font("TimesRoman", Font.BOLD, 18);
 9:         Font fi = new Font("TimesRoman", Font.ITALIC, 18);
10:         Font fbi = new Font("TimesRoman", Font.BOLD + Font.ITALIC,18);
11:
12:         g.setFont(f);
13:         g.drawString("This is a plain font", 10, 25);
14:         g.setFont(fb);
15:         g.drawString("This is a bold font", 10, 50);
16:         g.setFont(fi);
17:         g.drawString("This is an italic font", 10, 75);
18:         g.setFont(fbi);
19:         g.drawString("This is a bold italic font", 10, 100);
20:     }
21:
22: }
```

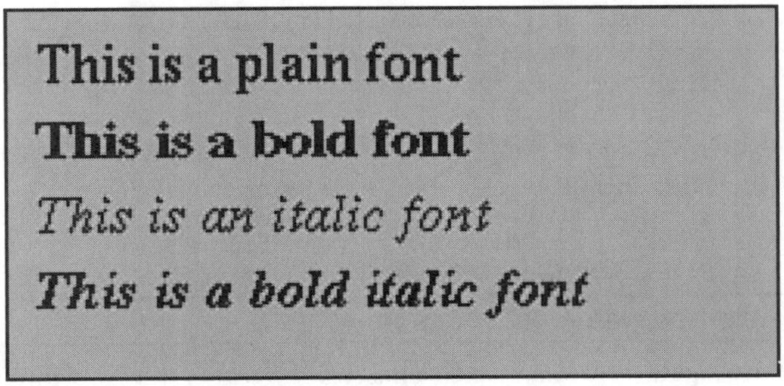

Figure 9.20 *The output of the ManyFonts applet.*

Finding Information About Fonts

Sometimes, you may want to make decisions in your Java program based on the qualities of the current font—for example, its point size or the total height of its characters. You can find out some basic information about fonts and font objects by using simple methods on Graphics and on the Font objects. Table 9.1 shows some of these methods:

Table 9.1   *Font Methods*

Method Name	In Object	Action
getFont()	Graphics	Returns the current font object as previously set by setFont()
getName()	Font	Returns the name of the font as a string
getSize()	Font	Returns the current font size (an integer)
getStyle()	Font	Returns the current style of the font (styles are integer constants: 0 is plain, 1 is bold, 2 is italic, 3 is bold italic)
isPlain()	Font	Returns true or false if the font's style is plain
isBold()	Font	Returns true or false if the font's style is bold
isItalic()	Font	Returns true or false if the font's style is italic

For more detailed information about the qualities of the current font (for example, the length or height of given characters), you need to work with font metrics. The FontMetrics class describes information specific to a given font: the leading between lines, the height and width of each character, and so on. To work with these sorts of values, you create a FontMetrics object based on the current font by using the applet method getFontMetrics:

```
Font f = new Font("TimesRoman", Font.BOLD, 36);
FontMetrics fmetrics = getFontMetrics(f);
g.setfont(f);
```

Table 9.2 shows some of the things you can find out using font metrics. All these methods should be called on a FontMetrics object.

Table 9.2   *FontMetrics Methods*

Method Name	Action
stringWidth(String)	Given a string, returns the full width of that string in pixels
charWidth(char)	Given a character, returns the width of that character

Method Name	Action
getAscent()	Returns the ascent of the font—that is, the distance between the font's baseline and the top of the characters
getDescent()	Returns the descent of the font—that is, the distance between the font's baseline and the bottoms of the characters (for characters such as p and q that drop below the baseline)
getLeading()	Returns the leading for the font, that is, the spacing between the descent of one line and the ascent of another line
getHeight()	Returns the total height of the font, which is the sum of the ascent, descent, and leading value

NOTE

You may have noticed that Java thinks of leading differently than most Mac applications, which define leading as the distance between baselines, rather than between the bottom of one line and the top of the next. For the record, Java's use of "leading" is the more correct use of the historical term.

As an example of the sorts of information you can use with font metrics, the following listing shows the Java code for an applet that automatically centers a string horizontally and vertically inside an applet. The centering position is different depending on the font and font size; by using font metrics to find out the actual size of a string, you can draw the string in the appropriate place.

Note the `Applet.size()` method here, which returns the width and height of the overall applet area as a `Dimension` object. You can then get to the individual width and height by using the `width` and `height` instance variables.

Figure 9.21 shows the result (less interesting than if you actually compile and experiment with various applet sizes).

```
 1: import java.awt.Font;
 2: import java.awt.Graphics;
 3: import java.awt.FontMetrics;
 4:
 5: public class Centered extends java.applet.Applet {
 6:
 7:     public void paint(Graphics g) {
 8:         Font f = new Font("TimesRoman", Font.PLAIN, 36);
 9:         FontMetrics fm = getFontMetrics(f);
10:         g.setFont(f);
11:
12:         String s = "This is how the world ends.";
13:         int xstart = (this.size().width - fm.stringWidth(s)) / 2;
```

```
14:          int ystart = (this.size().height - fm.getHeight()) / 2;
15:
16:          g.drawString(s, xstart, ystart);
17:    }
18:}
```

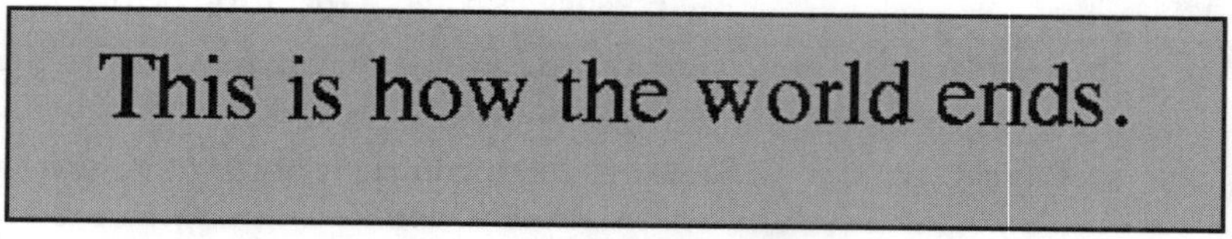

Figure 9.21 *The centered text.*

Color

Drawing black lines and tests on a gray background is all very nice, but being able to use different colors is much nicer. Java provides methods and behaviors for dealing with color in general through the Color class, and also provides methods for setting the current foreground and background colors so that you can draw with the colors you created.

Java's abstract color model uses 24-bit color, wherein a color is represented as a combination of red, green, and blue values. Each component of the color can have a number between 0 and 255. 0,0,0 is black, 255,255,255 is white, and Java can represent millions of colors between as well.

Java's abstract color model maps onto the color model of the platform Java is running on, which may have only 256 colors or fewer from which to choose. If a requested color in a color object is not available for display, the resulting color may be mapped to another or dithered, depending on how the browser viewing the color implemented it, and depending on the platform on which you're running. In other words, although Java gives the capability of managing millions of colors, keep in mind that the users viewing your applets may have fewer colors available to them.

Using Color Objects

To draw an object in a particular color, you must create an instance of the Color class to represent that color. The Color class defines a set of standard color objects, stored in class variables, that enable you quickly to get a color object for some of the more popular colors. For example, Color.red gives you a Color object representing red (RGB values of 255, 0, and 0), Color.white gives you a white color (RGB values of 255, 255, and 255), and so on. Table 9.3 shows the standard colors defined by variables in the Color class.

Table 9.3   *Standard Colors*

Color Name	RGB Value
Color.white	255,255,255
Color.black	0,0,0
Color.lightGray	192,192,192
Color.gray	128,128,128
Color.darkGray	64,64,64
Color.red	255,0,0
Color.green	0,255,0
Color.blue	0,0,255
Color.yellow	255,255,0
Color.magenta	255,0,255
Color.cyan	0,255,255
Color.pink	255,175,175
Color.orange	255,200,0

If the color you want to draw in is not one of the standard color objects, fear not. You can create a color object for any combination of red, green, or blue, as long as you have the values of the color you want. Just create a new color object:

```
Color c = new Color(140,140,140);
```

This line of Java code creates a color object representing a dark gray. You can use any combination of red, green, and blue values to construct a color object.

Alternatively, you can also create a color object using three floats from 0.0 to 1.0:

```
Color c = new Color(0.34,1.0,0.25)
```

Testing and Setting the Current Colors

To draw an object or text using a Color object, you have to set the current color to be that Color object, just as you have to set the current font to the font in which you want to draw. Use the setColor() method (a method for Graphics objects) to do this:

```
g.setColor(Color.green);
```

After setting the current color, all drawing operations will occur in that color.

In addition to setting the current color for the graphics context, you can also set the background and foreground colors for the applet itself by using the setBackground() and setForeground() methods. Both of these methods are defined in the java.awt.Component class, which Applet—and therefore your classes—automatically inherits.

The setBackground() method sets the background color of the applet, which is usually gray. It takes a single argument, a Color object:

```
setBackground(Color.white);
```

The setForeground() method also takes a single color as an argument, and affects everything that has been drawn on the applet, regardless of the color in which it has been drawn. You can use setForeground() to change the color of everything in the applet at once, rather than having to redraw everything:

```
setForeground(Color.black);
```

In addition to the setColor(), setForeground(), and setBackground() methods, there are corresponding "get" methods that enable you to retrieve the current graphics color of the background or foreground. Those methods are getColor (defined in Graphics objects), getForeground (defined in Applet), and getBackground (also in Applet). You can use these methods to choose colors based on existing colors in the applet:

```
setForeground(g.getColor());
```

A Single Color Example

Here is the code for an applet that fills the applet's drawing area with square boxes, each of which has a randomly chosen color in it. It's written so that it can handle any size of applet and automatically fill the area with the right number of boxes.

```
1:  import java.awt.Graphics;
2:  import java.awt.Color;
3:
4:  public class ColorBoxes extends java.applet.Applet {
5:
6:      public void paint(Graphics g) {
7:          int rval, gval, bval;
8:
9:          for (int j = 30; j < (this.size().height -25); j += 30)
10:             for (int i = 5; i < (this.size().width -25); i+= 30) {
11:                 rval = (int)Math.floor(Math.random() * 256);
12:                 gval = (int)Math.floor(Math.random() * 256);
13:                 bval = (int)Math.floor(Math.random() * 256);
```

```
14:
15:                     g.setColor(new Color(rval,gval,bval));
16:                     g.fillRect(i,j,25,25);
17:                     g.setColor(Color.black);
18:                     g.drawRect(i-1,j-1,25,25);
19:              }
20:       }
21: }
```

The two for loops are the heart of this example; the first one draws the rows, and the second draws the individual boxes within the row. When a box is drawn, the random color is calculated first, and then the box is drawn. A black outline is drawn around each box, because some of them tend to blend into the background of the applet.

Because this paint() method generates new colors each time the applet is painted, you can regenerate the colors by moving the window around or by covering the applet's window with another one. Figure 9.22 shows the final applet (although given that this picture is black and white, you can't get the full effect of the multicolored squares).

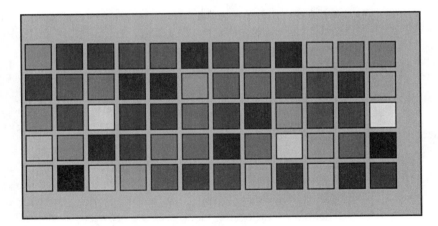

Figure 9.22   *The random colors applet.*

Summary

You present something on the screen by painting inside your applet: shapes, graphics, text, or images. Today you learned the basics of how to paint, including using the graphics primitives to draw rudimentary shapes, using fonts and font metrics to draw text, and using Color objects to change the color of what you're drawing on the screen. It's this foundation in painting that enables you to do animation inside an applet (which basically involves just painting repeatedly to the screen) and to work with image. These are topics you'll learn about tomorrow.

Questions and Answers

Q **In all the examples you show, and in all the tests I've made, the graphics primitives, such as `drawLine()` and `drawRect()`, produce lines that are one pixel wide. How can I draw thicker lines?**

A In the current state of the Java Graphics class, you can't; no methods exist for changing the default line width. If you really need a thicker line, you have to draw multiple lines one pixel apart to produce that effect.

Q **I wrote an applet to use Helvetica. It works fine on my system, but when I run it on my friend's system, everything is in Courier. Why?**

A Your friend most likely doesn't have the Helvetica font installed on his or her system. When Java can't find a font, it substitutes a default font instead—in your case, Courier. The best way to deal with this is to query the font list.

Q **I tried out the applet that draws boxes with random colors, but each time it draws, a lot of the boxes are the same color. If the colors are truly random, why is it doing this?**

A Two reasons. The first is that the random number generator I used in that code (from the Math class) isn't a very good random number generator; in fact, the documentation for that method says as much. For a better random number generator, use the Random class from the java.util package.

The second, more likely, reason is that there just aren't enough colors available in your browser or on your system to draw all the colors that the applet is generating. If your system can't produce the wide range of colors available using the Color class, or if the browser has allocated too many colors for other things, you may end up with duplicate colors in the boxes, depending on how the browser and the system has been written to handle that. Usually your applet won't use quite so many colors, so you won't run into this problem quite so often.

Q **I drew a rectangle that touched the left edge of the Applet Runner window, and then redrew it somewhere else. The very edge of the Applet Runner Window wasn't erased. What did I do wrong?**

A Nothing—it's a tiny bug in the Applet Runner, which will be fixed in a future release.

Simple Animation and Threads

by Laura Lemay with Timothy Webster

The first thing I ever saw Java do was an animation; a large red `"Hi there!"` ran across the screen from the right to the left. Even that simple form of animation was enough to make me stop and think, "This is really cool."

That sort of simple animation takes only a few methods to implement in Java, but those few methods are the basis for any Java applet that you want to update the screen dynamically. Starting with simple animations is a good way to build up to the more complicated applets. Today, you'll learn the fundamentals of animation in Java, and how the various parts of the system all work together so that you can create moving figures and dynamic applets. Specifically, you'll explore the following:

☐ How Java animations work—the `paint()` and `repaint()` methods, starting and stopping dynamic applets, and how to use and override these methods in your own applets

☐ Threads—what they are and how they can make your applets more well-behaved with other applets and with the Java system in general

☐ Reducing animation flicker, a common problem with animation in Java

Throughout today, you'll also work with lots of examples of real applets that create animations or perform some kind of dynamic movement.

Creating Animation in Java

Animation in Java involves two steps: constructing a frame of animation, and then asking Java to paint that frame. Repeat as necessary to create the illusion of movement. The basic, static applets that you created yesterday taught you how to accomplish the first part; all that's left is how to tell Java to paint a frame.

Painting and Repainting

The paint() method, as you learned yesterday, is called by Java whenever the applet needs to be painted—when the applet is initially drawn, when the window containing it is moved, or when another window is moved from over it. You can also, however, ask Java to repaint the applet at a time you choose. So, to change the appearance of what is on the screen, you construct the image or "frame" you want to paint, and then ask Java to paint this frame. If you do this repeatedly, and fast enough, you get animation inside your Java applet. That's all there is to it.

Where does all this take place? Not in the paint() method itself. All paint() does is put dots on the screen. paint(), in other words, is responsible only for the current frame of the animation at a time. The real work of changing what paint() does, of modifying the frame for an animation, actually occurs somewhere else in the definition of your applet.

In that "somewhere else," you construct the frame (set variables for paint() to use, create color or font or other objects that paint() will need), and then call the repaint() method. repaint() is the trigger that causes Java to call paint() and causes your frame to get drawn.

NOTE

> Because a Java applet can contain many different components that all need to be painted (as you'll learn later on this week), and in fact, applets are embedded inside a larger Java application that also paints to the screen in similar ways, when you call repaint() (and therefore paint()) you're not actually immediately drawing to the screen as you do in other window or graphics toolkits. Instead, repaint() is a *request* for Java to repaint your applet as soon as it can. Much of the time, the delay between the call and the actual repaint is negligible.

Starting and Stopping an Applet's Execution

Remember start() and stop() from Day 8? These are the methods that trigger your applet to start and stop running. You didn't use start() and stop() yesterday, because the applets on that day did nothing except paint once. With animations and other Java applets that are actually processing and running over time, you'll need to make use of start() and stop() to trigger the start of your applet's execution, and to stop it from running when you leave the page that contains that applet. For most applets, you'll want to override start() and stop() for just this reason.

The start() method triggers the execution of the applet. You can either do all the applet's work inside that method, or you can call other object's methods in order to do so. Usually, start() is used to create and begin execution of a thread so the applet can run in its own time.

stop(), on the other hand, suspends an applet's execution so when you move off the page on which the applet is displaying, it doesn't keep running and using up system resources. Most of the time when you create a start() method, you should also create a corresponding stop().

Putting It Together

Explaining how to do Java animation in text is more of a task than actually showing you how it works in code. An example or two will help make the relationship between all these methods clearer.

The following code shows a sample applet that, at first glance, uses basic applet animation to display the date and time and constantly updates it every second, creating a very simple animated digital clock (a frame from that clock is shown in Figure 10.1).

Sun Nov 05 20:43:02 PST 1995

Figure 10.1   *The digital clock.*

The words "at first glance" in the previous paragraph are very important: this applet doesn't work! However, despite the fact that it doesn't work, you can still learn a lot about basic animation with it, so working through the code will still be valuable. In the next section, you'll learn just what's wrong with it.

See whether you can figure out what's going on with this code before you go on to the analysis.

```
 1: import java.awt.Graphics;
 2: import java.awt.Font;
 3: import java.util.Date;
 4:
 5: public class DigitalClock extends java.applet.Applet {
 6:
 7:     Font theFont = new Font("TimesRoman",Font.BOLD,24);
 8:     Date theDate;
 9:
10:     public void start() {
```

```
11:            while (true) {
12:                theDate = new Date();
13:                repaint();
14:                try { Thread.sleep(1000); }
15:                catch (InterruptedException e) { }
16:            }
17:        }
18:
19:        public void paint(Graphics g) {
20:            g.setFont(theFont);
21:            g.drawString(theDate.toString(),10,50);
22:        }
23: }
```

Think you've got the basic idea? Let's go through it, line by line.

Lines 7 and 8 define two basic instance variables: theFont and theDate, which hold objects representing the current font and the current date, respectively. More about these later.

The start() method triggers the actual execution of the applet. Note the while loop inside this method; given that the test (true) always returns true, the loop never exits. A single animation frame is constructed inside that while loop, with the following steps:

☐ The Date class represents a date and time (Date is part of the java.util package—note that it was specifically imported in line 3). Line 12 creates a new instance of the Date class, which holds the current date and time, and assigns it to the theDate instance variable.

☐ The repaint() method is called.

☐ Lines 14 and 15, as complicated as they look, do nothing except pause for 1000 milliseconds (one second) before the loop repeats. The sleep() method there, part of the Thread class, is what causes the applet to pause. Without a specific sleep() method, the applet would run as fast as it possibly could, which, for faster computer systems, might be too fast for the eye to see. Using sleep() enables you to control exactly how fast the animation takes place. The try and catch stuff around it enables Java to manage errors if they occur. Such errors are called *exceptions* and are described on Day 17, next week.

On to the paint() method. Here, inside paint(), all that happens is that the current font (in the variable theFont) is set, and the date itself is printed to the screen (note that you have to call the toString() method to convert the date to a string). Because paint() is called repeatedly with whatever value happens to be in theDate, the string is updated every second to reflect the new date.

There are a few things to note about this example. First, you might think it would be easier to create the new Date object inside the paint() method. That way you could use a local variable and not need an instance variable to pass the Date object around. Although doing things that way creates cleaner code, it also results in a less efficient program. The paint() method is called every time a frame needs to be changed. In this case, it's not that important, but in an animation that needs to change frames very quickly, the paint() method has to pause to create that new object every time. By leaving paint() to do what it does best—painting the screen—and calculating new objects beforehand, you can make painting as efficient as possible. This is precisely the same reason why the Font object is also in an instance variable.

Threads: What They Are and Why You Need Them

Depending on your experience with operating systems and with environments within those systems, you may or may not have run into the concept of threads. Let's start from the beginning with some definitions.

When a program runs, it starts executing, runs its initialization code, calls methods or procedures, and continues running and processing until it's complete or until the program is exited. That program uses a single thread—where the thread is a single locus of control for the program.

Multithreading, as in Java, enables several different execution threads to run at the same time inside the same program, in parallel, without interfering with each other.

Here's a simple example. Suppose you have a long computation near the start of a program's execution. This long computation may not be needed until later on in the program's execution—it's actually tangential to the main point of the program, but it needs to get done eventually. In a single-threaded program, you have to wait for that computation to finish before the rest of the program can continue running. In a multithreaded system, you can put that computation into its own thread, enabling the rest of the program to continue running independently.

Using threads in Java, you can create an applet so that it runs in its own thread, and it will happily run all by itself without interfering with any other part of the system. Using threads, you can have lots of applets running at once on the same page. Depending on how many you have, you may eventually exhaust the system so that all of them will run slower, but all of them will run independently.

Even if you don't have lots of applets, using threads in your applets is good Java programming practice. The general rule of thumb for well-behaved applets: whenever you have any bit of processing that is likely to continue for a long time (such as an animation loop, or a bit of code that takes a long time to execute), put it in a thread.

The Problem with the Digital Clock Applet

The Digital Clock applet in the last section doesn't use threads. Instead, you put the while loop that cycles through the animation directly into the start() method so that when the applet starts running it keeps going until you quit the browser or applet viewer. Although this may seem like a good way to approach the problem, the digital clock won't work because the while loop in the start() method is monopolizing all the resources in the system—including painting. If you try compiling and running the digital clock applet, all you get is a blank screen. You also won't be able to stop the applet, because there's no way a stop() method can be called.

The solution to this problem is to rewrite the applet to use threads. Threads enable this applet to animate on its own without interfering with other system operations, enable it to be started and stopped, and enable you to run it in parallel with other applets.

Writing Applets with Threads

How do you create an applet that uses threads? There are several things you need to do. Fortunately, none of them are difficult, and a lot of the basics of using threads in applets is just boilerplate code that you can copy and paste from one applet to another. Because it's so easy, there's almost no reason *not* to use threads in your applets, given the benefits.

There are four modifications you need to make to create an applet that uses threads:

- ☐ Change the signature of your applet class to include the words implements Runnable.

- ☐ Include an instance variable to hold this applet's thread.

- ☐ Modify your start() method to do nothing but spawn a thread and start it running.

- ☐ Create a run() method that contains the actual code that starts your applet running.

The first change is to the first line of your class definition. You've already got something like this:

```
public class MyAppletClass extends java.applet.Applet {
...
}
```

You need to change it to the following:

```
public class MyAppletClass extends java.applet.Applet  implements Runnable {
...
}
```

What does this do? It includes support for the Runnable interface in your applet. If you think way back to Day 2, you'll remember that interfaces are a way to collect method names common to different classes, which can then be mixed in and implemented inside different classes that need to implement that behavior. Here, the Runnable interface defines the behavior your applet needs to run a thread; in particular, it gives you a default definition for the run() method. By implementing Runnable, you tell other classes that they can call the run() method on instances of this class.

The second step is to add an instance variable to hold this applet's thread. Call it anything you like; it's a variable of the type Thread (Thread is a class in java.lang, so you don't have to import it):

```
Thread runner;
```

Third, add a start() method or modify the existing one so that it does nothing but create a new thread and start it running. Here's a typical example of a start() method:

```
public void start() {
        if (runner == null); {
            runner = new Thread(this);
            runner.start();
        }
    }
```

If you modify start() to do nothing but spawn a thread, where does the body of your applet go? It goes into a new method, run(), which looks like this:

```
public void run() {
    // what your applet actually does
}
```

run() can contain anything you want to run in the separate thread: initialization code, the actual loop for your applet, or anything else that needs to run in its own thread. You also can create new objects and call methods from inside run(), and they'll also run inside that thread. The run method is the real heart of your applet.

Finally, now that you've got threads running and a start() method to start them, you should add a stop() method to suspend execution of that thread (and therefore whatever the applet is doing at the time) when the reader leaves the page. stop(), like start(), is usually something along these lines:

```
public void stop() {
      if (runner != null) {
            runner.stop();
            runner = null;
      }
}
```

The stop() method here does two things: it stops the thread from executing and also sets the thread's variable (runner) to null. Setting the variable to null makes the Thread object it previously contained available for garbage collection so that the applet can be removed from memory after a certain amount of time. If the reader comes back to this page and this applet, the start() method creates a new thread and starts up the applet once again.

And that's it! Four basic modifications, and now you have a well-behaved applet that runs in its own thread.

Fixing the Digital Clock

Remember the problems you had with the Digital Clock applet at the beginning of this section? Let's fix them so you can get an idea of how a real applet with threads looks. You'll follow the four steps outlined in the previous section.

First, modify the class definition to include the Runnable interface (the class is re-named to DigitalThreads instead of DigitalClock):

```
public class DigitalThreads extends java.applet.Applet
    implements Runnable {
    ...
```

Second, add an instance variable for the Thread:

```
Thread runner;
```

For the third step, swap the way you did things. Because the bulk of the applet is currently in a method called start(), but you want it to be in a method called run(), rather than do a lot of copying and pasting, just rename the existing start() to run():

```
public void run() {
      while (true) {
    ...
```

Finally, add the boilerplate start() and stop() methods:

```
public void start() {
      if (runner == null); {
```

```
            runner = new Thread(this);
            runner.start();
        }
    }

    public void stop() {
        if (runner != null) {
            runner.stop();
            runner = null;
        }
    }
}
```

You're finished! One applet converted to use threads in less than a minute flat. Here's the code for the final applet:

```
 1: import java.awt.Graphics;
 2: import java.awt.Font;
 3: import java.util.Date;
 4:
 5: public class DigitalThreads extends java.applet.Applet
 6:     implements Runnable {
 7:
 8:     Font theFont = new Font("TimesRoman",Font.BOLD,24);
 9:     Date theDate = new Date();
10:    Thread runner;
11:
12:    public void start() {
13:        if (runner == null); {
14:            runner = new Thread(this);
15:            runner.start();
16:        }
17:    }
18:
19:    public void stop() {
20:        if (runner != null) {
21:            runner.stop();
22:            runner = null;
23:        }
24:    }
25:
26: public void run() {
27:        while (true) {
28:            theDate = new Date();
29:            repaint();
30:            try { Thread.sleep(1000); }
31:            catch (InterruptedException e) { }
32:        }
33:    }
34:
```

```
35:     public void paint(Graphics g) {
36:         g.setFont(theFont);
37:         g.drawString(theDate.toString(),10,50);
38:     }
39: }
40:
```

Reducing Animation Flicker

If you've been following along with this book and trying the examples as you go, rather than reading this book on the airplane or in the bathtub, you may have noticed that when the date program runs, every once in a while, there's an annoying flicker in the animation. This isn't a mistake or an error in the program; in fact, that flicker is a side effect of creating animations in Java. Because it is really annoying, however, you'll learn how to reduce flicker in this part of today's lesson so that your animations run cleaner and look better on the screen.

Flicker and How to Avoid It

Flicker is caused by the way Java paints and repaints each frame of an applet. At the beginning of today's lesson, you learned that when you call the repaint() method, repaint() calls paint(). That's not precisely true. A call to paint() does indeed occur in response to a repaint(), but what actually happens are the following steps:

1. The call to repaint() results in a call to the method update().

2. The update() method clears the screen of any existing contents (in essence, fills it with the current background color), and then calls paint().

3. The paint() method then draws the contents of the current frame.

It's Step 2, the call to update(), that causes animation flicker. Because the screen is cleared between frames, the parts of the screen that don't change alternate rapidly between being painted and being cleared. Hence, flickering.

There are two major ways to avoid flicker in your Java applets:

☐ Override update() either not to clear the screen at all, or to clear only the parts of the screen you've changed.

☐ Override both update() and paint(), and use double-buffering.

If the second way sounds complicated, that's because it is. Double-buffering involves drawing to an offscreen graphics surface and then copying that entire surface to the screen. Because it's more complicated, you'll explore that one tomorrow. Today, let's cover the easier solution: overriding update().

How to Override update()

The cause of flickering lies in the update() method. To reduce flickering, therefore, override both update() and paint(). Here's what the default version of update() does (in the Component class, which you'll learn more about on Day 13):

```
public void update(Graphics g) {
    g.setColor(getBackground());
    g.fillRect(0, 0, width, height);
    g.setColor(getForeground());
    paint(g);
}
```

Basically, update() clears the screen (or, to be exact, fills the applet's bounding rectangle with the background color), sets things back to normal, and then calls paint(). When you override update(), you have to keep these two things in mind and make sure that your version of update() does something similar. In the next two sections, you'll work through some examples of overriding update() in different cases to reduce flicker.

Solution One: Don't Clear the Screen

The first solution to reducing flicker is not to clear the screen at all. This works only for some applets, of course. Here's an example of an applet of this type. The Color-Swirl applet prints a single string to the screen ("All the swirly colors"), but that string is presented in different colors that fade into each other dynamically. This applet flickers terribly when its run. Here is the source for this applet, and Figure 10.2 shows the result.

```
1:  import java.awt.Graphics;
2:  import java.awt.Color;
3:  import java.awt.Font;
4:
5:  public class ColorSwirl extends java.applet.Applet
6:      implements Runnable {
7:
8:      Font f = new Font("TimesRoman",Font.BOLD,48);
9:      Color colors[] = new Color[50];
10:     Thread runThread;
11:
12:     public void start() {
13:         if (runThread == null) {
14:             runThread = new Thread(this);
15:             runThread.start();
16:         }
17:     }
18:
```

```
19:     public void stop() {
20:         if (runThread != null) {
21:             runThread.stop();
22:             runThread = null;
23:         }
24:     }
25:
26:     public void run() {
27:
28:         // initialize the color array
29:         float c = 0;
30:         for (int i = 0; i < colors.length; i++) {
31:             colors[i] =
32:             Color.getHSBColor(c, (float)1.0,(float)1.0);
33:             c += .02;
34:         }
35:
36:         // cycle through the colors
37:         int i = 0;
38:         while (true) {
39:             setForeground(colors[i]);
40:             repaint();
41:             i++;
42:             try { Thread.sleep(50); }
43:             catch (InterruptedException e) { }
44:             if (i == colors.length ) i = 0;
45:         }
46:     }
47:
48:     public void paint(Graphics g) {
49:         g.setFont(f);
50:         g.drawString("All the Swirly Colors", 15,50);
51:     }
52: }
```

Figure 10.2   *The ColorSwirl applet.*

There are three new things to note about this applet that might look strange to you:

☐ When the applet starts, the first thing you do (in lines 28 through 34) is to create an array of Color objects that contains all the colors the text will display.

By creating all the colors beforehand, you can then just draw text in, one at a time; it's faster to precompute all the colors at once.

☐ To create the different colors, a method in the `Color` class called `getHSBColor()` creates a color object based on values for hue, saturation, and brightness, rather than the standard red, green, and blue. This is easier; by incrementing the hue value and keeping saturation and brightness constant, you can create a range of colors without having to know the RGB for each one. If you don't understand this, don't worry about it; it's just an easy way to create the color array.

☐ The applet then cycles through the array of colors, setting the foreground to each one in turn and calling `repaint()`. When it gets to the end of the array, it starts over again (line 44), so the process repeats over and over ad infinitum.

Now that you understand what the applet does, let's fix the flicker. Flicker here results because each time the applet is painted, there's a moment where the screen is cleared. Instead of the text cycling neatly from red to a nice pink to purple, it's going from red to gray, to pink to gray, to purple to gray, and so on—not very nice-looking at all.

Because the screen clearing is all that's causing the problem, the solution is easy: override `update()` and remove the part where the screen gets cleared. It doesn't really need to get cleared anyhow, because nothing is changing except the color of the text. With the screen clearing behavior removed from `update()`, all `update` needs to do is call `paint()`. Here's what the `update()` method looks like in this applet:

```
public void update(Graphics g) {
        paint(g);
    }
```

With that—with one small three-line addition—no more flicker. Wasn't that easy? (The flicker-free version of the applet is saved on the CD-ROM as ColorSwirl2.)

Solution Two: Redraw Only What You Have To

For some applets, it won't be quite that easy. Here's another example. In this applet, called Checkers, a red oval (a checker piece) moves from a black square to a white square, as if on a checkerboard. Here's the code for this applet, and Figure 10.3 shows the applet itself.

```
1:    import java.awt.Graphics;
2:      import java.awt.Color;
3:
4:    public class Checkers extends java.applet.Applet
5:        implements Runnable {
6:
```

```
 7:        Thread runner;
 8:        int xpos;
 9:
10:        public void start() {
11:            if (runner == null); {
12:                runner = new Thread(this);
13:                runner.start();
14:            }
15:        }
16:
17:        public void stop() {
18:            if (runner != null) {
19:                runner.stop();
20:                runner = null;
21:            }
22:        }
23:
24: public void run() {
25:            setBackground(Color.blue);
26:            while (true) {
27:                for (xpos = 5; xpos <= 105; xpos+=4) {
28:                    repaint();
29:                    try { Thread.sleep(100); }
30:                    catch (InterruptedException e) { }
31:                }
32:                for (xpos = 105; xpos > 5; xpos -=4) {
33:                    repaint();
34:                    try { Thread.sleep(100); }
35:                    catch (InterruptedException e) { }
36:                }
37:            }
38:        }
39:
40:        public void paint(Graphics g) {
41:            // Draw background
42:            g.setColor(Color.black);
43:            g.fillRect(0,0,100,100);
44:            g.setColor(Color.white);
45:            g.fillRect(101,0,100,100);
46:
47:            // Draw checker
48:            g.setColor(Color.red);
49:            g.fillOval(xpos,5,90,90);
50:        }
51: }
```

Figure 10.3   *The Checkers applet.*

Here's a quick run-through of what this applet does: an instance variable, xpos, keeps track of the current starting position of the checker (because it moves horizontally, the y stays constant and the x changes). In the run() method, you change the value of x and repaint, waiting 50 milliseconds between each move. The checker moves from one side of the screen to the other and then moves back (hence the two for loops in that method).

In the actual paint() method, the background squares are painted (one black and one white), and then the checker is drawn at its current position.

This applet, like the Swirling Colors applet, also has a terrible flicker. (In line 25, the background is blue to emphasize it, so if you run this applet you'll definitely see the flicker.)

However, the solution to solving the flicker problem for this applet is more difficult than for the last one, because you actually want to clear the screen before the next frame is drawn. Otherwise, the red checker won't have the appearance of leaving one position and moving to another; it'll just leave a red smear from one side of the checkerboard to the other.

How do you get around this? You still clear the screen, in order to get the animation effect, but, rather than clearing the entire screen, you clear only the part that you actually changed. By limiting the redraw to only a small area, you can eliminate much of the flicker you get from redrawing the entire screen.

To limit what gets redrawn, you need a couple of things. First, you need a way to restrict the drawing area so that each time paint() is called, only the part that needs to get redrawn actually gets redrawn. Fortunately, this is easy by using a mechanism called clipping.

NEW TERM   *Clipping*, part of the Graphics class, enables you to restrict the drawing area to a small portion of the full screen; although the entire screen may get instructions to redraw, only the portions inside the clipping area are actually drawn.

The second thing you need is a way to keep track of the actual area to redraw. Both the left and right edges of the drawing area change for each frame of the animation (one side to draw the new oval, the other to erase the bit of the oval left over from the previous frame), so to keep track of those two x values, you need instance variables for both the left side and the right.

With those two concepts in mind, let's start modifying the Checkers applet to redraw only what needs to be redrawn. First, you'll add instance variables for the left and right edges of the drawing area. Let's call those instance variables ux1 and ux2 (u for update), where ux1 is the left side of the area to draw and ux2 the right.

```
int ux1,ux2;
```

Now let's modify the run() method so that it keeps track of the actual area to be drawn, which you would think is easy—just update each side for each iteration of the animation. Here, however, things can get complicated because of the way Java uses paint() and repaint().

The problem with updating the edges of the drawing area with each frame of the animation is that for every call to repaint() there may not be an individual corresponding paint(). If system resources get tight (because of other programs running on the system or for any other reason), paint() may not get executed immediately and several calls to paint() may queue up waiting for their turn to change the pixels on the screen. In this case, rather than trying to make all those calls to paint() in order (and be potentially behind all the time), Java catches up by executing only the *most recent* call to paint(), and skips all the others.

If you update the edges of the drawing area with each repaint(), and a couple of calls to paint() are skipped, you end up with bits of the drawing surface not being updated and bits of the oval left behind. There's a simple way around this: update the leading edge of the oval each time the frame updates, but only update the trailing edge if the most recent paint has actually occurred. This way, if a couple of calls to paint() get skipped, the drawing area will get larger for each frame, and when paint() finally gets caught up, everything will get repainted correctly.

Yes, this is horrifyingly complex. If I could have written this applet simpler, I would have, but without this mechanism the applet will not get repainted correctly. Let's step through it slowly in the code so you can get a better grasp of what's going on at each step.

Let's start with `run()`, where each frame of the animation takes place. Here's where you calculate each side of the drawing area based on the old position of the oval and the new position of the oval. When the oval is moving toward the left side of the screen, this is easy. The value of ux1 (the left side of the drawing area) is the previous oval's x position (xpos), and the value of ux2 is the x position of the current oval plus the width of that oval (90 pixels in this example).

Here's what the old `run()` method looked like, to refresh your memory:

```
public void run() {
    setBackground(Color.blue);
    while (true) {
        for (xpos = 5; xpos <= 105; xpos+=4) {
            repaint();
            try { Thread.sleep(100); }
            catch (InterruptedException e) { }
        }
        for (xpos = 105; xpos > 5; xpos -=4) {
            repaint();
            try { Thread.sleep(100); }
            catch (InterruptedException e) { }
        }
    }
}
```

In the first `for` loop in the `run()` method, where the oval is moving toward the right, you first update ux2 (the right edge of the drawing area):

```
ux2 = xpos + 90;
```

Then, after the `repaint()` has occurred, you update ux1 to reflect the old x position of the oval. However, you want to update this value only if the paint actually happened. How can you tell if the paint actually happened? You can reset ux1 in `paint()` to a given value (0), and then test to see whether you can update that value or whether you have to wait for the `paint()` to occur:

```
if (ux1 == 0) ux1 = xpos;
```

Here's the new, completed `for` loop for when the oval is moving to the right:

```
for (xpos = 5; xpos <= 105; xpos+=4) {
    ux2 = xpos + 90;
    repaint();
    try { Thread.sleep(100); }
    catch (InterruptedException e) { }
    if (ux1 == 0) ux1 = xpos;
}
```

When the oval is moving to the left, everything flips. ux1, the left side, is the leading edge of the oval that gets updated every time, and ux2, the right side, has to wait to make sure it gets updated. So, in the second for loop, you first update ux1 to be the x position of the current oval:

```
ux1 = xpos;
```

Then, after the repaint() is called, you test to make sure the paint happened and update ux2:

```
if (ux2 == 0) ux2 = xpos + 90;
```

Here's the new version of the second for loop inside run():

```
for (xpos = 105; xpos > 5; xpos -=4) {
    ux1 = xpos;
    repaint();
    try { Thread.sleep(100); }
    catch (InterruptedException e) { }
    if (ux2 == 0) ux2 = xpos + 90;
}
```

Those are the only modifications run() needs. Let's override update() to limit the region that is being painted to the left and right edges of the drawing area that you set inside run(). To clip the drawing area to a specific rectangle, use the clipRect() method. clipRect(), like drawRect(), fillRect(), and clearRect(), is defined for graphics objects and takes four arguments: x and y starting positions, and width and height of the region.

Here's where ux1 and ux2 come into play. ux1 is the x point of the top corner of the region; then use ux2 to get the width of the region by subtracting ux1 from that value. Finally, to finish update(), you call paint():

```
public void update(Graphics g) {
        g.clipRect(ux1, 5, ux2 - ux1, 95);
        paint(g);
    }
```

Note that with the clipping region in place, you don't have to do anything to the actual paint() method. paint() goes ahead and draws to the entire screen each time, but only the areas inside the clipping region actually get changed onscreen.

You need to update the trailing edge of each drawing area inside paint() in case several calls to paint() were skipped. Because you are testing for a value of 0 inside run(), you merely reset ux1 and ux2 to 0 after drawing everything:

```
ux1 = ux2 = 0;
```

Those are the only changes you have to make to this applet in order to draw only the parts of the applet that changed (and to manage the case where some frames don't get updated immediately). Although this doesn't totally eliminate flickering in the animation, it does reduce it a great deal. Try it and see. Here is the final code for the Checkers applet.

```
1: import java.awt.Graphics;
2: import java.awt.Color;
3:
4: public class Checkers2 extends java.applet.Applet implements Runnable {
5:
6:     Thread runner;
7:     int xpos;
8:     int ux1,ux2;
9:
10:     public void start() {
11:         if (runner == null); {
12:             runner = new Thread(this);
13:             runner.start();
14:         }
15:     }
16:
17:     public void stop() {
18:         if (runner != null) {
19:             runner.stop();
20:             runner = null;
21:         }
22:     }
23:
24:     public void run() {
25:         setBackground(Color.blue);
26:         while (true) {
27:             for (xpos = 5; xpos <= 105; xpos+=4) {
28:                 ux2 = xpos + 90;
29:                 repaint();
30:                 try { Thread.sleep(100); }
31:                 catch (InterruptedException e) { }
32:                 if (ux1 == 0) ux1 = xpos;
33:             }
34:             for (xpos = 105; xpos > 5; xpos -=4) {
35:                 ux1 = xpos;
36:                 repaint();
37:                 try { Thread.sleep(100); }
38:                 catch (InterruptedException e) { }
39:                 if (ux2 == 0) ux2 = xpos + 90;
40:             }
41:         }
42:     }
```

```
43:    public void update(Graphics g) {
44:        g.clipRect(ux1, 5, ux2 - ux1, 95);
45:        paint(g);
46:    }
47:
48:    public void paint(Graphics g) {
49:        // Draw background
50:        g.setColor(Color.black);
51:        g.fillRect(0,0,100,100);
52:        g.setColor(Color.white);
53:        g.fillRect(101,0,100,100);
54:
55:        // Draw checker
56:        g.setColor(Color.red);
57:        g.fillOval(xpos,5,90,90);
58:
59:        // reset the drawing area
60:        ux1 = ux2 = 0;
61:    }
62: }
```

Summary

Congratulations on getting through Day 10! This day was a bit rough; you've learned a lot, and it all might seem overwhelming. You learned about a plethora of methods to use and override: start(), stop(), paint(), repaint(), run(), and update()—and you got a solid foundation in creating and using threads.

After today, you're over the worst hurdles in terms of understanding applets. Other than handling bitmap images, which you'll learn about tomorrow, you now have the basic background to create just about any animation you want in Java.

Questions and Answers

Q Why all the indirection with paint() and repaint() and update() and all that? Why not have a simple paint() method that just puts stuff on the screen when you want it there?

A The Java AWT toolkit enables you to nest drawable surfaces within other drawable surfaces. When a paint takes place, all the parts of the system are redrawn, starting from the outermost surface and moving downward into the most nested one. Because the drawing of your applet takes place at the same time everything else is drawn, your applet doesn't get any special treatment. Your applet will be painted when everything else is painted. Although with this system you sacrifice some of the immediacy of instant painting, it enables your applet to coexist with the rest of the system more cleanly.

Q Are Java threads like threads on other systems?

A Java threads have been influenced by other thread systems, and if you're used to working with threads, many of the concepts in Java threads will be very familiar to you. You learned the basics today; you'll learn more next week on Day 18.

Q When an applet uses threads, I just have to tell the thread to start and it starts, and tell it to stop and it stops? That's it? I don't have to test anything in my loops or keep track of its state? It just stops?

A It just stops. When you put your applet into a thread, Java can control the execution of your applet much more readily. By causing the thread to stop, your applet just stops running, and then resumes when the thread starts up again. Yes, it's all automatic. Neat, isn't it?

Q The ColorSwirl applet seems to display only five or six colors. What's going on here?

A This is the same problem that you ran into yesterday wherein, on some systems, there might not be enough colors to be able to display all of them reliably. If you're running into this problem, other than upgrading your hardware, you might try quitting other applications running on your system that use color. Other browsers or color tools in particular might be hogging colors that Java wants to use.

Q Even with the changes you made, the Checkers applet still flickers.

A And, unfortunately, it will continue to do so. Reducing the size of the drawing area by using clipping does significantly reduce the flickering, but it doesn't stop it entirely. For many applets, using either of the methods described today may be enough to reduce animation flicker to the point where your applet works right. To get totally flicker-free animation, you'll use a technique called double-buffering, which you'll learn about tomorrow.

More Animation, Images, and Sound

by Laura Lemay with Timothy Webster

Animations are fun and easy to do in Java, but there's only so much you can do with the built-in Java methods for lines and fonts and colors. For really interesting animations, you have to provide your own images for each frame of the animation—and having sounds is nice as well. Today, you'll do more with animations, incorporating images and sounds into Java applets.

Specifically, you'll explore the following topics:

☐ Using images—getting them from the server, loading them into Java, and displaying them in your applet

☐ Creating animations by using images, including an extensive example

☐ Using sounds—getting them and playing them at the appropriate times

☐ Sun's Animator applet—an easy way to organize animations and sounds in Java

☐ Double-buffering—hardcore flicker avoidance

Retrieving and Using Images

Basic image handling in Java is easy. The Image class in java.awt provides abstract methods to represent common image behavior, and special methods defined in Applet and Graphics give you everything you need to load and display images in your applet as easily as drawing a rectangle. In this section, you'll learn about how to get and draw images in your Java applets.

Getting Images

To display an image in your applet, you first must load that image over the Net into your Java program. Images are stored as separate files from your Java class files, so you have to tell Java where to find them.

The Applet class provides a method called getImage, which loads an image and automatically creates an instance of the Image class for you. To use it, all you have to do is import the java.awt.Image class, and then give getImage the URL of the image you want to load. There are two ways of doing the latter step:

- [ ] The getImage method with a single argument (an object of type URL) retrieves the image at that URL.

- [ ] The getImage method with two arguments: the base URL (also a URL object) and a string representing the path or filename of the actual image (relative to the base).

Although the first way may seem easier (just plug in the URL as a URL object), the second is more flexible. Remember, because you're compiling Java files, if you include a hard-coded URL of an image and then move your files around to a different location, you have to recompile all your Java files.

The latter form, therefore, is usually the one to use. The Applet class also provides two methods that will help with the base URL argument to getImage:

- [ ] The getDocumentBase() method returns a URL object representing the directory of the HTML file that contains this applet. So, for example, if the HTML file is located at http://www.myserver.com/htmlfiles/javahtml/, getDocumentBase() returns a URL pointing to that path.

☐ The getCodeBase() method returns a string representing the directory in which this applet is contained—which may or may not be the same directory as the HTML file, depending on whether the CODEBASE attribute in <APPLET> is set or not.

Whether you use getDocumentBase() or getCodeBase() depends on whether your images are relative to your HTML files or relative to your Java class files. Use whichever one applies better to your situation. Note that either of these methods is more flexible than hard-coding a URL or pathname into the getImage method; using either getDocumentBase() or getCodeBase() enables you to move your HTML files and applets around and Java can still find your images.

Here are a few examples of getImage to give you an idea of how to use it. This first call to getImage retrieves the file at that specific URL ("http://www.server.com/files/image.gif"). If any part of that URL changes, you have to recompile your Java applet to take the new path into account:

```
Image img = getImage(
    new URL("http://www.server.com/files/image.gif"));
```

In the following form of getImage, the image.gif file is in the same folder as the HTML files that refer to this applet:

```
Image img = getImage(getDocumentBase(), "image.gif")
```

In this similar form, the file image.gif is in the same folder as the applet itself:

```
Image img = getImage(getCodeBase(), "image.gif")
```

If you have lots of image files, it's common to put them into their own folder *inside* the folder that contains the HTML and applet. This form of getImage looks for the file image.gif in the folder images, which in turn is in the same directory as the Java applet:

```
Image img = getImage(getCodeBase(), "images/image.gif")
```

In the examples above, because the images are in the same folder (or subfolder) as your applet, they're on you're Mac—right? Roaster's Applet Viewer can run them without a hitch.

NOTE If you're using the TestFile project and TestFile.java file to enter the examples in this section, you will have to copy the appropriate images folder (the one in the folder for the example you're working on) from the CD into the TestFile folder you're working with.

If Java can't find the file you've indicated, getImage returns null. Your program will continue to run—you just won't see that image on your screen when you try to draw it.

NOTE Currently, Java supports images in the GIF and JPEG formats; Roaster plays only GIFs. Other image formats may be available later; however, for now, your images should be in either GIF or JPEG.

Drawing Images

All that stuff with getImage does nothing except go off and retrieve an image and stuff it into an instance of the Image class. Now that you have an image, you have to do something with it.

The most likely thing you're going to want to do is display it as you would a rectangle or a text string. The Graphics class provides two methods to do just that, both called drawImage.

The first version of drawImage takes four arguments: the image to display, the x and y positions of the top left corner, and this:

```
public void paint() {
    g.drawImage(img, 10, 10, this);
}
```

This first form does what you would expect it to: it draws the image in its original dimensions with the top left corner at the given x and y positions. What follows is the code for a very simple applet that loads in an image called ladybug.gif and displays it. Figure 11.1 shows the obvious result.

```
1: import java.awt.Graphics;
```

```
 2: import java.awt.Image;
 3:
 4: public class LadyBug extends java.applet.Applet {
 5:
 6:     Image bugimg;
 7:
 8:     public void init() {
 9:         bugimg = getImage(getCodeBase(),
10:             "images/ladybug.gif");
11:     }
12:
13:     public void paint(Graphics g) {
14:       g.drawImage(bugimg,10,10,this);
15:     }
16: }
```

Figure 11.1   *The ladybug image.*

The second form of drawImage takes six arguments: the image to draw, the x and y coordinates, a width and height of the image bounding box, and this. If the width and height arguments for the bounding box are smaller or larger than the actual image, the image is automatically scaled to fit. Using those extra arguments enables you to squeeze and expand images into whatever space you need them to fit in (keep in mind, however, that there may be some image degradation from scaling it smaller or larger than its intended size).

One helpful hint for scaling images is to find the size of the actual image that you've loaded, so you can then scale it to a specific percentage and avoid distortion in either direction. Two methods defined for the Image class enable you do this: getWidth() and getHeight(). Both take a single argument, an instance of ImageObserver, which is used to track the loading of the image (more about this later). Most of the time, you can use just this as an argument to either getWidth() or getHeight().

If you stored the ladybug image in a variable called bugimg, for example, this line returns the width of that image, in pixels:

```
theWidth = bugimg.getWidth(this);
```

The following code shows another use of the ladybug image, this time scaled several times to different sizes (Figure 11.2 shows the result).

```
 1: import java.awt.Graphics;
 2: import java.awt.Image;
 3:
 4: public class LadyBug2 extends java.applet.Applet {
 5:
 6:     Image bugimg;
 7:
 8:     public void init() {
 9:         bugimg = getImage(getCodeBase(),
10:             "images/ladybug.gif");
11:     }
12:
13:     public void paint(Graphics g) {
14:         int iwidth = bugimg.getWidth(this);
15:         int iheight = bugimg.getHeight(this);
16:         int xpos = 10;
17:
18:         // 25 %
19:       g.drawImage(bugimg,xpos,10,
20:             iwidth / 4, iheight / 4, this);
21:
22:         // 50 %
23:         xpos += (iwidth / 4) + 10;
24:         g.drawImage(bugimg, xpos , 10,
25:            iwidth / 2, iheight / 2, this);
26:
27:         // 100%
28:         xpos += (iwidth / 2) + 10;
29:         g.drawImage (bugimg, xpos, 10, this);
30:
31:         // 150% x, 25% y
32:         g.drawImage(bugimg, 10, iheight + 30,
33:             (int)(iwidth * 1.5), iheight / 4, this);
34:     }
35: }
```

Figure 11.2 *The second ladybug applet.*

I've been steadfastly avoiding mentioning that last argument to drawImage: the mysterious this, which also appears as an argument to getWidth() and getHeight(). Why is this argument used? Its official use is to pass in an object that functions as an ImageObserver (that is, an object that implements the ImageObserver interface). Image observers enable you to watch the progress of an image in the loading process and to make decisions when the image is only fully or partially loaded. The Applet class, from which your applet inherits, contains default behavior for watching for images that should work in the majority of cases—hence, the this argument to drawImage, getWidth(), and getHeight(). The only reason you'll want to use an alternate argument in its place is if you are tracking lots of images loading asynchronously. See the java.awt.image.ImageObserver class for more details.

Modifying Images

In addition to the basics and handling images described in this section, the java.awt.image package provides more classes and interfaces that enable you to modify images and their internal colors or to create bitmap images by hand. Most of these classes require background knowledge in image processing, including a good grasp of color models and bitwise operations. All these things are outside the scope of an introductory book on Java, but if you have this background (or you're interested in trying it out), the classes in `java.awt.image` will be helpful to you. Take a look at the sample code for creating and using images that comes with the Java Development Kit for examples of how to use the image classes.

Creating Animation Using Images

Creating animations using images is much the same as creating images using fonts, colors, or shapes—you use the same methods, the same procedures for painting, repainting, and reducing flicker that you learned about yesterday. The only difference is that you have a stack of images to flip through rather than a set of painting methods.

The best way to show you how to use images for animation is simply to walk through an example. Here's an extensive one of an animation of a small cat called Neko.

An Example: Neko

Neko was a small Macintosh animation/game written and drawn by Kenji Gotoh in 1989. "Neko" is Japanese for "cat," and the animation is of a small kitten that chases the mouse pointer around the screen, sleeps, scratches, and generally acts cute. The Neko program has since been ported to just about every possible platform, as well as rewritten as a popular screensaver.

For this example, you'll implement a small animation based on the original Neko graphics. Because the original Neko the cat was autonomous (it could "sense" the edges of the window and turn and run in a different direction), this applet merely causes Neko to run in from the left side of the screen, stop in the middle, yawn, scratch its ear, sleep a little, and then run off to the right.

NOTE
This is by far the largest of the applets discussed in this book, and if I either print it here and then describe it, or build it up line by line, you'll be here for days. Instead, I'm going to describe the parts of this applet independently, and I'm going to leave out the basics—the stuff you learned yesterday about starting and stopping threads, what the `run()` method does, and so on. All the code is printed later today so that you can put it all together.

Before you begin writing Java code to construct an animation, you should have all the images that form the animation itself. For this version of Neko there are nine of them (the original has 36), as shown in Figure 11.3.

Figure 11.3   *The images for Neko.*

Where you store your images isn't all that important, but you should take note of where you've put them, because you'll need that information.

Now, on to the applet. The basic idea of animation by using images is that you have a set of images and you display them one at a time, rapidly, so they give the appearance of movement. The easiest way to manage this in Java is to store the images in an array of class Image, and then to have a special variable that stores a reference to the current image.

NOTE

> The java.util class contains a class (HashTable) that implements a hash table. For large numbers of images, a hash table is faster to find and retrieve images from than an array is. Because you have a relatively small number of images here, and because arrays are easier to deal with, I'll use an array here.

For the Neko applet, you'll include instance variables to implement both these things: an array to hold the images called nekopics, and a variable of type Image to hold the current image:

```
Image nekopics[] = new Image[9];
```

```
Image currentimg;
```

Because you'll need to pass the position of the current image around between the methods in this applet, you'll also need to keep track of the current x and y positions. The y stays constant for this particular applet, but the x may vary. Let's add two instance variables for those two positions:

```
int xpos;
```

```
int ypos = 50;
```

Now, on to the body of the applet. During the applet's initialization, you'll read in all the images and store them in the nekopics array. This is the sort of operation that works especially well in an init() method.

Given that you have nine images with nine different filenames, you could do a separate call to getImage for each one. You can save at least a little typing, however, by creating an array of the filenames (nekosrc, an array of strings) and then just using a for loop to iterate over each one. Here's the init() method for the Neko applet that loads all the images into the nekopics array:

```
public void init() {

    String nekosrc[] = { "right1.gif", "right2.gif",
            "stop.gif", "yawn.gif", "scratch1.gif",
            "scratch2.gif","sleep1.gif", "sleep2.gif",
            "awake.gif" };
    for (int i=0; i < nekopics.length; i++) {
        nekopics[i] = getImage(getCodeBase(),
            "images/" + nekosrc[i]);
    }
}
```

Note here in the call to getImage that the folder that these images are stored in is included as part of the path.

With the images loaded, the next step is to start animating the bits of the applet. You do this inside the applet's thread's run() method. In this applet, Neko does five main things:

- □ Runs in from the left side of the screen
- □ Stops in the middle and yawns
- □ Scratches four times
- □ Sleeps
- □ Wakes up and runs off to the right side of the screen

Because you could animate this applet by merely painting the right image to the screen at the right time, it makes more sense to write this applet so that many of Neko's activities are contained in individual methods. This way, you can reuse some of the activities (the animation of Neko running, in particular) if you want Neko to do things in a different order.

Let's start by creating a method to make Neko run. Because you're going to be using this one twice, making it generic is a good plan. Let's create the nekorun method, which takes two arguments: the x position to start, and the x position to end. Neko then runs between those two positions (the y remains constant).

There are two images that represent Neko running; so, to create the running effect, you need to alternate between those two images (stored in positions 0 and 1 of the image array) as well as move them across the screen. The moving part is a simple for loop between the start and end arguments, setting the global x position to the current loop value. Swapping the images means merely testing to see which one is active at any turn of the loop and assigning the other one to the current image. Finally, at each new frame, you'll call `repaint()` and `sleep()` for a bit.

Actually, given that during this animation there will be a lot of sleeping of various intervals, it makes sense to create a method that does the sleeping for the appropriate time interval. Call it pause—here's its definition:

```
void pause(int time) {
    try { Thread.sleep(time); }
    catch (InterruptedException e) { }
}
```

Back to the nekorun method. To summarize, nekorun iterates from the start position to the end position. For each turn of the loop, it sets the current x position, sets currentimg to the right animation frame, calls `repaint()`, and pauses. Got it? Here's the definition of nekorun:

```
void nekorun(int start, int end) {
    for (int i = start; i < end; i+=10) {
        this.xpos = i;
        // swap images
        if (currentimg == nekopics[0])
            currentimg = nekopics[1];
        else if (currentimg == nekopics[1])
            currentimg = nekopics[0];
        repaint();
        pause(150);
    }
}
```

Note that in that second line you increment the loop by ten pixels. Why ten pixels, and not, say, five or eight? The answer is determined mostly through trial and error to see what looks right. Ten seems to work best for the animation. When you write your own animations, you have to play with both the distances and the sleep times until you get an animation you like.

Speaking of `repaint()`, let's cover the `paint()` method, which paints each frame. Here the `paint()` method is trivially simple; all `paint()` is responsible for is painting the current image at the curent x and y positions. All that information is stored in instance variables, so the `paint()` method has only two lines in it:

```
public void paint(Graphics g) {
if (currentimg != null)
    g.drawImage(currentimg, xpos, ypos, this);
}
```

Now let's back up to the run() method, where the main processing of this animation is happening. You've created the necorun method; in run() you'll call that method with the appropriate values to make Neko run from the left edge of the screen to the center:

```
// run from one side of the screen to the middle
nekorun(0, this.size().width / 2);
```

The second major thing Neko does in this animation is stop and yawn. You have a single frame for each of these things (in positions 2 and 3 in the array), so you don't really need a separate method for them. All you need to do is set the appropriate image, call repaint(), and pause for the right amount of time. This example pauses for a second each time for both stopping and yawning—again, using trial and error. Here's the code:

```
// stop and pause
currentimg = nekopics[2];
repaint();
pause(1000);

// yawn
currentimg = nekopics[3];
repaint();
pause(1000);
```

Let's move on to the third part of the animation: scratching. There's no horizontal for this part of the animation. You alternate between the two scratching images (stored in positions 4 and 5 of the image array). Because scratching is a distinct action, however, let's create a separate method for it.

The nekoscratch method takes a single argument: the number of times to scratch. With that argument, you can iterate, and then, inside the loop, alternate between the two scratching images and repaint() each time:

```
void nekoscratch(int numtimes) {
    for (int i = numtimes; i > 0; i--) {
        currentimg = nekopics[4];
        repaint();
        pause(150);
        currentimg = nekopics[5];
        repaint();
        pause(150);
    }
}
```

Inside the `run()` method, you can then call `nekoscratch` with an argument of 4:

```
// scratch four times
nekoscratch(4);
```

Onward! After scratching, Neko sleeps. Again, you have two images for sleeping (in positions 6 and 7 of the array), which you'll alternate a certain number of times. Here's the `nekosleep` method, which takes a single number argument, and animates for that many "turns":

```
void nekosleep(int numtimes) {
    for (int i = numtimes; i > 0; i--) {
        currentimg = nekopics[6];
        repaint();
        pause(250);
        currentimg = nekopics[7];
        repaint();
        pause(250);
    }
}
```

Call `nekosleep` in the `run()` method like this:

```
// sleep for 5 "turns"
nekosleep(5);
```

Finally, to finish off the applet, Neko wakes up and runs to the right side of the screen. `awake.gif` is your last image in the array (position eight), and you can reuse the `nekorun` method to finish:

```
// wake up and run off
currentimg = nekopics[8];
repaint();
pause(500);
nekorun(xpos, this.size().width + 10);
```

There's one more thing left to do to finish the applet. The images for the animation all have white backgrounds. Drawing those images on the default applet background (a medium gray) means an unsightly white box around each image. To get around the problem, merely set the applet's background to `white` at the start of the `run()` method:

```
setBackground(Color.white);
```

Got all that? There's a lot of code in this applet, and a lot of individual methods to accomplish a rather simple animation, but it's not all that complicated. The heart of it, as in the heart of all Java animations, is to set up the frame and then call `repaint()` to enable the screen to be drawn.

Note that you don't do anything to reduce the amount of flicker in this applet. It turns out that the images are small enough, and the drawing area also small enough, that flicker is not a problem for this applet. It's always a good idea to write your animations to do the simplest thing first, and then add behavior to make them run cleaner.

When you first run the Neko applet with Applet Runner, you may find the animation quite jerky and flickery. This is because the first time Roaster displays each image, it has to load it from the disk. After Neko has run off the screen, try choosing Restart, Reload, or Close from the Applet menu. You should find the animation much smoother this time.

To finish up this section, here is the complete code for the Neko applet.

```
36:  import java.awt.Graphics;
37:  import java.awt.Image;
38:  import java.awt.Color;
39:
40:  public class Neko extends java.applet.Applet
41:      implements Runnable {
42:
43:      Image nekopics[] = new Image[9];
44:      Image currentimg;
45:      Thread runner;
46:      int xpos;
47:      int ypos = 50;
48:
49:      public void init() {
50:              String nekosrc[] = { "right1.gif", "right2.gif",
51:              "stop.gif", "yawn.gif", "scratch1.gif",
52:              "scratch2.gif","sleep1.gif", "sleep2.gif",
53:              "awake.gif" };
54:
55:          for (int i=0; i < nekopics.length; i++) {
56:              nekopics[i] = getImage(getCodeBase(),
57:              "images/" + nekosrc[i]);
58:          }
59:
60:      public void start() {
61:          if (runner == null) {
62:              runner = new Thread(this);
63:              runner.start();
64:          }
65:      }
66:
67:      public void stop() {
68:          if (runner != null) {
```

```
69:                 runner.stop();
70:                 runner = null;
71:             }
72:         }
73:
74:     public void run() {
75:
76:         setBackground(Color.white);
77:
78:         // run from one side of the screen to the middle
79:         nekorun(0, this.size().width / 2);
80:
81:         // stop and pause
82:         currentimg = nekopics[2];
83:         repaint();
84:         pause(1000);
85:
86:         // yawn
87:         currentimg = nekopics[3];
88:         repaint();
89:         pause(1000);
90:
91:         // scratch four times
92:         nekoscratch(4);
93:
94:         // sleep for 5 "turns"
95:         nekosleep(5);
96:
97:         // wake up and run off
98:         currentimg = nekopics[8];
99:         repaint();
100:          pause(500);
101:          nekorun(xpos, this.size().width + 10);
102:     }
103:
104:     void nekorun(int start, int end) {
105:         for (int i = start; i < end; i+=10) {
106:             this.xpos = i;
107:             // swap images
108:             if (currentimg == nekopics[0])
109:         currentimg = nekopics[1];
110:             else if (currentimg == nekopics[1])
111:         currentimg = nekopics[0];
112:             else currentimg = nekopics[0];
113:
114:             repaint();
115:             pause(150);
116:         }
117:     }
```

```
118:
119:     void nekoscratch(int numtimes) {
120:         for (int i = numtimes; i > 0; i--) {
121:             currentimg = nekopics[4];
122:             repaint();
123:             pause(150);
124:             currentimg = nekopics[5];
125:             repaint();
126:             pause(150);
127:         }
128:     }
129:
130:     void nekosleep(int numtimes) {
131:         for (int i = numtimes; i > 0; i--) {
132:             currentimg = nekopics[6];
133:             repaint();
134:             pause(250);
135:             currentimg = nekopics[7];
136:             repaint();
137:             pause(250);
138:         }
139:
140:     void pause(int time) {
141:         try { Thread.sleep(time); }
142:         catch (InterruptedException e) { }
143:     }
144:
145:     public void paint(Graphics g) {
146:     if (currentimg != null)
147:         g.drawImage(currentimg, xpos, ypos, this);
148:     }
149: }
```

Retrieving and Using Sounds

Java has built-in support for playing sounds in conjunction with running animations or for sounds on their own. In fact, support for sound, like support for images, is built into the Applet and awt classes, so using sound in your Java applets is as easy as loading and using images.

Currently, the only sound format that Java supports is Sun's AU format, sometimes called μ-law format. AU files tend to be smaller than sound files in other formats, but the sound quality is not very good. If you're especially concerned with sound quality, you may want your sound clips to be references in the traditional HTML way (as links to external files) rather than included in a Java applet.

The simplest way to retrieve and play a sound is through the `play()` method, part of the `Applet` class and therefore available to you in your applets. The `play()` method is similar to the `getImage` method in that it takes one of two forms:

☐ `play` with one argument, a `URL` object, loads and plays the given audio clip at that URL.

☐ `play()` with two arguments, one a base `URL` and one a pathname, loads and plays that audio file. The first argument can most usefully be either a call to `getDocumentBase()` or `getCodeBase()`.

For example, the following line of code retrieves and plays the sound meow.au, which is contained in the audio folder. The audio folder, in turn, is located in the same folder as this applet:

```
play(getCodeBase(), "audio/meow.au");
```

The `play()` method retrieves and plays the given sound as soon as possible after it is called. If it can't find the sound, you won't get an error; you just won't get any audio when you expect it.

If you want to play a sound repeatedly, start and stop the sound clip, or run the clip as a loop (play it over and over), things are slightly more complicated—but not much more so. In this case, you use the applet method `getAudioClip()` to load the sound clip into an instance of the class `AudioClip` (part of `java.applet`—don't forget to import it) and then operate directly on that `AudioClip` object.

Suppose, for example, that you have a sound loop that you want to play in the background of your applet. In your initialization code, you can use this line to get the audio clip:

```
AudioClip clip = getAudioClip(getCodeBase(),
    "audio/loop.au");
```

Then, to play the clip once, use the `play()` method:

```
clip.play();
```

To stop a currently playing sound clip, use the `stop()` method:

```
clip.stop();
```

To loop the clip (play it repeatedly), use the `loop()` method:

```
clip.loop();
```

If the `getAudioClip()` method can't find the sound you indicate or can't load it for any reason, it returns `null`. It's a good idea to test for this case in your code before trying to play the audio clip, because trying to call the play(), stop(), and loop() methods on a null object will result in an error (actually, an exception).

In your applet, you can play as many audio clips as you need; all the sounds you use play concurrently as your applet executes.

Note that if you use a background sound—a sound clip that loops repeatedly—that sound clip will not stop playing automatically when you suspend the applet's thread. This means that even if your reader moves to another page, the first applet's sounds will continue to play. You can fix this problem by stopping the applet's background sound in your stop() method:

```
public void stop() {
    if (runner != null) {
        if (bgsound!= null)
            bgsound.stop();
        runner.stop();
        runner = null;
    }
}
```

The following code shows a simple framework for an applet that plays two sounds. The first, a background sound called loop.au, plays repeatedly. The second, a horn honking (beep.au) plays every five seconds. (I won't bother giving you a picture of this applet, because it doesn't actually display anything other than a simple string to the screen).

```
 1: import java.awt.Graphics;
 2: import java.applet.AudioClip;
 3:
 4: public class AudioLoop extends java.applet.Applet
 5:  implements Runnable {
 6:
 7: AudioClip bgsound;
 8: AudioClip beep;
 9:     Thread runner;
10:
11:     public void start() {
12:         if (runner == null) {
13:             runner = new Thread(this);
14:             runner.start();
15:         }
16:     }
17:
18:     public void stop() {
19:         if (runner != null) {
20:             if (bgsound != null) bgsound.stop();
```

```
21:                runner.stop();
22:                runner = null;
23:            }
24:        }
25:
26:        public void init() {
27:            bgsound = getAudioClip(getCodeBase(),"audio/loop.au");
28:            beep = getAudioClip(getCodeBase(), "audio/beep.au");
29:        }
30:
31:        public void run() {
32:            if (bgsound != null) bgsound.loop();
33:            while (runner != null) {
34:                try { Thread.sleep(5000); }
35:                catch (InterruptedException e) { }
36:                if (bgsound != null) beep.play();
37:            }
38:        }
39:
40:        public void paint(Graphics g) {
41:            g.drawString("Playing Sounds....", 10, 10);
42:        }
43: }
```

Sun's Animator Applet

Because most Java animations have a lot of code in common, being able to reuse all that code as much as possible makes creating animations with images and sounds much easier, particularly for Java developers who aren't as good at the programming side of Java. For just this reason, Sun provides an Animator class as part of the standard Java release.

The Animator applet provides a simple, general-purpose animation interface. You compile the code and create an HTML file with the appropriate parameters for the animation. Using the Animator applet, you can do the following:

☐ Create an animation loop—that is, an animation that plays repeatedly

☐ Add a soundtrack to the applet

☐ Add sounds to be played at individual frames

☐ Indicate the speed at which the animation is to occur

☐ Specify the order of the frames in the animation—which means that you can reuse frames that repeat during the course of the animation

Even if you don't intend to use Sun's Animator code, it's a great example of how animations work in Java and the sorts of clever tricks you can use in a Java applet.

The Animator class is part of the Java distribution. You can find the source and HTML files in the folder Roaster DR2:java:demo:Animator.

More About Flicker: Double-Buffering

Yesterday you learned two simple ways to reduce flickering in animation. Although you learned specifically about animation using drawing, flicker can also result from animation using images. In addition to the two flicker-reducing methods described yesterday, there is one other way to reduce flicker in an application: double-buffering.

NEW TERM

With *double-buffering*, you create a second surface (offscreen, so to speak), do all your painting to that offscreen surface, and then draw the whole surface at once onto the actual applet (and onto the screen) at the end—rather than drawing to the applet's actual graphics surface. Because all the work actually goes on behind the scenes, there's no opportunity for interim parts of the drawing process to appear accidentally and disrupt the smoothness of the animation.

Double-buffering isn't always the best solution. If your applet is suffering from flicker, try overriding update() and drawing only portions of the screen first; that may solve your problem. Double-buffering is less efficient than regular buffering, and also takes up more memory and space, so if you can avoid it, make an effort to do so. In terms of nearly eliminating animation flicker, however, double-buffering works exceptionally well.

Creating Applets with Double-Buffering

To execute double-buffering, you need two things: an image and a graphics context for that image. Those two together mimic the effect of the applet's drawing surface: the graphics context (an instance of Graphics) to provide the drawing methods, such as drawImage and drawString, and the Image to hold the dots that are drawn.

There are four major steps to adding double-buffering to your applet. First, your offscreen image and graphics context need to be stored in instance variables so that you can pass them to the paint() method. Declare the following instance variables in your class definition:

```
Image offscreenImage;
Graphics offscreenGraphics;
```

Second, during the initialization of the applet, you'll create an `Image` and a `Graphics` object and assign them to these variables (you have to wait until initialization so you know how big they're going to be). The `createImage` method gives you an instance of `Image`, which you can then send the `getGraphics()` method in order to get a new graphics context for that image:

```
offscreenImage = createImage(this.size().width,
    this.size().height);
offscreenGraphics = offscreenImage.getGraphics();
```

Now, whenever you have to draw to the screen (usually in your `paint` method), rather than drawing to `paint`'s graphics, draw to the offscreen graphics. For example, to draw an image called `img` at position `10,10` use this line:

```
offscreenGraphics.drawImage(img,10,10,this);
```

Finally, at the end of your `paint()` method, after all the drawing to the offscreen image is done, add the following line to print the offscreen buffer to the real screen:

```
g.drawImage(offscreenImage, 0, 0, this);
```

Of course, you most likely will want to override `update` so that it doesn't clear the screen between paintings:

```
public void update(Graphics g) {
    paint(g);
}
```

Let's review those four steps:

☐ Add instance variables to hold the image and graphics contexts for the off-screen buffer

☐ Create an image and a graphics context when your applet is initialized

☐ Do all your applet painting to the offscreen buffer, not the applet's drawing surface

☐ At the end of your `paint` method, draw the offscreen buffer to the real screen

An Example: Checkers Revisited

Yesterday's example featured the animated moving red oval to demonstrate animation flicker and how to reduce it. Even with the operations you did yesterday, however, the Checkers applet still flashed occasionally. Let's revise that applet to include double-buffering.

First, add the instance variables for the offscreen image and its graphics context:

```
Image offscreenImg;
Graphics offscreenG;
```

Second, add an init() method to initialize the offscreen buffer:

```
public void init() {
    offscreenImg = createImage(this.size().width,
    this.size().height);
    offscreenG = offscreenImg.getGraphics();
}
```

Third, modify the paint() method to draw to the offscreen buffer instead of to the main graphics buffer:

```
public void paint(Graphics g) {
    // Draw background
    offscreenG.setColor(Color.black);
    offscreenG.fillRect(0,0,100,100);
    offscreenG.setColor(Color.white);
    offscreenG.fillRect(100,0,100,100);

    // Draw checker
    offscreenG.setColor(Color.red);
    offscreenG.fillOval(xpos,5,90,90);

    g.drawImage(offscreenImg,0,0,this);
}
```

Note that you're still clipping the main graphics rectangle in the update() method, as you did yesterday; you don't have to change that part. The only part that is relevant is that final paint() method wherein everything is drawn offscreen before finally being displayed.

Summary

Three major topics were the focus of today's lesson. First, you learned about using images in your applets—locating them, loading them, and using the drawImage method to display them, either at their normal size or scaled to different sizes. You also learned how to create animations using images.

Second, you learned how to use sounds, which can be included in your applets any time you need them—at specific moments or as background sounds that can be repeated while the applet executes. You learned how to locate, load, and play sounds both using the play() and the getAudioClip() methods.

Finally, you learned about double-buffering, a technique that enables you virtually to eliminate flicker in animations, at some expense of animation efficiency and speed. Using images and graphics contexts, you can create an offscreen buffer to draw to, the result of which is then displayed to the screen at the last possible moment.

Questions and Answers

Q **In the Neko program, you put the image loading into the `init()` method. It seems to me that it might take Java a long time to load all those images, and because `init()` isn't in the main thread of the applet, there's going to be a distinct pause there. Why not put the image loading at the beginning of the `run()` method instead?**

A There are sneaky things going on behind the scenes. The `getImage` method doesn't actually load the image; in fact, it returns an `Image` object almost instantaneously, so it isn't taking up a large amount of processing time during initialization. The image data that `getImage` points to isn't actually loaded until the image is needed. This way, Java doesn't have to keep enormous images around in memory if the program is going to use only a small piece. Instead, it can just keep a reference to that data and retrieve what it needs later.

Q **If I use double-buffering, do I still have to clip to a small region of the screen? Because double-buffering eliminates flicker, it seems easier to draw the whole frame every time.**

A Easier, yes, but less efficient. Drawing only part of the screen not only reduces flicker, it also limits the amount of work your applet has to do in the `paint()` method. The faster the `paint()` method works, the faster and smoother your animation will run. Using clip regions and drawing only what is necessary is a good practice to follow in general—not just if you have a problem with flicker.

Managing Simple Events and Interactivity

by Laura Lemay with Timothy Webster

Java events are part of the Java AWT (Abstract Window Toolkit) package. An event is the way that the AWT communicates to you, as the programmer, and to other Java AWT components that *something* has happened. That something can be input from the user (mouse movements or clicks, keypresses), changes in the system environment (a window opening or closing, the window being scrolled up or down), or a host of other things that might, in some way, be interesting to the operation of the program.

NOTE
> Java's Abstract Window Toolkit is a package of classes that implements most common UI components, such as windows, buttons, menus, and so on. It is also specifically the AWT, and not Java, that generates and manages events.

In other words, whenever just about anything happens to a Java AWT component, including an applet, an event is generated. Some events are handled by the AWT or by the browser without your needing to do anything. paint() methods, for example, are generated and handled by the browser—all you have to do is tell the AWT what you want painted when it gets to your part of the window. Some events, however—for example, a mouse click inside the boundaries of your applet—you may need to know about. Writing your Java programs to handle these kinds of events enables you to get input from the user and have your applet change its behavior based on that input.

Today, you'll learn about managing simple events, including the following basics:

☐ Mouse clicks

☐ Mouse movements, including mouse dragging

☐ Keyboard actions

You'll also learn about the handleEvent() method, which is the basis for collecting, handling, and passing on events of all kinds from your applet to other UI components in the window or in your applet itself. Tomorrow, you'll learn how to combine events with the AWT to create a complete interface for your applet.

Mouse Clicks

Let's start with the most common event you might be interested in: mouse clicks. Mouse-click events occur when the user clicks the mouse somewhere in the body of your applet. You can use mouse clicks to accomplish very simple things—for example, to toggle the sound on and off in your applet, to move to the next slide in a presentation, or to clear the screen and start over—or you can use mouse clicks in conjunction with mouse movements to perform more complex actions inside your applet.

mouseDown and mouseUp

When you click the mouse once, the AWT generates two events: a mouseDown event when the mouse button is pressed, and a mouseUp event when the button is released. Why two individual events for a single mouse action? Because you may want to do different things for the "down" and the "up." For example, look at a pull-down menu. The mouseDown extends the menu, and the mouseUp selects an item (with mouseDrags between—but you'll learn about that one later). If you have only one event for both actions (mouseUp and mouseDown), you cannot implement that sort of user interaction.

Handling mouse events in your applet is easy—all you have to do is override the right method definition in your applet. That method will be called when that particular event occurs. Here's an example of the method signature for a mouseDown event:

```
public boolean mouseDown(Event evt, int x, int y) {
...
}
```

The mouseDown() method (and the mouseUp() method as well) takes three parameters: the event itself and the x and y coordinates where the mouseDown or mouseUp event occurred.

The event argument is an instance of the class Event. All system events generate an instance of the Event class, which contains information about where and when the event took place, the kind of event it is, and other information that you might want to know about this event. Sometimes having a reference to that event object is useful, as you'll discover later in this section.

The x and the y coordinates of the event, as passed in through the x and y arguments, are particularly nice to know because you can use them to determine precisely where the mouse click took place.

For example, here's a simple method that prints out information about a mouseDown when it occurs:

```
public boolean mouseDown(Event evt, int x, int y) {
    System.out.println("Mouse down at " + x + "," + y);
    return true;
}
```

By including this method in your applet, every time your user clicks the mouse inside your applet, this message will get printed.

Note that this method, unlike the other system methods you've studied this far, returns a boolean value instead of not returning anything (void). This will become important tomorrow when you create user interfaces and then manage input to these interfaces; having an event handler return true or false determines whether a given UI component can intercept an event or whether it needs to pass it on to the enclosing component. The general rule is that if your method deals with the event, it should return true, which for the focus of today's lesson is almost always the case.

The second half of the mouse click is the mouseUp() method, which is called when the mouse button is released. To handle a mouseUp event, add the mouseUp() method to your applet. mouseUp() looks just like mouseDown():

```
public boolean mouseUp(Event evt, int x, int y) {
    ....
}
```

An Example: Spots

In this section, you'll create an example of an applet that uses mouse events—mouseDown events in particular. The Spots applet starts with a blank screen and then sits and waits. When you click the mouse on that screen, a blue dot is drawn. You can place up to ten dots on the screen. Figure 12.1 shows the Spots applet.

Let's start from the beginning and build this applet, starting from the initial class definition:

```
import java.awt.Graphics;
import java.awt.Color;
import java.awt.Event;

public class Spots extends java.applet.Applet {
```

```
final int MAXSPOTS = 10;
int xspots[] = new int[MAXSPOTS];
int yspots[] = new int[MAXSPOTS];
int currspots = 0;

}
```

This class uses three other AWT classes: Graphics, Color, and Event. That last class, Event, needs to be imported in any applets that use events. The class has four instance variables: a constant to determine the maximum number of spots that can be drawn, two arrays to store the x and y coordinates of the spots that have already been drawn, and an integer to keep track of the number of the current spot.

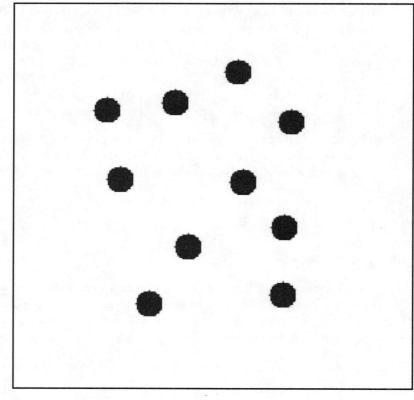

Figure 12.1   *The Spots applet.*

NOTE This class doesn't include the `implements Runnable` words in its definition. As you'll see later on as you build this applet, it also doesn't have a `run()` method. Why not? Because it doesn't actually do anything on its own—all it does is wait for input and then do stuff when input happens. There's no need for threads if your applet isn't actively doing something all the time.

Let's start with the `init()` method, which has one line, to set the background to white:

```
public void init() {
        setBackground(Color.white);
}
```

Set the background here instead of in `paint()`, because `paint()` is called repeatedly each time a new spot is added. Because you really need to set the background only once, putting it in the `paint()` method unnecessarily slows down that method. Putting it here is a much better idea.

The main action of this applet occurs on the `mouseDown()` method, so let's add that one now:

```
public boolean mouseDown(Event evt, int x, int y) {
    if (currspots < MAXSPOTS)
            addspot(x,y);
        else System.out.println("Too many spots.");
        return true;
}
```

When the mouse click occurs, the `mouseDown()` method tests to see whether there are less than ten spots. If so, it calls the `addspot()` method (which you'll write soon). If not, it just prints an error message. Finally, it returns true, because all the event methods have to return a boolean value (usually true).

What does `addspot()` do? It adds the coordinates of the spot to the arrays that store the coordinates, increments the `currspots` variable, and then calls `repaint()`:

```
void addspot(int x,int y) {
        xspots[currspots] = x;
        yspots[currspots] = y;
        currspots++;
        repaint();
    }
```

You may be wondering why you have to keep track of all the past spots in addition to the current spot. The reason is because of repaint(): each time you paint the screen, you have to paint all the old spots in addition to the newest spot. Otherwise, each time you painted a new spot, the older spots would be erased. Now, on to the paint() method:

```
public void paint(Graphics g) {
        g.setColor(Color.blue);
        for (int i = 0; i < currspots; i++) {
            g.fillOval(xspots[i] -10, yspots[i] -10,20,20);
        }
    }
```

Inside paint(), you just loop through the spots you've stored in the xspots and yspots arrays, painting each one (actually, painting them a little to the right and upward so that the spot is painted around the mouse pointer rather than below and to the right).

That's it! That's all you need to create an applet that handles mouse clicks. Everything else is handled for you. You have to add the appropriate behavior to mouseDown() or mouseUp() to intercept and handle that event. Here is the full text for the Spots applet.

```
 1: import java.awt.Graphics;
 2: import java.awt.Color;
 3: import java.awt.Event;
 4:
 5: public class Spots extends java.applet.Applet {
 6:
 7: final int MAXSPOTS = 10;
 8:     int xspots[] = new int[MAXSPOTS];
 9:     int yspots[] = new int[MAXSPOTS];
10:     int currspots = 0;
11:
12:     public void init() {
13:         setBackground(Color.white);
14:     }
15:
16:     public boolean mouseDown(Event evt, int x, int y) {
17:         if (currspots < MAXSPOTS)
18:             addspot(x,y);
19:         else System.out.println("Too many spots.");
20:         return true;
21: }
22:
```

```
23:     void addspot(int x,int y) {
24:         xspots[currspots] = x;
25:         yspots[currspots] = y;
26:         currspots++;
27:         repaint();
28:     }
29:
30:     public void paint(Graphics g) {
31:         g.setColor(Color.blue);
32:         for (int i = 0; i < currspots; i++) {
33:             g.fillOval(xspots[i] -10, yspots[i] -10,20,20);
34:         }
35:     }
36: }
```

NOTE

If you run this applet and click repeatedly, you will notice that nothing seems to happen after you exceed MAXSPOTS spots. However, if you open the AppletViewer.log file in the folder containing the Spots class, you should see one or more lines reading "Too many spots." As you may recall from Day 1, when you're running an applet with Roaster's Applet Runner, whatever you pass to System.out.println()—as we do in line 19—is written to the AppletViewer.log file (not shown in a window as with an application).

Mouse Movements

Every time the mouse is moved a single pixel in any direction, a mouse move event is generated. There are two mouse movement events: mouse drags, where the movement occurs with the mouse button pressed down, and plain mouse movements, where the mouse button isn't pressed.

To manage mouse movement events, use the mouseDrag() and mouseMove() methods.

mouseDrag() and mouseMove()

The mouseDrag() and mouseMove() methods, when included in your applet code, intercept and handle mouse movement events. The mouseMove() method, for plain mouse pointer movements without the mouse button pressed, looks much like the mouse-click methods:

```
public boolean mouseMove(Event evt, int x, int y) {
    ...
}
```

The mouseDrag() method handles mouse movements made with the mouse button pressed down (a complete dragging movement consists of a mouseDown event, a series of mouseDrag events for each pixel the mouse is moved, and a mouseUp event when the button is released). The mouseDrag() method looks like this:

```
public boolean mouseDrag(Event evt, int x, int y) {
    ...
}
```

mouseEnter() and mouseExit()

Finally, there are the mouseEnter() and mouseExit() methods. These two methods are called when the mouse pointer enters the applet or when it exits the applet. (In case you're wondering why you might need to know this, it's more useful on components of user interfaces that you might put inside an applet. You'll learn more about UI tomorrow.)

Both mouseEnter() and mouseExit() have similar signatures—three arguments: the event object and the x and y coordinates of the point where the mouse entered or exited the applet.

```
public boolean mouseEnter(Event evt, int x, int y) {
    ...
}
```

```
public boolean mouseExit(Event evt, int x, int y) {
    ...
}
```

An Example: Drawing Lines

Examples always help to make concepts more concrete. In this section you'll create an applet that enables you to draw straight lines on the screen by dragging from the startpoint to the endpoint. Figure 12.2 shows the applet at work.

Figure 12.2   *Drawing lines.*

As with the Spots applet (on which this applet is based), let's start with the basic definition and work our way through it. The following code shows the top of the Lines applet.

```
 1: import java.awt.Graphics;
 2: import java.awt.Color;
 3: import java.awt.Event;
 4: import java.awt.Point;
 5:
 6: public class Lines extends java.applet.Applet {
 7:
 8:     final int MAXLINES = 10;
 9:     Point starts[] = new Point[MAXLINES]; // starting points
10:     Point ends[] = new Point[10];     // ending points
11:     Point anchor;     // start of current line
12:     Point currentpoint; // current end of line
13:     int currline = 0; // number of lines
```

```
14:
15:    public void init() {
16:        setBackground(Color.white);
17:    }
18:
```

Compared to Spots, this applet added a few extra things. Unlike Spots, which keeps track of individual integer coordinates, this one keeps track of Point objects. Points represent an x and a y coordinate, encapsulated in a single object. To deal with points, you import the Point class (line 4) and set up a bunch of instance variables that hold points:

- The starts array holds points representing the starts of lines already drawn.

- The ends array holds the endpoints of those same lines.

- anchor holds the starting point of the line currently being drawn.

- currentpoint holds the current endpoint of the line currently being drawn.

- currline holds the current number of lines (to make sure you don't go over MAXLINES).

Finally, the init() method (lines 15 through 17), as in the Spots applet, sets the background of the applet to white.

The three main events this applet deals with are mouseDown, to set the anchor point for the current line, mouseDrag, to animate the current line as it's being drawn, and mouseUp, to set the ending point for the new line. Given that you have instance variables to hold each of these values, it's merely a matter of plugging the right variables into the right methods. Here's mouseDown, which sets the anchor point:

```
public boolean mouseDown(Event evt, int x, int y) {
    anchor = new Point(x,y);
    return true;
}
```

While the mouse is being dragged to draw the line, the applet animates the line being drawn. As you drag the mouse around, the new line moves with it from the anchor point to the tip of the mouse. The mouseDrag event contains the current point each time the mouse moves, so use that method to keep track of the current point (and to repaint for each movement so the line "animates"):

```
public boolean mouseDrag(Event evt, int x, int y) {
    currentpoint = new Point(x,y);
    repaint();
    return true;
}
```

The new line doesn't get added to the arrays of old lines until the mouse button is released. Here's mouseUp(), which tests to make sure you haven't exceeded the maximum number of lines before calling the addline() method (described next):

```
public boolean mouseUp(Event evt, int x, int y) {
    if (currline < MAXLINES)
        addline(x,y);
    else System.out.println("Too many lines.");
    return true;
}
```

The addline() method is where the arrays of lines get updated and where the applet is repainted to take the new line into effect:

```
void addline(int x,int y) {
    starts[currline] = anchor;
    ends[currline] = new Point(x,y);
    currline++;
    currentpoint = null;
    repaint();
}
```

Note that in this line you also set currentpoint to null. Why? Because the current line in process is over. By setting currentpoint to null, you can test for that value in the paint() method.

Painting the applet means drawing all the old lines stored in the starts and ends arrays, as well as drawing the current line in process (whose endpoints are in anchor and currentpoint, respectively). To show the animation of the current line, draw it in blue. Here's the paint() method for the Lines applet:

```
public void paint(Graphics g) {

    // Draw existing lines
    for (int i = 0; i < currline; i++) {
        g.drawLine(starts[i].x, starts[i].y,
            ends[i].x, ends[i].y);
    }

    // draw current line
    g.setColor(Color.blue);
    if (currentpoint != null)
        g.drawLine(anchor.x,anchor.y,
            currentpoint.x,currentpoint.y);
}
```

In paint(), when you're drawing the current line, you test first to see whether currentpoint is null. If it is, the applet isn't in the middle of drawing a line, so there's no reason to try drawing a line that doesn't exist. By testing for currentpoint (and by setting currentpoint to null in the addline() method), you can paint only what you need.

That's it—just 60 lines of code and a few basic methods, and you have a very basic drawing application in your Web browser. Here is the full text of the Lines applet, so that you can put the pieces together.

```
 1: import java.awt.Graphics;
 2: import java.awt.Color;
 3: import java.awt.Event;
 4: import java.awt.Point;
 5:
 6: public class Lines extends java.applet.Applet {
 7:
 8:     final int MAXLINES = 10;
 9:     Point starts[] = new Point[MAXLINES]; // starting points
10:     Point ends[] = new Point[10];    // endingpoints
11:     Point anchor;    // start of current line
12:     Point currentpoint; // current end of line
13:     int currline = 0; // number of lines
14:
15:     public void init() {
16:         setBackground(Color.white);
17:     }
18:
19:     public boolean mouseDown(Event evt, int x, int y) {
20:         anchor = new Point(x,y);
21:         return true;
22:     }
23:
24:     public boolean mouseUp(Event evt, int x, int y) {
25:         if (currline < MAXSPOTS)
26:             addline(x,y);
27:         else System.out.println("Too many lines.");
28:         return true;
29:     }
30:
31:     public boolean mouseDrag(Event evt, int x, int y) {
32:         currentpoint = new Point(x,y);
33:         repaint();
34:         return true;
35:     }
36:
37:     void addline(int x,int y) {
```

```
38:            starts[currline] = anchor;
39:            ends[currline] = new Point(x,y);
40:            currline++;
41:            currentpoint = null;
42:            repaint();
43:        }
44:
45:    public void paint(Graphics g) {
46:
47:        // Draw existing lines
48:        for (int i = 0; i < currline; i++) {
49:            g.drawLine(starts[i].x, starts[i].y,
50:                ends[i].x, ends[i].y);
51:        }
52:
53:        // draw current line
54:        g.setColor(Color.blue);
55:        if (currentpoint != null)
56:            g.drawLine(anchor.x,anchor.y,
57:                currentpoint.x,currentpoint.y);
58:        }
59: }
```

Keyboard Events

Keyboard events are generated whenever users press a key on the keyboard. By using key events, you can get hold of the values of the keys they pressed to perform an action or merely to get character input from the users of your applet.

The keyDown() Method

To capture a keyboard event, use the keyDown() method:

```
public boolean keyDown(Event evt, int key) {
    ...
}
```

The keys generated by keyDown events (and passed into keyDown() as the key argument) are integers representing ASCII character values, which include alphanumeric characters, function keys, tabs, returns, and so on. To use them as characters (for example, to print them), you need to cast them to characters:

```
currentchar = (char)key;
```

Here's a simple example of a keyDown() method that does nothing but print the key you just typed in both its ASCII and character representation:

```
public boolean keyDown(Event evt, int key) {
    System.out.println("ASCII value: " + key);
    System.out.println("Character: " + (char)key);
    return true;
}
```

Default Keys

The Event class provides a set of class variables that refer to several standard nonal-phanumeric keys, such as the arrow keys. If your interface uses these keys, you can provide more readable code by testing for these names in your keyDown() method rather than testing for their numeric values. For example, to test whether the up arrow was pressed, you might use the following snippet of code:

```
if (key == Event.UP) {
    ...
}
```

Because the values these class variables hold are integers, you also can use the switch statement to test for them.

Table 12.1 shows the standard event class variables for various keys and the actual keys they represent.

Table 12.1   *Standard Keys Defined by the Event Class*

Class Variable	Represented Key
Event.HOME	The Home key
Event.END	The End key
Event.PGUP	The Page Up key
Event.PGDN	The Page Down key
Event.UP	The up arrow
Event.DOWN	The down arrow
Event.LEFT	The left arrow
Event.RIGHT	The right arrow

An Example: Entering, Displaying, and Moving Characters

Let's look at an applet that demonstrates keyboard events. This one enables you to type a character, and it displays that character in the center of the applet window. You then can move that character around on the screen by using the arrow keys. Typing another character at any time changes the character as it's currently displayed. Figure 12.3 shows an example.

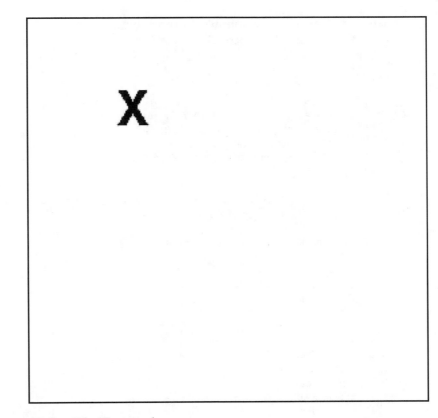

Figure 12.3   *The Keys applet.*

This applet is actually less complicated than the previous applets you've used. This one has only three methods: init(), keyDown(), and paint(). The instance variables are also simpler, because the only things you need to keep track of are the x any y positions of the current character and the values of that character itself. Here's the top of this class definition:

```
import java.awt.Graphics;
import java.awt.Event;
import java.awt.Font;

public class Keys extends java.applet.Applet {

    char currkey;
    int currx;
    int curry;
```

The init() method is responsible for three things: setting the background color, setting the applet's font (here, 36 point Helvetica bold), and setting the beginning position for the character (the middle of the screen, minus a few points to nudge it up and to the right):

```
public void init() {
    currx = (this.size().width / 2) -8;  // default
    curry = (this.size().height / 2) -16;
    setBackground(Color.white);
    setFont(new Font("Helvetica",Font.BOLD,36));
}
```

Because this applet's behavior is based on keyboard input, the keyDown() method is where most of the work of the applet takes place:

```
public boolean keyDown(Event evt, int key) {
    switch (key) {
    case Event.DOWN:
        curry += 5;
        break;
    case Event.UP:
        curry -= 5;
        break;
    case Event.LEFT:
        currx -= 5;
        break;
    case Event.RIGHT:
        currx += 5;
        break;
    default:
        currkey = (char)key;
    }
    repaint();
    return true;
}
```

In the center of the keyDown() applet is a switch statement that tests for different key events. If the event is an arrow key, the appropriate change is made to the character's position. If the event is any other key, the character itself is changed. The method finishes up with a repaint() and returns true.

The paint() method here is almost trivial; just display the current character at the current position. However, note that when the applet starts up, there's no initial character and nothing to draw, so you have to take that into account. The currkey variable is initialized to 0, so you paint the applet only if currkey has an actual value:

```
public void paint(Graphics g) {
    if (currkey != 0) {
        g.drawString(String.valueOf(currkey), currx,curry);
    }
}
```

Here is the complete source for the Keys applet:

```
1: import java.awt.Graphics;
2: import java.awt.Event;
3: import java.awt.Font;
4:
5: public class Keys extends java.applet.Applet {
6:
7:     char currkey;
8:     int currx;
9:     int curry;
10:
11:     public void init() {
12:         currx = (this.size().width / 2) -8;   // default
13:         curry = (this.size().height / 2) -16;
14:
15:         setBackground(Color.white);
16:         setFont(new Font("Helvetica",Font.BOLD,36));
17:     }
18:
19:     public boolean keyDown(Event evt, int key) {
20:         switch (key) {
21:         case Event.DOWN:
22:             curry += 5;
23:             break;
24:         case Event.UP:
25:             curry -= 5;
26:             break;
27:         case Event.LEFT:
28:             currx -= 5;
29:             break;
30:         case Event.RIGHT:
31:             currx += 5;
32:             break;
33:     default:
34:             currkey = (char)key;
35:         }
36:
37:         repaint();
38:         return true;
39:     }
40:
```

```
41:     public void paint(Graphics g) {
42:         if (currkey != 0) {
43:             g.drawString(String.valueOf(currkey), currx,curry);
44:         }
45:     }
46: }
```

When you run this applet, it may not work at first (nothing will happen when you press a key). You may have to click in the applet's window before it will start responding to your keystrokes. This is due to a minor bug in the current Roaster Applet Runner.

Testing for Modifier Keys

Shift, Control, and meta are modifier keys. They don't generate key events themselves, but when you get an ordinary mouse or keyboard event, you can test to see whether those keys were held down when the event occurred. Sometimes it may be obvious—shifted alphanumeric keys produce different key events than unshifted ones, for example. For other events, however—mouse events in particular—you may want to handle an event with a modifier key held down differently from a regular version of that event.

The Event class provides three methods for testing whether or not a modifier key is held down: shiftDown(), metaDown(), and controlDown(). The meta key maps to the ⌘ key on the Mac system. All return boolean values based on whether that modifier key is indeed held down. You can use these three methods in any of the event handling methods (mouse or keyboard) by calling them on the event object passed into that method:

```
public boolean mouseDown(Event evt, int x, int y ) {
    if (evt.shiftDown())
        // handle shift-click
    else // handle regular click
}
```

The AWT Event Handler

The default methods you've learned about today for handling basic events in applets are actually called by a generic event handler method called handleEvent(). The handleEvent() method is how the AWT generically deals with events that occur between application components and events based on user input.

In the default handleEvent() method, basic events are processed and the methods you learned about today are called. To handle events other than those mentioned here, to change the default event handling behavior, or to create and pass around your own events, you need to override `handleEvent()` in your own Java programs. The `handleEvent()` method looks like this:

```
public boolean handleEvent(Event evt) {
    ...
}
```

To test for specific events, examine the `id` instance variable of the `Event` object that gets passed in. The event ID is an integer, but fortunately, the `Event` class defines a whole set of event IDs as class variables that you can test for in the body of the `handleEvent()`. Because these class variables are integer constants, a `switch` statement works particularly well. For example, here's a simple `handleEvent()` method to print out debugging information about mouse events:

```
public boolean handleEvent(Event evt) {
    switch (evt.id) {
    case Event.MOUSE_DOWN:
        System.out.println("MouseDown: " +
                evt.x + "," + evt.y);
        return true;
    case Event.MOUSE_UP:
        System.out.println("MouseUp: " +
                evt.x + "," + evt.y);
        return true;
    case Event.MOUSE_MOVE:
        System.out.println("MouseMove: " +
                evt.x + "," + evt.y);
        return true;
    case Event.MOUSE_DRAG:
        System.out.println("MouseDown: " +
                evt.x + "," + evt.y);
        return true;
    default:
        return false;
    }
}
```

You can test for the following keyboard events:

☐ `Event.KEY_PRESS` is generated when a key is pressed (the same as the `keyDown()` method).

☐ `Event.KEY_RELEASE` is generated when a key is released.

☐ `Event.KEY_ACTION` is generated when a key action (a press and a release) occurs.

You can test for these mouse events:

☐ Event.MOUSE_DOWN is generated when the mouse button is pressed (the same as the mouseDown() method).

☐ Event.MOUSE_UP is generated when the mouse button is released (the same as the mouseUp() method).

☐ Event.MOUSE_MOVE is generated when the mouse is moved (the same as the mouseMove() method).

☐ Event.MOUSE_DRAG is generated when the mouse is moved with the button pressed (the same as the mouseDrag() method).

☐ Event.MOUSE_ENTER is generated when the mouse enters the applet (or a component of that applet). You can also use the mouseEnter() method.

☐ Event.MOUSE_EXIT is generated when the mouse exits the applet. You can also use the mouseExit() method.

In addition to these events, the Event class has a whole suite of methods for handling UI components. You'll learn more about these events tomorrow.

Note that if you override handleEvent() in your class, none of the default event handling methods you learned about today will get called unless you explicitly call them in the body of handleEvent(), so be careful if you decide to do this. One way to get around this is to test for the event you're interested in, and if that event isn't it, to call super.handleEvent() so that the superclass that defines handleEvent() can process things. Here's an example of how to do this:

```
public boolean handleEvent(Event evt) {
    if (evt.id == Event.MOUSE_DOWN) {
        // process the mouse down
        return true;
    } else {
        return super.handleEvent(evt);
    }
}
```

Summary

Handling events in Java's Abstract Window Toolkit (AWT) is easy. Most of the time, all you need to do is stick the right method in your applet code, and your applet intercepts and handles that method. Here are some of the basic events you can manage in this way:

- ☐ Mouse clicks—`mouseUp()` and `mouseDown()` methods for each part of a mouse click

- ☐ Mouse movements—`mouseMove()` and `mouseDrag()` for mouse movement with the mouse button released and pressed, respectively, as well as `mouseEnter()` and `mouseExit()` for when the mouse enters and exits the applet area

- ☐ `keyDown()` for when a key on the keyboard is pressed

All events in the AWT generate an `Event` object; inside that object, you can find out information about the event, when it occurred, and its x and y coordinates (if applicable). You can also test that event to see whether a modifier key was pressed when the event occurred, by using the `shiftDown()`, `controlDown()`, and `metaDown()` methods.

Finally, there is the `handleEvent()`, the "parent" of the individual event methods. The `handleEvent()` method is actually what the Java system calls to manage events; the default implementation calls the individual method events where necessary. To override how methods are managed in your applet, override `handleEvent()`.

Questions and Answers

Q In the Spots applet, the spot coordinates are stored in arrays, which have a limited size. How can I modify this applet so that it will draw an unlimited number of spots?

A You can do one of a couple things:

The first thing to do is test, in your `addspot()` method, whether the number of spots has exceeded `MAXSPOTS`. Then create a bigger array, copy the elements of the old array into that bigger array (use the `System.arraycopy()` method to do that), and reassign the x and y arrays to that new, bigger array.

The second thing to do is to use the `Vector` class. `Vector`, part of the `java.util` package, implements an array that is automatically growable—sort of like a linked list is in other languages. The disadvantage of `Vector` is that to put something into `Vector`, it has to be an actual object. This means you'll have to cast integers to `Integer` objects, and then extract their values from `Integer` objects to treat them as integers again. The Vector class enables you to access and change elements in the Vector just as you can in an array (by using method calls, rather than array syntax). Check it out.

Q   **What's a meta key?**

A   It's popular in Unix systems. On the Mac, it's mapped to the ⌘ key, and it's mapped to Alt on most PC keyboards. Because Shift and Ctrl are much more popular and widespread, it's probably a good idea to base your interfaces on those modifier keys if you can.

Q   **How do I test to see whether the Return key has been pressed?**

A   Different platforms may send different keys for the actual key marked "Return." In particular, Macintoshes send carriage returns, Unix systems send line feeds, and DOS systems send both. In Unicode, Return (line feed) is character 10; Enter (carriage return) is character 13. So, to provide a cross-platform behavior, you may want to test for both line feed and carriage return.

The word from the Java team is that a Return is a Return is a Return regardless of the platform. However, at the time of this writing, it is questionable whether or not this is currently true in the Java developer's kit. You may want to check the API documentation for the Event class to see whether this has changed in the interim.

Q   **I looked at the API for the Event class, and there are many more event types listed there than the ones you mention today.**

A   Yes. The Event class defines many different kinds of events, both for general user input, such as the mouse and keyboard events you learned about here, and also events for managing changes to the state of user interface components, such as windows and scroll bars. Tomorrow, you'll learn about those other events.

The Java Abstract Window Toolkit

by Laura Lemay with Timothy Webster

For the past five days you've concentrated on creating applets that do very simple things: display text, play an animation or a sound, or enable very basic interactions with the user. Once you get past that point, however, you may want to start creating more complex applets that behave like real applications embedded in a Web page—applets that start to look like Mac applications with buttons, menus, text fields, and other elements of a real application.

It's this sort of real work in Java applets and applications that Java's Abstract Window Toolkit, or AWT, was designed for. You've actually been using the AWT all along, as you might have guessed from the classes you've been importing. The Applet class and most of the classes you've been using this week are all integral parts of the AWT. The AWT provides the following:

☐ A full set of UI widgets and other components, including windows, menus, buttons, checkboxes, text fields, scrollbars, and scrolling lists

☐ Support for UI "containers," which can contain other embedded containers or UI widgets

☐ An event system for managing system and user events between and among parts of the AWT

☐ Mechanisms for laying out components in a way that enables platform-independent UI design

Today, you'll learn about how to use all these things in your Java applets. Tomorrow, you'll learn about creating windows, menus, and dialogs, which enable you to pop up separate windows from the browser window. In addition, you can use the AWT in stand-alone applications, so everything you've learned so far this week can still be used. If you find the framework of the Web browser too limiting, you can take your AWT background and start writing full-fledged Java applications.

Today, however, you'll continue focusing on applets.

An AWT Overview

The basic idea behind the AWT is that a Java window is a set of nested components, starting from the outermost window all the way down to the smallest UI component. Components can include things you can actually see on the screen, such as windows, menu bars, buttons, and text fields, and they can also include containers, which in turn can contain other components. Figure 13.1 shows how a sample page in a Java browser might include several different components, all of which are managed through the AWT.

This nesting of components within containers within other components creates a hierarchy of components, from the smallest checkbox inside an applet to the overall window on the screen. The hierarchy of components determines the arrangement of items on the screen and inside other items, the order in which they are painted, and how events are passed from one component to another.

These are the major components you can work with in the AWT:

☐ *Containers*. Containers are generic AWT components that can contain other components, including other containers. The most common form of container is the panel, which represents a container that can be displayed onscreen. Applets are a form of panel (in fact, the `Applet` class is a subclass of the `Panel` class).

☐ *Canvases*. A canvas is a simple drawing surface. Although you can draw on panels (as you've been doing all along), canvases are good for painting images or other graphics operations.

☐ *UI components*. These can include buttons, lists, simple popup menus, checkboxes, test fields, and other typical elements of a user interface.

☐ *Window construction components.* These include windows, frames, menu bars, and dialogs. These are listed separately from the other UI components because you'll use these less often—particularly in applets. In applets, the browser provides the main window and menu bar, so you don't have to use these. Your applet may create a new window, however, or you may want to write your own Java application that uses these components.

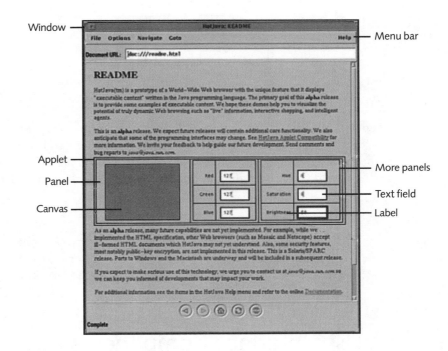

Figure 13.1   *AWT components.*

The classes inside the java.awt package are written and organized to mirror the abstract structure of containers, components, and individual UI components. Figure 13.2 shows some of the class hierarchy that makes up the main classes in the AWT. The root of most of the AWT components is the class Component, which provides basic display and event handling features. The classes Container, Canvas, TextComponent, and many of the other UI components inherit from Component. Inheriting from the Container class are objects that can contain other AWT components—the Panel and Window classes, in particular. Note that the java.applet.Applet class, even though it lives in its own package, inherits from Panel, so your applets are an integral part of the hierarchy of components in the AWT system.

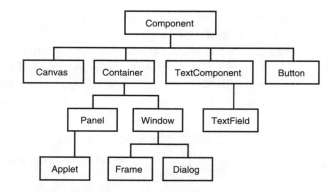

Figure 13.2   *A partial AWT class hierarchy.*

A graphical user interface-based application that you write by using the AWT can be as complex as you like, with dozens of nested containers and components inside each other. AWT was designed so that each component can play its part in the overall AWT system without needing to duplicate or keep track of the behavior of other parts in the system.

NOTE   If you've got the full version of Roaster, you might want to unstuff the AWT source code files from the src.zip archive on the Roaster CD and drop them all into a project called something like AWTtree. . Then, pick New > Class T ree (Command-C) to get a really good view of the AWT hierarchy.

The Basic User Interface Components

The simplest form of AWT component is the basic UI component. You can create and add these to your applet without needing to know anything about creating containers or panels—your applet, even before you start painting and drawing and handling events, is already an AWT container. Because an applet is a container, you can put other AWT components—such as UI components or other containers—into it.

In this section, you'll learn about the basic UI components: labels, buttons, checkboxes, choice menus, and text fields. In each case, the procedure for creating the component is the same—you first create the component, and then add it to the panel that holds it, at which point it is displayed on the screen. To add a component to a panel (such as your applet, for example), use the add() method:

```
public void init() {
    Button b = new Button("OK");
```

```
    add(b);
}
```

Note that where the component appears in the panel depends on the layout that panel is defined to have. The default layout for panels such as applets is `FlowLayout`, with a centered alignment, which means that components are added from left to right in rows, and then row by row as they fit, with each row centered. This explains why some of the examples in this section look a little funny. You'll learn more about panels and layouts in the next section.

Note also that each of these components has an action associated with it—that is, something that component does when it's activated. Actions generally trigger events or other activities in your applet (often called callbacks in other window toolkits). In this section, you'll focus on creating the components themselves; you'll learn about adding actions to them later in today's lesson.

On to the components!

Labels

The simplest form of UI component is the label.

NEW TERM   *Labels* are, effectively, text strings that you can use to label other UI components.

The advantages that a label has over an ordinary text string are that it follows the layout of the given panel and you don't have to worry about repainting it every time the panel is redrawn. Labels also can be easily aligned within a panel, enabling you to attach labels to other UI components without knowing exact pixel positions.

To create a label, use one of the following constructors:

☐ `Label()` creates an empty label, with its text aligned left.

☐ `Label(String)` creates a label with the given text string, also aligned left.

☐ `Label(String, int)` creates a label with the given text string and the given alignment. The available alignments are stored in class variables in `Label`, making them easier to remember: `Label.RIGHT`, `Label.LEFT`, and `Label.CENTER`.

The label's font is determined by the overall font for the component (as set by the `setFont()` method).

Here's some simple code to create a few labels. Figure 13.3 shows how this looks onscreen:

```
add(new Label("aligned left "));
add(new Label("aligned center", Label.CENTER));
add(new Label(" aligned right", Label.RIGHT));
```

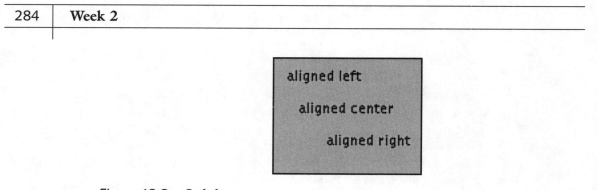

Figure 13.3   *Labels.*

After you have a label object, you can use methods defined in the Label class to get and set the values of the text as shown in Table 13.1.

Table 13.1   *Label Methods*

Method	Action
getText()	Returns a string containing this label's text
setText(String)	Changes the text of this label
getAlignment()	Returns an integer representing the alignment of this label: 0 is Label.LEFT, 1 is Label.CENTER, 2 is Label.RIGHT
setAlignment(int)	Changes the alignment of this label to the given integer or class variable

Buttons

The second user interface component to explore is the button.

NEW TERM *Buttons* are simple UI components that trigger some action in your interface when they are pressed. For example, a calculator applet might have buttons for each number and operator, or a dialog box might have buttons for "OK" and "Cancel."

To create a button, use one of the following constructors:

☐ Button() creates an empty button with no label.

☐ Button(String) creates a button with the given string object as a label.

After you have a button object, you can get the value of the button's label by using the getLabel() method and set the label using the setLabel(String) methods.

Figure 13.4 shows some simple buttons, created using the following code:

```
add(new Button("Rewind"));
add(new Button("Play"));
add(new Button("Fast Forward"));
add(new Button("Stop"));
```

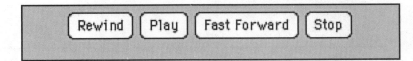

Figure 13.4   *Buttons.*

Checkboxes

Checkboxes can be selected or deselected to provide options.

NEW TERM   *Checkboxes* are user interface components that have two states: on and off (or checked and unchecked, selected and unselected, true and false, and so on). Unlike buttons, checkboxes usually don't trigger direct actions in a UI but, instead, are used to indicate optional features of some other action.

Checkboxes can be used in two ways:

☐ Nonexclusive, meaning that given a series of checkboxes, any of them can be selected

☐ Exclusive, meaning that within one series, only one checkbox can be selected at a time

The latter kind of checkboxes are called radio buttons or checkbox groups, and are described in the next section.

Nonexclusive checkboxes can be created by using the Checkbox class. You can create a checkbox by using one of the following constructors:

☐ Checkbox() creates an empty checkbox, unselected.

☐ Checkbox(*String*) creates a checkbox with the given string as a label.

☐ Checkbox(*String, null, boolean*) creates a checkbox that is either selected or unselected based on whether the boolean argument is true or false, respectively. (The null is used as a placeholder for a group argument. Only radio buttons have groups, as you'll learn in the next section.)

Table 13.2 lists the checkbox methods. Figure 13.5 shows a few simple checkboxes (only Underwear is selected) generated using the following code:

```
add(new Checkbox("Shoes"));
add(new Checkbox("Socks"));
add(new Checkbox("Pants"));
add(new Checkbox("Underwear", null, true));
add(new Checkbox("Shirt"));
```

Table 13.2   *Checkbox Methods*

Method	Action
getLabel()	Returns a string containing this checkbox's label
setLabel(String)	Changes the text of the checkbox's label
getState()	Returns true or false, based on whether the checkbox is selected or not
setState(boolean)	Changes the checkbox's state to selected (true) or unselected (false)

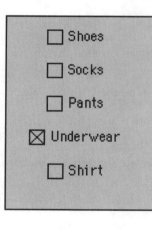

Figure 13.5   *Checkboxes.*

Radio Buttons

Radio buttons, like checkboxes, are used to select options.

NEW TERM

Radio buttons are used to select a single option at a time from a series of options. (On some platforms, radio buttons have the same appearance as checkboxes, which is one reason that AWT implements radio buttons as a special case of the Checkbox class.)

To create a series of radio buttons, first create an instance of CheckboxGroup:

```
CheckboxGroup cbg = new CheckboxGroup();
```

Then create and add the individual checkboxes, using the group as the second argument, and whether or not that checkbox is selected (only one in the series can be selected):

```
add(new Checkbox("Yes", cbg, true);
add(new Checkbox("no", cbg, false);
```

Here's a simple example (the results of which are shown in Figure 13.6):

```
CheckboxGroup cbg = new CheckboxGroup();

add(new Checkbox("Red", cbg, true));
add(new Checkbox("Blue", cbg, false));
add(new Checkbox("Yellow", cbg, false));
add(new Checkbox("Green", cbg, false));
add(new Checkbox("Orange", cbg, false));
add(new Checkbox("Purple", cbg, false));
```

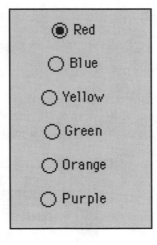

Figure 13.6   *Radio buttons.*

All the checkbox methods defined in the previous section can be used with the radio buttons in the group. In addition, you can use the getCheckboxGroup() and setCheckboxGroup() methods to access and change the group of any given radio button.

Finally, the getCurrent() and setCurrent(Checkbox) methods, defined in the checkbox group, can be used to get or set the currently selected radio button.

Choice Menus

The choice menu is a more complex UI component than labels, buttons, or checkboxes.

NEW TERM

Choice menus are popup (or pulldown) menus that enable you to select an item from that menu. The menu then displays that choice on the screen.

To create a choice menu, create an instance of the Choice class, and then use the addItem() method to add individual items to it in the order in which they should appear:

```
Choice c = new Choice();

c.addItem("Apples");
c.addItem("Oranges");
c.addItem("Strawberries");
c.addItem("Blueberries");
c.addItem("Bananas");
```

Finally, add the entire choice menu to the panel in the usual way:

```
add(c);
```

Figure 13.7 shows two simple choice menus: the top one shows how a choice menu looks when it's just sitting on a panel, and the lower one, generated from the code in the previous example, shows how a choice menu looks when an item is being selected.

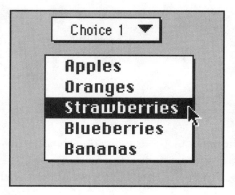

Figure 13.7   *Choice menus.*

Choice menus permit only one selection per menu. If you want to select multiple items, use a scrolling list instead.

After your choice menu is created, regardless of whether it's added to a panel, you can continue to add items to that menu by using the addItem() method. Table 13.3 shows some other methods that may be useful in working with choice menus.

Table 13.3 *Choice Menu Methods*

Method	Action
getItem(int)	Returns the string item at the given position (items inside a choice begin at 0, same as arrays)
countItems()	Returns the number of items in the menu
getSelectedIndex()	Returns the index position of the item that's selected
getSelectedItem()	Returns the currently selected item as a string
select(int)	Selects the item at the given position
select(String)	Selects the item with that string

Text Fields

Unlike the UI components up to this point, which enable you to select only among several options to perform an action, text fields enable you to enter any values.

NEW TERM *Text fields* enable your reader to enter text.

To create a text field, use one of the following constructors:

☐ TextField() creates an empty TextField 0 characters wide.

☐ TextField(int) creates an empty text field with the given width in characters.

☐ TextField(String) creates a text field 0 characters wide, initialized with the given string.

☐ TextField(String, int) creates a text field with the given width in characters and containing the given string. If the string is longer than the width, you can select and drag portions of the text within the field and the box will scroll left or right.

For example, the following line creates a text field 30 characters wide with the string "Enter Your Name" as its initial contents.

```
TextField tf = new TextField("Enter Your Name",30);
add(tf);
```

NOTE
> Text fields include only the editable field itself. You usually need to include a label with a text field to indicate what belongs in that text field.

NOTE
> Text fields are different from text areas; text fields are limited in size and are best used for one-line items, whereas text areas have scrollbars and are better for larger text windows. Both can be edited and enable selections with the mouse. You'll learn about text areas later today.

You can also create a text field that obscures the characters typed into it—for example, for password fields. To do this, first create the text fields itself, and then use the setEchoCharacter() method to set the character that is echoed on the screen. Here is an example:

```
TextField tf = new TextField(30);
tf.setEchoCharacter('*');
```

NOTE

> The setEchoCharacter() method does not work in the current release of Roaster.

Figure 13.8 shows three text boxes (and labels) that were created by using the following code:

```
add(new Label("Enter your Name"));
add(new TextField("your name here",45));
add(new Label("Enter your phone number"));
add(new TextField(12));
add(new Label("Enter your password"));
TextField t = new TextField(20);
t.setEchoCharacter('*');
add(t);
```

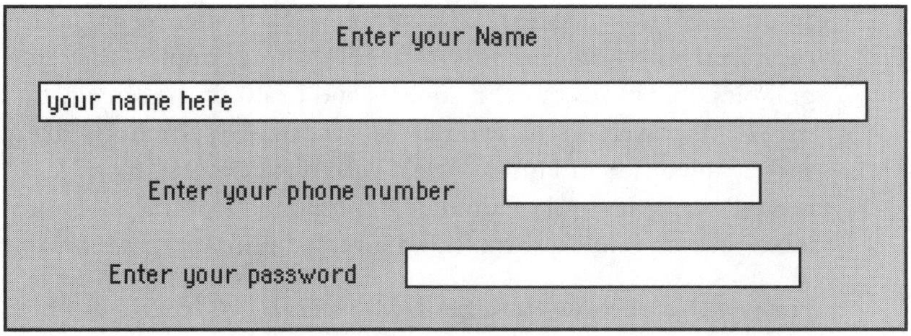

Figure 13.8 *Text fields.*

Text fields inherit from the class TextComponent and have a whole suite of methods, both inherited from that class and defined in its own class, that may be useful to you in your Java programs. Table 13.4 shows a selection of those methods.

Table 13.4   *Text Field Methods*

Method	Action
getText()	Returns the text this text field contains (as a string)
setText(String)	Puts the given text string into the field
getColumns()	Returns the width of this text field
select(int, int)	Selects the text between the two integer positions (positions start from 0)
selectAll()	Selects all the text in the field
isEditable()	Returns true or false based on whether the text is editable or not
setEditable(boolean)	true (the default) enables text to be edited; false freezes the text
getEchoChar()	Returns the character used for masking input
echoCharIsSet()	Returns true or false whether the field has a masking character or not

Panels and Layout

You know at this point that an AWT panel can contain UI components or other panels. The question now is how those components are actually arranged and displayed on the screen.

In other window systems, UI components are often arranged using hard-coded pixel measurements—put text field tf at 10,30, for example—the same way you used the graphics operations to paint squares and ovals on the screen. In the AWT, the window may be displayed on many different windowing systems on many different screens and with many different kinds of fonts with different font metrics. Therefore, you need a more flexible method of arranging components on the screen so that a layout that looks nice on one platform isn't a jumbled unusable mess on another.

For just this purpose, Java has layout managers, insets, and hints that each component can provide for helping lay out the screen.

Note that the nice thing about AWT components and user interface items is that you don't have to paint them—the AWT system manages all that for you. If you have graphical components or images, or you want to create animations inside panels, you still have to do that by hand, but for most of the basic components, all you have to do is put them on the screen, and Java will handle the rest.

Layout Managers

The actual appearance of the AWT components on the screen is determined by two things: the order in which they are added to the panel that holds them, and the layout manager that panel is currently using to lay out the screen. The layout manager determines how portions of the screen will be sectioned and how components within that panel will be placed.

Note that each panel on the screen can have its own layout manager. By nesting panels within panels, and using the appropriate layout manager for each one, you can often arrange your UI to group and arrange components in a way that is both functionally useful and also looks good on a variety of platforms and windowing systems. You'll learn about nesting panels in a later section.

The AWT provides five basic layout managers: FlowLayout, GridLayout, GridBagLayout, BorderLayout, and CardLayout. To create a layout manager for a given panel, use the setLayout() method for that panel:

```
public void init() {
    this.setLayout(new FlowLayout());
}
```

Setting the default layout manager, like defining the user interface components, is best done during the applet's or class's initialization, which is why it's included here.

After the layout manager is set, you can start adding components to the panel. The order in which components are added is often significant, depending on which layout manager is currently active. Read on for information about the specific layout managers and how they present components within the panel to which they apply.

The following sections describe the five basic Java AWT layout managers.

The FlowLayout Class

The FlowLayout class is the most basic of layouts. Using the flow layout, components are added to the panel one at a time, row by row. If a component doesn't fit onto a row, it's wrapped onto the next row. The flow layout also has an alignment, which determines the alignment of each row. By default, each row is center-aligned. Figure 13.9 shows a flow layout at its best—a simple row of buttons, centered on a line.

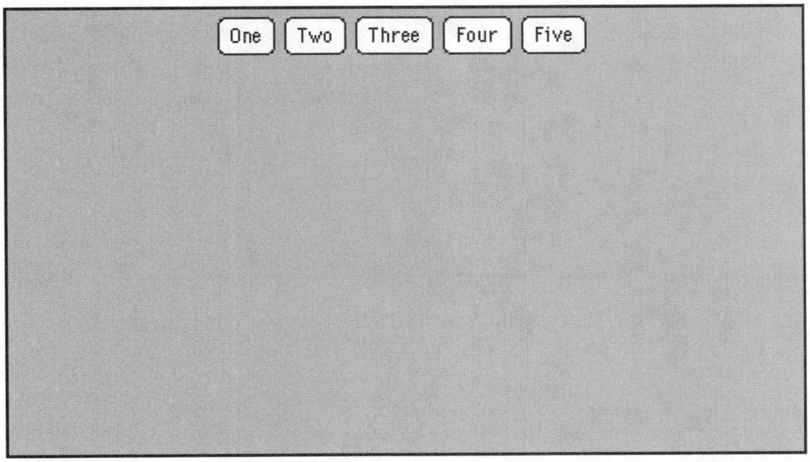

Figure 13.9   *Flow layout.*

To create a basic flow layout with a centered alignment, use the following line of code in your panel's initialization (because this is the default panel layout, you don't need to include this line if that is your intent):

```
setLayout(new FlowLayout());
```

To create a flow layout with an alignment other than centered, add the FlowLayout.RIGHT or FlowLayout.LEFT class variable as an argument:

```
setLayout(new FlowLayout(FlowLayout.LEFT));
```

You can also set horizontal and vertical gap values by using flow layouts. The gap is the number of pixels between components in a panel; by default, the horizontal and vertical gap values are three pixels, which can be very close indeed. Horizontal gap spreads out components to the left and to the right, vertical gap to the top and bottom of each component. Add integer arguments to the flow layout constructor to increase the gap (a layout gap of 10 points in both the horizontal and vertical directions is shown in Figure 13.10):

```
setLayout(new FlowLayout(FlowLayout.LEFT),10,10);
```

Figure 13.10 *Flow layout with a gap of 10 points.*

Grid Layouts

Grid layouts use a layout that offers more control over the placement of components inside a panel. Using a grid layout, you portion off the area of the panel into rows and columns. Each component you then add to the panel is placed in a "cell" of the grid, starting from the top row and progressing through each row from left to right (here's where the order of calls to the add() method are very relevant to how the screen is laid out). By using grid layouts and nested grids, you can often approximate the use of hard-coded pixel values to place your UI components precisely where you want them. Figure 13.11 shows a grid layout with three columns and three rows.

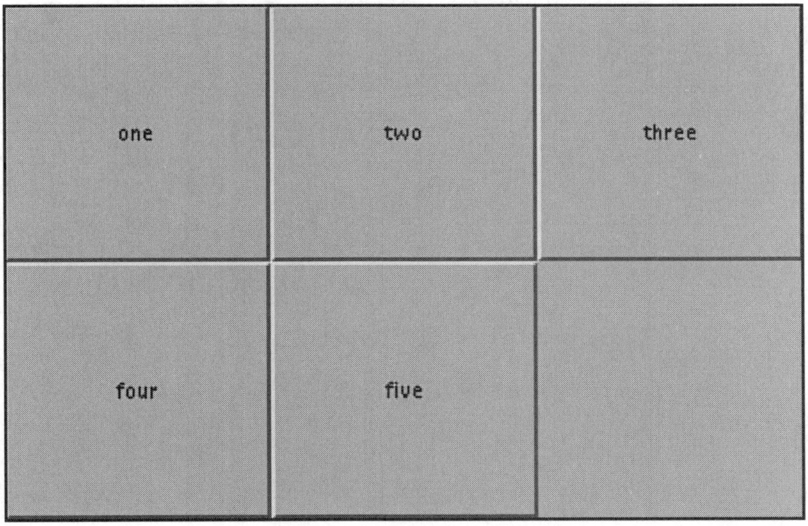

Figure 13.11   *Grid layout.*

To create a grid layout, indicate the number of rows and columns you want the grid to have when you create a new instance of the GridLayout class:

```
setLayout(new GridLayout(3,3));
```

Grid layouts can also have a horizontal and vertical gap between components; to create gaps, add those pixel values:

```
setLayout(new GridLayout(3,3,10,15));
```

Figure 13.12 shows a grid layout with a 10-pixel horizontal gap and a 15-pixel vertical gap.

GridBag Layouts

GridBag layouts, as implemented by the GridBagLayout class, are variations on grid layouts. GridBag layouts also enable you to lay out your user interface elements in a rectangular grid, but with GridBag layouts you have much more control over the presentation of each element in the grid. GridBag layouts use a helper class, GridBagConstraints, to indicate how each cell in the grid is to be formatted.

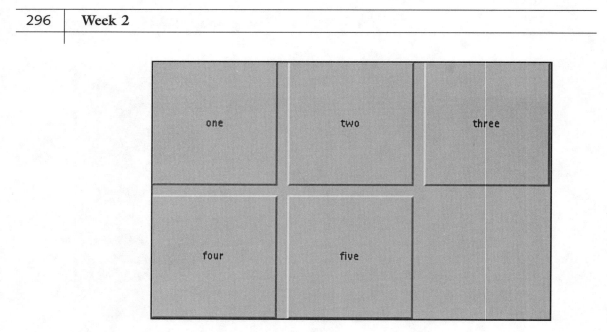

Figure 13.12   *Grid layouts with horizontal and vertical gap.*

The GridBagConstraints object contains information about a component's placement in the layout, and how the component behaves when the layout is resized. Typically, you will make a single GridBagConstraints instance and pass it as a parameter in the add() method—the layout method keeps track of the added component's contraints. In other words, you *don't* have to maintain separate GridBagConstraints instances for each of the components in your container.

A GridBagConstraints object has many instance variables that control how a component appears; for complete documentation of the use of these values, refer to Sun's API documentation at http://java.sun.com and examine the well-commented source code on the CD-ROM, in the files Roaster™:java:src:java:awt:GridBag and Roaster™:java:src:java:awt:GridBagConstraints.

The following snippet of code, taken from the API documentation, shows how you might set up a GridBagConstraints object:

```
1:  GridBagLayout gridbag = new GridBagLayout();
2:  GridBagConstraints c = new GridBagConstraints();
3:  c.fill = GridBagConstraints.BOTH;
4:  c.weightx = 1.0;
5:  makebutton("Button1", gridbag, c);
6:  makebutton("Button2", gridbag, c);
7:  makebutton("Button3", gridbag, c);
```

Lines 5 through 7 call the user-definded method makebutton(), which actually adds the buttons to the container. The code segment below shows the complete listing for the makebutton() method:

```
1:  protected void makebutton(String name,
2:                            GridBagLayout gridbag,
3:                            GridBagConstraints c) {
4:      Button button = new Button(name);
5:      gridbag.setConstraints(button, c);
6:      add(button);
7:  }
```

Line 5 calls the GridBagLayout method setConstraints(), which sets up the button in the layout using the information in the GridBagConstraints instance. After this information has been passed along to the layout manager, you can forget about it and use the GridBagConstraints instance to store layout information about the next component you wish to add. Here's how it works in the API's sample program:

```
1:  c.gridwidth = GridBagConstraints.REMAINDER;
2:  makebutton("Button4", gridbag, c);
3:
4:  c.weightx = 0.0;
5:  makebutton("Button5", gridbag, c);
// ...and the rest of the buttons are added in a similar fashion.
```

In lines 1 and 3, you write over the information about the first buttons, because the information is safely stored in the layout manager. In other words, GridBagConstraints is one big, complicated *dummy variable,* used to pass things to a method rather than to store important information.

Figure 13.13 shows the applet whose code is listed in the API documentation:

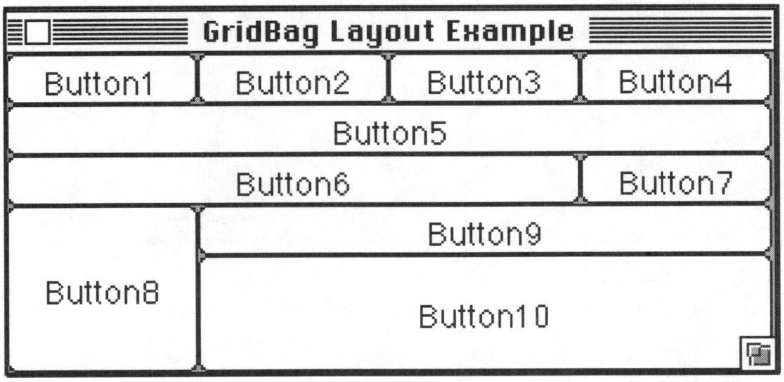

Figure 13.13 *The GridBagLayout.*

Yes, this is confusing. What values should you give the instance variable? GridBag-Layout's flexibility precludes an easy answer to this question: you'll have to experiment with different values, guided by the API documentation, to get a feel for what each of the instance variables controls.

Border Layouts

Border layouts behave differently from flow and grid layouts. When you add a component to a panel that uses a BorderLayout, you indicate its placement as a geographic direction: north, south, east, west, and center (see Figure 13.14). The components around all the edges are laid out with as much size as they need; the component in the center, if any, gets any space left over.

To use a border layout, you create it as you do the other layouts:

```
setLayout(new BorderLayout());
```

Then you add the individual components by using a special add() method: the first argument to add() is a string indicating the position of the component within the layout:

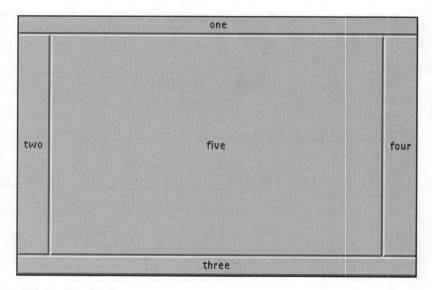

Figure 13.14   *Border layout.*

```
add("North", new TextField("Title",50));
add("South", new TextField("Status",50));
```

You can also use this form of add() for the other layout managers; the string argument will just be ignored if it's not needed.

Border layouts can also have horizontal and vertical gaps. Note that the north and south components extend all the way to the edge of the panel, so the gap will result in less space for the east, right, and center components. To add gaps to a border layout, include those pixel values as before:

```
setLayout(new BorderLayout(10,10));
```

Card Layouts

Card layouts are different from the other layouts. Unlike with the other three layouts, when you add components to a card layout, they are not all displayed on the screen at once. Card layouts are used to produce slide shows of components, one at a time. If you've ever used the HyperCard program on the Macintosh, you've worked with the same basic idea.

Generally when you create a card layout, the components you add to it will be other container components—usually panels. You can then use different layouts for those individual "cards" so that each screen has its own look.

When you add each "card" to the panel, you can give it a name. Then you can use methods defined on the CardLayout class to move back and forth between different cards in the layout.

For example, here's how to create a card layout containing three cards:

```
setLayout(new CardLayout());
Panel one = new Panel()
add("first", one);
Panel two = new Panel()
add("second", two);
Panel three = new Panel()
add("third", three);
show(this, "second");
```

Insets

Whereas horizontal gap and vertical gap are used to determine the amount of space between components in a panel, insets are used to determine the amount of space around the panel itself. The insets class provides values for the top, bottom, left, and right insets, which are then used when the panel itself is drawn. Figure 13.15 shows an inset in a GridLayout.

To include an inset, override the insets() method in your class (your Applet class or other class that serves as a panel):

```
public Insets insets() {
        return new Insets(10,10,10,10);
}
```

The arguments to the Insets constructor provide pixel insets for the top, left, bottom, and right edges of the panel. This particular example provides an inset of 10 pixels on all four sides of the panel.

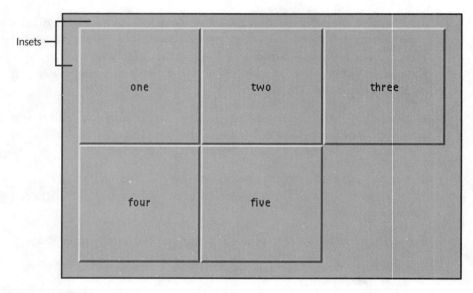

Figure 13.15   *Insets.*

Handling UI Actions and Events

If you stopped reading today's lesson right now, you could go out and create an applet that had lots of little UI components, nicely laid out on the screen with the proper layout manager, gap, and insets. If you did stop right here, however, your applet would be really dull, because none of your UI components would actually do anything when they were pressed or typed into or selected.

For your UI components to do something when they are activated, you need to hook up the UI's action with an operation.

Testing for an action by a UI component is a form of event management—the things you learned yesterday about events will come in handy here. In particular, UI components produce the special kind of event called an action. To intercept an action by any UI component, you define an action() method in your applet or class:

```
public boolean action(Event evt, Object arg) {
    ...
}
```

The action() method should look familiar to the basic mouse and keyboard event methods. Like those methods, it gets passed the event object that represents this event. It also gets an extra object, which can be of any type of object. What's that second argument for?

The second argument to the action method depends on the UI component that's generating the event. The basic definition is that it's any arbitrary argument—when a component generates an event, it can pass along any extra information that might later be needed. Because that extra information may be useful for you, it's passed on through the action() method.

All the basic UI components (except for labels, which have no action) have different actions and arguments:

- ☐ Buttons create actions when they are selected, and a button's argument is the label of the button.

- ☐ Checkboxes, both exclusive and nonexclusive, generate actions when a box is checked. The argument is always true.

- ☐ Choice menus generate an action when a menu item is selected, and the argument is that item.

- ☐ Text fields create actions when the user presses Return inside that text field. Note that if the user tabs to a different text field or uses the mouse to change the input focus, an action is *not* generated. Only a Return triggers the action.

Note that with actions, unlike with ordinary events, you can have many different kinds of objects generating the event, as opposed to a single event such as a mouseDown. To deal with those different UI components and the actions they generate, you have to test for the type of object that sent the event in the first place inside the body of your action() method. That object is stored in the event's target instance variable, and you can use the instanceof operator to find out what kind of UI component sent it:

```
public boolean action(Event evt, Object arg) {
    if (evt.target instanceof TextField)
        handleText(evt.target);
```

```
    else if (evt.target instanceof Choice)
        handleChoice(arg);
...
}
```

Although you can handle UI actions in the body of the action() method, it's much more common simply to define a handler method and call that method from action() instead. Here, there are two handler methods: one to handle the action on the text field (handleText()) and one to handle the action on the choice menu (handleChoice()). Depending on the action you want to handle, you may also want to pass on the argument from the action, the UI component that sent it, or any other information that the event might contain.

Here's a simple applet that has five buttons labeled with colors. The action() method tests for a button action and then passes off the word to a method called changeColor(), which changes the background color of the applet based on which button was pressed (see Figure 13.16 to see the applet in action):

```
import java.awt.*;

public class ButtonActionsTest extends java.applet.Applet {

    public void init() {
        setBackground(Color.white);

        add(new Button("Red"));
        add(new Button("Blue"));
        add(new Button("Green"));
        add(new Button("White"));
        add(new Button("Black"));
    }

    public boolean action(Event evt, Object arg) {
        if (evt.target instanceof Button)
            changeColor((String)arg);
        return true;
    }

    void changeColor(String bname) {
        if (bname.equals("Red")) setBackground(Color.red);
        else if (bname.equals("Blue")) setBackground(Color.blue);
        else if (bname.equals("Green")) setBackground(Color.green);
        else if (bname.equals("White")) setBackground(Color.white);
        else setBackground(Color.black);
repaint();
    }
}
```

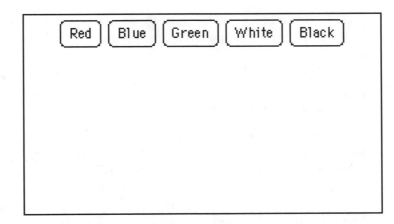

Figure 13.16 *The ButtonAction applet.*

Nesting Panels and Components

Adding UI components to individual applets is fun, but applets begin to turn into lots of fun when you begin working with nested panels. By nesting different panels inside your applet, and panels inside those panels, you can create different layouts for different parts of the overall applet area, isolate background and foreground colors and fonts to individual parts of an applet, and manage the design of your UI components much more cleanly and simply. The more complex the layout of your applet, the more likely you're going to want to use nested panels.

Nested Panels

Panels, as you've already learned, are components that can be actually displayed on screen; Panel's superclass Container provides the generic behavior for holding other components inside it. The Applet class, which your applets all inherit from, is a subclass of Panel. To nest other panels inside an applet, you merely create a new panel and add it to the applet, just as you would add any other UI component:

```
setLayout(new GridLayout(1,2,10,10));
Panel panel1 = new Panel();
Panel panel2 = new Panel();
add(panel1);
add(panel2);
```

You can then set up an independent layout for those subpanels and add AWT components to them (including still more subpanels) by calling the add() method in the appropriate panel:

```
panel1.setLayout(new FlowLayout());
panel1.add(new Button("Up"));
panel1.add(new Button("Down"));
```

Although you can do all this in a single class, it's common in applets that make heavy use of the panels to factor out the layout and behavior of the subpanels into separate classes, and to communicate between the panels by using method calls. You'll look at an extensive example of this later in today's lesson.

Events and Nested Panels

When you create applets with nested panels, those panels form a hierarchy from the outermost panel (the applet, usually) to the innermost UI component. This hierarchy is important to how each component in an applet interacts with the other components in the applet or with the browser that contains that applet; in particular, the component hierarchy determines the order in which components are painted to the screen.

More importantly, the hierarchy also affects event handling, particularly for user input events such as mouse and keyboard events.

Events are received by the innermost component in the component hierarchy and passed up the chain to the root. Suppose, for example, that you have an applet with a subpanel that can handle mouse events (using the mouseDown() and mouseUp() methods) and that panel contains a button. Clicking the button means that the button receives the event before the panel does; if the button isn't interested in that mouseDown(), the event gets passed to the panel, which can then process it or pass it further up the hierarchy.

Remember the discussion about the basic event methods yesterday? You learned that the basic event methods all return boolean values. Those boolean values become important when you're talking about handling events or passing them on.

An event handling method, whether it is the set of basic event methods or the more generic handleEvent(), can do one of three things, given any random event:

☐ Not be interested in the event (this is usually true only for handleEvent(), which receives all the events generated by the system). If this is the case, the event is passed on up the hierarchy until a component processes it (or it is ignored altogether). In this case, the event handling method should return false.

□ Intercept the event, process it, and return `true`. In this case, the event stops with that event method. Recall that this is the case with the basic `mouseDown()` and `keyDown()` methods that you learned about yesterday.

□ Intercept the method, process it, and pass it on to the next event handler. This is a more unusual case, but you may create a user interface by using nested components that will want to do this. In this case, the event method should return `false` to pass the event on to the next handler in the chain.

More UI Components

After you master the basic UI components and how to add them to panels and manage their events, you can add more UI components. In this section, you'll learn about text areas, scrolling lists, scrollbars, and canvases.

Note that the UI components in this section do not produce actions, so you can't use the `action()` method to handle their behavior. Instead, you have to use a generic `handleEvent()` method to test for specific events that these UI components generate. You'll learn more about this in the next section.

Text Areas

Text areas are like text fields, except they have more functionality for handling large amounts of text. Because text fields are limited in size and don't scroll, they are better for one-line responses and text entry; text areas can be any given width and height and have scrollbars by default, so you can deal with larger amounts of text more easily.

To create a text area, use one of the following constructors:

□ `TextArea()` creates an empty text area 0 rows long and 0 characters wide. Given that a text area with no dimensions can't be displayed, you should make sure you change the dimensions of this new text area before adding it to a panel (or just use the next constructor instead).

□ `TextArea(int, int)` creates an empty text area with the given rows and columns (characters).

□ `TextArea(String)` creates a text area displaying the given string, 0 rows by 0 columns.

□ `TextArea(String, int, int)` creates a text area by displaying the given string and with the given dimensions.

Figure 13.17 shows a simple text area generated from the following code:

```
String str = "Once upon a midnight dreary, while I pondered, weak and weary,\n" +
    "Over many a quaint and curious volume of forgotten lore,\n" +
    "While I nodded, nearly napping, suddenly there came a tapping,\n" +
    "As of some one gently rapping, rapping at my chamber door.\n" +
    "\"'Tis some visitor,\" I muttered, \"tapping at my chamber door-\n";

add(new TextArea(str,10,60));
```

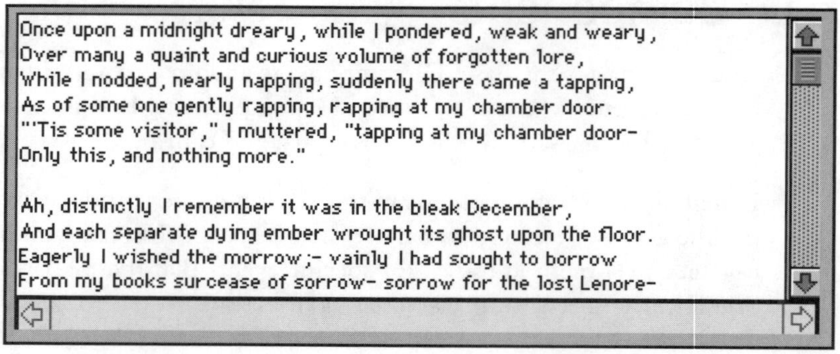

```
Once upon a midnight dreary, while I pondered, weak and weary,
Over many a quaint and curious volume of forgotten lore,
While I nodded, nearly napping, suddenly there came a tapping,
As of some one gently rapping, rapping at my chamber door.
"'Tis some visitor," I muttered, "tapping at my chamber door-
Only this, and nothing more."

Ah, distinctly I remember it was in the bleak December,
And each separate dying ember wrought its ghost upon the floor.
Eagerly I wished the morrow;- vainly I had sought to borrow
From my books surcease of sorrow- sorrow for the lost Lenore-
```

Figure 13.17   *A text area.*

Both text areas and text fields inherit from the TextComponent class, so a lot of the behavior for text fields (particularly getting and setting text and selections) is usable on text areas as well (refer to Table 13.4). Text areas also have a number of their own methods that you may find useful. Table 13.5 shows a sampling of those methods.

Table 13.5   *Text Area Methods*

Method	Action
getColumns()	Returns the width of the text area, in characters or columns
getRows()	Returns the number of rows in the text area (not the number of rows of text that the text area contains)
insertText(String, int)	Inserts the string at the given position in the text (text positions start at 0)
replaceText(String, int, int)	Replace the text between the given integer positions with the new string

Scrolling Lists

Remember the choice menu, which enables you to choose one of several different options? A scrolling list is functionally similar to a choice menu in that it lets you pick several options from a list. Scrolling lists differ in two significant ways:

☐ Scrolling lists are not popup menus. They're lists of items in which you can choose one or more items from a list. If the number of items is larger than the list box, a scrollbar is automatically provided so that you can see the other items.

☐ A scrolling list can be defined to accept only one item at a time (exclusive) or multiple items (nonexclusive).

To create a scrolling list, create an instance of the List class and then add individual items to that list. The List class has two constructors:

☐ List() creates an empty scrolling list that enables only one selection at a time.

☐ List(int, boolean) creates a scrolling list with the given number of visible lines on the screen (you're unlimited as to the number of actual items you can add to the list). The boolean argument indicates whether this list enables multiple selections (true) or not (false).

After creating a List object, add items to it using the addItem() method and then add the list itself to the panel that contains it. Here's an example, the result of which is shown in Figure 13.18:

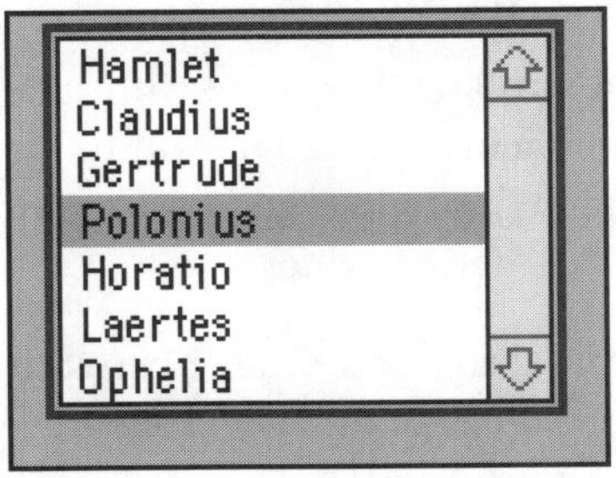

Figure 13.18   *A scrolling list.*

```
List lst = new List(5, true);

lst.addItem("Hamlet");
lst.addItem("Claudius");
lst.addItem("Gertrude");
lst.addItem("Polonius");
```

```
lst.addItem("Horatio");
lst.addItem("Laertes");
lst.addItem("Ophelia");

add(lst);
```

Table 13.6 shows some of the methods available to scrolling lists. See the API documentation for a complete set.

Table 13.6 *Scrolling List Methods*

Method	Action
getItem(int)	Returns the string item at the given position
countItems()	Returns the number of items in the menu
getSelectedIndex()	Returns the index position of the item that's selected (used for lists that enable only single selections)
getSelectedIndexes()	Returns an array of index positions (used for lists that enable multiple selections)
getSelectedItem()	Returns the currently selected item as a string
getSelectedItems()	Returns an array of strings containing all the selected items
select(int)	Selects the item at the given position
select(String)	Selects the item with that string

Scrollbars and Sliders

Text areas and scrolling lists come with their own scrollbars, which are built into those UI components and enable you to manage both the body of the area or the list and its scrollbar as a single unit. You can also create individual scrollbars, or sliders, to manipulate a range of values.

Scrollbars are used to select a value between a maximum and a minimum value. To change the current value of that scrollbar, you can use three different parts of the scrollbar (see Figure 13.19):

☐ Arrows on either end, which increment or decrement the values by some small unit (1 by default).

☐ A range in the middle, which increments or decrements the value by a larger amount (10 by default).

☐ A box in the middle, often called an *elevator* or *thumb*, whose position shows where in the range of values the current value is located. Moving this box with the mouse causes an absolute change in the value, based on the position of the box within the scrollbar.

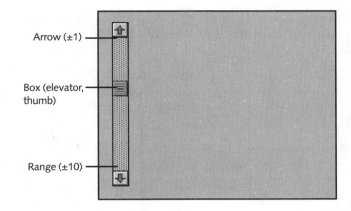

Figure 13.19 *Scrollbar parts.*

Choosing any of these visual elements causes a change in the scrollbar's value; you don't have to update anything or handle any events. All you have to do is give the scrollbar a maximum and minimum, and Java handles the rest.

To create a scrollbar, you can use one of three constructors:

☐ Scrollbar() creates a scrollbar with 0, 0 as its initial maximum and initial minimum values, in a vertical orientation.

☐ Scrollbar(int) creates a scrollbar with 0, 0 as its initial maximum and initial minimum values. The argument represents an orientation, for which you can use the class variables Scrollbar.HORIZONTAL and Scrollbar.VERTICAL.

☐ Scrollbar(int, int, int, int, int) creates a scrollbar with the following arguments (each one is an integer, and must be presented in this order):

The first argument is the orientation of the scrollbar: Scrollbar.HORIZONTAL and Scrollbar.VERTICAL.

The second argument is the initial value of the scrollbar, which should be a value between the scrollbar's maximum and minimum values.

The third argument is the the overall width (or height, depending on the orientation) of the scrollbar's box. On the Macintosh, the box for every scrollbar is the same size; on other platforms, however, the box is of variable size, and a larger box implies that a larger amount of the total range is currently showing.

The fourth and fifth arguments are the minimum and maximum values for the scrollbar.

Here's a simple example of a scrollbar that increments a single value (see Figure 13.20). The label to the left of the scrollbar is updated each time the scrollbar's value changes:

```java
import java.awt.*;

public class SliderTest extends java.applet.Applet {
    Label l;

    public void init() {
        l = new Label("0");
        add(l);
        add(new Scrollbar(Scrollbar.HORIZONTAL, 1, 0, 1, 100));
    }

    public boolean handleEvent(Event evt) {
        if (evt.target instanceof Scrollbar) {
            int v = ((Scrollbar)evt.target).getValue();
            l.setText(String.valueOf(v));
        }
        return true;
    }
}
```

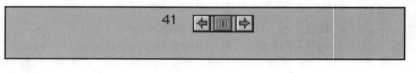

Figure 13.20   *A scrollbar.*

The Scrollbar class provides several methods for managing the values within scrollbars (see Table 13.7).

Table 13.7   *Scrollbar Methods*

Method	Action
getMaximum()	Returns the maximum value
getMinimum()	Returns the minimum value
getOrientation()	Returns the orientation of this scrollbar: 0 for vertical, 1 for horizontal
getValue()	Returns the scrollbar's current value
setValue(int)	Sets the current value of the scrollbar

Canvases

Although you can draw on most AWT components, such as panels, canvases do little *except* let you draw on them. They can't contain other components, but they can accept events, and you can create animations and display images on them. Canvases, in other words, should be used for much of the stuff you learned about earlier this week.

NEW TERM   A *canvas* is a component on which you can draw.

To create a canvas, use the Canvas class and add it to a panel as you would any other component:

```
Canvas can = new Canvas();
add(can);
```

More UI Events

Yesterday, you learned about some basic event types that are generated from user input to the mouse or the keyboard. These event types are stored in the Event object as the event ID, and can be tested for in the body of a handleEvent() method by using class variables defined in Event. For many basic events, such as mouseDown and keyDown, you can define methods for those events to handle the event directly. You learned a similar mechanism today for UI actions where creating an action() method handled a specifc action generated by a UI component.

The most general way of managing events, however, continues to be the handleEvent() method. For events relating to scrollbars and scrolling lists, the only way to intercept these events is to override handleEvent().

To intercept a specific event, test for that event's ID. The available IDs are defined as class variables in the Event class, so you can test them by name. You learned about some of the basic events yesterday. Table 13.8 shows additonal events that may be useful to you for the components you've learned about today (or that you might find useful in general).

Table 13.8   *Additional Events*

Event ID	What It Represents
ACTION_EVENT	Generated when a UI component action occurs
KEY_ACTION	Generated when text field action occurs
LIST_DESELECT	Generated when an item in a scrolling list is deselected

continues

Table 13.8 *Continued*

Event ID	What It Represents
LIST_SELECT	Generated when an item in a scrolling list is selected
SCROLL_ABSOLUTE	Generated when a scrollbar's box has been moved
SCROLL_LINE_DOWN	Generated when a scrollbar's bottom endpoint (or left endpoint) is selected
SCROLL_LINE_UP	Generated when a scrollbar's top endpoint (or right endpoint) is selected
SCROLL_PAGE_DOWN	Generated when the scrollbar's field below (or to the left of) the box is selected
SCROLL_PAGE_UP	Generated when the scrollbar's field above (or to the right of) the box is selected

A Complete Example: RGB to HSB Converter

Let's take a break here from theory and smaller examples to create a larger, more complex example that puts together much of what you've learned so far. The following applet example demonstrates layouts, nesting panels, creating user interface components, and catching and handling actions, as well as using multiple classes to put together a single applet. In short, it's probably the most complex applet you'll create so far.

Figure 13.21 shows the applet you'll be creating in this example. The ColorTest applet enables you to pick colors based on RGB (red, green, and blue) and HSB (hue, saturation, and brightness) values.

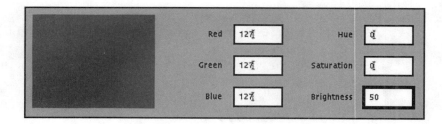

Figure 13.21 *The ColorTest applet.*

The ColorTest applet has three main parts: a colored box on the left side and two groups of text fields on the right. The first group indicates RGB values, the right,

HSB. By changing any of the values in any of the text boxes, the colored box is updated to the new color, as are the values in the other group of text boxes.

This applet uses two classes:

☐ ColorTest, which inherits from Applet. This is the controlling class for the applet itself.

☐ ColorControls, which inherits from Panel. You'll create this class to represent a group of three text fields and to handle actions from those text fields. Two instances of this class, one for the RGB values and one for the HSB ones, will be created and added to the applet.

Let's work through this step by step, because it's very complicated and can get confusing. All the code for this applet will be shown at the end of this section.

Create the Applet Layout

The best way to start creating an applet that uses AWT components is to worry about the layout first and then worry about the functionality. When dealing with the layout, you also should start with the outermost panel first and work inward.

Making a sketch of your UI design can help you figure out how to organize the panels inside your applet or window to best take advantage of layout and space. Figure 13.22 shows the ColorTest applet with a grid drawn over it so that you can get an idea of how the panels and embedded panels work.

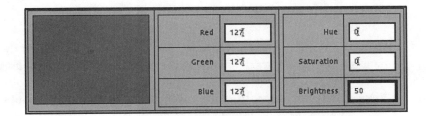

Figure 13.22   *The ColorTest applet panels and components.*

Create the Panel Layout

Let's start with the outermost panel—the applet itself. This panel has three parts: the color box on the left, the RGB text fields in the middle, and the HSB fields on the right.

Because this is the applet, your `ColorTest` class will be the applet class and inherit from `Applet`. You'll also import the AWT classes here (note that because you use so many of them in this program, it's easiest to just import the entire package):

```
import java.awt.*;

public class ColorTest extends java.applet.Applet {
...
}
```

Let's start with the `init()` method, where all the basic initialization and layout takes place. There are four major steps:

1. Set the layout for the big parts of the panel. Although a flow layout would work, a grid layout with one row and three columns is a much better idea.

2. Create the three components of this applet: a canvas for the color box and two subpanels for the text fields.

3. Add those components to the applet.

4. Finally, initialize the default color and update all the panels to reflect that default color.

Before you do any of that, let's set up instance variables to hold the three major components of this applet. You need to keep hold of these objects so you can update things when a value changes.

The color box is easy—it's just a canvas. Call it `swatch`.

```
Canvas swatch;
```

Now on to the subpanels. There are two of them, and although they have different labels and values, they're essentially the same panel. You could just create code for each one here, but you'd end up duplicating a lot of the same code. This is a perfect opportunity, therefore, to create another class to represent the subpanels with the text fields on them. Call them `ColorControls` (you'll get around to creating the class later) and define two variables, `RGBcontrols` and `HSBcontrols`, to hold them:

```
ColorControls RGBcontrols, HSBcontrols;
```

Back to the `init()` method. Step one is the layout. Let's use a grid layout and a gap of ten points to separate each of the components:

```
setLayout(new GridLayout(1,3,10,10));
```

Step two is creating the components, the canvas first. You have an instance variable to hold that one:

```
swatch = new Canvas();
```

You need to create two instances of your as-of-yet nonexistent ColorControls panels here as well, but you don't know exactly what you need to create them yet, so let's put in some basic constructors and fill in the details later:

```
RGBcontrols = new ColorControls()
HSBcontrols = new ColorControls();
```

Step three is adding them to the panel:

```
add(swatch);
add(RGBcontrols);
add(HSBcontrols);
```

While you're working on layout, add an inset just for fun—ten points along all the edges:

```
public Insets insets() {
    return new Insets(10,10,10,10);
}
```

Got it so far? Now you have a skeleton init() method and an insets() method in your ColorTest class. Let's move on now to creating the subpanel layout—to creating that ColorControls class.

Define the Subpanels

The ColorControls class will have behavior for laying out and handling the subpanels that represent the RGB and HSB values for the color. ColorControls doesn't need to be a subclass of Applet because it isn't actually an applet, it's just a panel. Define it to inherit from Panel:

```
class ColorControls extends Panel {
    ...
}
```

NOTE You can put the ColorControls class in the same file as the ColorTest class. You haven't been doing this so far because the applets and applications you've been creating had only one class. If you remember way back to Day 1, however, you learned that you can have multiple class definitions in a single file as long as only one of those definitions is declared public. In this case, the ColorTest class is public (it's an applet, so it has to be), but the ColorControls class doesn't need to be, so everything works out fine.

You need a couple of instance variables in this class. The first thing you need is a hook back up to the applet class that contains this panel. Why? The applet class is the class that oversees how the subcomponents work, so it's going to be the class that updates everything. Eventually, you're going to have to call a method in that class to indicate that something in this panel has changed. Without an actual reference to that outer class, there's no way to do this. So, instance variable number one is a reference to the class ColorTest:

```
ColorTest outerparent;
```

If you figure that the applet class is the one that's going to be updating everything, that class is going to need a way to get hold of the pieces inside this class. In particular, it's going to be interested in the individual text fields, so you're going to need instance variables to hold those. This creates three of them:

```
TextField f1, f2, f3;
```

Now for the constructor for this class. Again, this isn't an applet, so you don't use init(); all you need is a constructor method.

What do you need inside that constructor? You need to set the layout for the sub-panel, create the text fields, and add them to the panel. The goal here is to make the ColorControls class generic enough so that you can use it for both the RGB fields and the HSB fields.

The two different panels differ in two respects: the labels for the text fields and the initial values for the text fields. That's six values to get before you can create the object. You can pass those six values in through the constructors in ColorTest. You also need one more. Because you need that hook back to the applet class, you should also pass in a reference to that object as part of the constructor.

You now have seven arguments to the basic constructor for the ColorControls class. Here's the signature for that constructor:

```
ColorControls(ColorTest target,
        String l1, String l2, String l3,
        int v1, int v2, int v3) {
}
```

Given those arguments, you can assign the right values to your instance variables:

```
outerparent = target;

f1 = new TextField(String.valueOf(v1),10);
f2 = new TextField(String.valueOf(v2),10);
f3 = new TextField(String.valueOf(v3),10);
```

Note that because the first argument to the TextField constructor is a string and the values that you passed in were integers, you have to use the valueOf() class method (defined in String) to convert the integer to a string before creating each text field.

Next, you create the layout for this panel. You also use a grid layout for these sub-panels, as you did for the applet panel, but this time the grid will have three rows (one for each of the text field and label pairs) and two columns (one for the labels and one for the fields).

Given the 3-by-2 grid, you can now add the text fields and labels to that panel. Note that by separating the labels and the text fields into separate cells in the grid, you can align the labels, creating a nice aligned layout.

```
add(new Label(l1, Label.RIGHT));
add(f1);
add(new Label(l2, Label.RIGHT));
add(f2);
add(new Label(l3, Label.RIGHT));
add(f3);
```

Finally (because I like insets), you'll inset the contents of the subpanel a bit—only on the top and bottom edges—by including an insets() method:

```
public Insets insets() {
        return new Insets(10,10,0,0);
 }
```

You're almost there. You have 98 percent of the layout in place and ready to go, but you're missing two things: creating the ColorControls objects in ColorTest, and initializing everything so that all the components have the right values.

For both, you need to go back to the ColorTest class and the init() method you defined there. Let's start with the initialization part, because that's easy. The default color is black. Set up a local variable to hold that color object:

```
Color theColor = new Color(0,0,0);
```

To set the initial color of the color box, all you need to do is set its background:

```
swatch.setBackground(theColor);
```

Now, let's finally tackle initializing those subpanels. The constructor for ColorControls has seven arguments: the ColorTest object, three labels (strings), and three initial values for the text fields (integers). Let's do the RGB controls first, because you can easily extract the initial red, green, and blue values out of the Color object:

```
RGBcontrols = new ColorControls(this, "Red", "Green", "Blue",
        theColor.getRed(), theColor.getGreen(),
        theColor.getBlue());
```

Things get complicated on the HSB side of the panel. The Color class provides you with a method to get the HSB values out of a Color object, but there are two problems:

☐ The RGBtoHSB() method is a single class method that insists on returning an array of the three values.

☐ The HSB values are measured in floating-point values. I prefer to think of HSB as integers, wherein the hue is a degree value around a color wheel (0 through 360), and saturation and brightness are percentages from 0 to 100. Having HSB as integer values also enables you to have a generic subpanel, as was the intent.

Initializing the HSB subpanel is going to be a little difficult.

First, let's extract those HSB values. Given that the method takes three RGB arguments—an array of three floats—and returns an array of three floats, you have to go through this process to get those values:

```
float[] HSB = Color.RGBtoHSB(theColor.getRed(),
    theColor.getGreen(), theColor.getBlue(),(new float[3]));
```

Now you have an array of floats, where HSB[0] is the hue, HSB[1] is the saturation, and HSB[2] is the brightness. You can now (finally!) initialize the HSB side of the applet, making sure that when you pass those HSB values into the subpanel, you multiply them by the right values (360 for the hues, 100 for the saturation and the brightness) and convert them to integers:

```
HSBcontrols = new ColorControls(this,
        "Hue", "Saturation", "Brightness",
        (int)(HSB[0] * 360), (int)(HSB[1] * 100),
        (int)(HSB[2] * 100));
```

Ready to give up? Fear not—you've done the hard part. From here, it's (mostly) easy. Once you have your layout working, you can compile your Java program and see it how it looks. None of your UI components actually does anything, but perfecting the layout is half the battle.

Handle the Actions

After creating the layout, you set up actions with the UI components so that when the user interacts with the applet, the applet can respond.

The action of this applet occurs when the user changes a value in any of the text fields. By causing an action in a text field, the color changes, the color box updates to the new color, and the values of the fields in the opposite subpanel change to reflect the new color.

The ColorTest class is responsible for actually doing the updating, because it keeps track of all the subpanels. You should be tracking and intercepting events in the subpanel in which they occur, however. Because the action of the applet is an actual text action, you can use an action() method to intercept it:

```
public boolean action(Event evt, Object arg) {
        if (evt.target instanceof TextField) {
            this.outerparent.update(this);
            return true;
        }
        else return false;
    }
```

In the action() method, you test to make sure the action was indeed generated by a text field (because there are only text fields available, that's the only action you'll get, but it's a good idea to test for it anyhow). If so, call the update() method, defined in ColorTest, to update the applet to reflect all the new values. Because the outer applet is responsible for doing all the updating, this is precisely why you need that hook back to the applet—so you can call the right method at the right time.

Update the Result

The only part left now is to update all the values and the color swatch if one of the values changes. For this, you define the update() method in the ColorTest class. This update() method takes a single argument—the ColorControls instance that contains the changed value (you get that argument from the action() method in the subpanel).

NOTE   Won't this update() method interfere with the system's update() method? Nope. Remember, methods can have the same names, but different signatures and definitions. Because this update() has a single argument of type ColorControls, it doesn't interfere with the other version of update().

The update() method is responsible for updating all the panels in the applet. To know which panel to update, you need to know which panel changed. You can find out by testing to see whether the argument passed is the same as the subpanels you have stored in the RGBcontrols and HSBcontrols instance variables:

```
void update(ColorControls in) {

    if (in == RGBcontrols) { // the change was in RGB
        ...
    }
    else { // change was in HSB
}
```

This test is the heart of the update() method. Let's start with that first case—a number has been changed in the RGB text fields. So now, based on those new RGB values, you have to generate a new color object and update the values on the HSB panel. To reduce some typing, you create a few local variables to hold some basic values. In particular, the values of the text fields are strings, and you get into them by accessing the text field instance variables for the ColorControls panel (f1, f2, f3) and then using the getText() method to extract the actual values. Extract those values and store them in string variables so that you don't have to keep typing:

```
String v1 = in.f1.getText();
String v2 = in.f2.getText();
String v3 = in.f3.getText();
```

Given those string values for RGB, you now create a color object by converting those strings to integers:

```
Color c;
c = new Color(Integer.parseInt(v1),Integer.parseInt(v2),
              Integer.parseInt(v3));
```

NOTE   This part of the example isn't very robust; it assumes that the user has indeed entered real numbers into the text fields. A better version of this would test to make sure that no parsing errors had occurred (I was trying to keep this example small).

Since Integer.parseInt() throws an exception and we're not checking for it in our code, entering anything other than a number will produce an error message. On Day 17, you'll learn more about exceptions and how to handle them.

When you have a color object, you can update the color swatch:

```
swatch.setBackground(c);
```

The next step is to update the HSB panel to the new HSB values. Doing this in the init() method is no fun at all, and it's even less fun here. To do this, you call RGBtoHSB to get the floating-point values, convert them to integers with the right values, convert them to strings, and then put them back into the text fields for the HSB subpanel. Got all that? Here's the code:

```
float[] HSB = Color.RGBtoHSB(c.getRed(),c.getGreen(),
         c.getBlue(), (new float[3]));
HSB[0] *= 360;
HSB[1] *= 100;
HSB[2] *= 100;
HSBcontrols.f1.setText(String.valueOf((int)HSB[0]));
HSBcontrols.f2.setText(String.valueOf((int)HSB[1]));
HSBcontrols.f3.setText(String.valueOf((int)HSB[2]));
```

The second part of the update() method is called when a value on the HSB side of the panel is changed. This is the "else" in the if-else that determines what to update, given a change.

Believe it or not, it's easier to update RGB values given HSB than it is to do it the other way around. First, convert the string values from the HSB text fields to integers by using these lines:

```
int f1 = Integer.parseInt(v1);
int f2 = Integer.parseInt(v2);
int f3 = Integer.parseInt(v3);
```

There's a class method in the Color class that creates a new color object when given three HSB values. The catch is that those values are floats, and they're not the values you currently have. To call getHSBColor() (that's the name of the method), convert the integers to floats and divide by the right amounts:

```
c = Color.getHSBColor((float)f1 / 360, (float)f2 / 100, (float)f3/100);
```

Now that you have a color object, the rest is easy. Set the color swatch:

```
swatch.setBackground(c);
```

Then update the RGB text fields with the new RGB values from the color object:

```
RGBcontrols.f1.setText(String.valueOf(c.getRed()));
RGBcontrols.f2.setText(String.valueOf(c.getGreen()));
RGBcontrols.f3.setText(String.valueOf(c.getBlue()));
```

The Complete Source Code

What follows is the complete source code; often it's easier to figure out what's going on in this applet when it's all in one place and you can follow the method calls and how values are passed back and forth. Start with the init() method in applet, and go from there.

```
import java.awt.*;

public class ColorTest extends java.applet.Applet {
    ColorControls RGBcontrols, HSBcontrols;
    Canvas swatch;

    public void init() {
        Color theColor = new Color(0,0,0);
        float[] HSB = Color.RGBtoHSB(theColor.getRed(),
            theColor.getGreen(), theColor.getBlue(),
            (new float[3]));

        setLayout(new GridLayout(1,3,10,10));

        // The color swatch
        swatch = new Canvas();
        swatch.setBackground(theColor);

        // the control panels
        RGBcontrols = new ColorControls(this,
            "Red", "Green", "Blue",
            theColor.getRed(), theColor.getGreen(),
            theColor.getBlue());

        HSBcontrols = new ColorControls(this,
            "Hue", "Saturation", "Brightness",
            (int)(HSB[0] * 360), (int)(HSB[1] * 100),
            (int)(HSB[2] * 100));

        add(swatch);
        add(RGBcontrols);
        add(HSBcontrols);

    }

    public Insets insets() {
        return new Insets(10,10,10,10);
    }

    void update(ColorControls in) {
        Color c;
```

```
        String v1 = in.f1.getText();
        String v2 = in.f2.getText();
        String v3 = in.f3.getText();

        if (in == RGBcontrols) {    // change to RGB
            c = new Color(Integer.parseInt(v1),
                    Integer.parseInt(v2),
                    Integer.parseInt(v3));
            swatch.setBackground(c);

            float[] HSB = Color.RGBtoHSB(c.getRed(),c.getGreen(),
                    c.getBlue(), (new float[3]));
            HSB[0] *= 360;
            HSB[1] *= 100;
            HSB[2] *= 100;
            HSBcontrols.f1.setText(String.valueOf((int)HSB[0]));
            HSBcontrols.f2.setText(String.valueOf((int)HSB[1]));
            HSBcontrols.f3.setText(String.valueOf((int)HSB[2]));
        }
        else {     // change to HSB
            int f1 = Integer.parseInt(v1);
            int f2 = Integer.parseInt(v2);
            int f3 = Integer.parseInt(v3);
            c = Color.getHSBColor((float)f1 / 360,
                    (float)f2 / 100, (float)f3/100);
            swatch.setBackground(c);
            RGBcontrols.f1.setText(String.valueOf(c.getRed()));
            RGBcontrols.f2.setText(String.valueOf(
                c.getGreen()));
            RGBcontrols.f3.setText(String.valueOf(c.getBlue()));
        }
    }
}


class ColorControls extends Panel {
    TextField f1, f2, f3;
    ColorTest outerparent;

    ColorControls(ColorTest target,
            String l1, String l2, String l3,
            int v1, int v2, int v3) {

        this.outerparent = target;
        setLayout(new GridLayout(3,4,10,10));

        f1 = new TextField(String.valueOf(v1),10);
        f2 = new TextField(String.valueOf(v2),10);
```

```
            f3 = new TextField(String.valueOf(v3),10);

            add(new Label(l1, Label.RIGHT));
            add(f1);
            add(new Label(l2, Label.RIGHT));
            add(f2);
            add(new Label(l3, Label.RIGHT));
            add(f3);
        }

        public Insets insets() {
            return new Insets(10,10,0,0);
        }

        public boolean action(Event evt, Object arg) {
            if (evt.target instanceof TextField) {
                this.outerparent.update(this);
                retrue true;
            }
            else return false;
        }
    }
```

Summary

The Java AWT, or Abstract Window Toolkit, is a package of Java classes and interfaces for creating full-fledged access to a window-based graphical user interface system, with mechanisms for graphics display, event management, text and graphics primitives, user interface components, and cross-platform layout. The AWT is used by the HotJava browser itself for all its functionality. Applets are also an integral part of the AWT toolkit.

Today has been a big day; the lesson has brought together everything you've learned up to this point about simple applet management and added a lot more about creating applets, panels, and user interface components and managing the interactions between all of them. With the information you got today and the few bits that you'll learn tomorrow, you can create cross-platform Java applications that do just about anything you want.

Questions and Answers

Q You've mentioned a lot about the `Component` and `Container` classes, but it looks like the only `Container` objects that ever get created are `Panels`. What do the `Component` and `Container` classes give me?

A Those classes factor out the behavior for components (generic AWT components) and containers (components that can contain other components). Although you don't necessarily create direct instances of these classes, you can
create subclasses of them if you want to add behavior to the AWT that the
default classes do not provide. As with most of the Java classes, any time you
need a superclass's behavior, don't hesitate to extend that class by using your
own subclass.

Q Can I put a UI component at a specific x and y position on the screen?

A By using the existing layout managers supplied with the AWT, no. This is
actually a good thing because you don't know what kind of display environment your applet will be run under, what kind of fonts are installed, or what
kind of fonts are being currently used. By using the layout managers provided
with the AWT, you can be sure that every portion of your window will be view-
able and readable and usable. You can't guarantee that with hard-coded
layouts.

**Q I was exploring the AWT package, and I saw this subpackage called peer.
There's also references to the peer classes sprinkled throughout the API
documentation. What do peers do?**

A Peers are responsible for the platform-specific parts of the AWT. For example,
when you create a Java AWT window, you have an instance of the Window class
that provides generic window behavior, and then you have an instance of Win-
dowPeer that creates the very specific window for that platform—a Macintosh-
style window under MacOS, a motif window under X Windows, or a Windows
95 window under Windows 95. The peers also handle communication between
the window system and the Java window itself. By separating the generic component behavior (the AWT classes) from the actual system implementation and
appearance (the peer classes), you can focus on providing behavior in your Java
application and let the Java implementation deal with the platform-specific
details.

**Q There's a whole lot of functionality in the AWT that you haven't talked
about here.**

A Given that even a basic introduction took this long, I figured that if I put in
even more detail than I already have that this book would turn into *Teach Yourself Java for Macintosh in 21 Days Plus a Few Extra for the AWT Stuff*.

As it is, I've left windows, menus, and dialogs until tomorrow, so you'll have to
wait for those. But you can find out about a lot of the other features of AWT
merely by exploring the API documentation. Start with the Applet class and
examine the sorts of methods you can call. Then look at Panel, from which

applet inherits—you have all that class's functionality as well. The superclass of Panel is Container, which provides still more interesting detail. Component comes next. Explore the API and see what you can do with it. You might find something interesting.

Windows, Networking, and Other Tidbits

by Laura Lemay with Timothy Webster

Here you are on the last day of the second week, and you're just about finished with applets and the AWT. With the information you'll learn today, you can create a wide variety of applets and applications using Java. Next week's lessons provide more of the advanced stuff that you'll need to start doing really serious work in Java.

Today, to finish up this week, there are three very different topics:

- ☐ Windows, menus, and dialog boxes—the last of the AWT classes that enable you to pop up real windows from applets and to create stand-alone Java applications that have their own windows

- ☐ Networking—how to load new HTML files from an applet-capable browser, how to retrieve files from Web sites, and some basics on how to work with generic sockets in Java

- ☐ Extra tidbits—the smaller stuff that didn't fit in anywhere else, but that might be useful to you as you write your Java applets and applications.

NOTE

In the early releases of Roaster's Applet Runner, some of the classes and methods covered in this chapter do not do exactly what they are supposed to do. Some of these inconsistencies have been noted in the text; if you notice any other problems, you can expect them to be fixed very soon in one of the next updates to Roaster.

Windows, Menus, and Dialog Boxes

Today, you'll finish up the last bits of the AWT that didn't fit into yesterday's lesson. In addition to all the graphics, events, UI, and layout mechanisms that the AWT provides, it also provides windows, menus, and dialog boxes, enabling to you create full-featured applications either as part of your applet or independently for stand-alone Java applications.

Frames

The AWT Window class enables you to create windows that are independent of the browser window containing the applet—that is, separate popup windows with their own titles, resize handles, and menu bars.

The Window class provides basic behavior for windows. Most commonly, instead of using the Window class, you'll use Window's subclasses, Frame and Dialog. The Frame class enables you to create a fully functioning window with a menu bar. Dialog is a more limited window for dialog boxes. You'll learn more about dialog boxes later in this section.

To create a frame, use one of the following constructors:

☐ new Frame() creates a basic frame without a title.

☐ new Frame(*String*) creates a basic frame with the given title.

Frames are containers, just like panels are, so you can add other components to them just as you would regular panels, using the add() method. The default layout for windows is BorderLayout:

```
win = new Frame("My Cool Window");
win.setLayout(new BorderLayout(10,20));
win.add("North", new Button("start"));
win.add("Center", new Button("Move"));
```

To set a size for the new window, use the resize() method. To set a location for where the window appears, use the move() method. Note that the location() method can tell you where the applet window is on the screen so that you can pop up the extra window in a relative position to that window (all these methods are defined for all containers, so you can use them for applets, windows, and the components inside them, subject to the current layout):

```
win.resize(100,200);
Dimension d = location();
win.move(d.width + 50, d.height + 50);
```

When you initially create a window, it's invisible. You need to use the `show()` method to make the window appear on the screen (you can use `hide()` to hide it again):

```
win.show();
```

The following code shows an example of a simple applet with a popup window (both the applet and the window are shown in Figure 14.1). The applet has two buttons: one to show the window, and one to hide the window. The window itself, created from a subclass called `MyFrame`, has a single label: `"This is a Window."` You'll use this basic window and applet all through this section, so the more you understand what's going on here the easier it will be later.

```java
public class GUI extends java.applet.Applet {
    Frame window;

    public void init() {
        add(new Button("Open Window"));
        add(new Button("Close Window"));

        window = new MyFrame("A Popup Window");
        window.resize(150,150);
        window.move(100,100);
        window.show();
    }

    public boolean action(Event evt, Object arg) {
        if (evt.target instanceof Button) {
            String label = (String)arg;
            if (label.equals("Open Window")) {
                if (!window.isShowing())
                window.show();
            }
            else if (label == "Close Window") {
                if (window.isShowing())
                    window.hide();
            }
            return true;
        }
        else return false;
    }
}

class MyFrame extends Frame {
    Label l;

    MyFrame(String title) {
        super(title);
```

```
        setLayout(new GridLayout(1,1));
        l = new Label("This is a Window", Label.CENTER);
        add(l);
    }
```

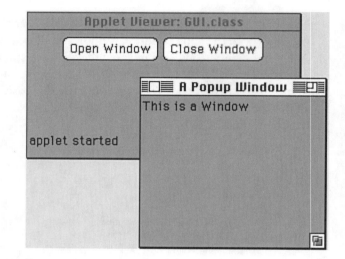

Figure 14.1   *Windows.*

Menus

Each new window you create can have its own menu bar along the top of the screen. Each menu bar can have a number of menus, and each menu, in turn, can have menu items. The AWT provides classes for all these things called, respectively, MenuBar, Menu, and MenuItem.

Menus and Menu Bars

To create a menu bar for a given window, create a new instance of the class MenuBar:

```
MenuBar mb = new MenuBar();
```

To set this menu bar as the default menu for the window, use the setMenuBar() method on the window:

```
window.setMenuBar(mb);
```

Add individual menus (File, Edit, and so on) to the menu bar by creating them and then adding them to the menu bar:

```
Menu m = new Menu("File");
mb.add(m);
```

Some systems enable you to indicate a special help menu, which may be drawn on the right side of the menu bar. You can indicate that a specific menu is the help menu by using the setHelpMenu() method. The given menu should already be added to the menu itself:

```
Menu hm = new Menu("Help");
mb.add(hm);
mb.setHelpMenu(hm);
```

If, for any reason, you want to prevent a user from selecting a menu, you can use the disable() command on that menu (and the enable() command to make it available again):

```
m.disable();
```

Menu Items

There are four kinds of items you can add to individual menus:

- ☐ Instances of the class MenuItem, for regular menu items
- ☐ Instances of the class CheckBoxMenuItem, for toggled menu items
- ☐ Other menus, with their own menu items
- ☐ Separators, for lines that separate groups of items on menus

Regular menu items are added by using the MenuItem class. Add them to a menu using the add() method:

```
Menu m = new Menu("Tools");
m.add(new MenuItem("Info"));
m.add(new MenuItem("Colors"));
m.add(new MenuItem("Sizes"));
```

Submenus can be added simply by creating a new instance of Menu and adding it to the first menu. You can then add items to *that* menu:

```
Menu sb = new Menu("Sizes");
m.add(sb);
sb.add(new MenuItem("Small"));
```

```
sb.add(new MenuItem("Medium"));
sb.add(new MenuItem("Large"));
```

The `CheckBoxMenuItem` class creates a menu item with a checkbox on it, enabling the menu state to be toggled on and off (selecting it once makes the checkbox appear selected; selecting it again unselects the checkbox). Create and add a checkbox menu item the same way you create and add regular menu items:

```
CheckboxMenuItem coords =
    new CheckboxMenuItem("Show Coordinates");
m.add(coords);
```

Finally, to add a separator to a menu (a line used to separate groups of items in a menu), create and add a menu item with the label "-".

```
MenuItem msep = new MenuItem("-");
m.add(msep);
```

Any menu item can be disabled by using the `disable()` method and enabled again using `enable()`. Disabled menu items cannot be selected:

```
MenuItem mi = new MenuItem("Fill");
m.addItem(mi);
mi.disable();
```

Menu Actions

The act of selecting a menu item causes an action event to be generated. You can handle that action the same way you handle other `action` methods—by overriding `action()`. Both regular menu items and checkbox menu items have actions that generate an extra argument representing the label for that menu. You can use that label to determine which action to take. Note, also, that because `CheckBoxMenuItem` is a subclass of `MenuItem`, you don't have to treat that menu item as a special case:

```
public boolean action(Event evt, Object arg) {
    if (evt.target instanceof MenuItem) {
        String label = (String)arg;
        if (label.equals("Show Coordinates")) toggleCoords();
        else if (label.equals("Fill")) fillcurrentArea();
```

```
        return true;
    }
    else return false;
}
```

An Example

Let's add a menu to the window you created in the previous section. Add it to the constructor method in the MyFrame class (Figure 14.2 shows the resulting menu):

```
MyFrame(String title) {
    super(title);
    MenuBar mb = new MenuBar();
    Menu m = new Menu("Colors");
    m.add(new MenuItem("Red"));
    m.add(new MenuItem("Blue"));
    m.add(new MenuItem("Green"));
    m.add(new MenuItem("-"));
    m.add(new CheckboxMenuItem("Reverse Text"));
    mb.add(m);
    mb.setHelpMenu(m);
    setMenuBar(mb);
...
}
```

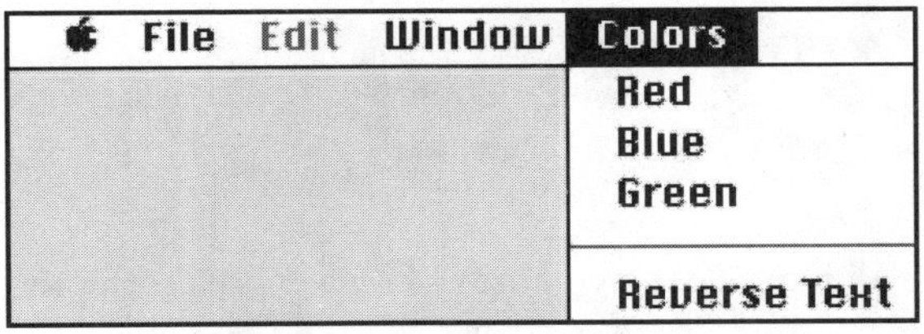

Figure 14.2 *A menu.*

This menu has four items: one each for the colors red, blue, and green (which, when selected, change the background of the window), and one checkbox menu item for reversing the color of the text to white. To handle these menu items, you need an action() method:

```
public boolean action(Event evt, Object arg) {
    if (evt.target instanceof MenuItem) {
        String label = (String)arg;
        if (label.equals("Red")) setBackground(Color.red);
        else if (label.equals("Blue")) setBackground(Color.blue);
        else if (label.equals("Green")) setBackground(Color.green);
        else if (label.equals("Reverse Text")) {
            if (getForeground() == Color.black)
                setForeground(Color.white);
            else setForeground(Color.black);
        }
        return true;
    }
    else return false;
}
```

Dialog Boxes

Dialog boxes are functionally similar to frames in that they pop up new windows on the screen. However, dialog boxes are intended to be used for transient windows—for example, windows that let you know about warnings, windows that ask you for specific information, and so on. Dialogs don't usually have title bars or many of the more general features that windows have (although you can create one with a title bar), and they can be made nonresizable or modal.

NEW TERM

A *modal dialog* prevents input to any of the other windows on the screen until that dialog is dismissed.

The AWT provides two kinds of dialog boxes: the Dialog class, which provides a generic dialog, and FileDialog, which produces a platform-specific dialog to choose files to save or open.

To create a generic dialog, use one of these constructors:

☐ Dialog(Frame, boolean) creates an initially invisible dialog, attached to the current frame, which is either modal (true) or not (false).

☐ Dialog(Frame, String, boolean) is the same as the previous constructor, with the addition of a title bar and a title indicated by the string argument.

Note that because you have to give a dialog a Frame argument, you can attach dialogs only to windows that already exist independently of the applet itself.

The dialog window, like the frame window, is a panel on which you can lay out and draw UI components and perform graphics operations, just as you would any other panel. Like other windows, the dialog is initially invisible, but you can show it with show() and hide it with hide().

Let's add a dialog to that same example with the popup window. You'll add a menu item for changing the text of the window, which brings up the Change Text dialog box (see Figure 14.3).

Figure 14.3 *The Change Text dialog.*

WARNING

With the DR1.1 version of Roaster, trying to display this dialog may cause the Applet Runner to crash. Because of this, we have removed the menu item from the version of the applet on the CD-ROM.

To add this dialog, first add a menu item to that window (the constructor method for the MyFrame class) to change the text the popup window displays:

```
m.add(new MenuItem("Set Text..."));
```

In that same method, you can create the dialog and lay out the parts of it (it's invisible by default, so you can do whatever you want to it and it won't appear on screen until you show it):

```
dl = new Dialog(this, "Enter Text",true);
dl.setLayout(new GridLayout(2,1,30,30));
tf = new TextField(l.getText(),20);
dl.add(tf);
dl.add(new Button("OK"));
dl.resize(150,75);
```

The action of choosing the menu item you just added brings up the dialog; choosing the OK button dismisses it. You need to add behavior to this class's action method so that the dialog works correctly. To the menu item tests, add a line for the new menu item:

```
if (evt.target instanceof MenuItem) {
    if (label.equals("Red")) setBackground(Color.red);
    if (label.equals("Blue")) setBackground(Color.blue);
    if (label.equals("Green")) setBackground(Color.green);
    if (label.equals("Set Text...")) dl.show();
}
```

Then, because OK is a button, you have to add a special case for that button separate from the menu items. In this special case, set the text of the window to the text that was typed into the text field, and then hide the dialog again:

```
if (evt.target instanceof Button) {
    if (label.equals("OK")) {
        l.setText(tf.getText());
        dl.hide();
    }
}
```

File Dialogs

FileDialog provides a basic file open/save dialog box that enables you to access the file system. The FileDialog class is system-independent, but each platform brings up its own platform's standard Open File dialog.

NOTE

The current version of Roaster doesn't support the FileDialog object; you can code it, and your code will compile, but the Applet Runner will crash. The implementation of this feature is still in the planning stages; it's too early to say which version of Roaster will implement FileDialog. In the meantime, you can test your Roaster-compiled code with the Sun Applet Viewer.

NOTE

For applets, you can bring up the file dialog, but due to security restrictions you can't do anything with it (or, if you can, access to any files on the local system is severely restricted). FileDialog is much more useful in stand-alone applications.

To create a file dialog, use the following constructors:

☐ `FileDialog(`*`Frame`*`, `*`String`*`)` creates an Open File dialog, attached to the given frame, with the given title. This form creates a dialog to load a file.

☐ `FileDialog(`*`Frame`*`, `*`String`*`, `*`int`*`)` also creates a file dialog, but that integer argument is used to determine whether the dialog is for loading a file or saving a file (the only difference is the labels on the buttons; the file dialog does not actually open or save anything). The possible options for the mode argument are `FileDialog.LOAD` and `FileDialog.SAVE`.

After you create a `FileDialog` instance, use `show()` to display it:

```
FileDialog fd = new FileDialog(this, "FileDialog");
fd.show();
```

When the reader chooses a file in the file dialog and dismisses it, you can then get to the file they chose by using the `getDirectory()` and `getFile()` methods; both return strings indicating the values that the reader chose. You can then open that file by using the stream and file handling methods (which you'll learn about next week) and then read from or write to that file.

NOTE

You probably know that the "directory" in the `getDirectory()` means "folder" in Mac-speak. `getDirectory()` returns the file's location in a slightly different way than you might be used to seeing if you've programmed on the Mac in AppleScript or HyperCard. The regular Mac approach is like this:

```
MyHardDrive:MyFolder:MySubfolder:
```

(Some applications, like BBEdit, adopt this system of identifying directory paths, too.) `getDirectory()` returns the directory path delimited with slashes, with a slash in front of your hard disk's name, too, like this:

```
/MyHardDrive/MyFolder/MySubfolder
```

Note that there's no slash after the last file's name.

Window Events

Yesterday you learned about writing your own event handler methods, and you noted that the `Event` class defines many standard events for which you can test. Window events are part of that list, so if you use windows, these events may be of interest to you. Table 14.1 shows those events.

Table 14.1 *Window Events from the Event Class*

WINDOW_DESTROY	Generated when a window is destroyed (for example, when the browser or applet viewer has quit)
WINDOW_EXPOSE	Generated when the window is brought forward from behind other windows
WINDOW_ICONIFY	Generated when the window is iconified
WINDOW_DEICONIFY	Generated when the window is restored from an icon
WINDOW_MOVED	Generated when the window is moved

Using AWT Windows in Stand-Alone Applications

Because frames are general-purpose mechanisms for creating AWT windows with panels, you can use them in your stand-alone Java applications and easily take advantage of all the applet capabilities you learned about this week. To do this, write your application as if it were an applet (inheriting from the Applet class and using threads, graphics, and UI components as necessary), and then add a main() method. Here's one for a class called MyAWTClass:

```
public static void main(String args[]) {
    Frame f = new Frame("My Window");
    MyAWTClass mac = new MyAWTClass();
    mac.init();
    mac.start();

    f.add("Center", mac);
    f.resize(300, 300);
    f.show();
}
```

This main() method does five things:

☐ It creates a new frame to hold the applet.

☐ It creates an instance of the class that defines that method.

☐ It duplicates the applet environment calls to init() and start().

☐ It adds the applet to the frame and resizes the frame to be 300 pixels square.

☐ It shows the frame on the screen.

By using this mechanism, you can create a Java program that can function equally well as an applet or an application—just include init() for applets and main() for applications.

If you do create an application that uses this mechanism, be careful of your `init()` methods that get parameters from an HTML file. When you run an applet as an application, you don't have the HTML parameters passed into the `init()` method. Pass them using Roaster's Preferences (⌘-;) command instead, and handle them in your `main()` method. Then set a flag so that the `init()` method doesn't try to read parameters that don't exist.

Networking in Java

Networking is the capability of making connections from your applet or application to a system over the network. Networking in Java involves classes in the `java.net` package, which provide cross-platform abstractions for simple networking operations, including connecting and retrieving files by using common Web protocols and creating basic Unix-like sockets. Used in conjunction with input and output streams (which you'll learn much more about next week), reading and writing files over the network becomes as easy as reading or writing to files on the local disk.

There are restrictions, of course. Java applets' capability to read or write from the disk on the machine that's running them is limited or nonexistent, depending on how the end user has set the browser. Applets may only connect to the server that they were stored on in the first place. Even given these restrictions, you can still accomplish a great deal and take advantage of the Web to read and process information over the Net.

This section describes three ways you can communicate with systems on the Net:

☐ `showDocument()`, which enables an applet to tell the browser to load and link to another page on the Web

☐ `openStream()`, a method that opens a connection to a URL and enables you to extract data from that connection

☐ The socket classes `Socket` and `ServerSocket`, which enable you to open standard socket connections to hosts and read to and write from those connections

Creating Links Inside Applets

Probably the easiest way to use networking inside an applet is to tell the browser running that applet to load a new page. You can use this, for example, to create animated imagemaps that, when clicked, load a new page.

To link to a new page, you create a new instance of the class URL. You saw some of this when you worked with images, but let's go over it a little more thoroughly here.

The URL class represents a uniform resource locator. To create a new URL, you can use one of four different forms:

- ☐ URL(String, *String, int, String*) creates a new URL object, given a protocol (http, ftp, gopher, file), a host name (www.lne.com, ftp.netcom.com), a port number (80 for http), and a filename or pathname.

- ☐ URL(*String, String, String*) does the same thing as the previous form, minus the port number.

- ☐ URL(*URL, String*) creates a URL, given a base path and a relative path. For the base, you can use getDocumentBase() for the URL of the current HTML file, or getCodeBase for the URL of the Java class file. The relative path is tacked onto the last directory in those base URLs (just like with images and sounds).

- ☐ URL(*String*) creates a URL object from a URL string (which should include the protocol, hostname, optional port name, and filename).

For that last one (creating a URL from a string), you have to catch a malformed URL exception, so surround the URL constructor with a try...catch:

```
String url = "http://www.yahoo.com/";
try { theURL = new URL(url); }
catch ( MalformedURLException e) {
    System.out.println("Bad URL: " + theURL);
}
```

(We'll cover exceptions (error-handling) in detail next week, on Day 17.)

Getting a URL object is the hard part. After you have one, all you have to do is pass it to the browser. Do this by using this single line of code, where theURL is the URL object to link to:

```
getAppletContext().showDocument(theURL);
```

The browser that contains your URL then loads and displays the document at that URL.

NOTE
The following applet won't work with Roaster's Applet Runner *or* Sun's Applet Viewer, because neither one parses much HTML—just <APPLET> tags. This applet was intended to run under a Java-savvy Web browser, such as the Java beta of Netscape Navigator 2.0 or the Atlas preview version of Navigator 3.0.

The following listing shows a simple applet that displays three buttons that represent important Web locations (the buttons are shown in Figure 14.4). Clicking the buttons causes the document to be loaded from the locations to which those buttons refer.

```java
import java.awt.*;
import java.net.URL;
import java.net.MalformedURLException;

public class ButtonLink extends java.applet.Applet {

    Bookmark bmlist[] = new Bookmark[3];

    public void init() {
        bmlist[0] = new Bookmark("Laura's Home Page",
            "http://www.lne.com/lemay/");
        bmlist[1] = new Bookmark("Yahoo",
            "http://www.yahoo.com");
        bmlist[2]= new Bookmark("Java Home Page",
            "http://java.sun.com");

        setLayout(new GridLayout(bmlist.length,1,10,10));
        for (int i = 0; i < bmlist.length; i++) {
            add(new Button(bmlist[i].name));
        }
    }

    public boolean action(Event evt, Object arg) {
        if (evt.target instanceof Button) {
            LinkTo((String)arg);
            return true;
        }
        else retrurn false;
    }

    void LinkTo(String name) {
        URL theURL = null;
        for (int i = 0; i < bmlist.length; i++) {
            if (name.equals(bmlist[i].name))
                theURL = bmlist[i].url;
        }
        if (theURL != null)
            getAppletContext().showDocument(theURL);
    }
}

class Bookmark {
    String name;
    URL url;
```

```
Bookmark(String name, String theURL) {
    this.name = name;
    try { this.url = new URL(theURL); }
    catch ( MalformedURLException e) {
        System.out.println("Bad URL: " + theURL);
    }
}
}
```

Two classes make up this applet: the first implements the actual applet itself, the second is a class representing a bookmark. Bookmarks have two parts: a name and a URL.

This particular applet creates three bookmark instances and stores them in an array of bookmarks (this applet could be easily modified to make bookmarks as parameters from an HTML file). For each bookmark, a button is created whose label is the value of the bookmark's name.

When the buttons are pressed, the linkTo() method is called, which tells the browser to load the URL referenced by that bookmark.

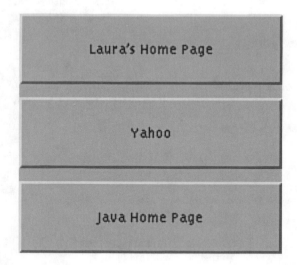

Figure 14.4   *Bookmark buttons.*

Opening Web Connections

Rather than asking the browser to just load the contents of a file, sometimes you might want to get that file's contents so that your applet can use them. If the file you want to grab is stored on the Web and can be accessed using the more common URL forms (`http`, `ftp`, and so on), your applet can use the URL class to get it.

Note that for security reasons, applets can connect back only to the same host from which they originally loaded. This means that if you have your applets stored on a system called www.myhost.com, the only machine your applet can open a connection to will be that same host (and that same host *name*, so be careful with host aliases). If the file the applet wants to retrieve is on that same system, using URL connections is the easiest way to get it.

openStream()

URL defines a method called `openStream()`, which opens a network connection using the given URL and returns an instance of the class `InputStream` (part of the `java.io` package). If you convert that stream to a `DataInputStream` (with a `BufferedInputStream` in the middle for better performance), you can then read characters and lines from that stream (you'll learn all about streams on Day 19). For example, these lines open a connection to the URL stored in the variable `theURL`, and then read and echo each line of the file to the standard output:

```
try {
    InputStream in = theURL.openStream();
    DataInputStream data = new DataInputStream(
        new BufferedInputStream(in);

    String line;
    while ((line = data.readLine()) != null) {
        System.out.println("line");
    }
}
catch (IOException e) {
    System.out.println("IO Error: " + e.getMessage());
}
```

NOTE   You need to wrap all those lines in a `try...catch` statement to catch `IOException` exceptions.

Here's an example of an applet that uses the `openStream()` method to open a connection to a Web site, reads a file from that connection (Edgar Allen Poe's poem "The Raven"), and displays the result in a text area. Figure 14.5 shows the result after the file has been read.

```
1: import java.awt.*;
2: import java.io.DataInputStream;
3: import java.io.BufferedInputStream;
```

```
4: import java.io.IOException;
5: import java.net.URL;
6: import java.net.URLConnection;
7: import java.net.MalformedURLException;
8:
9: public class GetRaven extends java.applet.Applet
10:     implements Runnable {
11:
12:     URL theURL;
13:     Thread runner;
14:     TextArea ta = new TextArea("Getting text...",30,70);
15:
16:     public void init() {
17:
18: String url = "http://www.roaster.com/raven.txt"
19:         try { this.theURL = new URL(url); }
20:         catch ( MalformedURLException e) {
21:             System.out.println("Bad URL: " + theURL);
22:         }
23:         add(ta);
24:     }
25:
26:     public Insets insets() {
27:         return new Insets(10,10,10,10);
28:     }
29:
30:     public void start() {
31:         if (runner == null) {
32:             runner = new Thread(this);
33:             runner.start();
34:         }
35:     }
36:
37:     public void stop() {
38:         if (runner != null) {
39:             runner.stop();
40:             runner = null;
41:         }
42:     }
43:
44:     public void run() {
45:         InputStream conn = null;
46:         DataInputStream data = null;
47:         String line;
48:         StringBuffer buf = new StringBuffer();
49:
50:         try {
51:             conn = this.theURL.openStream();
```

```
52:             data = new DataInputStream(new BufferedInputStream(
53:                 conn));
54:
55:             while ((line = data.readLine()) != null) {
56:                 buf.append(line + "\n");
57:             }
58:
59:             ta.setText(buf.toString());
60:         }
61:     catch (IOException e) {
62:         System.out.println("IO Error:" + e.getMessage());
63:     }
64:   }
65: }
```

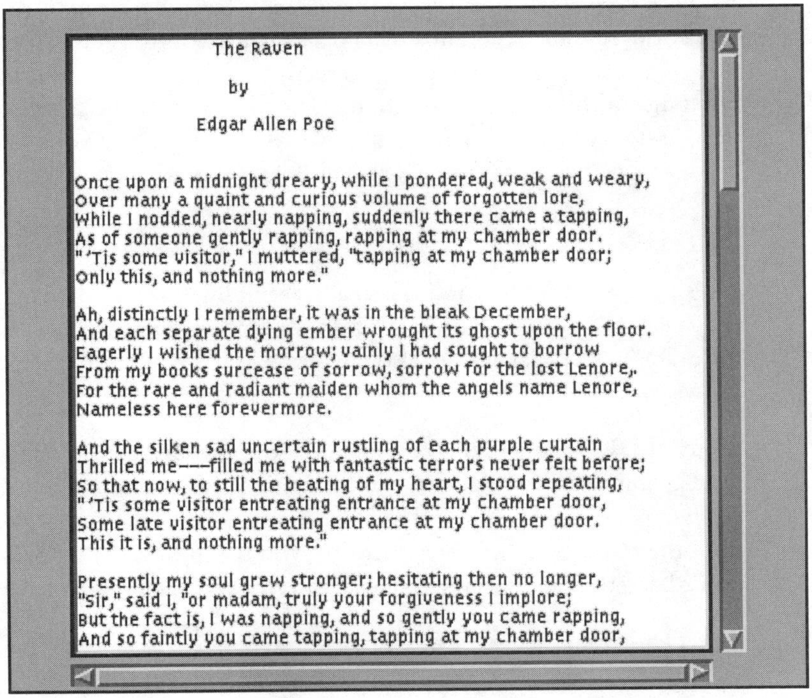

Figure 14.5 *The* GetRaven *class.*

The init() method (lines 16 to 24) sets up the URL and the text area in which that file will be displayed. The URL could be easily passed into the applet via an HTML parameter; here, it's just hard-coded for simplicity.

Because it might take some time to load the file over the network, you put that routine into its own thread and use the familiar start(), stop(), and run() methods to control that thread.

Inside run() (lines 44 to 64), the work takes place. Here, you initialize a bunch of variables and then open the connection to the URL (using the openStream() method in line 51). After the connection is open, you set up an input stream in lines 52 to 56 and read from it, line by line, putting the result into an instance of StringBuffer (a string buffer is a modifiable string).

When all the data has been read, line 59 converts the StringBuffer object into a real string and then puts that result in the text area.

One other thing to note about this example is that the part of the code that opened a network connection, read from the file, and created a string is surrounded by a try and catch statement. If any errors occur while you're trying to read or process the file, these statements enable you to recover from them without the entire program crashing (in this case, the program exits with an error, because there's little else to be done if the applet can't read the file). try and catch give you the capability of handling and recovering from errors. You'll learn more about exceptions on Day 17.

The URLconnection Class

URL's openStream() method is actually a simplified use of the URLconnection class. URLconnection provides a way to retrieve files by using URLs—on Web or FTP sites, for example. URLconnection also enables you to create output streams if the protocol allows it.

To use a URL connection, you first create a new instance of the class URLconnection, set its parameters (whether it enables writing, for example), and then use the connect() method to open the connection. Keep in mind that, with a URL connection, the class handles the protocol for you based on the first part of the URL, so you don't have to make specific requests to retrieve a file; all you have to do is read it.

Sockets

For networking applications beyond what the URL and URLconnection classes offer (for example, for other protocols or for more general networking applications), Java provides the Socket and ServerSocket classes as an abstraction of standard socket programming techniques.

The Socket class provides a client-side socket interface similar to standard Unix sockets. To open a connection, create a new instance of Socket (where *hostname* is the host to connect to, and *portnum* is the port number):

```
Socket connection = new Socket(hostname, portnum);
```

When the socket is open, you can use input and output streams to read and write from that socket (you'll learn all about input and output streams on Day 19):

```
DataInputStream in = new DataInputStream(
    new BufferedInputStream(connection.getInputStream()));
DataOutputStream out= new DataOutputStream(
    new BufferedOutputStream(connection.getOutputStream()));
```

After you're done with the socket, don't forget to close it (this also closes all the input and ouput streams you may have set up for that socket):

```
connection.close();
```

Server-side sockets work similarly, with the exception of the accept() method. A server socket listens on a TCP port for a connection for a client; when a client connects to that port, the accept() method accepts a connection from that client. By using both client and server sockets, you can create applications that communicate with each other over the network.

To create a server socket and bind it to a port, create a new instance of ServerSocket with the port number:

```
ServerSocket sconnection = new ServerSocket(8888);
```

To listen on that port (and to accept a connection from any clients if one is made), use the accept() method:

```
sconnection.accept();
```

After the socket connection is made, you can use input and output streams to read from and write to the client.

See the java.net package for more information about Java sockets.

Other Applet Hints

On this, the last section of the last day of the second week, let's finish up with some small hints that didn't fit in anywhere else: using showStatus() to print messages in the browser status window, providing applet information, and communicating between multiple applets on the same page.

The showStatus() Method

The showStatus() method, available in the applet class, enables you to display a string in the status bar of the browser, which contains the applet. (Roaster's Applet Runner creates a status bar at the bottom of each Applet's window; Sun's Applet Viewer shows status bar messages in the main program window—not the applet's window.) You can use this for printing error, link, help, or other status messages:

```
getAppletContext().showStatus("Change the color");
```

The getAppletContext() method enables your applet to access features of the browser that contains it. You already saw a use of this with links, wherein you could use the showDocument() method to tell the browser to load a page. showStatus() uses that same mechanism to print status messages.

NOTE

showStatus() may not be supported in all browsers, so do not depend on it for your applet's functionality or interface. It is a useful way of communicating optional information to your user—if you need a more reliable method of communication, set up a label in your applet and update it to reflect changes in its message.

Applet Information

The AWT gives you a mechanism for associating information with your applet. Usually, there is a mechanism in the browser for viewing display information. You can use this mechanism to sign your name or your organization to your applet, or to provide contact information for users.

To provide information about your applet, override the getAppletInfo() method:

```
public String getAppletInfo() {
    return "GetRaven copyright 1995 Laura Lemay";
}
```

Communicating Between Applets

Sometimes you want to have an HTML page that has several different applets on it. To do this, all you have to do is include several different iterations of the applet tag— the browser will create different instances of your applet for each one that appears on the HTML page.

What if you want to communicate between those applets? What if you want a change in one applet to affect the other applets in some way?

The best way to do this is to use the applet context to get to different applets on the same page. You've already seen the use of the getAppletContext() method for several other uses; you can also use it to get the other applets on the page. For example, to call a method in all the applets on a page (including the current applet), use the getApplets() method and a for loop that looks something like this:

```
for (Enumeration e = getAppletContext().getApplets();
        e.hasMoreElements();) {
    Applet current = (Applet)(e.nextElement());
  current.sendMessage();
}
```

The getApplets() method returns an Enumeration object with a list of the applets on the page. Iterating over the Enumeration object in this way enables you to access each element in the Enumeration in turn.

If you want to call a method in a specific applet, it's slightly more complicated. To do this, you give your applets a name and then refer to them by name inside the body of code for that applet.

To give an applet a name, use the NAME parameter in your HTML file:

```
<P>This applet sends information:
<APPLET CODE="MyApplet.class" WIDTH=100 HEIGHT=150
    NAME="sender"> </APPLET>
<P>This applet receives information from the sender:
<APPLET CODE="MyApplet.class" WIDTH=100 HEIGHT=150
    NAME="receiver"> </APPLET>
```

To get a reference to another applet on the same page, use the getApplet() method from the applet context with the name of that applet. This gives you a reference to the applet of that name. You can then refer to that applet as if it were just another object: call methods, set its instance variables, and so on:

```
// get ahold of the receiver applet
Applet receiver = getAppletContext().getApplet("receiver");
// tell it to update itself.
reciever.update(text, value);
```

In this example, you use the getApplet() method to get a reference to the applet with the name receiver. Given that reference, you can then call methods in that applet as if it were just another object in your own environment. Here, for example, if both applets have an update() method, you can tell receiver to update itself by using the information the current applet has.

Naming your applets and then referring to them by using the methods described in this section enables your applets to communicate and stay in sync with each other, providing uniform behavior for all the applets on your page.

Summary

Congratulations! Take a deep breath—you're finished with Week 2. This week has been full of useful information about creating applets and using the Java AWT classes to display, draw, animate, process input, and create fully fledged interfaces in your applets.

Today, you finished exploring applets and the AWT by learning about three concepts.

First, you learned about windows, frames, menus, and dialogs, which enable you to create a framework for your applets—or enable your Java applications to take advantage of applet features.

Second, you had a brief introduction to Java networking through some of the classes in the java.net package. Applet networking includes things as simple as pointing the browser to another page from inside your applet, but can also include retrieving files from the Web by using standard Web protocols (http, ftp, and so on). For more advanced networking capabilities, Java provides basic socket interfaces that can be used to implement many basic network-oriented applets—client-server interactions, chat sessions, and so on.

Finally, you finished up with the tidbits—small features of the Java AWT and of applets that didn't fit anywhere else, including showStatus(), producing information for your applet, and communicating between multiple applets on a single page.

Questions and Answers

Q When I create popup windows, they all show up with this big red bar that says `Warning: applet window`. What does this mean?

A The warning is to tell you (and the users of your applet) that the window being displayed was generated by an applet, and not by the browser itself. This is a security feature to keep an applet programmer from popping up a window that masquerades as a browser window and, for example, asks users for their passwords.

There's nothing you can do to hide or obscure the warning.

The current release of Roaster does not display this warning, but it will be implemented in a future version.

Q What good is having a file dialog box if you can't read or write files from the local file system?

A Applets can't necessarily read or write from the local file system, but because you can use AWT components in Java applications as well as applets, the file dialog box is very useful for that purpose.

Q How can I mimic an HTML form submission in a Java applet?

A Currently, applets make it difficult to do this. The best (and easiest) way is to use GET notation to get the browser to submit the form contents for you.

HTML forms can be submitted in two ways: by using the GET request or by using POST. If you use GET, your form information is encoded in the URL itself, something like this:

```
http://www.blah.com/cgi-bin/myscript?foo=1&bar=2&name=Laura
```

Because the form input is encoded in the URL, you can write a Java applet to mimic a form, get input from the user, and then construct a new URL object with the form data included on the end. Then just pass that URL to the browser by using `getAppletContext().showDocument()`, and the browser will submit the form results itself. For simple forms, this is all you need.

Q How can I do POST form submissions?

A You'll have to mimic what a browser does to send forms using POST: open a socket to the server and send the data, which looks something like this (the exact format is determined by the HTTP protocol; this is only a subset of it):

```
POST /cgi-bin/mailto.cgi HTTP/1.0
Content-type: application/x-www-form-urlencoded
Content-length: 36

{your encoded form data here}
```

If you've done it right, you get the CGI form output back from the server. It's then up to your applet to handle that output properly. Note that if the output is in HTML, there really isn't a way to pass that output to the browser that is running your applet. If you get back a URL, however, you can redirect the browser to that URL.

Q: It looks like the `openStream()` method and the `Socket` classes both implement TCP sockets. Does Java support UDP (datagram) sockets?

A: The JDK 1.0 provides two classes, `DatagramSocket` and `DaragramPacket`, which implement UDP sockets. The `DatagramSocket` class operates similarly to the `Socket` class. Use instances of `DatagramPacket` for each packet you send or receive over the socket.

See the API documentation for the java.net package for more information.

Q: I've seen something called applet properties in the Java documentation. What are properties?

A: Properties are features of applets and the applet environments that you can test for and make decisions in your code based on their values. At the time this book is being written, properties are still very new. See the latest Java documentation for more information on properties.

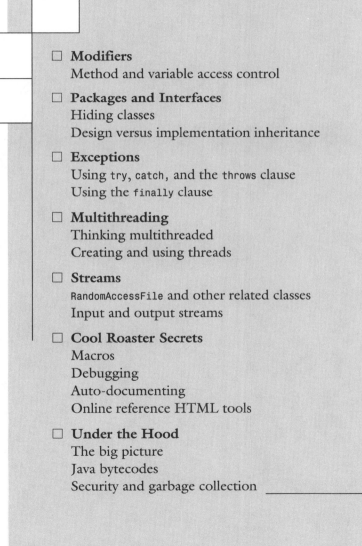

Week 3

- ☐ **Modifiers**
  Method and variable access control

- ☐ **Packages and Interfaces**
  Hiding classes
  Design versus implementation inheritance

- ☐ **Exceptions**
  Using try, catch, and the throws clause
  Using the finally clause

- ☐ **Multithreading**
  Thinking multithreaded
  Creating and using threads

- ☐ **Streams**
  RandomAccessFile and other related classes
  Input and output streams

- ☐ **Cool Roaster Secrets**
  Macros
  Debugging
  Auto-documenting
  Online reference HTML tools

- ☐ **Under the Hood**
  The big picture
  Java bytecodes
  Security and garbage collection

Modifiers

by Charles L. Perkins with Timothy Webster

After programming in Java for a while, you'll discover that making all your classes, methods, and variables public can begin to seem oversimplistic—just what are those modifiers for, if you're not going to use them? The larger your program becomes, and the more you reuse your classes for new projects, the more you will want some sort of control over their visibility. One of the large-scale solutions to this problem, packages, must wait until tomorrow, but today you'll explore what you can do within a class.

Today, you'll learn how to create and use the following:

☐ Methods and variables that control their access by other classes

☐ Class variables and methods

☐ Constant variables, classes that cannot be subclassed, and methods that cannot be overridden

☐ Abstract classes and methods

Modifiers are prefixes that can be applied in various combinations to the methods and variables within a class and, some, to the class itself.

There is a long and varied list of modifiers. The order of modifiers is irrelevant to their meaning—your order can vary and is really a matter of taste. Pick a style and then be consistent with it throughout all your classes. Here is the recommended order:

```
<access> static abstract synchronized <unusual> final native
```

where `<access>` can be public, private protected, or private, and `<unusual>` includes volatile and transient.

NOTE After the alpha release, `threadsafe` has been replaced by `volatile`. Both have to do with multithreading; no more will be said about them here (see Day 18). `transient` is a special modifier used to declare a variable to be outside the persistent part of an object. This makes persistent object storage systems easier to implement in Java, and though the compiler supports it, it is not used by the current Java system.

All the modifiers are essentially optional; none have to appear in a declaration. Good style suggests adding as many as are needed to best describe the intended use of, and restrictions on, what you're declaring. In some special situations (inside an interface, for example, as described tomorrow), certain modifiers are implicitly defined for you, and you needn't type them—they will be assumed to be there.

The synchronized modifier is covered on Day 18; it has to do with multithreaded methods. The `native` modifier specifies that a method is implemented in the native language of your computer (usually C), rather than in Java; the use of native methods is not yet supported in either Roaster or Sun's JDK for the Mac. How <access> modifiers apply to classes is covered tomorrow.

Method and Variable Access Control

Access control is about controlling visibility. When a method or variable is visible to another class, its methods can reference (call or modify) that method or variable. To "protect" a method or variable from such references, you use the four levels of visibility described in the next sections. Each, in turn, is more restrictive, and thus provides more protection than the one before it.

The Four Ps of Protection

Learning your four Ps (`public`, `package`, `private protected`, and `private`) comes down to understanding the fundamental relationships that a method or variable within a class can have to the other classes in the system.

public

Because any class is an island unto itself, the first of these relationships builds on the distinction between the inside and the outside of the class. Any method or variable is visible to the class in which it is defined, but what if you want to make it visible to all the classes outside this class?

The answer is obvious: simply declare the method or variable to have `public` access. Almost every method and variable defined in the rest of this book has been declared, for simplicity's sake, `public`. When you use any of the examples provided in your own code, you'll probably decide to restrict this access further. Because you're just learning now, it's not a bad idea to begin with the widest possible access you can imagine and then narrow it down as you gain design experience, until the access that each of your variables and methods should have becomes second nature. Here are some examples of `public` declarations:

```
public class  APublicClass {
    public int      aPublicInt;
    public String  aPublicString;

    public float    aPublicMethod() {
        . . .
    }
}
```

NOTE

> The two (or more) spaces after the prefix of modifiers and type in these declarations are intentional. They make finding the variable or method name within each line a little easier. Further in the book, you'll see that the type and the name are sometimes separately lined up in a column to make it even more evident what is what. When you get enough modifiers on a line, you'll begin to appreciate these small touches.

A variable or method with `public` access has the widest possible visibility. Anyone can see it. Anyone can use it. Of course, this may not always be what you want—which brings us to the next level of protection.

package

In C, there is the notion of hiding a name so that only the functions within a given source file can see it. In Java, source files are replaced by the more explicit notion of packages, which can group classes (you learn about these tomorrow). For now, all you need to know is that the relationship you want to support is of a class to its fellow implementors of one piece of a system, library, or program (or to any other grouping of related classes). This defines the next level of increased protection and narrowed visibility.

Due to an idiosyncrasy of the Java language, this next level of access has no precise name. It is indicated by the lack of any access modifier in a declaration. Historically, it has been called various suggestive names, including "friendly" and "package." The latter usage seems most appropriate and is the one used here. Perhaps in a later release of the system, it will be possible to say `package` explicitly, but for now it is simply the default protection when none has been specified.

NOTE Why would anyone want to make more typing for themselves and explicitly say package? It is a matter of consistency and clarity. If you have a pattern of declarations with varying access modifier prefixes, you may always want the modifier to be stated explicitly, both for the reader's benefit and because, in some contexts, different "default" levels of protection are being assumed, and you want the compiler to notice your intentions and warn you of any conflicts.

Most of the declarations you've seen in the past two weeks have used this default level of protection. Here's a reminder of what they look like:

```
public class  ALessPublicClass {
    int     aPackageInt    = 2;
    String  aPackageString = "a 1 and a ";

    float   aPackageMethod() {    // no access modifier means "package"
        . . .
    }
}

public class  AClassInTheSamePackage {
    public void   testUse() {
        ALessPublicClass  aLPC = new ALessPublicClass();

        System.out.println(aLPC.aPackageString + aLPC.aPackageInt);
        aLPC.aPackageMethod();           // all of these are A.O.K.
    }
}
```

NOTE If a class from any other package tried to access aLPC the way that `AClassInTheSame-Package` does in this example, it would generate compile-time errors. (You'll learn how to create such classes tomorrow.)

Why was package made a default? When you're designing a large system and you partition your classes into work groups to implement smaller pieces of that system, the classes often need to share a lot more with one another than with the outside world. The need for this level of sharing is common enough that it was made the default level of protection.

What if you have some details of your implementation that you don't want to share with these "friends"? The answer to this question leads us naturally to the next level of protection.

private protected

The third relationship is between a class and its present and future subclasses. These subclasses are much closer to a parent class than to any other "outside" classes for the following reasons:

- ☐ Subclasses are usually more intimately aware of the internals of a parent class.

- ☐ Subclasses are often written by you or by someone to whom you've given your source code.

- ☐ Subclasses frequently need to modify or enhance the representation of the data within a parent class.

No one else is permitted this level of access; they must be content with the public face that the class presents.

To support the level of intimacy reserved for subclasses, modern programming languages have invented an intermediate level of access between the previous two levels and full privacy. This level gives more protection and narrows visibility still further, but still allows subclasses full access. In Java, this level of protection is called, appropriately enough, `private protected`:

```
public class  AProtectedClassSubclass {
    private protected int     aProtectedInt    = 4;
    private protected String  aProtectedString = "and a 3 and a ";

    private protected float   aProtectedMethod() {
        . . .
    }
}

public class  AProtectedClassSubclass extends AProtectedClassSubclass {
    public void  testUse() {
        AProtectedClassSubclass  aPCs = new AProtectedClassSubclass();

        System.out.println(aPCs.aProtectedString + aPCs.aProtectedInt);
        aPCs.aProtectedMethod();              // all of these are A.O.K.
    }
}

public class  AnyClassInTheSamePackage {
    public void  testUse() {
        AProtectedClassSubclass  aPCs = new AProtectedClassSubclass();

        System.out.println(aPCs.aProtectedString + aPCs.aProtectedInt);
        aPCs.aProtectedMethod();              // NONE of these are legal
    }
}
```

Even though `AnyClassInTheSamePackage` is in the same package as `AProtectedClass`, it is not a subclass of it (it's a subclass of `Object`). Only subclasses are allowed to see, and use, `private protected` variables and methods.

The declarations in `AProtectedClassSubclass` are prefixed by `private protected` because as of version 1.0 of the Java API, adding `private` is required to get the behavior described here. `protected` alone allows both subclasses and classes in the same package access, thus providing a combined (fifth) level of protection.

One of the most striking examples of the need for this special level of access is when you are supporting a public abstraction with your class. As far as the outside world is concerned, you have a simple, public interface (via methods) to whatever abstraction you've built for your users. A more complex representation, and the implementation that depends on it, is hidden inside. When subclasses extend and modify this representation, or even just your implementation of it, they need to get to the underlying, concrete representation and not simply to the abstraction:

```
public class  SortedList {
    private protected BinaryTree  theBinaryTree;

    . . .

    public Object[]  theList() {
        return theBinaryTree.asArray();
    }

    public void      add(Object o) {
        theBinaryTree.addObject(o);
    }
}

public class  InsertSortedList extends SortedList {
    public void      insert(Object o, int position) {
        theBinaryTree.insertObject(o,     position);
    }
}
```

Without being able to access `theBinaryTree` directly, the `insert()` method has to get the list as an array of `Object`s, via the public method `theList()`, allocate a new, bigger array, and insert the new object by hand. By "seeing" that its parent is using a `BinaryTree` to implement the sorted list, it can call upon `BinaryTree`'s built-in method `insertObject()` to get the job done.

Some languages, such as CLU, have experimented with more explicit ways of "raising" and "lowering" your level of abstraction to solve this same problem in a more general way. In Java, `private protected` solves only a part of the problem, by enabling you to separate the concrete from the abstract; the rest is up to you.

private

The final relationship comes full circle, back to the distinction between the inside and outside of the class. private is the most narrowly visible, highest level of protection that you can get—the diametric opposite of public. private methods and variables cannot be seen by any class other than the one in which they are defined:

```
public class  APrivateClass {
    private int     aPrivateInt;
    private String  aPrivateString;

    private float   aPrivateMethod() {
        . . .
    }
}
```

This might seem extremely restrictive, but it is, in fact, a commonly used level of protection. Any private data, internal state, or representations unique to your implementation—anything that shouldn't be directly shared with subclasses—is private. Remember that an an object's primary job is to encapsulate its data—to hide it from the world's sight and limit its manipulation. The best way to do that is to make as much data as private as possible. Your methods can always be less restrictive, as you'll see next, but keeping a tight rein on your internal representation is important. It separates design from implementation, minimizes the amount of information one class needs to know about another to get its job done, and reduces the extent of the code changes you will need when your representation changes.

The Conventions of Instance Variable Access

A good rule of thumb is that unless an instance variable is constant (you'll soon see how to specify this), it should almost certainly be private. If you don't do this, you have the following problem:

```
public class  AFoolishClass {
    public String  aUsefulString;
    . . . // set up the useful value of the string
}
```

This class may have thought of setting up aUsefulString for the use of other classes, expecting them to (only) read it. Because it isn't private, however, they can say:

```
AFoolishClass  aFC = new AFoolishClass();

aFC.aUsefulString = "oops!";
```

Because there is no way to specify separately the level of protection for reading from and writing to instance variables, they should almost always be private.

NOTE The careful reader may notice that this rule is violated in many examples in this book. Most of these were just for clarity's sake and to make the examples shorter and pithier. (You'll see soon that it takes more space to do the right thing.) One use cannot be avoided: the `System.out.print()` calls scattered throughout the book must use the `public` variable `out` directly. You cannot change this `final` system class (which you might have written differently). You can imagine the disastrous results if anyone accidentally modifies the contents of this (global) `public` variable!

Accessor Methods

If instance variables are `private`, how do you give access to them to the outside world? The answer is to write "accessor" methods:

```
public class  ACorrectClass {
    private    String  aUsefulString;

    public     String  aUsefulString() {              // "get" the value
        return aUsefulString;
    }

    private protected void    aUsefulString(String s) {    // "set" the value
        aUsefulString = s;
    }
}
```

Using methods to access an instance variable is one of the most frequently used idioms in object-oriented programs. Applying it liberally throughout all your classes repays you many times over with more robust and reusable programs. Notice how separating the reading and writing of the instance variable enables you to specify a `public` method to return its value and a `private protected` method to set it. This is often a useful pattern of protections, because everyone probably needs to be able to ask for the value, but only you (and your subclasses) should be able to change it. If it is a particularly private piece of data, you could make its "set" method `private` and its "get" method `private protected`, or any other combination that suits the data's sensitivity to the light of the outside world.

NOTE One of the alternative conventions for the naming of accessor methods is to prepend the variable name with the prefixes `get` and `set`. Besides making you type more—for a little less clarity—this style forces you (by the capitalization conventions of Java) to write method names such as `setAnnoyingFirstCapitalLetter()`. All this is, of course, a matter of taste—just be consistent in using whatever convention you adopt.

Whenever you want to append to your own instance variable, try writing this:

```
aUsefulString(aUsefulString() + " some appended text");
```

Just like someone outside the class, you're using accessor methods to change aUsefulString. Why do this?

You protected the variable in the first place so that changes to your representation would not affect the use of your class by others, but it still will affect the use of your class by you! As in the abstract versus concrete discussion earlier, you should be protected from knowing too much about your own representation, except in those few places that actually need to know about it. Then, if you must change something about aUsefulString, it will not affect every use of that variable in your class (as it would without accessor methods); rather, it affects only the implementations of its accessor.

There's a powerful side effect of maintaining this level of indirection when accessing your own instance variables. If, at some later date, some special code needs to be performed each time aUsefulString is accessed, you can put that code in one place, and all the other methods in your class (and in everyone else's) will correctly call that special code. Here's an example:

```
private protected void  aUsefulString(String s) {   // the "set" method
    aUsefulString = s;
    performSomeImportantBookkeepingOn(s);
}
```

It might seem a little difficult to get used to saying this:

```
x(12 + 5 * x());
```

... rather than this:

```
x = 12 + 5 * x;
```

... but the minor inconvenience will reward you with a rosy future of reusability and easy maintenance.

Class Variables and Methods

What if you want to create a shared variable that all your instances can see and use? If you use an instance variable, each instance has its own copy of the variable, defeating its whole purpose. If you place it in the class itself, however, there is only one copy, and all the instances of the class share it. This is called a class variable:

```
public class  Circle {
    public static float  pi = 3.14159265F;

    public float  area(float r) {
        return  pi * r * r;
    }
}
```

Because of its historical ties to C, Java uses the word `static` to declare class variables and methods. Whenever you see the word `static`, remember to think "class."

Instances can refer to their own class's variables as though they were instance variables, like so:

```
Circle c = new Circle();
float x  = c.pi;
```

Because `pi` is declared `public`, methods in other classes can also refer to `pi`:

```
float  circumference = 2 * Circle.pi * r;
```

NOTE Instances of `Circle` can also use this form of access. In most cases, for clarity, this is the preferred form, even for instances, where `Circle` is implied and need not be written out. It clarifies that a class variable is being used, and helps the reader to know instantly where it's used and that the variable is global to all instances. This may seem pedantic, but if you try it yourself, you'll see that it can make things clearer.

By the way, if you might change your mind later about how a class variable is accessed, created, and so forth, you should create instance (or even class) accessor methods to hide any uses of it from these changes.

Class methods are defined analogously. They can be accessed in the same two ways by instances of their class, but only via the full class name by instances of other classes. Here's a class that defines class methods to help it count its own instances:

```
public class  InstanceCounter {
    private    static int  instanceCount = 0;   // a class variable

    private protected static int  instanceCount() {    // a class method
        return instanceCount;
    }
```

```
    private   static void  incrementCount() {
        ++instanceCount;
    }

    InstanceCounter() {
        InstanceCounter.incrementCount();
    }
}
```

In this example, an explicit use of the class name calls the method `incrementCount()`. Though this may seem verbose, in a larger program it immediately tells the reader which object (the class, rather than the instance) is expected to handle the method. This is especially useful if the reader needs to find where that method is declared in a large class that places all its class methods at the top (the recommended practice, by the way).

Note the initialization of `instanceCount` to 0. Just as an instance variable is initialized when its instance is created, a class variable is initialized when its class is created. This class initialization happens essentially before anything else can happen to that class, or its instances, so the class in the example will work as planned.

Finally, the conventions you learned for accessing an instance variable are applied in this example to access a class variable. The accessor methods are therefore class methods. (There is no "set" method here, just an increment method, because no one is allowed to set `instanceCount` directly.) Note that only subclasses are allowed to ask what the `instanceCount` is, because that is a (relatively) intimate detail. Here's a test of `InstanceCounter` in action:

```
public class  InstanceCounterTester extends InstanceCounter {
    public static void  main(String args[]) {
        for (int i = 0;  i < 10;  ++i)
            new InstanceCounter();
        System.out.println("made " + InstanceCounter.instanceCount());
    }
}
```

Not shockingly, this example prints the following:

```
made 10
```

The `final` Modifier

Although it's not the final modifier discussed, the `final` modifier is very versatile:

☐ When the `final` modifier is applied to a class, it means that the class cannot be subclassed.

☐ When it is applied to a variable, it means that the variable is constant.

☐ When it is applied to a method, it means that the method cannot be overridden by subclasses.

`final` Classes

Here's a `final` class declaration:

```
public final class  AFinalClass {
    . . .
}
```

You declare a class `final` for only two reasons. The first is security. You expect to use its instances as unforgeable capabilities, and you don't want anyone else to be able to subclass and create new and different instances of them. The second is efficiency. You want to count on instances of only that one class (and no subclasses) being around in the system so that you can optimize for them.

NOTE

The Java class library uses `final` classes extensively. You can flip through the class hierarchy diagrams in Appendix B to see them (`final` classes are shaded darker than `public` classes). Examples of the first reason to use `final` are the classes `java.lang.System` and, from the package `java.net`, `InetAddress` and `Socket`. A good example of the use of `final` for efficiency's sake is `java.lang.String`. Strings are so common in Java, and so central to it, that the run-time handles them specially.

It will be a rare event for you to create a `final` class yourself, although you'll have plenty of opportunity to be upset at certain system classes being `final` (thus making extending them annoyingly difficult). Such is the price of security and efficiency. Let's hope that efficiency will be less of an issue soon, and some of these classes will become `public` once again.

`final` Variables

To declare constants in Java, use `final` variables:

```
public class  AnotherFinalClass {
    public static final int     aConstantInt    = 123;
    public          final String aConstantString = "Hello world!";
}
```

NOTE The unusual spacing in the last line of the example makes it clearer that the top variable is a class variable and the bottom isn't, but that both are `public` and `final`.

`final` class and instance variables can be used in expressions just like normal class and instance variables, but they cannot be modified. As a result, `final` variables must be given their (constant) value at the time of declaration. These variables function like a better, typed version of the `#define` constants of C. Classes can provide useful constants to other classes via `final` class variables such as the one discussed previously. Other classes reference them just as before: `AnotherFinalClass.aConstantInt`.

Local variables (those inside blocks of code surrounded by braces, for example, in `while` or `for` loops) can't be declared `final`. (This would be just a convenience, really, because `final` instance variables work almost as well in this case.) In fact, local variables can have no modifiers in front of them at all:

```
{
    int  aLocalVariable;    // I'm so sad without my modifiers...
    . . .
}
```

`final` Methods

Here's an example of using `final` methods:

```
public class  MyPenultimateFinalClass {
    public static final void  aUniqueAndReallyUsefulMethod() {
        . . .
    }

    public        final void  noOneGetsToDoThisButMe() {
        . . .
    }
}
```

`final` methods cannot be overridden by subclasses. It is a rare thing that a method truly wants to declare itself the final word on its own implementation, so why does this modifier apply to methods?

The answer is efficiency. If you declare a method `final`, the compiler can then "inline" it right in the middle of methods that call it, because it "knows" that no one else can ever subclass and override the method to change its meaning. Although you might not use `final` right away when writing a class, as you tune the system later, you may discover that a few methods have to be `final` to make your class fast enough. Almost all your methods will be fine, however, just as they are.

The Java class library declares a lot of commonly used methods final so that you'll benefit from the speed-up. In the case of classes that are already final, this makes perfect sense and is a wise choice. The few final methods declared in non-final classes will annoy you—your subclasses can no longer override them. When efficiency becomes less of an issue for the Java environment, many of these final methods can be "unfrozen" again, restoring this lost flexibility to the system.

NOTE

private methods are effectively final, as are all methods declared in a final class. Marking these latter methods final (as the Java library sometimes does) is legal, but redundant; the compiler already treats them as final.

It's possible to use final methods for some of the same security reasons you use final classes, but it's a much rarer event.

If you use accessor methods often—and you should—and you are worried about efficiency, consider this rewrite of ACorrectClass that's much faster:

```
public class  ACorrectFinalClass {
    private           String  aUsefulString;

    public    final String  aUsefulString() {    // now faster to use
        return aUsefulString;
    }

    private protected final void    aUsefulString(String s) { // also faster
        aUsefulString = s;
    }
}
```

NOTE

Future Java compilers will almost certainly be smart enough to "in-line" simple methods automatically, so you probably won't need to use final in such cases for much longer.

abstract Methods and Classes

Whenever you arrange classes into an inheritance hierarchy, the presumption is that "higher" classes are more abstract and general, whereas "lower" subclasses are more concrete and specific. Often, as you design a set of classes, you factor out common design and implementation into a shared superclass. If the primary reason that a superclass exists is to act as this common, shared repository of methods and properties, and if only its subclasses expect to be used, that superclass is called an abstract class.

abstract classes can create no instances, but they can contain anything a normal class can contain and, in addition, are allowed to prefix any of their methods with the modifier abstract. Non-abstract classes are not allowed to use this modifier; using it on even one of your methods requires that the whole class that contains it be declared abstract. Here's an example:

```
public abstract class  MyFirstAbstractClass {
    int  anInstanceVariable;

    public abstract int aMethodMyNonAbstractSubclassesMustImplement();

    public void  doSomething() {
        . . .    // a normal method
    }
}

public class  AConcreteSubClass extends MyFirstAbstractClass {
    public int  aMethodMyNonAbstractSubclassesMustImplement() {
        . . .    // we *must* implement this method
    }
}
```

... and some attempted uses of these classes:

```
Object  a = new MyFirstAbstractClass();    // illegal, is abstract
Object  c = new AConcreteSubClass();       // OK, a concrete subclass
```

Notice that abstract methods need no implementation; it is required that non-abstract subclasses provide an implementation. The abstract class simply provides the template for the methods, which are implemented by others later. In fact, in the Java class library, there are several abstract classes that have no documented sub-classes in the system, but simply provide a base from which you can subclass in your own programs. If you look at the diagrams in Appendix B, abstract classes are shaded even darker than final classes and are quite common in the library.

Using an abstract class to embody a pure design—that is, nothing but abstract methods—is better accomplished in Java by using an interface (discussed tomorrow). Whenever a design calls for an abstraction that includes instance state and/or a partial implementation, however, an abstract class is your only choice.

In previous object-oriented languages, abstract classes were simply a convention. They proved so valuable that Java supports them not only in the form described here, but also in the purer, richer form of interfaces, which will be described tomorrow.

Summary

Today, you learned how variables and methods can control their visibility and access by other classes via the four Ps of protection: public, package, private protected, and private. You also learned that, although instance variables are most often declared private, declaring accessor methods enables you to control the reading and writing of them separately. Protection levels enable you, for example, to separate cleanly your public abstractions from their concrete representations.

You also learned how to create class variables and methods, which are associated with the class itself, and how to declare final variables, methods, and classes to represent constants, fast or secure methods, and classes, respectively.

Finally, you discovered how to declare and use abstract classes, which cannot be instantiated, and abstract methods, which have no implementation and must be overridden in subclasses. Together, they provide a template for subclasses to fill in and act as a variant of the powerful interfaces of Java that you'll study tomorrow.

Questions and Answers

Q Why are there so many different levels of protection in Java?

A Each level of protection, or visibility, provides a different view of your class to the outside world. One view is tailored for everyone, one for classes in your own package, another for your class and its subclasses only, and the final one for just within your class. Each is a logically well-defined and useful separation that Java supports directly in the language (as opposed to, for example, accessor methods, which are a convention you must follow).

Q Won't using accessor methods everywhere slow down my Java code?

A Not always. Soon, Java compilers will be smart enough to make them fast automatically, but if you're concerned about speed, you can always declare accessor methods to be final, and they'll be just as fast as direct instance variable accesses.

Q Are class (static) methods inherited just like instance methods?

A Yes and no. The compiler enables you to inherit them, but according to one of the oddest clauses in the =current language specifications, static (class) methods are now final by default. How, then, can you ever declare a non-final class method? The answer is that you can't! Inheritance of class methods is not allowed, breaking the symmetry with instance methods. Because this goes against a part of Java's philosophy (of making everything as simple as possible) perhaps it will be reversed in a later release.

Q Based on what I've learned, it seems like final abstract or private abstract methods or classes don't make sense. Are they legal?

A Nope, they're compile-time errors, as you have guessed. To be useful, abstract methods must be overridden, and abstract classes must be subclassed, but neither of those two operations would be legal if they were also private or final.

Q What about static transient or final transient?

A Those are also compile-time errors. Because a "transient" part of an object's state is assumed to be changing within each instance, it cannot be static or final. This restriction matters only in the future, though, when transient is actually used by Java.

Packages and Interfaces

by Charles L. Perkins with Timothy Webster

When you examine a new language feature, you should ask yourself two questions:

1. How can I use it to better organize the methods and classes of my Java program?

2. How can I use it while writing the Java code in my methods?

The first is often called programming in the large, and the second, programming in the small. Bill Joy, a founder of Sun Microsystems, likes to say that Java feels like C when programming in the small and like SmallTalk when programming in the large. What he means is that Java is familiar and powerful like any C-like language while you're coding, but has the extensibility and expressive power of a pure object-oriented language like SmallTalk while you're designing.

The separation of designing from coding was one of the most fundamental advances in programming in the past few decades, and object-oriented languages such as Java implement a strong form of this separation. The first part of this separation has already been described on previous days: when you develop a Java program, first you design the classes and decide on the relationships between these classes, and then you implement the Java code needed for each of the methods in your design. If you are careful enough with both these processes, you can change your mind about aspects of the design without affecting anything but small, local pieces of your Java code, and you can change the implementation of any method without affecting the rest of the design.

As you begin to explore more advanced Java programming, however, you'll find that this simple model becomes too limiting. Today, you'll explore these limitations, for programming in the large and in the small, to motivate the need for packages and interfaces. Let's start with packages.

Packages

Packages are Java's way of doing large-scale design and organization. They are used to both categorize and group classes. Let's explore why you might need to use packages.

Programming in the Large

When you begin to develop Java programs that use a large number of classes, you will quickly discover some limitations in the model presented thus far for designing and building them.

For one thing, as the number of classes grows, the likelihood of your wanting to reuse the short, simple name of some class increases. If you use classes that you've built in the past or that someone else has built for you (such as the classes in the Java library), you may not remember—or even know—that these class names are in conflict. Being able to "hide" a class inside a package becomes useful.

Here's a simple example of the creation of a package in a Java source file:

```
package  myFirstPackage;

public class  MyPublicClass extends ItsSuperclass {
    . . .
}
```

NOTE If a package statement appears in a Java source file, it must be the first thing in that file (except for comments and white space, of course).

Notice that when you compile a class that's part of a package with Roaster, the package that the class belongs to is added as the "subhead" of the package in the project window. In Figure 16.1, you can see that MyPublicClass belongs to myFirstPackage.

You first declare the name of the package by using a package statement. Then you define a class, just as you would normally. That class, and any other classes also declared inside this same package name, are grouped together. (These other classes are usually located in other, separate source files.)

Packages can be further organized into a hierarchy somewhat analogous to the inheritance hierarchy, where each "level" usually represents a smaller, more specific grouping of classes. The Java class library itself is organized along these lines (see the diagrams in Appendix B). The top level is called java; the next level includes names such as io, net, util, and awt. The last has an even lower level, which includes the package image. The ColorModel class, located in the package image, can be uniquely referred to anywhere in your Java code as java.awt.image.ColorModel.

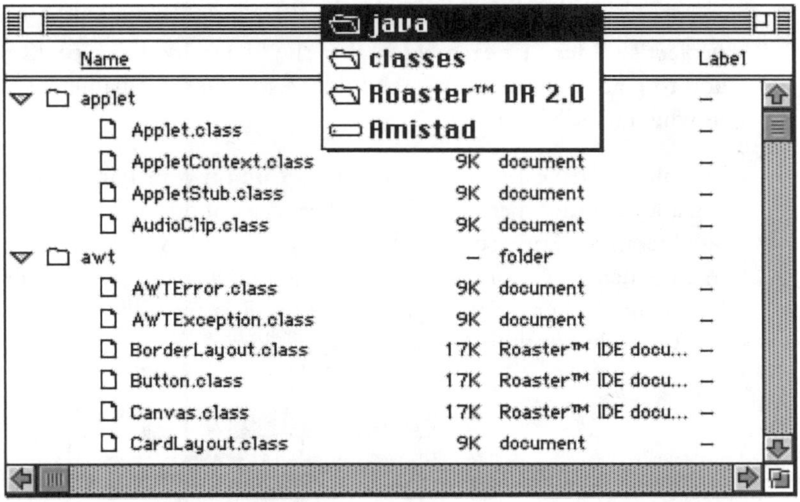

Figure 16.1   *The Roaster project window identifies the package of each class.*

NOTE

By convention, the first level of the hierarchy specifies the (globally unique) name of the company that developed the Java package(s). For example, Sun Microsystem's classes, which are not part of the standard Java environment, all begin with the prefix sun. The standard package, java, is an exception to this rule because it is so fundamental and because it might someday be implemented by multiple companies.

Sun has specified a more formal procedure for package naming to be followed in the future. The top-level package name space now reserves, for the use of this procedure, all the uppercase abbreviations used for top-level domains on the Internet (EDU, COM, GOV, FR, US, and so on). These reserved names form the first part of all new package names, which are prefixed by a reversed version of your domain name. By this procedure, the sun packages would be called COM.sun. If you're further down in your company's or university's domain tree, you can keep reversing to your heart's content: EDU.harvard.cs.projects.ai.learning.myPackage. Because domain names are already guaranteed to be unique globally, this nicely solves that thorny problem, and as a bonus, the applets and packages from the potentially millions of Java programmers out there will automatically be stored into a growing hierarchy below your classes directory, giving you a way to find and categorize them all in a comprehensible manner.

Because each Java class should be located in a separate source file, the grouping of classes provided by a hierarchy of packages is analogous to the grouping of files into a hierarchy of directories on your file system. The Java compiler reinforces this analogy by requiring you to store your packaged classes in a folder hierarchy inside your project's folder that exactly matches the hierarchy of the packages you have created, and to place each class into the folder with the same name (and level) as the package in which it's defined.

You already have one such hierarchy set up on your hard disk: the Roaster folder includes a folder hierarchy for the Java class library that exactly mirrors the java package hierarchy. For example, the class referenced as java.awt.image.ColorModel is stored in a file named ColorModel.class in the folder image, which in turn is in the folder awt, which is in the folder java inside the Roaster folder. Figure 16.2 shows the Finder's expanded outline view of the java folder.

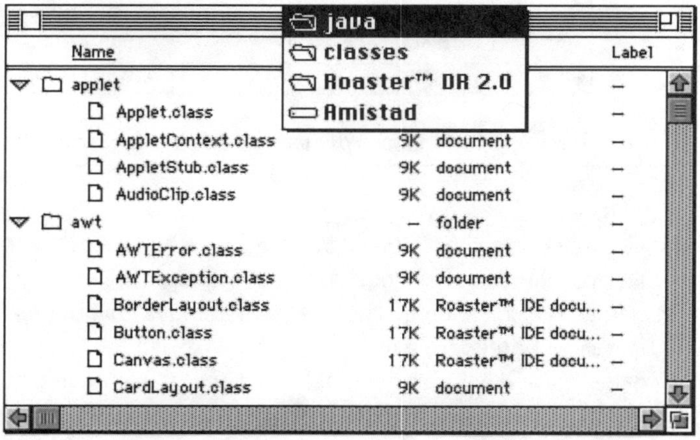

Figure 16.2   *The* java *package's hierarchical structure, mirrored in the organization of folders and files in the Finder.*

In particular, if you have created a package within myFirstPackage called mySecondPackage, by declaring a class...

```
package  myFirstPackage.mySecondPackage;

public class  AnotherPublicClass extends AnotherSuperclass {
    . . .
}
```

... the class file (called AnotherPublicClass.class) must be put in a folder inside the folder mySecondPackage in the folder myFirstPackage in the project's base folder for

Roaster's compiler to find it. When Roaster compiles AnotherPublicClass.java, it puts the resulting class file in the same folder as the source file—no matter where the source file is located, or where the class file should be for other classes to refer to it.

NOTE

This also means that, for today's first example, the source file would be named APublicClass.java and should be stored in the folder myFirstPackage. What happens when, as in earlier examples in the book, classes are defined without a package statement? The compiler places such classes in a default, unnamed package—hence the <default> subhead that appears over your program's name in the Roaster project window.

Roaster's Class Browser Tool

Roaster provides a special tool for navigating the hierarchy of packages and classes. It's called the class browser tool, and you can invoke it with File > New > Class Browser (Command-B).

Like the class tree tool, the class browser is used for visualization and navigation—it doesn't directly affect the code. The browser's three panels show all of the packages in the current project, all of the classes in the selected package, and all of the methods and instance variables in the selected method. The class browser also includes a little source code editor window that displays the definition of the item selected in the members panel.

Figure 16.3 shows how the class browser displays the package and class structure of javaTree.π, a project that includes the entire java.* hierarchy.

The new class browser displays a list of the packages in the leftmost panel. When we choose a package, say, java.awt, and click its name, all of the classes in the java.awt package (and included in the current project) are displayed in the middle panel. If we choose one of java.awt's classes, such as java.awt.polygon, and click its name in the middle panel, the classes' methods and variables appear in the rightmost panel. If we click a method or variable, the code that defines the element appears in the source code window. (By the way, double-clicking in any of these panels jumps to the source code file that defines the label that you double-click.) Figure 16.4 shows this sample navigation, with the method addPoint() selected.

This is an excellent way to get to know the Java source code and, because the source code is very well documented with comments, the browser is a great online reference source to complement the QuickView documentation.

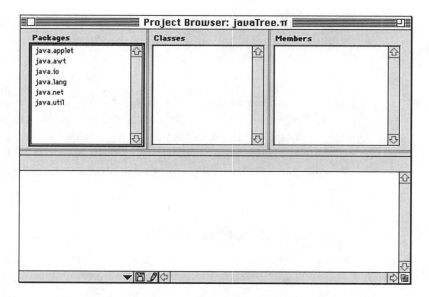

Figure 16.3 *The class browser tool provides an easy way to view the Java source file packages.*

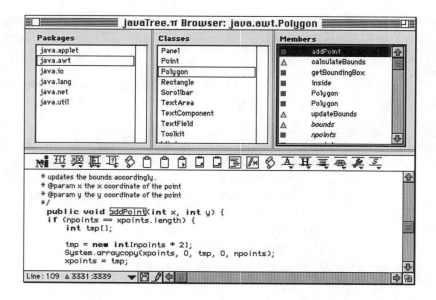

Figure 16.4 *Using the class browser to navigate to* java.awt.Polygon.addPoint().

Programming in the Small

When you refer to a class by name in your Java code, you are using a package. Most of the time you aren't aware of it because many of the most commonly used classes in the system are in a package that the Java compiler automatically imports for you, called `java.lang`. So whenever you saw this, for example...

```
String  aString;
```

... something more interesting than you might have thought was occurring. What if you want to refer to the class you created at the start of this section, the one in the package `myFirstPackage`? If you try this...

```
MyPublicClass  someName;
```

... the compiler complains—the class `MyPublicClass` is not defined in the package `java.lang`. To solve this problem, Java allows any class name to be prefixed by the name of the package in which it was defined to form a unique reference to the class:

```
myFirstPackage.MyPublicClass  someName;
```

> **NOTE**
>
> Recall that by convention, package names tend to begin with a lowercase letter to distinguish them from class names. Thus, for example, in the full name of the built-in `String` class, `java.lang.String`, it's easier to separate visually the package name from the class name.

Suppose you want to use a lot of classes from a package, a package with a long name, or both. You don't want to have to refer to your classes as `that.really.long.package.name.ClassName`. Java enables you to "import" the names of those classes into your program. They then act just as `java.lang` classes do, and you can refer to them without a prefix. For example, to use the really long class name in the last example more easily, you can write the following:

```
import that.really.long.package.name.ClassName;

ClassName  anObject;
// and you can use ClassName directly as many times as you like
```

> **NOTE**
>
> All `import` statements must appear after any `package` statement but before any class definitions. Thus, they are "stuck" at the top of your source file.

What if you want to use several classes from that same package? Here's an attempt from a (soon-to-be-tired) programmer:

```
that.really.long.package.name.ClassOne     first;
that.really.long.package.name.ClassTwo     second;
that.really.long.package.name.ClassThree   andSoOn;
```

Here's one from a more savvy programmer, who knows how to import a whole package of public classes:

```
import that.really.long.package.name.*;
```

```
ClassOne    first;
ClassTwo    second;
ClassThree  andSoOn;
```

If you plan to use a class or a package only a few times in your source file, it's probably not worth importing it. The rule of thumb is to ask yourself: "Does the loss in clarity I'd introduce by referring to just the class name outweigh the convenience of not having to type the extra characters?" If it does, don't use import. Remember that the package name lets the reader know where to find more information about the class right at the place you're using it, rather than at the top of the file, where the import statements are located.

What if you have the following in class A's source file?

```
package  packageA;

public class  ClassName {
    . . .
}

public class  ClassA {
    . . .
}
```

... and in class B's source file you have this:

```
package  packageB;

public class  ClassName {
    . . .
}

public class  ClassB {
    . . .
}
```

Then you write the following, somewhere else:

```
import packageA.*;
import packageB.*;
```

```
ClassName  anObject;         // which ClassName did you mean?
```

There are two possible interpretations for the class you intended, one in `packageA` and one in `packageB`. Because this is ambiguous, what should the poor compiler do? It generates an error, of course, and you have to be more explicit about which one you intended. Here's an example:

```
import packageA.*;
import packageB.*;

packageA.ClassName  anObject;      // now OK
packageB.ClassName  anotherObject; // also OK

ClassA  anAObject;      // was never a problem
ClassB  aBObject;       // ditto
```

NOTE   You may wonder why so many declaration statements appear as examples in today's lesson. Declarations are good examples because they're the simplest possible way of referencing a class name. Any use of a class name (in your `extends` clause, for example, or in `new ClassName()`) obeys the same rules.

Hiding Classes

The astute reader may have noticed that the discussion of importing with an asterisk (`*`) stated that it imported a whole package of `public` classes. Why would you want to have classes of any other kind? Take a look at this:

```
package  collections;

public class  LinkedList {
    private Node  root;

    public  void  add(Object o) {
        root = new Node(o, root);
    }
    . . .
}

class  Node {                      // not public
    private Object  contents;
    private Node    next;

    Node(Object o, Node n) {
        contents = o;
        next     = n;
    }
```

```
    . . .
}
```

The goal of the `LinkedList` class is to provide a set of useful public methods (such as `add()`) to any other classes that might want to use them. These other classes couldn't care less about any support classes `LinkedList` needs to get its job done, and would prefer to not "see" them when using `LinkedList`. In addition, `LinkedList` may feel that the `Node` class is local to its implementation and should not be seen by any other classes.

For methods and variables, this would be addressed by the four Ps of protection discussed yesterday: `private`, `protected`, `package`, and `public`, listed in order of increasing visibility. You've already explored many `public` classes, and because both `private` and `protected` really make sense only when you're inside a class definition, you cannot put them outside of one as part of defining a new class. `LinkedList` might really like to say "only classes in my source file can see this class," but because, by convention, each class is located in a separate source file, this would be a little-needed, over-narrow approach.

Instead, `LinkedList` declares no protection modifier, which is equivalent to saying `package`. Now the class can be seen and used only by other classes in the same package in which it was defined. In this case, it's the `collections` package. You might use `LinkedList` as follows:

```
import collections.*;          // only imports public classes

LinkedList  aLinkedList;
/* Node  n; */             // would generate a compile-time error

aLinkedList.add(new Integer(1138));
aLinkedList.add("THX-");
. . .
```

One of the great powers of hidden classes is that even if you use them to introduce a great deal of complexity into the implementation of some public class, all the complexity is hidden when that class is imported. Thus, creating a good package consists of defining a small, clean set of public classes and methods for other classes to use, and then implementing them by using any number of hidden (package) support classes. You'll see another use for hidden classes later today.

Interfaces

Interfaces, like the abstract classes and methods you saw yesterday, provide templates of behavior that other classes are expected to implement, but they are much more powerful. Let's see why you might need such power.

Programming in the Large

When you first begin to design object-oriented programs, the class hierarchy seems almost miraculous. Within that single tree you can express a hierarchy of numeric types (number, complex, float, rational, integer), many simple to moderately complex relationships between objects and processes in the world, and any number of points along the axis from abstract/general to concrete/specific. After some deeper thought or more complex design experience, this wonderful tree begins to become restrictive. The very power and discipline you've achieved by carefully placing only one copy of each idea somewhere in the tree can come back to haunt you whenever you need to cross-fertilize disparate parts of that tree.

Some languages address these problems by introducing more flexible run-time power, such as the code block and the perform: method of SmallTalk; others choose to provide more complex inheritance hierarchies, such as multiple-inheritance. With the latter complexity comes a host of confusing and error-prone ambiguities and misunderstandings, and with the former, a harder time implementing safety and security and a harder language to explain and teach. Java has chosen to take neither of these paths but, in the spirit of objective-C's protocols, has adopted a separate hierarchy altogether to gain the expressive power needed to loosen the straitjacket.

This new hierarchy is a hierarchy of interfaces. Interfaces are not limited to a single superclass, so they enable a form of multiple-inheritance. But they pass on only method descriptions to their children, not method implementations nor instance variables, which helps to eliminate many of the complexities of full multiple-inheritance.

Interfaces, like classes, are declared in source files, one interface to a file. Like classes, they also are compiled into .class files. In fact, almost everywhere that this book has a class name in any of its examples or discussions, you can substitute an interface name.

Java programmers often say "class" when they actually mean "class or interface." Interfaces complement and extend the power of classes, and the two can be treated almost exactly the same. One of the few differences between them is that an interface cannot be instantiated: new can create only an instance of a class. Here's the declaration of an interface:

```
package  myFirstPackage;

public interface  MyFirstInterface extends Interface1, Interface2, ... {
    . . .
    // all methods in here will be public and abstract
    // all variables will be public, static, and final
}
```

This example is a rewritten version of the first example in today's lesson. It now adds a new public interface to the package myFirstPackage, instead of a new public class. Note that multiple parents can be listed in an interface's extends clause.

Any variables or methods defined in a public interface may accept a limited set of modifiers, and certain modifiers are implicitly prefixed to the variable or method. In the following example, the conditions on modifiers in an interface are listed in the comments. Exactly those modifiers can (optionally) appear, but no others:

```
public interface  MySecondInterface {
    public static final int  theAnswer = 42;  // both lines OK
    public abstract      int  lifeTheUniverseAndEverything();

    long  bingBangCounter = 0;  // OK, becomes public, static, final
    long  ageOfTheUniverse();   // OK, becomes public and abstract

    private protected int  aConstant;  // not OK
    private   int  getAnInt();  // not OK
}
```

Roaster and Interfaces

Remember that mysterious third panel in Roaster's class tree tool from Day 2? That's right—it's the Interface panel, and it shows the interfaces implemented by the currently selected class tree.

If you'd like to play around with this, take a look in the Day 16 folder on the CD-ROM. We've included the snippet of the previous example code in the file AnyClass.π.

As we can see in Figure 16.5, the class tree diagram in Roaster's class tree window shows your project's interfaces in floating boxes that aren't directly attached to the rest of the hierarchy. As an additional visual cue, interfaces are labelled with italic, rather than roman, type.

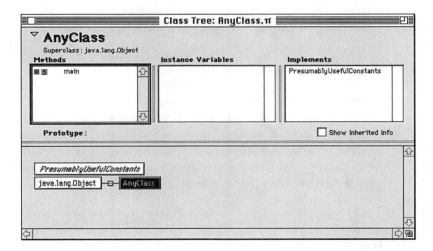

Figure 16.5   *Roaster's class tree tool also displays your project's interfaces.*

Design versus Implementation Revisited

One of the most powerful things interfaces add to Java is the capability of separating design inheritance from implementation inheritance. In the single-class inheritance tree, these two are inextricably bound. Sometimes, you want to be able to describe an interface to a class of objects abstractly, without having to implement a particular implementation of it yourself. You could create an abstract class, such as those described yesterday. In order for a new class to use this type of "interface," however, it has to become a subclass of the abstract class and accept its position in the tree. If this new class also needs to be a subclass of some other class in the tree, for implementation reasons, what could it do? What if it wants to use two such "interfaces" at once? Watch this:

```
class  FirstImplementor extends SomeClass implements    MySecondInterface {
    . . .
}

class  SecondImplementor implements MyFirstInterface,    MySecondInterface {
    . . .
}
```

The first class above is "stuck" in the single inheritance tree just below the class SomeClass but is free to implement an interface as well. The second class is stuck just below Object but has implemented two interfaces (it could have implemented any number of them). Implementing an interface means promising to implement all the methods specified in it.

NOTE Although an abstract class can ignore this strict requirement, and can implement any subset of the methods (or even none of them), all its non-abstract subclasses must still obey it.

Because interfaces are in a separate hierarchy, they can be "mixed in" to the classes in the single inheritance tree, enabling the designer to add an interface anywhere it is needed throughout the tree. The single-inheritance class tree can thus be viewed as containing only the implementation hierarchy; the design hierarchy (full of abstract methods, mostly) is contained in the multiple-inheritance interface tree. This is a powerful way of thinking about the organization of your program, and though it takes a little getting used to, it's also a highly recommended one.

Let's examine one simple example of this separation by creating the new class Orange. Suppose you already have a good implementation of the class Fruit, and an interface, Fruitlike, that represents what Fruits are expected to be able to do. You want an orange to be a fruit, but you also want it to be a spherical object that can be tossed, rotated, and so on. Here's how to express it all:

```
interface  Fruitlike extends Foodlike {
    void  decay();
    void  squish();
    . . .
}

class  Fruit extends Food implements Fruitlike {
    private Color  myColor;
    private int    daysTilIRot;
    . . .
```

```
}

interface  Spherelike {
    void  toss();
    void  rotate();
    . . .
}

class  Orange extends Fruit implements Spherelike {
    . . .  // toss()ing may squish() me (unique to me)
}
```

You'll use this example again later today. For now, notice that class `Orange` doesn't have to say `implements Fruitlike` because, by extending `Fruit`, it already has!

NOTE

The reverse is not true, however. Implementing an interface implies nothing about the implementation hierarchy of a class. By the way, if you had used a more traditional way of designing classes (though not necessarily better), the class `Fruit` would be the interface description, as well as being the implementation.

One of the nice things about this structure is that you can change your mind about what class `Orange` extends (if a really great `Sphere` class is suddenly implemented, for example), yet class `Orange` will still understand the same two interfaces:

```
class  Sphere implements Spherelike {   // extends Object
    private float  radius;
    . . .
}

class  Orange extends Sphere implements Fruitlike {
    . . .      // users of Orange never need know about the change!
}
```

The canonical use of the "mix-in" capability of interfaces is to allow several classes, scattered across the single-inheritance tree, to implement the same set of methods (or even just one). Although these classes share a common superclass (at worst, Object), it is likely that below this common parent are many subclasses that are not interested in this set of methods. Adding the methods to the parent class, or even creating a new abstract class to hold them and inserting it into the hierarchy above the parent, is not an ideal solution.

Instead, use an interface to specify the method(s). It can be implemented by every class that shares the need and by none of the other classes that would have been forced to "understand" them in the single-inheritance tree. (Design is applied only where needed.) Users of the interface can now specify variables and arguments to be of a new interface type that can refer to any of the classes that implement the interface (as you'll see below)—a powerful abstraction. Some examples of "mix-in" facilities are object persistence (via read() and write() methods), producing or consuming something (the Java library does this for images), and providing generally useful constants. The last of these might look like this:

```
public interface  PresumablyUsefulConstants {
    public static final int     oneOfThem   = 1234;
    public static final float    another     = 1.234F;
    public static final String   yetAnother  = "1234";
    . . .
}

public class  AnyClass implements PresumablyUsefulConstants {
    public static void  main(String argV[]) {
        double  calculation = oneOfThem * another;

        System.out.println("hello " + yetAnother + calculation);
        . . .
    }
}
```

This outputs the thoroughly meaningless hello 12341522.755981, but in the process demonstrates that the class AnyClass can refer directly to all the variables defined in the interface PresumablyUsefulConstants. Normally, you refer to such variables and constants via the class, as for the constant Integer.MIN_VALUE, which is provided by the Integer class. If a set of constants is large or is widely used, the shortcut of being able to refer to them directly (as oneOfThem rather than as PresumablyUsefulConstants. oneOfThem) makes it worth placing them into an interface and implementing it widely.

Programming in the Small

How do you actually use these interfaces? Remember that almost everywhere that you can use a class, you can use an interface instead. Let's try to make use of the interface MySecondInterface defined previously:

```
MySecondInterface  anObject = getTheRightObjectSomehow();

long  age = anObject.ageOfTheUniverse();
```

After you declare anObject to be of type MySecondInterface, you can use anObject as the receiver of any message that the interface defines (or inherits). What does the previous declaration really mean?

When a variable is declared to be of an interface type, it simply means that any object the variable refers to is expected to have implemented that interface—that is, it is expected to understand all the methods that interface specifies. It assumes that a promise made between the designer of the interface and its eventual implementors has been kept. Although this is a rather abstract notion, it allows, for example, the previous code to be written long before any classes that qualify are actually implemented (or even created!). In traditional object-oriented programming, you are forced to create a class with "stub" implementations to get the same effect.

Here's a more complicated example:

```
Orange      anOrange    = getAnOrange();
Fruit       aFruit      = (Fruit) getAnOrange();
Fruitlike   aFruitlike  = (Fruitlike) getAnOrange();
Spherelike  aSpherelike = (Spherelike) getAnOrange();

aFruit.decay();          // fruits decay
aFruitlike.squish();     //  and squish

aFruitlike.toss();       // not OK
aSpherelike.toss();      // OK

anOrange.decay();        // oranges can do it all
anOrange.squish();
anOrange.toss();
anOrange.rotate();
```

Declarations and casts are used in this example to restrict an orange to act more like a mere fruit or sphere, simply to demonstrate the flexibility of the structure built previously. If the second structure built (the one with the new Sphere class) were being used instead, most of this code would still work. (In the line bearing Fruit, all instances of Fruit need to be replaced by Sphere. The later use of aFruit.decay() could be replaced by, for example, aSphere.rotate(). Everything else is the same.)

NOTE The direct use of (implementation) class names is for demonstration purposes only. Normally, you would use only interface names in those declarations and casts so that none of the code in the example would have to change to support the new structure.

Interfaces are implemented and used throughout the Java class library, whenever a behavior is expected to be implemented by a number of disparate classes. In Appendix B you'll find, for example, the interfaces java.lang.Runnable, java.util.Enumeration, java.util.Observable, java.awt.image.ImageConsumer, and java.awt.image.ImageProducer. Let's use one of these interfaces, Enumeration, to revisit the LinkedList example—and to tie together today's lesson—by demonstrating a good use of packages and interfaces together:

```
package  collections;

public class  LinkedList {
    private Node  root;

    . . .
    public Enumeration  enumerate() {
        return new LinkedListEnumerator(root);
    }
}

class  Node {
    private Object  contents;
    private Node    next;

    . . .
    public  Object  contents() {
        return contents;
    }

    public  Node    next() {
        return next;
    }
}

class  LinkedListEnumerator implements Enumeration {
    private Node  currentNode;

    LinkedListEnumerator(Node  root) {
        currentNode = root;
    }

    public boolean  hasMoreElements() {
        return currentNode != null;
    }

    public Object   nextElement() {
        Object  anObject = currentNode.contents();

        currentNode = currentNode.next();
        return  anObject;
    }
}
```

Here is a typical use of the enumerator:

```
collections.LinkedList  aLinkedList = createLinkedList();
java.util.Enumeration   e = aLinkedList.enumerate();
```

```
while (e.hasMoreElements()) {
    Object  anObject = e.nextElement();
    // do something useful with anObject
}
```

Notice that although you are using the `Enumeration` e as though you know what it is, you actually do not. In fact, it is an instance of a hidden class (`LinkedListEnumerator`) that you cannot see or use directly. By a combination of packages and interfaces, the `LinkedList` class has managed to provide a transparent public interface to some of its most important behavior (via the already defined interface `java.util.Enumeration`) while still encapsulating (hiding) its two implementation (support) classes.

Handing out an object like this is sometimes called vending. Often, the "vendor" gives out an object that a receiver can't create itself, but that it knows how to use. By giving it back to the vendor, the receiver can prove it has a certain capability, authenticate itself, or do any number of useful tasks—all without knowing much about the vended object. This is a powerful metaphor that can be applied to a broad range of situations.

Summary

Today you learned how packages can be used to collect and categorize classes into meaningful groups. Packages are arranged in a hierarchy, which not only better organizes your programs, but allows you and the millions of Java programmers out on the Net to name and share their projects uniquely with one another.

You also learned how to use packages, both your own and the many preexisting ones in the Java class library.

You then discovered how to declare and use interfaces, a powerful mechanism for extending the traditional single-inheritance of Java's classes and for separating the design inheritance from the implementation inheritance in your programs. Interfaces are often used to call shared methods when the exact class involved is not known. You'll see further uses of interfaces tomorrow and the day after.

Finally, packages and interfaces can be combined to provide useful abstractions, such as `Enumeration`, that appear simple yet are actually hiding almost all their (complex) implementation from their users. This is a powerful technique.

Questions and Answers

Q What will happen to package/directory hierarchies when some sort of archiving is added to Java?

A Being able to download over the Net a whole archive of packages, classes, and resources is something that Java systems may soon be able to do. When this happens, the simple mapping between folder hierarchy and package hierarchy will break down, and you will not be able to tell as easily where each class is stored (that is, in which archive). Presumably these new, advanced Java systems will provide tools that make this task (and compiling and linking your program in general) much easier.

Q Can you say `import some.package.B*` to import all the classes in that package that begin with `B`?

A No, the `import` asterisk (*) does not act like a Unix or Windows command-line asterisk.

Q Then what exactly does `importing` with an * mean?

A Combining everything said previously, this precise definition emerges: it `imports` all the `public` classes that are directly inside the package named, and not inside one of its subpackages. (You can only `import` exactly this set of classes, or exactly one explicitly named class, from a given package.) By the way, Java only "loads" the information for a class when you actually refer to that class in your code, so the * form of import is no less efficient than naming each class individually.

Q Is there any way that a hidden (`package`) class can somehow be forced out of hiding?

A A bizarre case in which a hidden class can be forced into visibility occurs if it has a `public` superclass and someone casts an instance of it to the superclass. Any `public` methods of that superclass can now be called via your hidden class instance, even if those methods were not thought of by you as `public` when overridden in the hidden class. Usually, these `public()` methods are ones you don't mind having your instances perform, or you wouldn't have declared them to have that `public` superclass. This isn't always the case. Many of the system's built-in classes are `public`—you may have no choice. Luckily, this is a rare event.

Q Why is full multiple-inheritance so complex that Java abandoned it?

A It's not so much that it is too complex, but that it makes the language overly complicated—and as you'll learn on the final day, this can cause larger systems to be less trustworthy and thus, less secure. For example, if you were to inherit from two different parents, each having an instance variable with the same name, you would be forced to allow the conflict and explain how the exact same references to that variable name in each of your superclasses, and in you (all three), are now different. Instead of being able to call "super" methods to get more abstract behavior accomplished, you would always need to worry about which of the (possibly many) identical methods you actually wished to call in which parent. Java's run-time method dispatching would have to be more complex as well. Finally, because so many people would be providing classes for reuse on the Net, the normally manageable conflicts that would arise in your own program would be confounded by millions of users mixing and matching these fully multi-inherited classes at will. In the future, if all these issues are resolved, more powerful inheritance may be added to Java, but its current capabilities are already sufficient for 99 percent of your programs.

Q `abstract` **classes don't have to implement all the methods in an interface themselves, but do all their subclasses have to?**

A Actually, no. Because of inheritance, the precise rule is that an implementation must be provided by some class for each method, but it doesn't have to be your class. This is analogous to when you are the subclass of a class that implements an interface for you. Whatever the `abstract` class doesn't implement, the first non-`abstract` class below it must implement. Then, any further subclasses need do nothing further.

Q **You didn't mention callbacks. Aren't they an important use of interfaces?**

A Yes, but I didn't mention them because a good example would be too bulky in the text. These callbacks are often used in user interfaces (such as window systems) to specify what set of methods are going to be sent whenever the user does a certain set of things (such as clicking the mouse somewhere, typing, and so forth). Because the user interface classes should not "know" anything about the classes using them, an interface's capability to specify a set of methods separate from the class tree is crucial in this case. Callbacks using interfaces are not as general as using, for example, the `perform:()` method of SmallTalk, however, because a given object can request that a user interface object "call it back" only by using a single method name. Suppose that object wanted two user interfaces objects of the same class to call it back, using different names to tell them apart? It cannot do this in Java, and it is forced to use special state and tests to tell them apart. (I warned you that it was complicated!) So, although interfaces are quite valuable in this case, they are not the ideal callback facility.

Exceptions

by Charles L. Perkins with Timothy Webster

Today you'll learn about exceptional conditions in Java:

☐ How to declare when you are expecting one

☐ How to handle them in your code

☐ How to create them

☐ How your code is limited, yet made more robust by them

Let's begin by describing why new ways of handling exceptions were invented.

Programming languages have long labored to solve the following common problem:

```
int  status = callSomethingThatAlmostAlwaysWorks();

if (status == FUNNY_RETURN_VALUE) {
    . . .           // something unusual happened, handle it
    switch(someGlobalErrorIndicator) {
        . . .           // handle more specific problems
    }
} else {
    . . .           // all is well, go your merry way
}
```

Somehow this seems like a lot of work to do to handle a rare case. What's worse, if the function called returns an int as part of its normal answer, you must distinguish one special integer (FUNNY_RETURN_VALUE) to indicate an error. What if that function really needs all the integers? You must do something even more ugly.

Even if you manage to find a distinguished value (such as NULL in C for pointers, -1 for integers, and so forth), what if there are multiple errors that must be produced by the same function? Often, some global variable is used as an error indicator. The function stores a value in it and prays that no one else changes it before the caller gets to handle the error. Multiple errors propagate badly, if at all, and there are numerous problems with generalizing this to large programs, complex errors, and so forth.

Luckily, there is an alternative: using exceptions to help you handle exceptional conditions in your program, making the normal, nonexceptional code cleaner and easier to read.

NEW TERM An *exception* is any object that is an instance of the class Throwable (or any of its subclasses).

Programming in the Large

When you begin to build complex programs in Java, you discover that after you've designed the classes and interfaces and their methods descriptions, you still have not defined all the behavior of your objects. After all, an interface describes the normal way to use an object and doesn't include any strange, exceptional cases. In many systems, the documentation takes care of this problem by explicitly listing the distinguished values used in "hacks" like the previous example. Because the system knows nothing about these hacks, it cannot check them for consistency. In fact, the compiler can do nothing at all to help you with these exceptional conditions, in contrast to the helpful warnings and errors it produces if a method is used incorrectly.

More importantly, you have not captured in your design this important aspect of your program. Instead, you are forced to make up a way to describe it in the documentation and hope you have not made any mistakes when you implement it later. What's worse, everyone else makes up a different way of describing the same thing. Clearly, you need some uniform way of declaring the intentions of classes and methods with respect to these exceptional conditions. Java provides just such a way:

```
public class  MyFirstExceptionalClass {
    public void  anExceptionalMethod() throws MyFirstException {
       . . .
    }
}
```

Here, you warn the reader (and the compiler) that the code . . . may throw an exception called MyFirstException.

You can think of a method's description as a contract between the designer of that method (or class) and you, the caller of the method. Usually, this description tells the types of a method's arguments, what it returns, and the general semantics of what it normally does. You are now being told, as well, what abnormal things it can do. This is a promise, just like the method promises to return a value of a certain type, and you can count on it when writing your code. These new promises help to tease apart and make explicit all the places where exceptional conditions should be handled in your program, and that makes large-scale design easier.

Because exceptions are instances of classes, they can be put into a hierarchy that can naturally describe the relationships among the different types of exceptions. In fact, if you take a moment to glance in Appendix B at the diagrams for java.lang-errors and java.lang-exceptions, you'll see that the class Throwable actually has two large hierarchies of classes beneath it. The roots of these two hierarchies are subclasses of Throwable called Exception and Error. These hierarchies embody the rich set of relationships that exist between exceptions and errors in the Java run-time environment.

When you know that a particular kind of error or exception can occur in your method, you are supposed to either handle it yourself or explicitly warn potential callers about the possibility via the throws clause. Not all errors and exceptions must be listed; instances of either class Error or RuntimeException (or any of their subclasses) do not have to be listed in your throws clause. They get special treatment because they can occur anywhere within a Java program and are usually conditions that you, as the programmer, did not directly cause. One good example is the OutOfMemoryError, which can happen anywhere, at any time, and for any number of reasons.

NOTE

You can, of course, choose to list these errors and run-time exceptions if you like, and the callers of your methods will be forced to handle them, just like a non-run-time exception.

Whenever you see the word "exception" by itself, it almost always means "exception or error" (that is, an instance of Throwable). The previous discussion makes it clear that Exceptions and Errors actually form two separate hierarchies, but except for the throws clause rule, they act exactly the same.

If you examine the diagrams in Appendix B more carefully, you'll notice that there are only five types of exceptions (in java.lang) that must be listed in a throws clause (remember that all Errors and RuntimeExceptions are exempt):

☐ ClassNotFoundException

☐ IllegalAccessException

☐ InstantiationException

☐ InterrupedException

☐ NoSuchMethodException

Each of these names suggests something that is explicitly caused by the programmer, not some behind-the-scenes event such as OutOfMemoryError.

If you look further in Appendix B, near the bottom of the diagrams for java.util and java.io, you'll see that each package adds some new exceptions. The former is adding two exceptions somewhat akin to ArrayStoreException and IndexOutOfBoundsException, and so decides to place them under RuntimeException. The latter is adding a whole new tree of IOExceptions, which are more explicitly caused by the programmer, and so they are rooted under Exception. Thus, IOExceptions must be described in throws clauses. Finally, package java.awt defines one of each style, implicit and explicit.

The Java class library uses exceptions everywhere, and to good effect. If you examine Java's detailed API documentation or the class library source files included with the Roaster release, you see that many of the methods in the library have throws clauses, and some of them even document (when they believe it will make something clearer to the reader) when they may throw one of the implicit errors or exceptions. This is just a nicety on the documenter's part, because you are not required to catch conditions like that. If it wasn't obvious that such a condition could happen there, and for some reason you really cared about catching it, this would be useful information.

Programming in the Small

Now that you have a feeling for how exceptions can help you design a program and a class library better, how do you actually use exceptions? Let's try to use anExceptionalMethod() defined in today's first example:

```
public void  anotherExceptionalMethod() throws MyFirstException {
    MyFirstExceptionalClass  aMFEC = new MyFirstExceptionalClass();

    aMFEC.anExceptionalMethod();
}
```

Let's examine this example more closely. If you assume that MyFirstException is a subclass of Exception, it means that if you don't handle it in anotherExceptionalMethod()'s code, you must warn your callers about it. Because your code simply calls anExceptionalMethod() without doing anything about the fact that it may throw MyFirstException, you must add that exception to your throws clause. This is perfectly legal, but it does defer to your caller something that perhaps you should be responsible for doing yourself. (It depends on the circumstances, of course.)

Suppose that that you feel responsible today and decide to handle the exception. Because you're now declaring a method without a throws clause, you must "catch" the expected exception and do something useful with it:

```
public void  responsibleMethod() {
    MyFirstExceptionalClass  aMFEC = new MyFirstExceptionalClass();

    try {
        aMFEC.anExceptionalMethod();
    } catch (MyFirstException m) {
        . . .    // do something terribly significant and responsible
    }
}
```

The try statement says basically: "Try running the code inside these braces, and if there are exceptions thrown, I will attach handlers to take care of them." (You first heard about these on Day 10.) You can have as many catch clauses at the end of a try as you need. Each enables you to handle any and all exceptions that are instances of the class listed in parentheses, of any of its subclasses, or of a class that implements the interface listed in parentheses. In the catch in this example, exceptions of the class MyFirstException (or any of its subclasses) are being handled.

What if you want to combine both of the approaches shown so far? You'd like to handle the exception yourself, but also reflect it up to your caller. This can be done by explicitly rethrowing the exception:

```
public void  responsibleExceptionalMethod() throws MyFirstException {
    MyFirstExceptionalClass  aMFEC = new MyFirstExceptionalClass();

    try {
        aMFEC.anExceptionalMethod();
    } catch (MyFirstException m) {
        . . .            // do something responsible
        throw m;         // re-throw the exception
    }
}
```

This works because exception handlers can be nested. You handle the exception by doing something responsible with it, but decide that it is too important to not give an exception handler that might be in your caller a chance to handle it as well. Exceptions float all the way up the chain of method callers this way (usually not being handled by most of them) until at last, the system itself handles any uncaught ones by aborting your program and printing an error message. In a stand-alone program, this is not such a terrible result; but in an applet, it can cause the browser (and by extension, the operating system) to crash. Most browsers protect themselves from this disaster by catching all exceptions themselves whenever they run an applet, but you can never tell. If it's possible for you to catch an exception and do something intelligent with it, you should.

If an uncaught exception is thrown in Roaster's Applet Runner, the applet's execution will terminate, and a series of strings will be output to the `Applet Runner.out` window describing what the exception was and where it was thrown.

Let's see what `throwing` a new exception looks like. How about fleshing out today's first example:

```
public class  MyFirstExceptionalClass {
    public void  anExceptionalMethod() throws MyFirstException {
        . . .
        if (someThingUnusualHasHappened()) {
            throw new MyFirstException();
            // execution never reaches here
        }
    }
}
```

NOTE throw is like a break statement—nothing "beyond it" is executed.

This is the fundamental way that all exceptions are generated; someone, somewhere, had to create an exception object and throw it. In fact, the whole hierarchy under the class `Throwable` would be worth much less if there were not `throw` statements scattered throughout the code in the Java library at just the right places. Because exceptions propagate up from any depth down inside methods, any method call you make might generate a plethora of possible errors and exceptions. Luckily, only the ones listed in the `throws` clause of that method need be thought about; the rest travel silently past the method on their way to becoming an error message (or being caught and handled higher in the system).

Here's an unusual demonstration of this, where the `throw` and the handler that catches it are very close together:

```
System.out.print("Now ");
try {
    System.out.print("is ");
    throw new MyFirstException();
    System.out.print("a ");
} catch (MyFirstException m) {
    System.out.print("the ");
}
System.out.print("time.");
```

It prints: `Now is the time.`

Exceptions are a quite powerful way of partitioning the space of all possible error conditions into manageable pieces. Because the first `catch` clause that matches is executed, you can build chains such as the following:

```
try {
    someReallyExceptionalMethod();
} catch (NullPointerException n) {   // a subclass of RuntimeException
    . . .
} catch (RuntimeException r) {        // a subclass of Exception
    . . .
} catch (IOException i) {             // a subclass of Exception
    . . .
} catch (MyFirstException m) {        // our subclass of Exception
    . . .
} catch (Exception e) {               // a subclass of Throwable
    . . .
} catch (Throwable t) {
    . . . // Errors, plus anything not caught above are caught here
}
```

By listing subclasses before their parent classes, the parent catches anything it would normally catch that's also not one of the subclasses above it. By juggling chains like these, you can express almost any combination of tests. If there's some really obscure case you can't handle, perhaps you can use an interface to catch it instead. That enables you to design your (peculiar) exceptions hierarchy using multiple inheritance. Catching an interface rather than a class can also be used to test for a property that many exceptions share but that cannot be expressed in the single-inheritance tree alone.

Suppose, for example, that a scattered set of your exception classes require a reboot after being thrown. You create an interface called `NeedsReboot`, and all these classes implement the interface. (None of them needs to have a common parent exception class.) Then, the highest level of exception handler simply catches classes that implement `NeedsReboot` and performs a reboot:

```
public interface  NeedsReboot { }   // needs no contents at all

try {
    someMethodThatGeneratesExceptionsThatImplementNeedsReboot();
} catch (NeedsReboot n) {    // catch an interface
    . . .                    // cleanup
    SystemClass.reboot();    // reboot using a made-up system class
}
```

By the way, if you need really unusual behavior during an exception, you can place the behavior into the exception class itself! Remember that an exception is also a normal class, so it can contain instance variables and methods. Although using them is a little peculiar, it might be valuable on a few bizarre occasions. Here's what this might look like:

```
try {
    someExceptionallyStrangeMethod();
} catch (ComplexException e) {
    switch (e.internalState()) {     // probably an instance variable value
        case e.COMPLEX_CASE:         // a class variable of the exception
            e.performComplexBehavior(myState, theContext, etc);
            break;
        . . .
    }
}
```

The Limitations Placed on the Programmer

As powerful as all this sounds, isn't it a little limiting, too? For example, suppose you want to override one of the standard methods of the Object class, toString(), to be smarter about how you print yourself:

```
public class  MyIllegalClass {
    public String  toString() {
        someReallyExceptionalMethod();
        . . .            // returns some String
    }
}
```

Because the superclass (Object) defined the method declaration for toString() without a throws clause, any implementation of it in any subclass must obey this restriction. In particular, you cannot just call someReallyExceptionalMethod(), as you did previously, because it will generate a host of errors and exceptions, some of which are not exempt from being listed in a throws clause (such as IOException and MyFirstException). If all the exceptions thrown were exempt, you would have no problem, but because some are not, you have to catch at least those few exceptions for this to be legal Java:

```
public class  MyLegalClass {
    public String  toString() {
        try {
            someReallyExceptionalMethod();
        } catch (IOException e) {
        } catch (MyFirstException m) {
        }
```

```
    . . .          // returns some String
    }
}
```

In both cases, you elect to catch the exceptions and do absolutely nothing with them. Although this is legal, it is not always the right thing to do. You may need to think for a while to come up with the best, nontrivial behavior for any particular catch clause. This extra thought and care makes your program more robust, better able to handle unusual input, and more likely to work correctly when used by multiple threads (you'll see this tomorrow).

MyIllegalClass's toString() method produces a compiler error to remind you to reflect on these issues. This extra care will richly reward you as you reuse your classes in later projects and in larger and larger programs. Of course, the Java class library has been written with exactly this degree of care, and that's one of the reasons it's robust enough to be used in constructing all your Java projects.

The finally Clause

Finally, for finally. Suppose there is some action that you absolutely must do, no matter what happens. Usually, this critical action is something like freeing some external resource after acquiring it, closing a file after opening it, and so forth. To be sure that "no matter what" includes "no matter what exceptions," you use a clause of the try statement designed for exactly this sort of thing, finally:

```
SomeFileClass  f = new SomeFileClass();

if (f.open("/a/file/name/path")) {
    try {
        someReallyExceptionalMethod();
    } finally {
        f.close();
    }
}
```

This use of finally behaves very much like the following:

```
SomeFileClass  f = new SomeFileClass();

if (f.open("/a/file/name/path")) {
    try {
        someReallyExceptionalMethod();
    } catch (Throwable t) {
        f.close();
        throw t;
    }
}
```

... except that `finally` can also be used to clean up not only after exceptions but after return, break, and `continue` statements as well. Here's a complex demonstration:

```
public class  MyFinalExceptionalClass extends ContextClass {
    public static void  main(String argv[]) {
        int  mysteriousState = getContext();

        while (true) {
            System.out.print("Who ");
            try {
                System.out.print("is ");
                if (mysteriousState == 1)
                    return;
                System.out.print("that ");
                if (mysteriousState == 2)
                    break;
                System.out.print("strange ");
                if (mysteriousState == 3)
                    continue;
                System.out.print("but kindly ");
                if (mysteriousState == 4)
                    throw new UncaughtException();
                System.out.print("not at all ");
            } finally {
                System.out.print("amusing ");
            }
            System.out.print("yet compelling ");
        }
        System.out.print("man?");
    }
}
```

Here is the output produced depending on the value of `mysteriousState`:

```
1    Who is amusing
2    Who is that amusing man?
3    Who is that strange amusing Who is that strange amusing . . .
4    Who is that strange but kindly amusing
5    Who is that strange but kindly not at all amusing yet compelling man?
```

NOTE   In cases 3 and 5 the output never ends until you press ⌘-period. In 4, an error message generated by the `UncaughtException` is also printed.

Summary

Today you learned how exceptions aid your program's design, robustness, and multithreading capability (more on this tomorrow).

You also learned about the vast array of exceptions defined and thrown in the Java class library, and how to try methods while catching any of a hierarchically ordered set of possible exceptions and errors. Java's reliance on strict exception handling does place some restrictions on the programmer, but you learned that these restrictions are light compared to the rewards.

Finally, the finally clause was discussed, which provides a fool-proof way to be certain that something is accomplished.

Questions and Answers

Q I'm still not sure I understand the differences between Exceptions, Errors, and RuntimeExceptions. Is there another way of looking at them?

A Errors are caused by dynamic linking, or virtual machine problems, and are thus too low-level for most programs to care about (although sophisticated development libraries and environments probably care a great deal about them). RuntimeExceptions are generated by the normal execution of Java code, and though they occasionally reflect a condition you will want to handle explicitly, more often they reflect a coding mistake by the programmer and simply need to print an error to help flag that mistake. Exceptions that are not RuntimeExceptions (IOExceptions, for example) are conditions that, because of their nature, should be explicitly handled by any robust and well thought-out code. The Java class library was written using only a few of these, but they are extremely important to the safe and correct use of the system. The compiler helps you handle these exceptions properly via its throws clause checks and restrictions.

Q Is there any way to "get around" the strict restrictions placed on methods by the throws clause?

A Yes. Suppose you thought long and hard and have decided that you need to circumvent this restriction. This is almost never the case, because the right solution is to go back and redesign your methods to reflect the exceptions that you need to throw. Imagine, however, that for some reason a system class has you in a straitjacket. Your first solution is to subclass RuntimeException to make up a new, exempt exception of your own. Now you can throw it to your heart's content, because the throws clause that was annoying you does not need to include this new exception. If you need a lot of such exceptions, an elegant approach is to mix in some novel exception interfaces to your new Runtime classes. You're free to choose whatever subset of these new interfaces you want to catch (none of the normal Runtime exceptions need be caught), while any leftover (new) Runtime exceptions are (legally) allowed to go through that otherwise annoying standard method in the library.

Q I'm still a little confused by long chains of catch clauses. Can you label the previous example with which exceptions are handled by each line of code?

A Certainly, here it is:

```
try {
someReallyExceptionalMethod();
} catch (NullPointerException n) {
  . . . // handles NullPointerExceptions
} catch (RuntimeException r) {
  . . . // handles RuntimeExceptions that are not
➥NullPointerExceptions
} catch (IOException i) {
  . . . // handles IOExceptions
} catch (MyFirstException m) {
  . . . // handles MyFirstExceptions
} catch (Exception e) {  // handles Exceptions that are not
➥RuntimeExceptions
  . . .                  //              nor IOExceptions nor
➥MyFirstExceptions
} catch (Throwable t) {
  . . . // handles Throwables that are not Exceptions (i.e.,
➥Errors)
}
```

Q Given how annoying it can sometimes be to handle exceptional conditions properly, what's stopping me from surrounding any method with a throws clause as follows

```
try { thatAnnoyingMethod(); } catch (Throwable t) { }
```

... and simply ignoring all exceptions?

A Nothing, other than your own conscience. In some cases, you should do nothing, because it is the correct thing to do for your method's implementation. Otherwise, you should struggle through the annoyance and gain experience. Good style is a struggle even for the best programmer, but the rewards are rich indeed.

Multithreading

by Charles L. Perkins with Timothy Webster

Today, you'll learn more about the threads mentioned briefly in Week 2:

☐ How to "think multithreaded"

☐ How to protect your methods and variables from unintended thread conflicts

☐ How to create, start, and stop threads and threaded classes

☐ How the scheduler works in Java

First, let's begin by motivating the need for threads.

Threads are a relatively recent invention in the computer science world. Although processes, their larger parent, have been around for decades, threads have only recently been accepted into the mainstream. What's odd about this is that they are very valuable, and programs written with them are noticeably better, even to the casual user. In fact, some of the best individual, Herculean efforts over the years have involved implementing a threads-like facility by hand to give a program a more friendly feel to its users.

Imagine that you're using your favorite text editor on a large file. When it starts up, does it need to examine the entire file before it lets you edit? Does it need to make a copy of the file? If the file is huge, this can be a nightmare. Wouldn't it be nicer for it to show you the first page, enabling you to begin editing, and somehow (in the background) complete the slower tasks necessary for initialization? Threads allow exactly this kind of within-the-program parallelism.

Perhaps the best example of threading (or lack of it) is a WWW browser. Can your browser download an indefinite number of files and Web pages at once while still enabling you to continue browsing? While these pages are downloading, can your browser download all the pictures, sounds, and so forth in parallel, interleaving the fast and slow download times of multiple Internet servers? HotJava can do all of these things—and more—by using the built-in threading of the Java language.

The Problem with Parallelism

If threading is so wonderful, why doesn't every system have it? Many modern operating systems have the basic primitives needed to create and run threads, but they are missing a key ingredient. The rest of their environment is not thread-safe. (For the record, the Mac *began* to support multithreading with the Thread Manager extension, which is System 7-compatible and built into System 7.5; full support for pre-emptive multitasking will be introduced with System 8—the famous "Copland.")

NOTE For those programmers experienced with the Mac Toolbox who might be wondering—Roaster uses its own set of routines to implement multithreading, and does not rely on Apple's Thread Manager routines.

Imagine that you are in a thread, one of many, and each of you is sharing some important data managed by the system. If you were managing that data, you could take steps to protect it (as you'll see later today), but the system is managing it. Now visualize a piece of code in the system that reads some crucial value, thinks about it for a while, and then adds 1 to the value:

```
if (crucialValue > 0) {
    . . .                    // think about what to do
    crucialValue += 1;
}
```

Remember that any number of threads may be calling upon this part of the system at once. The disaster occurs when two threads have both executed the `if` test before either has incremented the `crucialValue`. In that case, the value is clobbered by them both with the same `crucialValue + 1`, and one of the increments has been lost. This may not seem so bad to you, but imagine instead that the crucial value affects the state of the screen as it is being displayed. Now, unfortunate ordering of the threads can cause the screen to be updated incorrectly. In the same way, mouse or keyboard events can be lost, databases can be inaccurately updated, and so forth.

This disaster is inescapable if any significant part of the system has not been written with threads in mind. Therein lies the barrier to a mainstream threaded environment—the large effort required to rewrite existing libraries for thread safety. Luckily, Java was written from scratch with this is mind, and every Java class in its library is thread-safe. Thus, you now have to worry only about your own synchronization and thread-ordering problems, because you can assume that the Java system will do the right thing.

NEW TERM

Atomic operations are operations that appear to happen "all at once"—exactly at the same time—to other threads.

NOTE

Some readers may wonder what the fundamental problem really is. Can't you just make the "think about what to do" segment in the example smaller and smaller to reduce or eliminate the problem? Without atomic operations, the answer is no. Even if the segment took zero time, you must first look at the value of some variable to make any decision and then change something to reflect that decision. These two steps can never be made to happen at the same time without an atomic operation. Unless you're given one by the system, it's literally impossible to create your own.

Even the one line `crucialValue += 1` involves three steps: get the current value, add one to it, and store it back where it was. (Using `++crucialValue` doesn't help either.) All three steps need to happen "all at once" (atomically) to be safe. Special Java primitives, at the lowest levels of the language, provide you with the basic atomic operations you need to build safe, threaded programs.

Thinking Multithreaded

Getting used to threads takes a little while and a new way of thinking. Rather than imagining that you always know exactly what's happening when you look at a method you've written, you have to ask yourself some additional questions. What will happen if more than one thread calls into this method at the same time? Do you need to protect it in some way? What about your class as a whole? Are you assuming that only one of its methods is running at the same time?

Often you make such assumptions, and a local instance variable will be messed up as a result. Let's make a few mistakes and then try to correct them. First, the simplest case:

```
public class  ThreadCounter {
    int  crucialValue;

    public void  countMe() {
        crucialValue += 1;
    }

    public int  howMany() {
        return crucialValue;
    }
}
```

This code suffers from the most pure form of the "synchronization problem:" the += takes more than one step, and you may miscount the number of threads as a result. (Don't worry about how threads are created yet, just imagine that a whole bunch of them are able to call countMe(), at once, at slightly different times.) Java enables you to fix this:

```
public class  SafeThreadCounter {
    int  crucialValue;

    public synchronized void  countMe() {
        crucialValue += 1;
    }

    public           int  howMany() {
        return crucialValue;
    }
}
```

The synchronized keyword tells Java to make the block of code in the method thread-safe. Only one thread will be allowed inside this method at once, and others have to wait until the currently running thread is finished with it before they can begin running it. This implies that synchronizing a large, long-running method is almost always a bad idea. All your threads would end up stuck at this bottleneck, waiting in single file to get their turn at this one slow method.

It's even worse than you might think for most unsynchronized variables. Because the compiler can keep variables' values around in registers during computations, and a thread's registers can't be seen by other threads (especially if they're on another processor in a true multiprocessor computer), a variable can be updated in such a way that no possible order of thread updates could have produced the result. This is completely incomprehensible to the programmer. To avoid this bizarre case, you can label a variable volatile, meaning that you know it will be updated asynchronously by multiprocessor-like threads. Java then loads and stores it each time it's needed and does not use registers.

NOTE

In earlier releases, variables that were safe from these bizarre effects were labeled threadsafe. Because most variables are safe to use, however, they are now assumed to be thread-safe unless you mark them volatile. Using volatile is an extremely rare event. In fact, in the current release, the Java library does not use volatile anywhere.

Points About Points

The method `howMany()` in the last example doesn't need to be `synchronized`, because it simply returns the current value of an instance variable. Someone higher in the call chain may need to be `synchronized`, though—someone who uses the value returned from the method. Here's an example:

```
public class  Point {
    private float  x, y;

    public  float  x() {          // needs no synchronization
        return x;
    }

    public  float  y() {          // ditto
        return y;
    }
    . . .     // methods to set and change x and y
}

public class  UnsafePointPrinter {
    public void  print(Point p) {
        System.out.println("The point's x is " + p.x()
                            + " and y is " + p.y() + ".");
    }
}
```

The analogous methods to `howMany()` are `x()` and `y()`. They need no synchronization, because they just return the values of instance variables. It is the responsibility of the caller of `x()` and `y()` to decide whether it needs to synchronize itself—and in this case, it does. Although the method `print()` simply reads values and prints them out, it reads two values. This means that there is a chance that some other thread, running between the call to `p.x()` and the call to `p.y()`, could have changed the value of x and y stored inside the `Point` p. Remember, you don't know how many other threads have a way to reach and call methods in this `Point` object! "Thinking multi-threaded" comes down to being careful any time you make an assumption that something has not happened between two parts of your program (even two parts of the same line, or the same expression, such as the string + expression in this example).

TryAgainPointPrinter

You could make a safe version of `print()` by simply adding the `synchronized` keyword modifier to it, but instead, let's try a slightly subtler, more efficient approach:

```
public class  TryAgainPointPrinter {
```

```
public void  print(Point p) {
    float  safeX, safeY;

    synchronized(this) {
        safeX = p.x();       // these two lines now
        safeY = p.y();       // happen atomically
    }
    System.out.print("The point's x is " + safeX
                                + " y is " + safeY);
    }
}
```

The synchronized statement takes an argument that says what object you would like to lock to prevent more than one thread from executing the enclosed block of code at the same time. Here, you use this (the instance itself), which is exactly the object that would have been locked by the synchronized method as a whole if you had changed print() to be like your safe countMe() method. You have an added bonus with this new form of synchronization: you can specify exactly what part of a method needs to be safe, and the rest can be left unsafe.

Notice how you took advantage of this freedom to make the protected part of the method as small as possible, while leaving the String creations, concatenations, and printing (which together take a small but nonzero amount of time) outside the "protected" area. This is both good style (as a guide to the reader of your code) and more efficient, because fewer threads get stuck waiting to get into protected areas.

SafePointPrinter

The astute reader, though, may still be worried by the last example. It seems as if you made sure that no one executes your calls to x() and y() out of order, but have you prevented the Point p from changing out from under you? The answer is no, you still have not solved the problem. You really do need the full power of the synchronized statement:

```
public class  SafePointPrinter {
    public void  print(Point p) {
        float  safeX, safeY;

        synchronized(p) {         // no one can change p
            safeX = p.x();        // while these two lines
            safeY = p.y();        // are happening atomically
        }
        System.out.print("The point's x is " + safeX
                                    + " y is " + safeY);
    }
}
```

Now you've got it. You actually needed to protect the Point p to protect from changes, so you lock it by giving it as the argument to your synchronized statement. Now when x() and y() happen together, they can be sure to get the current x and y of the Point p, without any other thread being able to call a modifying method between. You're still assuming, however, that the Point p has properly protected itself. (You can always assume this about system classes—but you wrote this Point class.) You can make sure by writing the only method that can change x and y inside p yourself:

```java
public class  Point {
    private float  x, y;

    . . .           // the x() and y() methods

    public synchronized void  setXAndY(float  newX,  float  newY) {
        x = newX;
        y = newY;
    }
}
```

By making the only "set" method in Point synchronized, you guarantee that any other thread trying to grab the Point p and change it out from under you has to wait: you've locked the Point p with your synchronized(p) statement, and any other thread has to try to lock the same Point p via the implicit synchronized(this) statement p now executes when entering setXAndY(). Thus, at last, you are thread-safe.

NOTE

> By the way, if Java had some way of returning more than one value at once, you could write a synchronized getXAndY() method for Points that returns both values safely. In the current Java language, such a method could return a new, unique Point to guarantee to its callers that no one else has a copy that might be changed. This sort of trick can be used to minimize the parts of the system that need to worry about synchronization.

ReallySafePoint

An added benefit of the use of the synchronized modifier on methods (or of synchronized(this) {. . .}) is that only one of these methods (or blocks of code) can run at once. You can use that knowledge to guarantee that only one of several crucial methods in a class will run at once:

```java
public class  ReallySafePoint {
```

```
    private float  x, y;

    public synchronized Point  getUniquePoint() {
        return new Point(x, y);     // can be a less safe Point
    }                               // because only the caller has it

    public synchronized void   setXAndY(float  newX,  float  newY) {
        x = newX;
        y = newY;
    }

    public synchronized void   scale(float  scaleX,  float  scaleY) {
        x *= scaleX;
        y *= scaleY;
    }

    public synchronized void   add(ReallySafePoint  aRSP) {
        Point  p = aRSP.getUniquePoint();

        x += p.x();
        y += p.y();
    }  // Point p is soon thrown away by GC; no one else ever saw it
}
```

This example combines several of the ideas mentioned previously. To avoid a caller's having to synchronize(p) whenever getting your x and y, you give them a synchronized way to get a unique Point (like returning multiple values). Each method that modifies the object's instance variables is also synchronized to prevent it from running between the x and y references in getUniquePoint() and from stepping on each other as they each modify the local x and y. Note that add() itself uses getUniquePoint() to avoid having to say synchronized(aRSP).

Classes that are this safe are a little unusual; it is more often your responsibility to protect yourself from other threads' use of commonly held objects (such as Points). Only when you know for certain that you're the only one that knows about an object can you fully relax. Of course, if you created the object and gave it to no one else, you can be that certain.

Protecting a Class Variable

Finally, suppose you want a class variable to collect some information across all a class's instances:

```
public class  StaticCounter {
    private static int  crucialValue;

    public synchronized void  countMe() {
        crucialValue += 1;
```

```
    }
}
```

Is this safe? If `crucialValue` were an instance variable, it would be. Because it's a class variable, however, and there is only one copy of it for all instances, you can still have multiple threads modifying it by using different instances of the class. (Remember, the `synchronized` modifier locks the object `this`—an instance.) Luckily, you already know the tools you need to solve this:

```
public class  StaticCounter {
    private static int  crucialValue;

    public void  countMe() {
        synchronized(getClass()) {   // can't directly reference StaticCounter
            crucialValue += 1;       // the (shared) class is now locked
        }
    }
}
```

The trick is to "lock" on a different object—not on an instance of the class, but on the class itself. Because a class variable is "inside" a class, just as an instance variable is inside an instance, this shouldn't be all that unexpected. In a similar way, classes can provide global resources that any instance (or other class) can access directly by using the class name, and lock by using that same class name. In this example, `crucialValue` is used from within an instance of `StaticCounter`, but if `crucialValue` were declared `public` instead, from anywhere in the program, it would be safe to say the following:

```
synchronized(new StaticCounter().getClass()) {
    StaticCounter.crucialValue += 1;
}
```

NOTE   The direct use of another object's variable is really bad style—it's used here simply to demonstrate a point quickly. `StaticCounter` normally provides a `countMe()`-like class method of its own to do this sort of dirty work.

You can appreciate how much work the Java team has done for you by thinking all these hard thoughts for each and every class (and method!) in the Java class library.

Creating and Using Threads

Now that you understand the power (and the dangers) of having many threads running at once, how are those threads actually created?

WARNING The system itself always has a few so-called daemon threads running, one of which is constantly doing the tedious task of garbage collection for you in the background. There is also a main user thread that listens for events from your mouse and keyboard. If you're not careful, you can sometimes lock out this main thread. If you do, no events are sent to your program and it appears to be dead.

Because there is a class `java.lang.Thread`, you might guess that you could create a thread of your own by subclassing it—and you are right:

```
public class  MyFirstThread extends Thread { // a.k.a., java.lang.Thread
    public void  run() {
        . . .                    // do something useful
    }
}
```

You now have a new type of `Thread` called `MyFirstThread`, which does something useful (unspecified) when its `run()` method is called. Of course, no one has created this thread or called its `run()` method, so it does absolutely nothing at the moment. To actually create and run an instance of your new thread class, you write the following:

```
MyFirstThread  aMFT = new MyFirstThread();

aMFT.start();     // calls our run() method
```

What could be simpler? You create a new instance of your thread class and then ask it to start running. Whenever you want to stop the thread, you use this:

```
aMFT.stop();
```

Besides responding to `start()` and `stop()`, a thread can also be temporarily suspended and later resumed:

```
Thread  t = new Thread();

t.suspend();
. . .             // do something special while t isn't running
t.resume();
```

A thread will automatically `suspend()` and then `resume()` when it's first blocked at a synchronized point and then later unblocked (when it's that thread's "turn" to run).

The Runnable Interface

This is all well and good if every time you want to create a `Thread` you have the luxury of being able to place it under the `Thread` class in the single-inheritance class tree.

What if it more naturally belongs under some other class, from which it needs to get most of its implementation? The interfaces of Day 16 come to the rescue:

```
public class  MySecondThread extends ImportantClass implements Runnable {
    public void  run() {
        . . .                // do something useful
    }
}
```

By implementing the interface Runnable, you declare your intention to run in a separate thread. In fact, the class Thread itself implements this interface, as you might expect from the design discussions on Day 16. As you also might guess from the example, the interface Runnable specifies only one method: run(). As in MyFirstThread, you expect someone to create an instance of a thread and somehow call your run() method. Here's how this is accomplished:

```
MySecondThread  aMST = new MySecondThread();
Thread          aThread = new Thread(aMST);

aThread.start();   // calls our run() method, indirectly
```

First, you create an instance of MySecondThread. Then, by passing this instance to the constructor making the new Thread, you make it the target of that Thread. Whenever that new Thread starts up, its run() method calls the run() method of the target it was given (assumed by the Thread to be an object that implements the Runnable interface). When start() is called, aThread (indirectly) calls your run() method. You can stop aThread with stop(). If you don't need to talk to the Thread explicitly or to the instance of MySecondThread, here's a one-line shortcut:

```
new Thread(new MySecondThread()).start();
```

NOTE

As you can see, the class name, MySecondThread, is a bit of a misnomer—it does not descend from Thread, nor is it actually the thread that you start() and stop(). It probably should have been called MySecondThreadedClass or ImportantRunnableClass.

ThreadTester

Here's a longer example:

```
public class  SimpleRunnable implements Runnable {
    public void  run() {
        System.out.println("in thread named '"
                        + Thread.currentThread().getName() + "'");
    } // any other methods run() calls are in current thread as well
}
```

```
public class  ThreadTester {
    public static void  main(String argv[]) {
        SimpleRunnable  aSR = new SimpleRunnable();

        while (true) {
            Thread  t = new Thread(aSR);

            System.out.println("new Thread() " + (t == null ?
                                        "fail" : "succeed") + "ed.");
            t.start();
            try { t.join(); } catch (InterruptedException ignored) { }
                    // waits for thread to finish its run() method
        }
    }
}
```

NOTE

You may be worried that only one instance of the class SimpleRunnable is created, but many new Threads are using it. Don't they get confused? Remember to separate in your mind the aSR instance (and the methods it understands) from the various threads of execution that can pass through it. aSR's methods provide a template for execution, and the multiple threads created are sharing that template. Each remembers where it is executing and whatever else it needs to make it distinct from the other running threads. They all share the same instance and the same methods. That's why you need to be so careful, when adding synchronization, to imagine numerous threads running rampant over each of your methods.

The class method currentThread() can be called to get the thread in which a method is currently executing. If the SimpleRunnable class were a subclass of Thread, its methods would know the answer already (it is the thread running). Because SimpleRunnable simply implements the interface Runnable, however, and counts on someone else (ThreadTester's main()) to create the thread, its run() method needs another way to get its hands on that thread. Often, you'll be deep inside methods called by your run() method when suddenly you need to get the current thread. The class method shown in the example works, no matter where you are.

WARNING

You can do some reasonably disastrous things with your knowledge of threads. For example, if you're running in the main thread of the system and, because you think you are in a different thread, you accidentally say the following:

```
Thread.currentThread().stop();
```

... it has unfortunate consequences for your (soon-to-be-dead) program!

The example then calls on getName(), the current thread to get the thread's name (usually something helpful, such as Thread-23) so it can tell the world in which thread run() is running. The final thing to note is the use of the method join(), which, when sent to a thread, means "I'm planning to wait forever for you to finish your run() method." You don't want to do this lightly: if you have anything else important you need to get done in your thread any time soon, you can't count on how long the join()ed thread may take to finish. In the example, its run() method is short and finishes quickly, so each loop can safely wait for the previous thread to die before creating the next one. (Of course, in this example, you didn't have anything else you wanted to do while waiting for join() anyway.) Here's the output produced:

```
new Thread() succeeded.
in thread named 'Thread-1'
new Thread() succeeded.
in thread named 'Thread-2'
new Thread() succeeded.
in thread named 'Thread-3'
^C
```

Use ⌘-period to interrupt the program, because it otherwise would continue forever.

NamedThreadTester

If you want your threads to have particular names, you can assign them yourself by using a two-argument form of Thread's constructor:

```
public class  NamedThreadTester {
    public static void  main(String argv[]) {
        SimpleRunnable  aSR = new SimpleRunnable();

        for (int  i = 1;  true;  ++i) {
            Thread  t = new Thread(aSR, "" + (100 - i)
                                        + " threads on the wall...");

            System.out.println("new Thread() " + (t == null ?
                                        "fail" : "succeed") + "ed.");
            t.start();
            try { t.join(); } catch (InterruptedException ignored) { }
        }
    }
}
```

... which takes a target object, as before, and a String, which names the new thread. Here's the output:

```
new Thread() succeeded.
in thread named '99 threads on the wall...'
new Thread() succeeded.
in thread named '98 threads on the wall...'
new Thread() succeeded.
in thread named '97 threads on the wall...'
^C
```

Naming a thread is one easy way to pass it some information. This information flows from the parent thread to its new child. It's also useful, for debugging purposes, to give threads meaningful names (such as network input) so that when they appear during an error—in a debugging session, for example—you can easily identify which thread caused the problem. You might also think of using names to help group or organize your threads, but Java actually provides you with a ThreadGroup class to perform this function. A ThreadGroup enables you to group threads, to control them all as a unit, and to keep them from being able to affect other threads (useful for security).

Knowing When a Thread Has Stopped

Let's imagine a different version of the last example, one that creates a thread and then hands the thread off to other parts of the program. Suppose the class that created the thread would like to know when that thread dies so that it can perform some cleanup operation. If SimpleRunnable were a subclass of Thread, you might try to catch stop() whenever it's sent—but look at Thread's declaration of the stop() method:

```
public final void  stop(); { . . . }
```

The final here means that you can't override this method in a subclass. In any case, SimpleRunnable is not a subclass of Thread, so how can this imagined example possibly catch the death of its thread? The answer is to use the following magic:

```
public class  SingleThreadTester {
    public static void  main(String argv[]) {
        Thread  t = new Thread(new SimpleRunnable());

        try {
            t.start();
            someMethodThatMightStopTheThread(t);
        } catch (ThreadDeath  aTD) {
            . . .              // do some required cleanup
            throw aTD;         // re-throw the error
        }
    }
}
```

You understand most of this magic from yesterday's lesson. All you need to know is that if the thread created in the example dies, it throws an error of class ThreadDeath.

The code catches that error and performs the required cleanup. It then rethrows the error, allowing the thread to die. The cleanup code is not called if the thread exits normally (its run() method completes), but that's fine; you posited that the cleanup was needed only when stop() was used on the thread.

NOTE Threads can die in other ways—for example, by throwing exceptions that no one catches. In these cases, stop() is never called, and the previous code is not sufficient. (If the cleanup always has to occur, even at the normal end of a thread's life, you can put it in a finally clause.) Because unexpected exceptions can come out of nowhere to kill a thread, multithreaded programs that carefully catch and handle all their exceptions are more predictable, robust, and easier to debug.

Thread Scheduling

You might wonder exactly what order your threads will be run in, and how you can control that order. Unfortunately, the current implementations of the Java system cannot precisely answer the former, though with a lot of work, you can always do the latter.

The part of the system that decides the real-time ordering of threads is called the scheduler.

Preemptive versus Nonpreemptive

Normally, any scheduler has two fundamentally different ways of looking at its job: nonpreemptive scheduling and preemptive time-slicing.

With nonpreemptive scheduling, the scheduler runs the current thread forever, requiring that thread explicitly to tell it when it is safe to start a different thread. With preemptive time-slicing, the scheduler runs the current thread until it has used up a certain tiny fraction of a second, and then "preempts" it, suspend()s it, and resume()s another thread for the next tiny fraction of a second.

Nonpreemptive scheduling is very courtly, always asking for permission to schedule, and is quite valuable in extremely time-critical, real-time applications where being interrupted at the wrong moment, or for too long, could mean crashing an airplane.

Most modern schedulers use preemptive time-slicing, because, except for a few time-critical cases, it has turned out to make writing multithreaded programs much easier. For one thing, it does not force each thread to decide exactly when it should "yield" control to another thread. Instead, every thread can just run blindly on, knowing that the scheduler will be fair about giving all the other threads their chance to run.

It turns out that this approach is still not the ideal way to schedule threads. You've given a little too much control to the scheduler. The final touch many modern schedulers add is to enable you to assign each thread a priority. This creates a total ordering of all threads, making some threads more "important" than others. Being higher priority often means that a thread gets run more often (or gets more total running time), but it always means that it can interrupt other, lower-priority threads, even before their "time-slice" has expired.

The current Java release does not precisely specify the behavior of its scheduler. Threads can be assigned priorities, and when a choice is made between several threads that all want to run, the highest-priority thread wins. However, among threads that are all the same priority, the behavior is not well-defined. In fact, the different platforms on which Java currently runs have different behaviors—some, including Roaster, behaving more like a preemptive scheduler, and some more like a nonpreemptive scheduler.

NOTE

> This incomplete specification of the scheduler is terribly annoying and, presumably, will be corrected in later releases. Not knowing the fine details of how scheduling occurs is perfectly all right, but not knowing whether equal priority threads must explicitly yield or face running forever is not all right. For example, all the threads you have created so far are equal priority threads, so you don't know their basic scheduling behavior!

Testing Your Scheduler

Here's a little application that tests what sort of scheduler the run-time system that's running the system uses:

```
public class  RunnablePotato implements Runnable {
    public void  run() {
        while (true)
            System.out.println(Thread.currentThread().getName());
    }
}


public class  PotatoThreadTester {
    public static void  main(String argv[]) {
        RunnablePotato  aRP = new RunnablePotato();

        new Thread(aRP, "one potato").start();
        new Thread(aRP, "two potato").start();
    }
}
```

Roaster uses a preemptive scheduler that time-slices. When the application runs, it repeats the line one potato a few times, followed by the same number of two potato lines, over and over:

```
one potato
one potato
...
one potato
two potato
two potato
...
two potato
. . .
```

... until you interrupt the program.

For a nonpreemptive scheduler, this prints the following:

```
one potato
one potato
one potato
. . .
```

... forever, until you interrupt the program.

What if you want to be sure the two threads will take turns, no matter what the system scheduler wants to do? You rewrite RunnablePotato as follows:

```
public class  RunnablePotato implements Runnable {
    public void  run() {
        while (true) {
            System.out.println(Thread.currentThread().getName());
            Thread.yield();  // let another thread run for a while
        }
    }
}
```

NOTE   Normally, you have to say Thread.currentThread().yield() to get your hands on the current thread, and then call yield(). Because this pattern is so common, however, the Thread class provides a shortcut.

The yield() method explicitly gives any other threads that want to run a chance to begin running. (If there are no threads waiting to run, the thread that made the yield() simply continues.) In our example, there's another thread that's just dying to run, so when you now run the class ThreadTester, it should output the following:

```
one potato
two potato
one potato
two potato
one potato
two potato
. . .
```

The revised version of ThreadTest will produce this output, even if you run it on a non-Mac implementation of Java with a nonpreemptive system scheduler, which would never normally run the second thread.

PriorityThreadTester

The current version of Roaster doesn't implement priority-based preemptive scheduling. For a demonstration, try this:

```
public class  PriorityThreadTester {
    public static void  main(String argv[]) {
        RunnablePotato  aRP = new RunnablePotato();
        Thread          t1  = new Thread(aRP, "one potato");
        Thread          t2  = new Thread(aRP, "two potato");

        t2.setPriority(t1.getPriority() + 1);
        t1.start();
        t2.start();   // at priority Thread.NORM_PRIORITY + 1
    }
}
```

NOTE

The values representing the lowest, normal, and highest priorities that threads can be assigned are stored in class variables of the Thread class: Thread.MIN_PRIORITY, Thread.NORM_PRIORITY, and Thread.MAX_PRIORITY. The system assigns new threads, by default, the priority Thread.NORM_PRIORITY. Priorities in Java are currently defined in a range from 1 to 10, with 5 being normal, but you shouldn't depend on these values; use the class variables, or tricks like the one shown in this example.

Roaster produces one potato as the first line of output, and hence does not preempt using priorities.

Why? Imagine that the first thread (t1) has just begun to run. Even before it has a chance to print anything, along comes a higher-priority thread (t2) that wants to run right away. That higher-priority thread should preempt (interrupt) the first, and get a chance to print two potato before t1 finishes printing anything. In fact, if you use the RunnablePotato class that never yield()s, t2 stays in control forever, printing two pota-to lines, because it's a higher priority than t1 and it never yields control. If you use the latest RunnablePotato class (with yield()), the output is alternating lines of one potato and two potato as before, but starting with two potato.

Here's a good, illustrative example of how complex threads behave:

```
public class  ComplexThread extends Thread {
    private int  delay;

    ComplexThread(String  name,  float  seconds) {
        super(name);
        delay = (int) seconds * 1000;    // delays are in milliseconds
        start();                         // start up ourself!
    }

    public void  run() {
        while (true) {
            System.out.println(Thread.currentThread().getName());
            try {
                Thread.sleep(delay);
            } catch (InterruptedException  ignored) {
                return;
            }
        }
    }

    public static void  main(String argv[]) {
        new ComplexThread("one potato",    1.1F);
        new ComplexThread("two potato",    0.3F);
        new ComplexThread("three potato", 0.5F);
        new ComplexThread("four",          0.7F);
    }
}
```

This example combines the thread and its tester into a single class. Its constructor takes care of naming (itself) and of starting (itself), because it is now a Thread. The main() method creates new instances of its own class, because that class is a subclass of Thread. run() is also more complicated, because it now uses, for the first time, a method that can throw an unexpected exception.

The Thread.sleep() method forces the current thread to yield() and then waits for at least the specified amount of time to elapse before allowing the thread to run again. It might be interrupted, however, while sleeping by another thread. In such a case, it throws an InterruptedException. Now, because run() is not defined as throwing this exception, you must "hide" the fact by catching and handling it yourself. Because interruptions are usually requests to stop, you should exit the thread, which you can do by simply returning from the run() method.

This program should output a repeating but complex pattern of four different lines, where every once in a while you see the following:

```
. . .
one potato
two potato
three potato
four
. . .
```

You should study the pattern output to prove to yourself that true parallelism is going on inside Java programs. You may also begin to appreciate that, if even this simple set of four threads can produce such complex behavior, many more threads must be capable of producing near chaos if not carefully controlled. Luckily, Java provides the synchronization and thread-safe libraries you need to control that chaos.

Summary

Today, you learned that parallelism is desirable and powerful, but introduces many new problems—methods and variables now need to be protected from thread conflicts—that can lead to chaos if not carefully controlled.

By "thinking multithreaded," you can detect the places in your programs that require synchronized statements (or modifiers) to make them thread-safe. A series of Point examples demonstrated the various levels of safety you can achieve and showed how subclasses of Thread, or classes that implement the Runnable interface, are created and run() to generate multithreaded programs.

You also learned how to yield(), how to start(), stop(), suspend(), and resume() your threads, and how to catch ThreadDeath whenever it happens.

Finally, you learned about preemptive and nonpreemptive scheduling, both with and without priorities, and that Roaster uses preemptive scheduling without priorities.

This wraps up the description of threads. You now know enough to write the most complex of programs: multithreaded ones. As you get more comfortable with threads, you may begin to use the ThreadGroup class or to use the enumeration methods of Thread to get your hands on all the threads in the system and manipulate them. Don't be afraid to experiment; you can't permanently break anything, and you learn only by trying.

Questions and Answers

Q If they're so important to Java, why haven't threads appeared throughout the entire book?

A Actually, they have. Every stand-alone program written so far has "created" at least one thread, the one in which it is running. (Of course the system created that Thread for it automatically.)

Q How exactly do these threads get created and run? What about applets?

A When a simple, stand-alone Java program starts up, the Applet Runner creates a main thread, and its run() method calls your main() method to start your program—you do nothing to get that Thread. Likewise, when a simple applet loads into Applet Runner or a Java-aware browser, a Thread has already been created, and its run() method calls your init() and start() methods to start your program. In either case, a new Thread() of some kind was done somewhere, by the Java environment itself.

Q The `ThreadTester` class had an infinite loop that created `Threads` and then `join()`ed with them. Is it really infinite?

A In theory, yes. In actuality, how far the loop runs determines the resource limits of (and tests the stability of) the threads package and garbage collector in your Java release. Over time, all Java releases will converge on making the loop truly infinite.

Q I know Java releases are still a little fuzzy about the scheduler's behavior, but what's the current story?

A Here are the gruesome details, relayed by Arthur van Hoff: the way Java schedules threads "... depends on the platform. It is usually preemptive, but not always time-sliced. Priorities are not always observed, depending on the underlying implementation." This final clause gives you a hint that all this confusion is an implementation problem, and that in a future release, the design and implementation will both be clear about scheduling behavior.

Q Does Java support more complex multithreaded concepts, such as semaphores?

A The class `Object` in Java provides methods that can be used to build up condition variables, semaphores, and any higher-level parallel construct you might need. The method wait() (and its two variants with a timeout) causes the current thread to wait until some condition has been satisfied. The method notify() (or notifyAll()), which must be called from within a synchronized method or block, tells the thread (or all threads) to wake up and check that condition again, because something has changed. By careful combinations of these two primitive methods, any data structure can be manipulated safely by a set of threads, and all the classical parallel primitives needed to implement published parallel algorithms can be built.

Q My parallel friends tell me I should worry about something called "deadlock." Should I?

A Not for simple multithreaded programs. However, in more complicated programs, one of the biggest worries does become one of avoiding a situation in which one thread has locked an object and is waiting for another thread to finish, while that other thread is waiting for the first thread to release that same object before it can finish. That's a deadlock—both threads will be stuck forever. Mutual dependencies like this involving more than two threads can be quite intricate, convoluted, and difficult to locate, much less rectify. They are one of the main challenges in writing complex multithreaded programs.

Streams

by Charles L. Perkins with Timothy Webster

Today you'll explore Java's streams:

☐ Input streams—and how to create, use, and detect the end of them—and filtered input streams, which can be nested to great effect

☐ Output streams, which are mostly analogous to (but the inverse of) input streams

You'll also learn about two stream interfaces that make the reading and writing of typed streams much easier (as well as about several utility classes used to access the file system). Let's begin with a little history behind the invention of streams.

One of the early inventions of the Unix operating system was the "pipe." There isn't really a Macintosh equivalent to the pipe—it's a system tool that enables you to redirect output—for example, to take text that would ordinarily go to the screen, and write it to a file or feed it to another program instead. It doesn't make a lot of sense in the Mac environment, where even the simplest programs output a great deal more than text strings. Perhaps the closest analogy—and it isn't very close—is the Mac's capability to move data between applications via Apple Events. By unifying many disparate ways of communicating into the single metaphor of the pipe, Unix paved the way for a whole series of related inventions, culminating in the abstraction known as streams.

NEW TERM   A *pipe* is an uninterpreted stream of bytes that can be used for communicating between programs or for reading and writing to peripheral devices and files.

NEW TERM   A *stream* is a path of communication between the source of some information and its destination.

The information that comprises an uninterpreted byte stream can come from any "pipe source," from the computer's memory, or even from the Internet. In fact, the source and destination of a stream are completely arbitrary producers and consumers of bytes, respectively. Therein lies the power of the abstraction. You don't need to know about the source of the information when reading from a stream, and you don't need to know about the final destination when writing to one.

General-purpose methods that can read from any source accept a stream argument to specify that source; general methods for writing accept a stream to specify the destination. Arbitrary processors (or filters) of data have two stream arguments. They read from the first, process the data, and write the results to the second. These processors have no idea of either the source or the destination of the data they are processing. Sources and destinations can vary widely: from two memory buffers on the same local computer, to the ELF transmissions to and from a submarine at sea, to the real-time data streams of a NASA probe in deep space.

By decoupling the consuming, processing, or producing of data from the sources and destinations of that data, you can mix and match any combination of them at will as you write your program. In the future, when new, previously nonexistent forms of source or destination (or consumer, processor, or producer) appear, they can be used within the same framework, with no changes to your classes. New stream abstractions, supporting higher levels of interpretation "on top of" the bytes, can be written completely independently of the underlying transport mechanisms for the bytes themselves.

At the pinnacle of this stream framework are the two abstract classes, InputStream and OutputStream. Below these classes is a virtual cornucopia of categorized classes, demonstrating the wide range of streams in the system, but also demonstrating an extremely well-designed hierarchy of relationships between these streams. (The java.io hierarchy is shown in Figure 19.1, and also included in Appendix B.) Let's begin with the parents and then work our way down this bushy tree.

Input Streams

All the methods you will explore today are declared to throw IOExceptions. This new subclass of Exception conceptually embodies all the possible I/O errors that might occur while using streams. Several subclasses of it define a few, more specific exceptions that can be thrown as well. For now, it is enough to know that you must either catch an IOException, or be in a method that can "pass it along," to be a well-behaved user of streams.

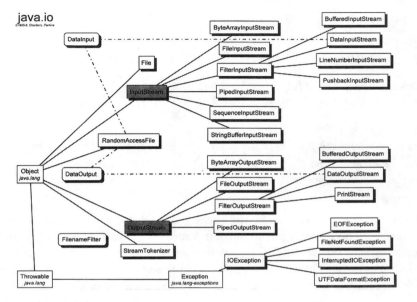

Figure 19.1 *The java.io hierarchy.*

The abstract Class InputStream

InputStream is an abstract class that defines the fundamental ways in which a destination consumer reads a stream of bytes from some source. The identity of the source and the manner of the creation and transport of the bytes are irrelevant. When using an input stream, you are the destination of those bytes, and that's all you need to know.

read()

The most important method to the consumer of an input stream is the one that reads bytes from the source. This method, read(), comes in many flavors, and each is demonstrated in an example in today's lesson.

Each of these read() methods is defined to "block" (wait) until all the input requested becomes available. Don't worry about this limitation; because of multithreading, you can do as many other things as you like while this one thread is waiting for input. In fact, it is a common idiom to assign a thread to each stream of input (and for each stream of output) that is solely responsible for reading from it (or writing to it). These input threads might then "hand off" the information to other threads for processing. This naturally overlaps the I/O time of your program with its compute time.

Here's the first form of read():

```
InputStream  s      = getAnInputStreamFromSomewhere();
byte[]       buffer = new byte[1024];   // any size will do

if (s.read(buffer) != buffer.length)
    System.out.println("I got less than I expected.");
```

NOTE

Here and throughout the rest of today's lesson, assume that either an import java.io appears before all the examples or that you mentally prefix all references to java.io classes with the prefix java.io.

This form of read() attempts to fill the entire buffer given. If it cannot (usually due to reaching the end of the input stream), it returns the actual number of bytes that were read into the buffer. After that, any further calls to read() return -1, indicating that you are at the end of the stream. Note that the if statement still works even in this case, because -1 != 1024 (this corresponds to an input stream with no bytes in it at all).

NOTE

Don't forget that, unlike in C, the -1 case in Java is not used to indicate an error. Any I/O errors throw instances of IOException (which you're not catching yet). You learned on Day 17 that all uses of distinguished values can be replaced by the use of exceptions, and so they should. The -1 in the last example is a bit of an historical anachronism. You'll soon see a better approach to indicating end of the stream using the class DataInputStream.

You can also read into a "slice" of your buffer by specifying the offset into the buffer, and the length desired, as arguments to read():

```
s.read(buffer, 100, 300);
```

This example tries to fill in bytes 100 through 399 and behaves otherwise exactly the same as the previous read() method. In fact, in the current release, the default implementation of the former version of read() uses the latter:

```
public int  read(byte[]  buffer) throws IOException {
    return  read(buffer, 0, buffer.length);
}
```

Finally, you can read in bytes one at a time:

```
InputStream  s = getAnInputStreamFromSomewhere();
byte         b;
int          byteOrMinus1;

while ((byteOrMinus1 = s.read()) != -1) {
b = (byte) byteOrMinus1;
. . .     // process the byte b
}
. . .     // reached end of stream
```

NOTE

Because of the nature of integer promotion in Java in general, and because in this case the read() method returns an int, using the byte type in your code may be a little frustrating. You'll find yourself constantly having explicitly to cast the result of arithmetic expressions, or of int return values, back to your size. Because read() really should be returning a byte in this case, I feel justified in declaring and using it as such (despite the pain)—it makes the size of the data being read clearer. In cases wherein you feel the range of a variable is naturally limited to a byte (or a short) rather than an int, please take the time to declare it that way and pay the small price necessary to gain the added clarity. By the way, a lot of the Java class library code simply stores the result of read() in an int. This proves that even the Java team is human—everyone makes style mistakes.

skip()

What if you want to skip over some of the bytes in a stream, or start reading a stream from other than its beginning? A method similar to read() does the trick:

```
if (s.skip(1024) != 1024)
    System.out.println("I skipped less than I expected.");
```

This skips over the next 1024 bytes in the input stream. skip() takes and returns a long integer, because streams are not required to be limited to any particular size. The default implementation of skip in this release simply uses read():

```
public long  skip(long n) throws IOException {
    byte[]  buffer = new byte[(int) n];

    return  read(buffer);
}
```

NOTE

> This implementation does not support large skips correctly, because its `long` argument is cast to an `int`. Subclasses must override this default implementation if they want to handle this more properly. This won't be as easy as you might think, because the current release of the Java system does not allow integer types larger than `int` to act as array subscripts.

available()

If for some reason you would like to know how many bytes are in the stream right now, you can ask:

```
if (s.available() < 1024)
    System.out.println("Too little is available right now.");
```

This tells you the number of bytes that you can `read()` without blocking. Because of the abstract nature of the source of these bytes, streams may or may not be able to tell you a reasonable answer to this question. For example, some streams always return 0. Unless you use specific subclasses of `InputStream` that you know provide reasonable answers to this question, it's not a good idea to rely upon this method. Remember, multithreading eliminates many of the problems associated with blocking while waiting for a stream to fill again. Thus, one of the strongest rationales for the use of `available()` goes away.

mark() and reset()

Some streams support the notion of marking a position in the stream, and then later resetting the stream to that position to reread the bytes there. Clearly, the stream would have to "remember" all those bytes, so there is a limitation on how far apart in a stream the mark and its subsequent reset can occur. There's also a method that asks whether or not the stream supports the notion of marking at all. Here's an example:

```
InputStream  s = getAnInputStreamFromSomewhere();

if (s.markSupported()) {     // does s support the notion?
    . . .              // read the stream for a while
    s.mark(1024);
    . . .              // read less than 1024 more bytes
    s.reset();
    . . .              // we can now reread those bytes
} else {
    . . .                        // no, perform some alternative
}
```

When marking a stream, you specify the maximum number of bytes you intend to allow to pass before resetting it. This allows the stream to limit the size of its byte "memory." If this number of bytes goes by and you have not yet reset(), the mark becomes invalid, and attempting to reset() will throw an exception.

Marking and resetting a stream is most valuable when you are attempting to identify the type of the stream (or the next part of the stream), but to do so, you must consume a significant piece of it in the process. Often, this is because you have several black-box parsers that you can hand the stream to, but they will consume some (unknown to you) number of bytes before making up their mind about whether the stream is of their type. Set a large size for the read limit above, and let each parser run until it either throws an error or completes a successful parse. If an error is thrown, reset() and try the next parser.

close()

Because you don't know what resources an open stream represents, nor how to deal with them properly when you're finished reading the stream, you must usually explicitly close down a stream so that it can release these resources. Of course, garbage collection and a finalization method can do this for you, but what if you need to reopen that stream or those resources before they have been freed by this asynchronous process? At best, this is annoying or confusing; at worst, it introduces an unexpected, obscure, and difficult-to-track-down bug. Because you're interacting with the outside world of external resources, it's safer to be explicit about when you're finished using them:

```
InputStream  s = alwaysMakesANewInputStream();

try {
    . . .        // use s to your heart's content
} finally {
    s.close();
}
```

Get used to this idiom (using finally); it's a useful way to be sure something (such as closing the stream) always gets done. Of course, you're assuming that the stream is always successfully created. If this is not always the case, and null is sometimes returned instead, here's the correct way to be safe:

```
InputStream  s = tryToMakeANewInputStream();

if (s != null) {
    try {
        . . .
```

```
    } finally {
        s.close();
    }
}
```

All input streams descend from the abstract class InputStream. All share the few methods described so far. Thus, stream s in the previous examples could have been any of the more complex input streams described in the next few sections.

ByteArrayInputStream

The "inverse" of some of the previous examples would be to create an input stream from an array of bytes. This is exactly what ByteArrayInputStream does:

```
byte[]  buffer = new byte[1024];

fillWithUsefulData(buffer);

InputStream  s = new ByteArrayInputStream(buffer);
```

Readers of the new stream s see a stream 1024 bytes long, containing the bytes in the array buffer. Just as read() has a form that takes an offset and a length, so does this class's constructor:

```
InputStream  s = new ByteArrayInputStream(buffer, 100, 300);
```

Here, the stream is 300 bytes long and consists of bytes 100-399 from the array buffer.

NOTE

Finally, you've seen your first examples of the creation of a stream. These new streams are attached to the simplest of all possible sources of data, an array of bytes in the memory of the local computer.

ByteArrayInputStreams only implement the standard set of methods that all input streams do. Here, however, the available() method has a particularly simple job—it returns 1024 and 300, respectively, for the two instances of ByteArrayInputStream you created previously, because it knows exactly how many bytes are available. Finally, calling reset() on a ByteArrayInputStream resets it to the beginning of the stream (buffer), no matter where the mark is set.

FileInputStream

One of the most common uses of streams, and historically the earliest, is to attach them to files in the file system. Here, for example, is the creation of such an input stream (remember, Java uses the Unix system for specifying file paths, with a "/"

before the name of the hard drive, and "/" between folders and subfolders, rather than the Mac system, which uses colons):

```
InputStream  s = new FileInputStream("/some/path/and/fileName");
```

> Applets attempting to open, read, or write streams based on files in the file system can cause security violations (depending on the paranoia level set by the user of the browser). Fortunately, Roaster's Applet Runner will let you work with files from an Applet, but you'll run into problems when users try to load your program with a Java-capable Web browser. Try to create applets that do not depend on files at all, by using servers to hold shared information. If that's impossible, limit your applet's I/O to a single file or directory to which the user can easily assign file access permission. (Standalone Java programs have none of these problems, of course.)

You also can create the stream from a previously opened file descriptor:

```
int         fd = openInputFileInTraditionalWays();
InputStream  s  = new FileInputStream(fd);
```

WARNING

> Don't forget that Roaster doesn't support the `FileDialog` object yet—so don't pass a file descriptor produced by one of `FileDialog`'s methods to `FileInputStream`.

In either case, because it's based on an actual (finite-length) file, the input stream created can implement `available()` precisely and can `skip()` like a champ (just as `ByteArrayInputStream` can, by the way). In addition, `FileInputStream` knows a few more tricks:

```
FileInputStream  aFIS = new FileInputStream("aFileName");

int  myFD = aFIS.getFD();

/* aFIS.finalize(); */  // will call close() when automatically called by GC
```

NOTE

> To call the new methods, you must declare the stream variable `aFIS` to be of type `FileInputStream`, because plain `InputStream`s don't know about them.

The first is obvious: `getFD()` returns the file descriptor of the file on which the stream is based. The second, though, is an interesting shortcut that enables you to create

FileInputStreams without worrying about closing them later. FileInputStream's implementation of finalize(), a protected method, closes the stream. Unlike in the previous contrived example in comments, you almost never can nor should call a finalize() method directly. The garbage collector calls it after noticing that the stream is no longer in use, but before actually destroying the stream. Thus, you can go merrily along using the stream, never closing it, and all will be well. The system takes care of closing it (eventually).

You can get away with this because streams based on files tie up very few resources, and these resources cannot be accidentally reused before garbage collection (these were the things worried about in the previous discussion of finalization and close()). Of course, if you were also writing to the file, you would have to be more careful. (Reopening the file too soon after writing might make it appear in an inconsistent state because the finalize()—and thus the close()—might not have happened yet). Just because you don't have to close the stream doesn't mean you might not want to do so anyway. For clarity, or if you don't know precisely what type of an InputStream you were handed, you might choose to call close() yourself.

FilterInputStream

This "abstract" class simply provides a "pass-through" for all the standard methods of InputStream. It holds inside itself another stream, by definition one further "down" the chain of filters, to which it forwards all method calls. It implements nothing new but allows itself to be nested:

```
InputStream          s  = getAnInputStreamFromSomewhere();
FilterInputStream   s1 = new FilterInputStream(s);
FilterInputStream   s2 = new FilterInputStream(s1);
FilterInputStream   s3 = new FilterInputStream(s2);

... s3.read() ...
```

Whenever a read is performed on the filtered stream s3, it passes along the request to s2; then s2 does the same to s1, and finally s is asked to provide the bytes. Subclasses of FilterInputStream will, of course, do some nontrivial processing of the bytes as they flow past. The rather verbose form of "chaining" in the previous example can be made more elegant:

```
s3 = new FilterInputStream(new FilterInputStream(new FilterInputStream(s)));
```

You should use this idiom in your code whenever you can. It clearly expresses the nesting of chained filters, and can easily be parsed and "read aloud" by starting at the innermost stream s and reading outward—each filter stream applying to the one within—until you reach the outermost stream s3.

NOTE

FilterInputStream is called "abstract," rather than abstract, because it is not actually declared to be abstract. This means that, as useless as they are, you can create instances of FilterInputStream directly. The same will hold for its output stream "brother" class, described later today.

Now let's examine each of the subclasses of FilterInputStream in turn.

BufferedInputStream

This is one of the most valuable of all streams. It implements the full complement of InputStream's methods, but it does so by using a buffered array of bytes that acts as a cache for future reading. This decouples the rate and the size of the "chunks" you're reading from the more regular, larger block sizes in which streams are most efficiently read (from, for example, peripheral devices, files in the file system, or the network). It also allows smart streams to read ahead when they expect that you will want more data soon.

Because the buffering of BufferedInputStream is so valuable, and it's also the only class to handle mark() and reset() properly, you might wish that every input stream could somehow share its valuable capabilities. Normally, because those stream classes do not implement them, you would be out of luck. Fortunately, you already saw a way that filter streams can wrap themselves "around" other streams. Suppose that you would like a buffered FileInputStream that can handle marking and resetting correctly. Et voilà:

```
InputStream  s = new BufferedInputStream(new FileInputStream("foo"));
```

You have a buffered input stream based on the file "foo" that can mark() and reset().

Now you can begin to see the power of nesting streams. Any capability provided by a filter input stream (or output stream, as you'll see soon) can be used by any other basic stream via nesting. Of course, any combination of these capabilities, and in any order, can be as easily accomplished by nesting the filter streams themselves.

DataInputStream

All the methods that instances of this class understand are defined in a separate interface, which both DataInputStream and RandomAccessFile (another class in java.io) implement. This interface is general-purpose enough that you might want to use it yourself in the classes you create. It is called DataInput.

The DataInput Interface

When you begin using streams to any degree, you'll quickly discover that byte streams are not a really helpful format into which to force all data. In particular, the primitive types of the Java language embody a rather nice way of looking at data, but with the streams you've been defining thus far in this book, you could not read data of these types. The DataInput interface specifies a higher-level set of methods that, when used for both reading and writing, can support a more complex, typed stream of data. Here are the set of methods this interface defines:

```
void    readFully(byte[] buffer)                          throws IOException;
void    readFully(byte[] buffer, int offset, int length) throws IOException;
int     skipBytes(int n)                                  throws IOException;

boolean readBoolean()         throws IOException;
byte    readByte()            throws IOException;
int     readUnsignedByte()    throws IOException;
short   readShort()           throws IOException;
int     readUnsignedShort()   throws IOException;
char    readChar()            throws IOException;
int     readInt()             throws IOException;
long    readLong()            throws IOException;
float   readFloat()           throws IOException;
double  readDouble()          throws IOException;

String  readLine()            throws IOException;
String  readUTF()             throws IOException;
```

The first three methods are simply new names for skip() and the two forms of read() you've seen previously. Each of the next ten methods reads in a primitive type or its unsigned counterpart (useful for using every bit efficiently in a binary stream). These latter methods must return an integer of a wider size than you might think; because integers are signed in Java, the unsigned value does not fit in anything smaller. The final two methods read a newline ('\r', '\n', or "\r\n") terminated string of characters from the stream—the first in ASCII and the second in Unicode.

Now that you know what the interface that DataInputStream implements looks like, let's see it in action:

```
DataInputStream  s = new DataInputStream(getNumericInputStream());

long  size = s.readLong();     // the number of items in the stream

while (size— > 0) {
```

```
        if (s.readBoolean()) {      // should I process this item?
            int     anInteger    = s.readInt();
            int     magicBitFlags = s.readUnsignedShort();
            double  aDouble      = s.readDouble();

            if ((magicBitFlags & 0100000) != 0) {
                . . .      // high bit set, do something special
            }
            . . .      // process anInteger and aDouble
        }
}
```

Because the class implements an interface for all its methods, you can also use the following interface:

```
DataInput  d = new DataInputStream(new FileInputStream("anything"));
String     line;

while ((line = d.readLine()) != null) {
    . . .      // process the line
}
```

The EOFException

One final point about most of DataInputStream's methods: when the end of the stream is reached, they throw an EOFException. This is tremendously useful and, in fact, enables you to rewrite all the kludgy uses of -1 you saw earlier today in a much nicer fashion:

```
DataInputStream  s = new DataInputStream(getAnInputStreamFromSomewhere());

try {
    while (true) {
    byte  b = (byte) s.readByte();
    . . .      // process the byte b
    }
} catch (EOFException e) {
    . . .      // reached end of stream
}
```

This works just as well for all but the last two of the read methods of DataInputStream.

WARNING   skipBytes() does nothing at all on end of stream, readLine() returns null, and readUTF() might throw a UTFDataFormatException, if it notices the problem at all.

LineNumberInputStream

In an editor or a debugger, line numbering is crucial. To add this valuable capability to your programs, use the filter stream LineNumberInputStream, which keeps track of line numbers as its stream flows through it. It's even smart enough to remember a line number and later restore it, during a mark() and reset(). You might use this class as follows:

```
LineNumberInputStream  aLNIS;
aLNIS = new LineNumberInputStream(new FileInputStream("source"));

DataInputStream  s = new DataInputStream(aLNIS);
String           line;

while ((line = s.readLine()) != null) {
    . . .    // process the line
    System.out.println("Did line number: " + aLNIS.getLineNumber());
}
```

Here, two filter streams are nested around the FileInputStream actually providing the data—the first to read lines one at a time and the second to keep track of the line numbers of these lines as they go by. You must explicitly name the intermediate filter stream, aLNIS, because if you did not, you couldn't call getLineNumber() later. Note that if you invert the order of the nested streams, reading from the DataInputStream does not cause the LineNumberInputStream to "see" the lines.

You must put any filter streams acting as "monitors" in the middle of the chain and "pull" the data from the outermost filter stream so that the data will pass through each of the monitors in turn. In the same way, buffering should occur as far inside the chain as possible, because it won't be able to do its job properly unless most of the streams that need buffering come after it in the flow. For example, here's a doubly silly order:

```
new BufferedInputStream(new LineNumberInputStream(
        _new DataInputStream(new FileInputStream("foo"));
```

... and here's a much better order:

```
new DataInputStream(new LineNumberInputStream(
        _new BufferedInputStream(new FileInputStream("foo"));
```

LineNumberInputStreams can also be told to setLineNumber(), for those few times when you know more than they do.

PushbackInputStream

The filter stream class PushbackInputStream is commonly used in parsers to "push back" a single character in the input (after reading it) while trying to determine what to do next—a simplified version of the mark() and reset() utility you learned about earlier. Its only addition to the standard set of InputStream methods is unread(), which as you might guess, pretends that it never read the byte passed in as its argument, and then gives that byte back as the return value of the next read().

The following is a simple implementation of readLine() using this class:

```
public class  SimpleLineReader {
    private FilterInputStream  s;

    public  SimpleLineReader(InputStream  anIS) {
        s = new DataInputStream(anIS);
    }

    . . .    // other read() methods using stream s

    public String  readLine() throws IOException {
        char[]  buffer = new char[100];
        int     offset = 0;
        byte    thisByte;

        try {
loop:       while (offset < buffer.length) {
                switch (thisByte = (byte) s.read()) {
                    case '\n':
                        break loop;
                    case '\r':
                        byte  nextByte = (byte) s.read();

                        if (nextByte != '\n') {
                            if (!(s instanceof PushbackInputStream)){
                                s = new PushbackInputStream(s);
                            }
                            ((PushbackInputStream) s).unread(nextByte);
                        }
                        break loop;
                    default:
                        buffer[offset++] = (char) thisByte;
                        break;
                }
            }
        }
```

```
        } catch (EOFException e) {
            if (offset == 0)
                return null;
        }
        return String.copyValueOf(buffer, 0, offset);
    }
}
```

This demonstrates numerous things. For the purpose of this example, readLine() is restricted to reading the first 100 characters of the line. In this respect, it demonstrates how not to write a general-purpose line processor (you should be able to read any size line). It also reminds you how to break out of an outer loop and how to produce a String from an array of characters (in this case, from a "slice" of the array of characters). This example also includes standard uses of InputStream's read() for reading bytes one at a time, and of determining the end of the stream by enclosing it in a DataInputStream and catching EOFException.

One of the more unusual aspects of the example is the way PushbackInputStream is used. To be sure that '\n' is ignored following '\r', you have to "look ahead" one character; but if it is not a '\n', you must push back that character. Look at the next two lines as if you didn't know much about the stream s. The general technique used is instructive. First, you see whether s is already an instanceof some kind of PushbackInputStream. If so, you can simply use it. If not, you enclose the current stream (whatever it is) inside a new PushbackInputStream and use this new stream. Now, let's jump back into the context of the example.

The line following wants to call the method unread(). The problem is that s has a "compile-time type" of FilterInputStream, and thus doesn't understand that method. The previous two lines have guaranteed, however, that the run-time type of the stream in s is PushbackInputStream, so you can safely cast it to that type and then safely call unread().

NOTE   This example was done in an unusual way for demonstration purposes. You could have simply declared a PushbackInputStream variable and always enclosed the DataInputStream in it. (Conversely, SimpleLineReader's constructor could have checked whether its argument was already of the right class, the way PushbackInputStream did, before creating a new DataInputStream.) The interesting thing about this approach of "wrapping a class only when needed" is that it works for any InputStream that you hand it, and it does additional work only if it needs to. Both of these are good general design principles.

All the subclasses of `FilterInputStream` have now been described. It's time to return to the direct subclasses of `InputStream`.

PipedInputStream

This class, along with its "brother" class `PipedOutputStream`, are covered later today (they need to be understood and demonstrated together). For now, all you need to know is that together they create a simple, two-way communication conduit between threads.

SequenceInputStream

Suppose you have two separate streams and you would like to make a composite stream that consists of one stream followed by the other (like appending two `String`s together). This is exactly what `SequenceInputStream` was created for:

```
InputStream  s1 = new FileInputStream("theFirstPart");
InputStream  s2 = new FileInputStream("theRest");

InputStream  s  = new SequenceInputStream(s1, s2);

... s.read() ...   // reads from each stream in turn
```

You could have "faked" this example by reading each file in turn—but what if you had to hand the composite stream s to some other method that was expecting only a single `InputStream`? Here's an example (using s) that line-numbers the two previous files with a common numbering scheme:

```
LineNumberInputStream  aLNIS = new LineNumberInputStream(s);

... aLNIS.getLineNumber() ...
```

NOTE   Stringing together streams this way is especially useful when the streams are of unknown length and origin and were just handed to you by someone else.

What if you want to string together more than two streams? You could try the following:

```
Vector  v = new Vector();
. . .   // set up all the streams and add each to the Vector
InputStream  s1 = new SequenceInputStream(v.elementAt(0), v.elementAt(1));
InputStream  s2 = new SequenceInputStream(s1, v.elementAt(2));
InputStream  s3 = new SequenceInputStream(s2, v.elementAt(3));
. . .
```

A `Vector` is an array of objects that can be filled, referenced (with `elementAt()`), and enumerated.

However, it's much easier to use a different constructor that `SequenceInputStream` provides:

```
InputStream  s  = new SequenceInputStream(v.elements());
```

It takes an enumeration of all the sequences you wish to combine and returns a single stream that reads through the data of each in turn.

StringBufferInputStream

`StringBufferInputStream` is exactly like `ByteArrayInputStream`, but instead of being based on a byte array, it's based on an array of characters (a `String`):

```
String      buffer = "Now is the time for all good men to come...";
InputStream  s     = new StringBufferInputStream(buffer);
```

All comments that were made about `ByteArrayInputStream` apply here as well. (See the earlier section on that class.)

NOTE `StringBufferInputStream` is a bit of a misnomer, because this input stream is actually based on a `String`. It should really be called `StringInputStream`.

Output Streams

`Output streams` are, in almost every case, paired with a "brother" `InputStream` that you've already learned. If an `InputStream` performs a certain operation, the "brother" `OutputStream` performs the inverse operation. You'll see more of what this means soon.

The abstract Class OutputStream

`OutputStream` is the `abstract` class that defines the fundamental ways in which a source (producer) writes a stream of bytes to some destination. The identity of the destination and the manner of the transport and storage of the bytes are irrelevant. When using an output stream, you are the source of those bytes, and that's all you need to know.

write()

The most important method to the producer of an output stream is the one that writes bytes to the destination. This method, write(), comes in many flavors, each demonstrated in an example coming up.

Every one of these write() methods is defined to "block" (wait) until all the output requested has been written. You don't need to worry about this limitation—see the note under InputStream's read() method if you don't remember why.

```
OutputStream  s      = getAnOutputStreamFromSomewhere();
byte[]        buffer = new byte[1024];    // any size will do

fillInData(buffer);    // the data we want to output
s.write(buffer);
```

You also can write a "slice" of your buffer by specifying the offset into the buffer, and the length desired, as arguments to write():

```
s.write(buffer, 100, 300);
```

This writes out bytes 100 through 399 and behaves otherwise exactly the same as the previous write() method. In fact, in the current release, the default implementation of the former version of write() uses the latter:

```
public void  write(byte[]  buffer) throws IOException {
    write(buffer, 0, buffer.length);
}
```

Finally, you can write out bytes one at a time:

```
while (thereAreMoreBytesToOutput()) {
    byte  b = getNextByteForOutput();

    s.write(b);
}
```

flush()

Because you don't know what an output stream is connected to, you might be required to flush your output through some buffered cache to get it to be written (in a timely manner, or at all). OutputStream's version of this method does nothing, but it is expected that subclasses that require flushing (for example, BufferedOutputStream and PrintStream) will override this version to do something nontrivial.

close()

Just like for an InputStream, you should (usually) explicitly close down an OutputStream so that it can release any resources it may have reserved on your behalf. (All the same notes and examples from InputStream's close() method apply here, with the prefix In replaced everywhere by Out.)

All output streams descend from the abstract class OutputStream. All share the previous few methods in common.

ByteArrayOutputStream

The inverse of ByteArrayInputStream, which creates an input stream from an array of bytes, is ByteArrayOutputStream, which directs an output stream into an array of bytes:

```
OutputStream  s = new ByteArrayOutputStream();

s.write(123);
. . .
```

The size of the (internal) byte array grows as needed to store a stream of any length. You can provide an initial capacity as an aid to the class, if you like:

```
OutputStream  s = new ByteArrayOutputStream(1024 * 1024);  // 1 Megabyte
```

NOTE
> You've just seen your first examples of the creation of an output stream. These new streams were attached to the simplest of all possible destinations of data, an array of bytes in the memory of the local computer.

After the ByteArrayOutputStream s has been "filled," it can be output to another output stream:

```
OutputStream            anotherOutputStream = getTheOtherOutputStream();
ByteArrayOutputStream   s = new ByteArrayOutputStream();

fillWithUsefulData(s);
s.writeTo(anotherOutputStream);
```

It also can be extracted as a byte array or converted to a String:

```
byte[]  buffer            = s.toByteArray();
String  bufferString      = s.toString();
String  bufferUnicodeString = s.toString(upperByteValue);
```

NOTE
> The last method enables you to "fake" Unicode (16-bit) characters by filling in their lower bytes with ASCII and then specifying a common upper byte (usually 0) to create a Unicode `String` result.

`ByteArrayOutputStreams` have two utility methods: one simply returns the current number of bytes stored in the internal byte array, and the other resets the array so that the stream can be rewritten from the beginning:

```
int  sizeOfMyByteArray = s.size();

s.reset();      // s.size() would now return 0
s.write(123);
. . .
```

FileOutputStream

One of the most common uses of streams is to attach them to files in the file system. Here, for example, is the creation of such an output stream using the Unix system of file notation:

```
OutputStream  s = new FileOutputStream("/some/path/and/fileName");
```

WARNING
> Applets attempting to open, read, or write streams based on files in the file system can cause security violations. See the note under `FileInputStream` for more details.

You also can create the stream from a previously opened file descriptor:

```
int           fd = openOutputFileInTraditionalWays();
OutputStream  s = new FileOutputStream(fd);
```

`FileOutputStream` is the inverse of `FileInputStream`, and it knows the same tricks:

```
FileOutputStream  aFOS = new FileOutputStream("aFileName");

int  myFD = aFOS.getFD();

/* aFOS.finalize(); */  // will call close() when automatically called by GC
```

NOTE
> To call the new methods, you must declare the stream variable aFOS to be of type `FileOutputStream`, because plain `OutputStreams` don't know about them.

The first is obvious. getFD() simply returns the file descriptor for the file on which the stream is based. The second, commented, contrived call to finalize() is there to remind you that you don't have to worry about closing the stream—it is done for you automatically. (See the discussion under FileInputStream for more.)

FilterOutputStream

This "abstract" class simply provides a "pass-through" for all the standard methods of OutputStream. It holds inside itself another stream, by definition one further "down" the chain of filters, to which it forwards all method calls. It implements nothing new but allows itself to be nested:

```
OutputStream        s  = getAnOutputStreamFromSomewhere();
FilterOutputStream  s1 = new FilterOutputStream(s);
FilterOutputStream  s2 = new FilterOutputStream(s1);
FilterOutputStream  s3 = new FilterOutputStream(s2);

... s3.write(123) ...
```

Whenever a write is performed on the filtered stream s3, it passes along the request to s2. Then s2 does the same to s1, and finally s is asked to output the bytes. Subclasses of FilterOutputStream, of course, do some nontrivial processing of the bytes as they flow past. This chain can be tightly nested—see its "brother" class, FilterInputStream, for more.

Now let's examine each of the subclasses of FilterOutputStream in turn.

BufferedOutputStream

BufferedOutputStream is one of the most valuable of all streams. All it does is implement the full complement of OutputStream's methods, but it does so by using a buffered array of bytes that acts as a cache for writing. This decouples the rate and the size of the "chunks" you're writing from the more regular, larger block sizes in which streams are most efficiently written (to peripheral devices, files in the file system, or the network, for example).

BufferedOutputStream is one of two classes in the Java library to implement flush(), which pushes the bytes you've written through the buffer and out the other side. Because buffering is so valuable, you might wish that every output stream could somehow be buffered. Fortunately, you can surround any output stream in such a way as to achieve just that:

```
OutputStream  s = new BufferedOutputStream(new FileOutputStream("foo"));
```

You now have a buffered output stream based on the file "foo" that can be flush()ed.

Just as for filter input streams, any capability provided by a filter output stream can be used by any other basic stream via nesting and any combination of these capabilities, in any order, can be as easily accomplished by nesting the filter streams themselves.

DataOutputStream

All the methods that instances of this class understand are defined in a separate interface, which both DataOutputStream and RandomAccessFile implement. This interface is general-purpose enough that you might want use it yourself in the classes you create. It is called DataOutput.

The DataOutput Interface

In cooperation with its "brother" inverse interface, DataInput, DataOutput provides a higher-level, typed-stream approach to the reading and writing of data. Rather than dealing with bytes, this interface deals with writing the primitive types of the Java language directly:

```
void  write(int i)                                       throws IOException;
void  write(byte[]  buffer)                              throws IOException;
void  write(byte[]  buffer, int  offset, int  length) throws IOException;

void  writeBoolean(boolean b) throws IOException;
void  writeByte(int i)        throws IOException;
void  writeShort(int i)       throws IOException;
void  writeChar(int i)        throws IOException;
void  writeInt(int i)         throws IOException;
void  writeLong(long l)       throws IOException;
void  writeFloat(float f)     throws IOException;
void  writeDouble(double d)   throws IOException;

void  writeBytes(String s) throws IOException;
void  writeChars(String s) throws IOException;
void  writeUTF(String s)   throws IOException;
```

Most of these methods have counterparts in the interface DataInput.

The first three methods mirror the three forms of write() you saw previously. Each of the next eight methods write out a primitive type. The final three methods write out a string of bytes or characters to the stream: the first one as 8-bit bytes; the second, as 16-bit Unicode characters; and the last, as a special Unicode stream (readable by DataInput's readUTF()).

NOTE

The unsigned read methods in `DataInput` have no counterparts here. You can write out the data they need via `DataOutput`'s signed methods because they accept `int` arguments and also because they write out the correct number of bits for the unsigned integer of a given size as a side effect of writing out the signed integer of that same size. It is the method that reads this integer that must interpret the sign bit correctly; the writer's job is easy.

Now that you know what the interface that `DataOutputStream` implements looks like, let's see it in action:

```
DataOutputStream  s    = new DataOutputStream(getNumericOutputStream());
long             size = getNumberOfItemsInNumericStream();

s.writeLong(size);

for (int  i = 0;  i < size;  ++i) {
    if (shouldProcessNumber(i)) {
        s.writeBoolean(true);       // should process this item
        s.writeInt(theIntegerForItemNumber(i));
        s.writeShort(theMagicBitFlagsForItemNumber(i));
        s.writeDouble(theDoubleForItemNumber(i));
    } else
        s.writeBoolean(false);
}
```

This is the exact inverse of the example that was given for `DataInput`. Together, they form a pair that can communicate a particular array of structured primitive types across any stream (or "transport layer"). Use this pair as a jumping-off point whenever you need to do something similar.

In addition to the interface above, the class itself implements one (self-explanatory) utility method:

```
int  theNumberOfBytesWrittenSoFar = s.size();
```

Processing a File

One of the most common idioms in file I/O is to open a file, read and process it line-by-line, and output it again to another file. Here's a prototypical example of how that would be done in Java:

```
DataInput   aDI = new DataInputStream(new FileInputStream("source"));
DataOutput  aDO = new DataOutputStream(new FileOutputStream("dest"));
String      line;
```

```
while ((line = aDI.readLine()) != null) {
    StringBuffer  modifiedLine = new StringBuffer(line);

    . . .        // process modifiedLine in place
    aDO.writeBytes(modifiedLine.toString());
}
aDI.close();
aDO.close();
```

If you want to process it byte-by-byte, use this:

```
try {
    while (true) {
        byte  b = (byte) aDI.readByte();

        . . .        // process b in place
        aDO.writeByte(b);
    }
} finally {
    aDI.close();
    aDO.close();
}
```

Here's a cute two-liner that just copies the file:

```
try { while (true) aDO.writeByte(aDI.readByte()); }
finally { aDI.close(); aDO.close(); }
```

NOTE Many of the examples in today's lesson (and the last two) assume that they appear inside a method that has IOException in its throws clause, so they don't have to "worry" about catching those exceptions and handling them more reasonably. Your code should be a little less cavalier.

PrintStream

You may not realize it, but you're already intimately familiar with the use of two methods of the PrintStream class. That's because whenever you use these method calls…

```
System.out.print(. . .)
System.out.println(. . .)
```

… you are actually using a PrintStream instance located in the System's class variable out to perform the output. System.err is also a PrintStream, and System.in is an InputStream.

PrintStream is uniquely an output stream class (it has no "brother"). Because it is usually attached to a screen output device of some kind, it provides an implementation of flush(). It also provides the familiar close() and write() methods, as well as a plethora of choices for outputting the primitive types and Strings of Java:

```
public void  write(int b);
public void  write(byte[]  buffer, int  offset, int  length);
public void  flush();
public void  close();

public void  print(Object o);
public void  print(String s);
public void  print(char[]  buffer);
public void  print(char c);
public void  print(int i);
public void  print(long l);
public void  print(float f);
public void  print(double d);
public void  print(boolean b);

public void  println(Object o);
public void  println(String s);
public void  println(char[]  buffer);
public void  println(char c);
public void  println(int i);
public void  println(long l);
public void  println(float f);
public void  println(double d);
public void  println(boolean b);

public void  println();    // output a blank line
```

PrintStream can also be wrapped around any output stream, just like a filter class:

```
PrintStream  s = PrintStream(new FileOutputStream("foo"));

s.println("Here's the first line of text in the file foo.");
```

If you provide a second argument to the constructor for PrintStream, it is a boolean that specifies whether the stream should auto-flush. If true, a flush() is sent after each character is written (or for the three-argument form of write(), after a whole group of characters has been written).

PipedOutputStream

Along with PipedInputStream, this pair of classes supports a Unix-pipe-like connection between two threads, implementing all the careful synchronization that allows this sort of "shared queue" to operate safely. To set up the connection:

```
PipedInputStream    sIn  = PipedInputStream();
PipedOutputStream   sOut = PipedOutputStream(sIn);
```

One thread writes to sOut, and the other reads from sIn. By setting up two such pairs, the threads can communicate safely in both directions.

Related Classes

The other classes and interfaces in java.io supplement the streams to provide a complete I/O system.

The File class abstracts "file" in a platform-independent way. Given a filename, it can respond to queries about the type, status, and properties of a file or directory in the file system.

A RandomAccessFile is created given a file, a filename, or a file descriptor. It combines in one class implementations of the DataInput and DataOutput interfaces, both tuned for "random access" to a file in the file system. In addition to these interfaces, RandomAccessFile provides certain traditional Unix-like facilities, such as seek()ing to a random point in the file.

Finally, the StreamTokenizer class takes an input stream and produces a sequence of tokens. By overriding its various methods in your own subclasses, you can create powerful lexical parsers.

You can learn more about any and all of these classes from the full (online) API descriptions in your Java release.

Summary

Today you learned about the general idea of streams and met input streams based on byte arrays, files, pipes, sequences of other streams, and string buffers, as well as input filters for buffering, typing data, line numbering, and pushing-back characters.

You also met the analogous "brother" output streams for byte arrays, files, and pipes, and output filters for buffering and typing data, and the unique output filter used for printing.

Along the way, you became familiar with the fundamental methods all streams understand (such as read() and write()), as well as the unique methods many streams add to this repertoire. You learned about catching IOExceptions—especially the most useful of them, EOFException.

Finally, the twice-useful `DataInput` and `DataOutput` interfaces formed the heart of `RandomAccessFile`, one of the several utility classes that round out Java's I/O facilities.

Java streams provide a powerful base on which you can build multithreaded, streaming interfaces of the most complex kinds, and the programs (such as HotJava) to interpret them. The higher-level Internet protocols and services of the future that your applets can build upon this base are really limited only by your imagination.

Questions and Answers

Q In an early `read()` example, you did something with the variable `byteOrMinus1` that seemed a little clumsy. Isn't there a better way? If not, why recommend the cast later?

A Yes, there is something a little odd about those statements. You might be tempted to try something like this instead:

```
while ((b = (byte) s.read()) != -1) {
. . .    // process the byte b
}
```

The problem with this shortcut occurs when `read()` returns the value `0xFF` (`0377`). Because this value is signed-extended before the test gets executed, it will appear to be identical to the integer value `-1` that indicates end of stream. Only saving that value in a separate integer variable, and then casting it later, will accomplish the desired result. The cast to `byte` is recommended in the note for orthogonal reasons—storing integer values in correctly sized variables is always good style (and besides, `read()` really should be returning something of `byte` size here and throwing an exception for end of stream).

Q What input streams in `java.io` actually implement `mark()`, `reset()`, and `markSupported()`?

A `InputStream` itself does, and in their default implementations, `markSupported()` returns `false`, `mark()` does nothing, and `reset()` throws an exception. The only input stream in the current release that correctly supports marking is `BufferedInputStream`, which overrides these defaults. `LineNumberInputStream` actually implements `mark()` and `reset()`, but in the current release, it doesn't answer `markSupported()` correctly, so it looks as if it does not.

Q Why is `available()` useful, if it sometimes gives the wrong answer?

A First, for many streams, it gives the right answer. Second, for some network streams, its implementation might be sending a special query to discover some information you couldn't get any other way (for example, the size of a file being transferred by `ftp`). If you were displaying a "progress bar" for network or file transfers, for example, `available()` would often give you the total size of the transfer, and if it did not—usually by returning 0—it would be obvious to you (and your users).

Q What's a good example use of the `DataInput`/`DataOutput` pair of interfaces?

A One common use of such a pair is when objects want to "pickle" themselves for storage or movement over a network. Each object implements read and write methods using these interfaces, effectively converting itself to a stream that can later be reconstituted "on the other end" into a copy of the original object.

Cool Roaster Secrets

by Timothy Webster

You've learned a lot about Java in the past 19 days, and you now have some powerful conceptual tools you can use to build Java programs.

In the real world, you'll also need some practical software tools to manage the task of building robust objects and applications that other programmers can understand and use. Fortunately, such tools are included as part of the Roaster IDE package, and future Roaster releases will include even more software to handle some of the drudgery of application development.

Tomorrow, we'll take a detailed look at the inner workings of Java and the Java Virtual machine—it will be a long and difficult day. Today we'll relax a little, and look at things that make working in Java a little easier. Specifically, we'll take a look at:

- ☐ Roaster's Debugger tool, which helps you to track down problems in your code
- ☐ Roaster's Macro feature
- ☐ Roaster's support for the `javadoc` compiler, which automatically creates HTML documentation for your code
- ☐ QuickView, an online Java reference package that comes bundled with Roaster
- ☐ Roaster's new HTML support tools

The Debugger

If you've had any programming experience at all, or if you've tried to improvise new programs from the examples in the book, you already know that nothing ever works in quite the same way you had imagined it would—often, your first versions of little methods to accomplish particular tasks don't work at all.

Keep in mind that we're talking about logic, not syntax, problems. The line

```
int y = math.sqrt(x);
```

is incorrect, because the word `math` should be `Math`. This is a syntax error, which the compiler will catch. It won't cause your program to do funny things—your program simply won't run until you've removed this sort of syntax error.

Logic errors are more subtle and pernicious. Your program will run, but it won't do what you intend it to do. These errors can be very simple. Consider the classic example:

```
1:  int x = 0;
2:  while (x < 5); {
3:    x++
4:    }
```

Because there's a semicolon after `(x < 5)` in line 2, the code above executes the empty statement between the right parenthesis and the semicolon, rather than the code block that contains line 3. `x` will never be incremented, and the program will never exit the loop.

The compiler can't catch this sort of error—the code in this example is syntactically correct, even though it doesn't work. You'll have to catch these kinds of mistakes yourself. Tracking down these sorts of errors, or bugs, is a significant part of the application development process.

The Simplest Approach to Debugging

You're already familiar with one of the most common techniques for debugging software: our old friend, `System.out.println`. Quite often you'll add diagnostic output to your program during the development stages: feedback intended for you, the programmer, rather than for the user. (Don't forget to remove these before you distribute your applet or application!) For example, you might add a new line to our new example code to see what's happening to `x`:

```
1:  int x = 0;
2:  while (x < 5); {
3:    x++
4:    System.out.println(x);
5:    }
```

No, the new line won't do anything—the code block between the brackets won't be executed just because you stuck another statement in there. *But,* if you're alert, you'll notice that the program isn't outputting your diagnostic, and from this you would probably surmise that the block is not being executed. With this information in hand, you might even notice that misplaced semicolon.

Roaster's Debugger

Throwing these kinds of diagnostics into your code is an ancient and time-honored technique, and in many, many cases, it's the easiest and most appropriate way to create a window into the workings of your code.

Often, however, it's impractical. A moderately complicated program can have dozens of methods and perhaps hundreds of variables stowed away in its objects: Even if you were inclined to add the code necessary to report on the status of all these players (and to remove the code afterwards, without removing something critical in the process), it's unlikely that you would be able to decipher the diagnostic messages as they whiz toward the bottom of the Applet.out window.

Here's where Roaster's Debugger comes in. The Debugger enables you to step through your software line by line, and to monitor the behavior of variables and keep track of which methods have been called. It's really quite handy for figuring out what's happening in your program.

NOTE   Roaster's Debugger is still a work in progress. The following description is based on the DR1.1 version of Roaster, which implemented a bytecode-level Debugger. The final Release 1 version of Roaster will feature both source-level and bytecode-level debugging; however, in the version of Roaster bundled with this book, the Debugger is still a "work in progress" and will most likely not behave correctly. In fact, you probably shouldn't even enable the Debugger in this version unless you're feeling adventurous. Nevertheless, the Debugger features described below should be substantially the same in the final release of Roaster, so you can read this section to get a head start on using these tools when they are finally implemented.

Let's use the Debugger to work through this little application:

```
1:  public class DebuggerExample {
2:
3:    public static void main (String Args[]) {
4:      Bug myBug = new Bug();
5:      myBug.crawl();
6:      myBug.report();
7:    }
8:  }
9:
```

```
10:  class Bug {
11:
12:  int x;
13:  int y;
14:
15:    Bug () {
15:      x = 0;
16:      y = 0;
17:    }
18:
19:    void crawl () {
20:      while (x < 5) {
21:      x++;
22:      y = 2*x;
23:      }
24:    }
25:
26:    void report () {
27:      System.out.println (x + "   " + y);
28:    }
29:  }
```

This application couldn't be simpler: it creates an instance of the class bug, calls bug's crawl() method, which increments bug's instance variables a few times in a loop, and then calls bug's report() method, which prints out the values of bug's instance variables to the screen.

The Debugger will keep track of vital information for us and display this information in its own windows. To begin the debugging session:

1. Enter and compile the Java code in the usual way.

2. Make sure that your application's project window is open, and your application (or applet) is selected.

3. Choose Enable Debugger (Command-Shift-D) from the Project menu.

4. Open the application's .class files—in this case, DebuggerExample.class and Bug.class.

5. Choose Run (Command-R) from the Project menu. The Applet Viewer application will launch.

6. Click one of the .class windows to go back to the Roaster IDE, or choose Roaster from the Finder's application menu.

7. Chooose Current Call Chain and Current Object Inspector from the Windows menu. Take a look at Figure 20.1 for a look at what your screen might look like (especially if everything's scrunched up on a PowerBook screen…).

```
import debuggerExample;
import Bug;
import java.lang.Object;

public
class debuggerExample extends java.lang.Object
    {
        public static void main(java.lang.String[])
        {
➡ 0x0000:          new Bug
  0x0003:          dup
  0x0004:          invokenonvirtual     Bug()
  0x0007:          astore_1
  0x0008:          aload_1
  0x0009:          invokevirtual    void crawl()
  0x000C:          aload_1
  0x000D:          invokevirtual    void report()
  0x0010:          return
        }

        public debuggerExample()
        {
  0x0000:          aload_0
  0x0001:          invokenonvirtual     java.lang.Object(
  0x0004:          return
        }
}
```
Line: 10 ▲ 174

Figure 20.1   *The Debugger's start state.*

See the little arrow next to the first line of DebuggerExample's main() method? The arrow points to the next line to be executed—and right now, you'd expect it to point to the first line of main().

NOTE

Here are those big, bad bytecodes—not so scary, are they? Because the skeletal structure and the variable names of the program are carried over to the .class file, it's fairly easy to figure out where you are, and most of the bytecodes are not so cryptic. Tomorrow, when we go over the Java virtual machine, we'll look at the meaning of all the Java bytecodes in detail.

You can set *breakpoints*—places where Applet Runner will pause as it runs through your code—by clicking next to a line of code. If you're using the DR 1.1 implementation of Roaster, I recommend that you simply step through, because Applet Runner seems to miss some of the breakpoints.

Start clicking! The Debugger controls are, from left to right:

Go	Runs the app to the next breakpoint. This button may be invisible, but it's still there.
Pause	Pauses execution.
Kill	Stops execution and quits Applet Runner.

continues

Step Over	Executes a method call, without showing you the grisly details of the method.
Step Through	Enters a method.
Step Out	Puts you back at the point where the method you're in was called.
Step Over Continuous	Executes repeated Step-Overs.
Step Through Continuous	Executes repeated Step-Throughs.

In Figure 20.2, we've stepped down and into the `Bug` method constructor. The Calling Chain window shows that we're in the constructor `Bug.Bug()`, and that constructor was called by DebuggerExample's `main()` method. The Current Object window shows the values of `Bug`'s instance variables.

Figure 20.2 *Into the* `Bug` *method constructor.*

In Figure 20.3, we've stepped into the `crawl()` method. As you've probably guessed, the line

```
0x000A:        putfield    Bug.x <int>
```

stores a new value in `MyBug`'s variable x. The Current Object window faithfully reports this value: `Bug.x` now has a value of 1. As you step through the `crawl()` method, you can watch the values of of x and y change.

```
0x0006:        putfield     Bug.x <int>
0x0009:        aload_0
0x000A:        iconst_0
0x000B:        putfield     Bug.y <int>
0x000E:        return
     }

     void crawl()
     {
0x0000:        goto    0x0017
0x0003:        aload_0
0x0004:        dup
0x0005:        getfield     Bug.x <int>
0x0008:        iconst_1
0x0009:        iadd
0x000A:        putfield     Bug.x <int>
0x000D:        aload_0
0x000E:        iconst_2
0x000F:        aload_0
0x0010:        getfield     Bug.x <int>
0x0013:        imul
0x0014:        putfield     Bug.y <int>
0x0017:        aload_0
0x0018:        getfield     Bug.x <int>
0x001B:        iconst_5
0x001C:        icmplt 0x0003
0x001F:        return
     }

     void report()
     {
0x0000:        getstatic    java.lang.System.out <java
```
Line: 36 △ 621

Figure 20.3   *Into the* crawl() *method.*

The ability to monitor the values of variables may seem trivial for code like

```
x++;
```

but all too soon, you'll find yourself writing things like

```
dx = ((x <= 0) || (x >= 500)) ? -dx : dx;
```

If you don't have extensive programming experience (and sometimes if you do) it's hard to evaluate the correctness of this sort of expression by looking at it. The easiest way to make sure it does what you think it does is to watch the values of the variables in the Debugger as it runs.

Remember, when Roaster's Debugger is released, it may be set up slightly differently, but the basic functions—setting breakpoints, stepping through code, and monitoring the values of variables—will be the same, and these functions will carry over to the source code Debugger as well.

Macros

At some point, typing things like

```
import java.awt.*;
public class MyApplet extends java.applet.Applet {
```

becomes more tedious than instructive. After all, you've been a computer programmer for at least 19 days, and you're using a computer—surely, there must be a way to automate this process.

There is. The Natural Intelligence team has included a macro feature in Roaster, and it's easy to configure Roaster to add commonly used statements to your source files. Roaster macros can contain meta-characters and other macros, and can be tied to keyboard shortcuts.

Suppose you want to create a macro for the lines in the example above. Here's how:

1. Find the macro icon on the source code editor's toolbar. If you haven't reconfigured the toolbar, the icon should be the fourth from the left; hold the cursor over the icon without clicking for a few seconds, and the word "Macro" should appear if you have the right icon. Select New Macro from the icon's menu.

2. Give the macro a name—preferably, something descriptive. (Give foo a rest!)

3. Give the macro an identifier. This will be used to embed the macro in other macros. (You probably won't be embedding the example into anything, but you might as well give it an identifier, in case you want to create an elaborate system of include macros.

4. Click OK. A new source window labelled Macro:Applet (or Macro: + whatever you've named your macro) will come up. Type in the text of the example, replacing MyApplet with the ¥ (Option-Y) character.

5. Save and close the macro's window.

6. Type a name for your applet into the source code editor window. (It's already open, or you wouldn't have a macro icon on-screen.) Double-click the applet's name to select it.

7. Click and hold on the macro icon. Your new macro's name has been added to the end of the icon's window. Select your macro from the menu.

8. Find the Natural Intelligence icon. If you haven't reconfigured your toolbar, it's the first icon on the right. Choose Configure HotKeys from the icon's menu.

9. Click on the macro icon in the Configure HotKeys window. Type a keyboard shortcut in the slot next to your macro's name. (Don't use a keyboard shortcut like Command-M that you use all the time!)

Notice that your macro has substituted the selected text for the ¥ character.

The Macro Options menu item under the macro icon menu includes a list of special strings that you can use for information like the current date and time. For example,

```
// %Date
// %Time
```

would add the current date and time (in a comment field) to your source code.

> **NOTE**   These special strings, like Java, are case-sensitive. %DATE will produce %DATE in your source code, rather than the current date.

QuickView—Roaster's Online Documentation

Roaster comes bundled with a demo version of Altura Software's QuickView multimedia player, and extensive documentation on Java in QuickView's own hypertext format. Using QuickView, you can very quickly search a *huge* database of information about the Java language, and use QuickView's Bookmarking and Note features to customize the database to your own needs.

Using QuickView is quite a bit like using Netscape Navigator:

☐ Text entries include clickable links marked with underlines.

☐ QuickView keeps a record of each browsing session: The QuickView's History button is almost exactly analogous to Navigator's Windows > History command.

☐ QuickView enables you to add locations in the database to a Bookmark menu.

If you've ever used a Web browser, QuickView will seem very intuitive to use.

> **NOTE**   The full version of QuickView enables users to alter the contents of a database. The version that comes with the book is a limited version, and you can't change any of the entries directly.

QuickView has a few nice features you *won't* find in Navigator. You can annotate pages with little sticky-note-style windows that you pull from a "pad" at the top of the QuickView window. The QuickView Find field supports type-ahead: After you've typed a few letters, QuickView will display the first matching keyword in gray type. Figure 20.4 shows how QuickView has guessed "filedialog" from "filedi".

Like Sun's freely distributed API documentation, QuickView provides a hypertext-based reference to the Java classes. However, the database contains a great deal more information that's useful when you're writing code: lists of all the methods that return objects of the given class (via the Returned-By link) methods that accept the objects of the class as parameters (via the Passed_To link), and other classes that use instances of the class as variables (via the Variable Type link).

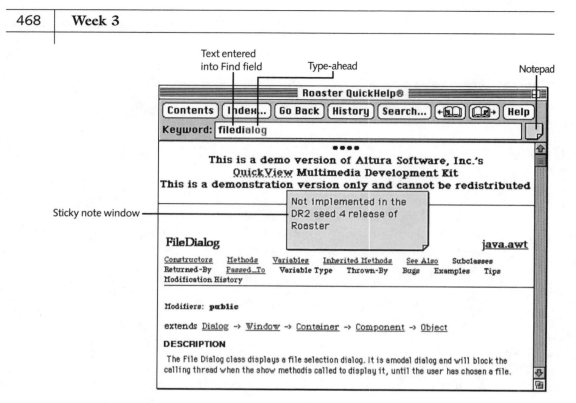

Figure 20.4 *QuickView's display of information about the* FileDialog *class.*

javadoc

Roaster supports a version of the javadoc compiler that automatically creates HTML documentation from comments in your source code.

We were not entirely honest when we told you that there are two ways of marking comments in Java code: In fact, there are three. Recall that you can use double slashes (//) or standard C/C++ style block comments (/* . . . */). Java also recognizes a special form of the block comment used for information to be included in the HTML documentation, with an extra asterisk in the opening string, like so:

```
/**
 *  The secret, third comment style
 */
```

(Notice that the source code editor marks these special comments with green, rather than red.) When you put such comments directly above a package, interface, class, method, or variable definition, the javadoc compiler builds a nifty HTML file that indexes, lists, and describes all such elements in your code. For example, take a look at the following code:

```
 1:   class autoDoc {
 2:       /**
 3:        * The size (in quarts) of the AutoDoc object.
 4:        */
 5:       int myInteger;
 6:       /**
 7:      * The state of the AutoDoc object:
 8:      * If true, the object is activated.
 9:      * If false, the object is idle.
10:      */
11:     boolean myBoolean;
12:     /**
13:      * The coordinates of the AutoDoc object.
14:      */
15:     Point myPoint;
16:       /**
17:        * Constructs an AutoDoc object with a string label.
18:        */
19:     autoDoc (String name) {}
20:       /**
21:        * Constructs an AutoDoc object of the given size.
22:        */
23:     autoDoc (int Size) {}
24:       /**
25:        * Constructs AutoDoc object at the given location.
26:        */
27:     autoDoc (Point Location) {}
28:       /**
29:        *
30:        * Rotates the AutoDoc object.
31:        */
32:     public void SpinAutoDoc (int arc) {}
33:   }
```

(I'm not sure what an autoDoc is, other than the fact that it's measured in quarts and it spins.) To compile this into HTML documentation, choose Edit > Preferences (Command-;), click Project, and make sure that the Collect Documentation Comments box is checked. Choose Project > Compile HTML Documentation. Roaster will deposit the finished HTML file in the Roaster:API Documentation folder with the name AutoDoc.html.

NOTE Roaster prepends package names to these file names, so if this file belonged to package MyPackage, Roaster would name the file MyPackage.AutoDoc.html. There isn't an easy way to set Roaster to redirect these files to another folder—if you want them somewhere else, you'll need to drag them out of the Documentation folder.

Figure 20.5 shows the top of the resulting HTML document, as displayed in Netscape Navigator. To view it in its full glory, take a look at the HTML file in Netscape Navigator.

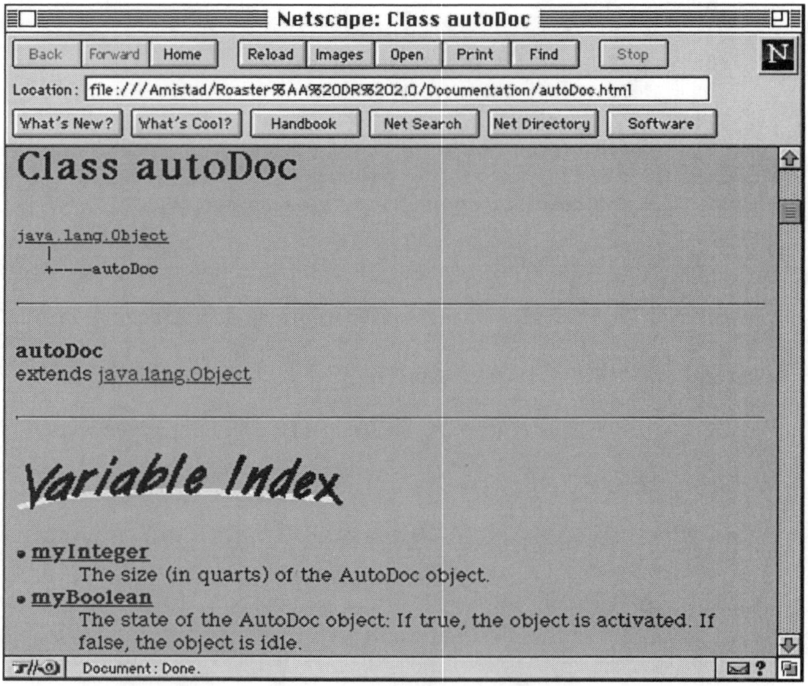

Figure 20.5   *The top of the HTML document.*

NOTE   When you look at these local documentation files with your Web browser, you'll notice that the headers and bullets are different from those included in Sun's online documentation. It turns out that these image files are not quite so freely distributed as Java itself, and so Natural Intelligence has provided alternative image files—and in this typographer's opinion, they're a vast improvement over Sun's "Love Boat" typeface.

Roaster's HTML Tools

The DR2 release of Roaster has added new tools that make the source code editor one of the best Mac-based HTML development tools on the MacOS.

We're not going to try to persuade you that Roaster is a WYSIWYG, drag-and-drop Web page editor, because it's not. It is, however, an excellent tool for working with HTML at the source code level, and it's perfect for fine-tuning pages created with an application like Adobe PageMill.

Installing the Tools

Roaster's HTML tools are stored in the source code editor's icon bar. These icons do not appear by default: You must use the Customize Toolbar command (described in "Before You Begin") to add them to the toolbar. They are:

HTML Font Tool

The HTML Font tool changes the size of the selected text in accordance with Netscape's <FONT> tag extension to HTML.

HTML Heading Tool

The HTML Heading tool adds the changes of the selected text to one of the six standard HTML head sizes.

The HTML List tool adds ordered list, unordered list, or one of several esoteric list format tags to the selected text. Each line of the selection becomes a separate list item.

The HTML Links tool adds images, applets, anchors, and frames to your pages. (We'll show you an example of the applet command below.) The Links tool also supports some special tags: paragraph, line break, and horizontal rule.

The HTML Styles tool supports all the standard text style tags, including seldom-used tags like "teletype" and "variable." The tool adds the tags to the selected text.

The HTML Tools tool includes all the previous tools (except the List tools) in one giant menu. Use it if you're pressed for toolbar real estate.

Editing HTML with Roaster

When you use the source code editor to create HTML documents, it's a good idea to save your files early in the process. Remember to give the file's name an .html or .htm extension so that the editor can mark HTML keywords and balance tags for you.

You may have noticed that Roaster's HTML tools don't provide head and body tags. It will save you a great deal of typing (and frustration) to build HTML header and footer macros, using the techniques described earlier today.

Naturally, the HTML tools handle <APPLET> tags, handling all of the many parameters in a fairly painless way. Let's revisit the MoreHelloApplet file from Day 8, creating an HTML file with the source code editor. (We've put a spare copy of the applet, and the HTML code, in the Day 20:HTML Editor folder on the CD-ROM.)

Choosing the Applet command from the HTML Links (or HTML Tools) icon's menu invokes the dialog box shown in Figure 20.6. We've put the applet in a folder called applets, and we use the Codebase field to indicate this alternate filepath. The Alt field contains a text string to be displayed if the Web page is viewed with a non-Java-capable browser.

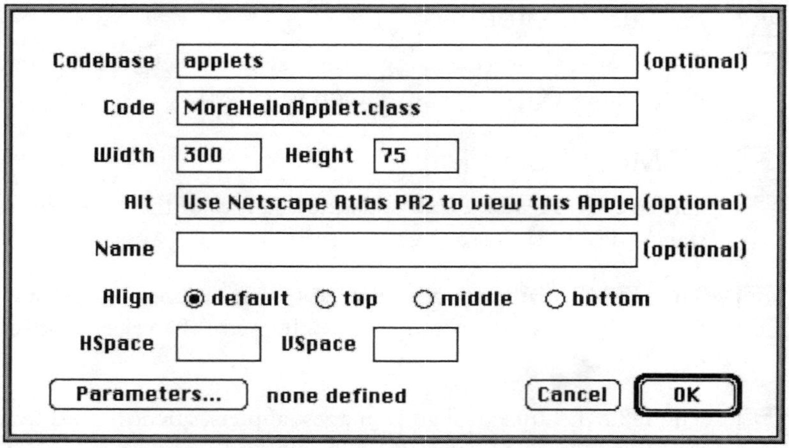

Figure 20.6   *The Applet dialog box.*

To add the applet parameters (i.e., the parameters that MoreHelloApplet is looking for, *not* the parameters of the <APPLET> tag) click the Parameters button. Roaster presents a dialog box, as shown in Figure 20.7.

Remember, although HTML isn't case-sensitive, Java is, and it's important to make sure that what you enter into the Parameter Name field(s) exactly matches the parameter names in your Java code.

Roaster takes the information from these dialog boxes and uses it to assemble the following HTML snippet:

```
<APPLET
     CODEBASE="applets"
     CODE="MoreHelloApplet.class"
     WIDTH="300"
     HEIGHT="75"
     ALT="Use Netscape Atlas PR2 or higher to view this applet">
```

```
      <PARAM name="name" value="Ratso">
</APPLET>
```

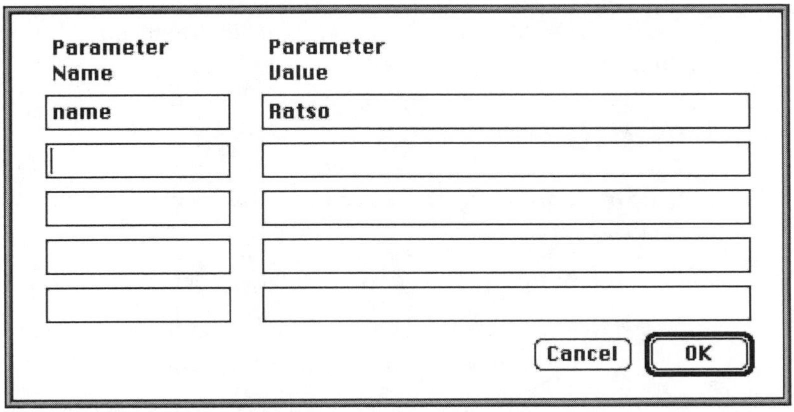

Figure 20.7 *The Parameters dialog box.*

Much cushier, isn't it? We used the Image command and two macros to finish off the HTML document, without writing any HTML by hand. Figure 20.8 shows how Netscape Atlas displays the results.

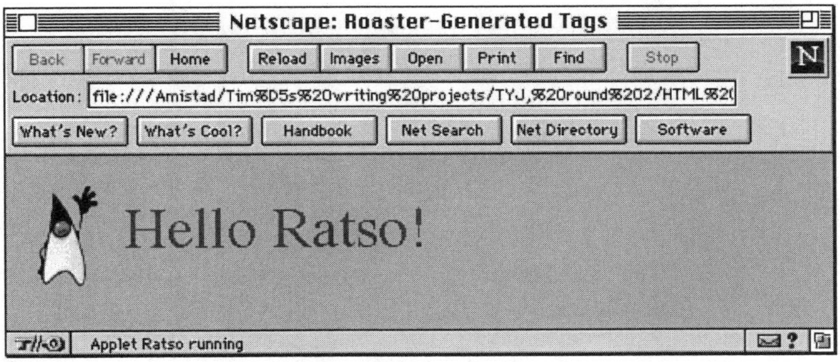

Figure 20.8 *Figure 8.6 revisited, with HTML tags generated by Roaster.*

Summary

Today, you learned about how the special tools that make Roaster easier to use: the Debugger, which lets you peek into the inner workings of your program as it runs; the macro feature, which enables you to quickly add commonly used phrases to your code;

javadoc, which generates HTML documentation from the comments in your code; QuickView, a complete online reference for the Java language; and Roaster's HTML tools, which enable you to easily generate HTML and add applets to Web pages.

Tomorrow, our final day, we'll take a look "under the hood" at how the Java virtual machine works.

Questions and Answers

Q What's in the future for Roaster and its planned successor, Roaster Professional?

A A just-in-time compiler, to make Java applets and applications run even faster.

A javah compiler, which will enable you to incorporate C routines into your Java programs (with a resulting gain in speed, but loss of portability).

A visual application-builder that will enable you to code parts of your programs with Apple's drag-and-drop technology.

Support for JDBC, Sun's specification for a database connectivity API, and for other database connectivity options. (The JDBC specification is still under development. For an interesting preview of similar technology, take a look at the Database Connectivity folder on the CD-ROM.)

Q Where can I learn more about scripting Roaster?

A As of this writing, there aren't any references available that specifically address scripting Roaster. The best place to start is inside the Scripts folder—open one of the scripts and have a look at it. Don't forget that you can peek at Roaster's Apple-Script "dictionary" by dragging the Roaster IDE icon onto the Script editor.

Q What are the Debugger's Object List, Runtime Stack, and Runtime Status windows for?

A They're for keeping track of what's going on inside the Java virtual machine. Specifically:

The Object List shows all of the objects that are running around inside the virtual machine, and the current address of the object in the virtual machine's memory. If you click an object's address, it will bring up the Object Inspector window for that object. Remember, this shows all the objects in the virtual machine, not just the objects that you've created.

The Runtime Stack and Runtime status show what's happening on the stack—where the program counter is, what the values of the bytes on the stack are, etc. What's a stack, you ask? We'll explain that tomorrow. Get a good night's sleep—tomorrow will be a long (and rewarding) day.

Under the Hood

by Charles L. Perkins with Timothy Webster

Today, your final day, the inner workings of the Java system will be revealed.

You'll find out all about Java's vision, Java's virtual machine, those bytecodes you've heard so much about, that mysterious garbage collector, and why you might worry about security but don't
have to.

Let's begin, however, with the big picture.

The Big Picture

The Java team is very ambitious. Their ultimate goal is nothing less than to revolutionize the way software is written and distributed. They've started with the Internet, where they believe much of the interesting software of the future will live.

To achieve such an ambitious goal, a large fraction of the Internet programming community itself must be marshalled behind a similar goal and given the tools to help achieve it. The Java language, with its four S's (small, simple, safe, secure), and its flexible, Net-oriented environment, hopes to become the focal point for the rallying of this new legion of programmers.

To this end, Sun Microsystems has done something rather gutsy. What was originally a secret, tens-of-millions-of-dollars research and development project, and 100 percent proprietary, has become a free, open, and relatively unencumbered technology standard upon which anyone can build. They are literally *giving it away* and reserving only the rights they need to maintain and grow the standard.

NOTE Actually, as Sun's lawyers have more and more time to think, the original intentions of the Java team get further obscured by legal details. It is still relatively unencumbered, but its earlier releases were completely unencumbered. Let's hope that this is not a pattern that will continue.

Any truly open standard must be supported by at least one excellent, freely available "demonstration" implementation. Sun has already shipped an alpha, and now a beta, to the Internet and plans a final release soon. In parallel, several universities, companies, and individuals have already expressed their intention to duplicate the Java environment, based on the open API that Sun has created.

Several other languages are even contemplating compiling down to Java bytecodes to help them become a more robust and commonplace standard for moving executable content around on the Net.

Why It's a Powerful Vision

One of the reasons this brilliant move on Sun's part has a real chance of success is the pent-up frustration of literally a whole generation of programmers who desperately want to share their code with one another. Right now, the computer science world is balkanized into factions at universities and companies all over the world, with hundreds of languages, dozens of them widely used, dividing and separating us all. It's the worst sort of Tower of Babel. Java hopes to build some bridges and help tear down that tower. Because it is so simple, because it's so useful for programming over the Internet, and because the Internet is so "hot" right now—this confluence of forces should help propel Java onto center stage.

It deserves to be there. It is the natural outgrowth of ideas that, since the early 1970s inside the Smalltalk group at Xerox PARC, have lain relatively dormant in the mainstream. (As you may know, Xerox PARC technology was the inspiration for the Macintosh.) Smalltalk, in fact, invented the first object-oriented bytecode interpreter and pioneered many of the deep ideas that Java builds on today. Those efforts, however, were not embraced over the intervening decades as a solution to the general problems of software. Today, with those problems becoming so much more obvious, and with the Net crying out for a new kind of programming, the soil is fertile for something stronger to grow from those old roots, something that just might spread like wildfire. (Is it a coincidence that Java's previous internal names were Green and OAK?)

This new vision of software is one in which the Net becomes an ocean of objects, classes, and the open APIs between them. Traditional applications have vanished,

Day 21 Under the Hood | 477

replaced by skeletal frameworks into which can be fitted any parts from this ocean, on demand, to suit any purpose. User interfaces will be mixed and matched, built in pieces and constructed to taste, whenever the need arises, *by their own users*. Menus of choices will be filled by dynamic lists of *all* the choices available for that function, at that exact moment, across the entire ocean (of the Net).

In such a world, software distribution is no longer an issue. Software will be *everywhere* and will be paid for via a plethora of new micro-accounting models, which charge tiny fractions of cents for the parts as they are assembled and used. Frameworks will come into existence to support entertainment, business, and the social (cyber-)spaces of the near future.

This is a dream that many of us have waited *all our lives* to be a part of. There are tremendous challenges to making it all come true, but the powerful winds of change we all feel must stir us into action, because, at last, there is a base on which to build that dream: Java.

(For a Macintosh-o-centric peek at how the framework end of this vision might look, check out the OpenDoc information at http://www.opendoc.apple.com.)

The Java Virtual Machine

To make visions like this possible, Java must be ubiquitous. It must be able to run on any computer and any operating system—now, and in the future. In order to achieve this level of portability, Java must be very precise not only about the language itself, but also about the environment in which the language lives. You can see, from earlier in the book and Appendix B, that the Java environment includes a generally useful set of packages of classes and a freely available implementation of them. This takes care of a part of what is needed, but it is crucial also to specify exactly how the run-time environment of Java behaves.

This final requirement is what has stymied many attempts at ubiquity in the past. If you base your system on any assumptions about what is "beneath" the run-time system, you lose. If you depend in any way on the computer or operating system below, you lose. Java solves this problem by *inventing* an abstract computer of its own and running on that.

This *virtual machine* runs a special set of instructions called bytecodes that are simply a stream of formatted bytes, each of which has a precise specification of exactly what each bytecode does to this virtual machine. The virtual machine is also responsible for certain fundamental capabilities of Java, such as object creation and garbage collection.

Finally, in order to be able to move bytecodes safely across the Internet, you need a bulletproof model of security—and how to maintain it—and a precise format for how this stream of bytecodes can be sent from one virtual machine to another.

Each of these requirements is addressed in today's lesson.

NOTE

This discussion blurs the distinction between the runtime and the virtual machine of Java. This is intentional but a little unconventional. Think of the virtual machine as providing *all* the capabilities, even those that are conventionally assigned to the runtime. This book uses the words "runtime" and "virtual machine" interchangeably. Equating the two highlights the single *environment* that must be created to support Java.

Much of the following description is based closely on the latest "Virtual Machine Specifications" documents, so if you delve more deeply into the details online, you will cover some familiar ground.

An Overview

It is worth quoting the introduction to the Java virtual machine documentation here, because it is so relevant to the vision outlined earlier:

The Java virtual machine specification has a purpose that is both like and unlike equivalent documents for other languages and abstract machines. It is intended to present an abstract, logical machine design free from the distraction of inconsequential details of any implementation. It does not anticipate an implementation technology, or an implementation host. At the same time it gives a reader sufficient information to allow implementation of the abstract design in a range of technologies.

However, the intent of the [...] Java project is to create a language [...] that will allow the interchange over the Internet of "executable content," which will be embodied by compiled Java code. The project specifically does not want Java to be a proprietary language and does not want to be the sole purveyor of Java language implementations. Rather, we hope to make documents like this one, and source code for our implementation, freely available for people to use as they choose.

This vision [...] can be achieved only if the executable content can be reliably shared between different Java implementations. These intentions prohibit the definition of the

Java virtual machine from being fully abstract. Rather, relevant logical elements of the design have to be made sufficiently concrete to allow the interchange of compiled Java code. This does not collapse the Java virtual machine specification to a description of a Java implementation; elements of the design that do not play a part in the interchange of executable content remain abstract. But it does force us to specify, in addition to the abstract machine design, a concrete interchange format for compiled Java code.

The Java virtual machine specification consists of the following:

- [ ] The bytecode syntax, including opcode and operand sizes, values, and types, and their alignment and endian-ness

- [ ] The values of any identifiers (for example, type identifiers) in bytecodes or in supporting structures

- [ ] The layout of the supporting structures that appear in compiled Java code (for example, the constant pool)

- [ ] The Java .class file format

Each of these is covered today.

Despite this degree of specificity, there are still several elements of the design that remain (purposely) abstract, including the following:

- [ ] The layout and management of the run-time data areas

- [ ] The particular garbage-collection algorithms, strategies, and constraints used

- [ ] The compiler, development environment, and run-time extensions (apart from the need to generate and read valid Java bytecodes)

- [ ] Any optimizations performed, once valid bytecodes are received

Here, the creativity of a virtual machine implementor has full rein.

The Fundamental Parts

The Java virtual machine can be deconstructed into five fundamental pieces:

- [ ] A bytecode instruction set

- [ ] A set of registers

- [ ] A stack

☐ A garbage-collected heap

☐ An area for storing methods

These might be implemented by using an interpreter, a native binary code compiler, or even a hardware chip—but all these logical, abstract components of the virtual machine must be supplied in *some* form in every Java system.

NOTE

> The memory areas used by the Java virtual machine are not required to be at any particular place in memory, to be in any particular order, or even to use contiguous memory. However, all but the method area must be able to represent 32-bit values (for example, the Java stack is 32 bits wide).

The virtual machine, and its supporting code, is often referred to as the run-time environment, and when this book refers to something being done at runtime, the virtual machine is what's doing it.

Java Bytecodes

The Java virtual machine instruction set is optimized to be small and compact. It is designed to travel across the Net, and so has traded speed of interpretation for space. (Given that both Net bandwidth and mass storage speeds increase less rapidly than CPU speed, this seems like an appropriate trade-off.)

 As mentioned, Java source code is "compiled" into bytecodes and stored in a .class file. On Sun's Java system, this is performed using the javac tool. (The current version of Roaster enables you to use javac to compile your code, and also provides its own not-quite-perfect homebrewed Java compiler.) javac is not exactly a traditional "compiler," because it translates source code into bytecodes, a lower-level format that cannot be run directly, but must be further interpreted by each computer. Of course, it is exactly this level of "indirection" that buys you the power, flexibility, and extreme portability of Java code.

NOTE

> Quotation marks are used around the word "compiler" when talking about javac. Later today you will also learn about the "just-in-time" compiler, which acts more like the back end of a traditional compiler. The use of the same word "compiler" for these two different pieces of Java technology is unfortunate, but somewhat reasonable, because each is really one-half (either the front or the back end) of a more traditional compiler.

A bytecode instruction consists of a one-byte opcode that serves to identify the instruction involved and zero or more operands, each of which may be more than one byte long, that encode the parameters the opcode requires.

> **NOTE**
>
> When operands are more than one byte long, they are stored in big-endian order, high-order byte first. These operands must be assembled from the byte stream at runtime. For example, a 16-bit parameter appears in the stream as two bytes so that its value is `first_byte * 256 + second_byte`. The bytecode instruction stream is only byte-aligned, and alignment of any larger quantities is not guaranteed (except for "within" the special bytecodes `lookupswitch` and `tableswitch`, which have special alignment rules of their own).

Bytecodes interpret data in the runtime's memory areas as belonging to a fixed set of types: the primitive types you've seen several times before, consisting of several signed integer types (8-bit `byte`, 16-bit `short`, 32-bit `int`, 64-bit `long`), one unsigned integer type (16-bit `char`), and two signed floating-point types (32-bit `float`, 64-bit `double`), plus the type "reference to an object" (a 32-bit pointer-like type). Some special bytecodes (for example, the `dup` instructions), treat run-time memory areas as raw data, without regard to type. This is the exception, however, not the rule.

These primitive types are distinguished and managed by the compiler, `javac`, not by the Java run-time environment. These types are not "tagged" in memory, and thus cannot be distinguished at run-time. Different bytecodes are designed to handle each of the various primitive types uniquely, and the compiler carefully chooses from this palette based on its knowledge of the actual types stored in the various memory areas. For example, when adding two integers, the compiler generates an `iadd` bytecode; for adding two floats, `fadd` is generated. (You'll see all this in gruesome detail later.)

Registers

The registers of the Java virtual machine are just like the registers inside a "real" computer.

> **NEW TERM**
>
> *Registers* hold the machine's state, affect its operation, and are updated after each bytecode is executed.

The following are the Java registers:

- ☐ pc, the program counter, which indicates what bytecode is being executed

- ☐ optop, a pointer to the top of the operand stack, which is used to evaluate all arithmetic expressions

- ☐ frame, a pointer to the execution environment of the current method, which includes an activation record for this method call and any associated debugging information

- ☐ vars, a pointer to the first local variable of the currently executing method

The virtual machine defines these registers to be 32 bits wide.

NOTE

Because the virtual machine is primarily stack-based, it does not use any registers for passing or receiving arguments. This is a conscious choice skewed toward bytecode simplicity and compactness. It also aids efficient implementation on register-poor architectures, which most of today's computers, unfortunately, are. Perhaps when the majority of CPUs out there are a little more sophisticated, this choice will be reexamined, though simplicity and compactness may still be reason enough!

By the way, the pc register is also used when the runtime handles exceptions; catch clauses are (ultimately) associated with ranges of the pc within a method's bytecodes.

The Stack

The Java virtual machine is stack-based. A Java stack frame is similar to the stack frame of a conventional programming language—it holds the state for a single method call. Frames for nested method calls are stacked on top of this frame.

NEW TERM

The *stack* is used to supply parameters to bytecodes and methods, and to receive results back from them.

Each stack frame contains three (possibly empty) sets of data: the local variables for the method call, its execution environment, and its operand stack. The sizes of these first two are fixed at the start of a method call, but the operand stack varies in size as bytecodes are executed in the method.

Local variables are stored in an array of 32-bit slots, indexed by the register vars. Most types take up one slot in the array, but the long and double types each take up two slots.

NOTE `long` and `double` values, stored or referenced via an index N, take up the (32-bit) slots N and N + 1. These 64-bit values are thus not guaranteed to be 64-bit-aligned. Implementors are free to decide the appropriate way to divide these values between the two slots.

The execution environment in a stack frame helps to maintain the stack itself. It contains a pointer to the previous stack frame, a pointer to the local variables of the method call, and pointers to the stack's current "base" and "top." Additional debugging information can also be placed into the execution environment.

The operand stack, a 32-bit first-in-first-out (FIFO) stack, is used to store the parameters and return values of most bytecode instructions. For example, the `iadd` bytecode expects two integers to be stored on the top of the stack. It pops them, adds them together, and pushes the resulting sum back onto the stack.

Each primitive data type has unique instructions that know how to extract, operate, and push back operands of that type. For example, `long` and `double` operands take two "slots" on the stack, and the special bytecodes that handle these operands take this into account. It is illegal for the types on the stack and the instruction operating on them to be incompatible (`javac` outputs bytecodes that always obey this rule).

NOTE The top of the operand stack and the top of the overall Java stack are almost always the same. Thus, "the stack" refers to both stacks, collectively.

The Heap

NEW TERM The *heap* is that part of memory from which newly created instances (objects) are allocated.

In Java, the heap is often assigned a large, fixed size when the Java run-time system is started, but on systems that support virtual memory, it can grow as needed, in a nearly unbounded fashion.

Because objects are automatically garbage-collected in Java, programmers do not have to (and, in fact, *cannot*) manually free the memory allocated to an object when they are finished using it.

Java objects are referenced indirectly at runtime, via handles, which are a kind of pointer into the heap.

Because objects are never referenced directly, parallel garbage collectors can be written that operate independent of your program, moving around objects in the heap at will. You'll learn more about garbage collection later.

The Method Area

Like the compiled code areas of conventional programming language environments or the TEXT segment in a Unix process, the method area stores the Java bytecodes that implement almost every method in the Java system. (Remember that some methods might be native, and thus implemented, for example, in C.) The method area also stores the symbol tables needed for dynamic linking, and any other additional information debuggers or development environments which might want to associate with each method's implementation.

Because bytecodes are stored as byte streams, the method area is aligned on byte boundaries. (The other areas are all aligned on 32-bit word boundaries.)

The Constant Pool

In the heap, each class has a constant pool "attached" to it. Usually created by javac, these constants encode all the names (of variables, methods, and so forth) used by any method in a class. The class contains a count of how many constants there are and an offset that specifies how far into the class description itself the array of constants begins. These constants are typed by using specially coded bytes and have a precisely defined format when they appear in the .class file for a class. Later today, a little of this file format is covered, but everything is fully specified by the virtual machine specifications in the Roaster release.

Limitations

The virtual machine, as currently defined, places some restrictions on legal Java programs by virtue of the choices it has made (some were previously described, and more will be detailed later today).

These limitations and their implications are:

- ☐ 32-bit pointers, which imply that the virtual machine can address only 4G of memory (this may be relaxed in later releases)

- ☐ Unsigned 16-bit indices into the exception, line number, and local variable tables, which limit the size of a method's bytecode implementation to 64K (this limitation may be eliminated in the final release)

- ☐ Unsigned 16-bit indices into the constant pool, which limits the number of constants in a class to 64K (a limit on the complexity of a class)

In addition, Sun's implementation of the virtual machine uses so-called _quick byte-codes, which further limit the system. Unsigned 8-bit offsets into objects may limit the number of methods in a class to 256 (this limit may not exist in the final release), and unsigned 8-bit argument counts limit the size of the argument list to 255 32-bit words. (Although this means that you can have up to 255 arguments of most types, you can have only 127 of them if they're all long or double.)

Bytecodes in More Detail

One of the main tasks of the virtual machine is the fast, efficient execution of the Java bytecodes in methods. This is a case where speed is of the utmost importance. Every Java program suffers from a slow implementation here, so the runtime must use as many "tricks" as possible to make bytecodes run fast. The only other goal (or limitation) is that Java programmers must not be able to see these tricks in the behavior of their programs.

A Java run-time implementer must be extremely clever to satisfy both these goals.

The Bytecode Interpreter

A bytecode interpreter examines each opcode byte (bytecode) in a method's byte-code stream, in turn, and executes a unique action for that bytecode. This might consume further bytes for the operands of the bytecode and might affect which byte-code will be examined next. It operates like the hardware CPU in a computer, which examines memory for instructions to carry out in exactly the same manner. It is the software CPU of the Java virtual machine.

Your first, naive attempt to write such a bytecode interpreter will almost certainly be disastrously slow. The inner loop, which dispatches one bytecode each time through the loop, is notoriously difficult to optimize. In fact, smart people have been thinking about this problem, in one form or another, for more than 20 years. Luckily, they've gotten results that can be applied to Java.

The final result is that the interpreter shipped in the current release of Roaster has an extremely fast inner loop. In fact, on even a relatively slow computer, Java interpreters have been timed as performing more than 590,000 bytecodes per second! This is really quite good, because the CPU in that computer does only about 30 times better using *hardware*.

This interpreter is fast enough for most Java programs—but what if a smart implementor wants to do better?

The Just-in-Time Compiler

About a decade ago, a really clever trick was discovered by Peter Deutsch while he was trying to make Smalltalk run faster. He called it "dynamic translation" during interpretation. Sun calls it "just-in-time" compiling.

The trick is to notice that the really fast interpreter you've just written—in C, for example—already has a useful sequence of native binary code for each bytecode that it interprets: *the binary code that the interpreter itself is executing.* Because the interpreter has already been compiled from C into native binary code, for each bytecode that it interprets, it passes through a sequence of native code instructions for the hardware CPU on which it is running. By saving a copy of each binary instruction as it "goes by," the interpreter can keep a running log of the binary code it has run to interpret a bytecode. It can just as easily keep a log of the set of bytecodes that it ran to interpret an entire method.

You take that log of instructions and "peephole-optimize" it, just as a smart compiler does. This eliminates redundant or unnecessary instructions from the log, and makes it look just like the optimized binary code that a good compiler might have produced.

NOTE

This is where the name compiler comes from in "just-in-time" compiler, but it's really only the back end of a traditional compiler—the part that does code generation. By the way, the front end is `javac`.

Here's where the trick comes in. The next time that method is run (in exactly the same way), the interpreter can now simply execute directly the stored log of binary native code. Because this optimizes out the inner-loop overhead of each bytecode, as well as any other redundancies between the bytecodes in a method, it can gain a factor of 10 or more in speed. In fact, an experimental version of this technology at Sun has shown that Java programs using it can run as fast as compiled C programs.

NOTE

The parenthetical, "in exactly the same way," in the last paragraph is needed because if anything is different about the input to the method, it takes a different path through the interpreter and must be relogged. (There are, however, sophisticated versions of this technology that solve this, and other, difficulties.) The cache of native code for a method must be invalidated whenever the method has changed, and the interpreter must pay a small cost up front each time a method is run for the first time. However, these small bookkeeping costs are far outweighed by the amazing gains in speed.

The `java2c` Translator

Another, simpler trick, which works well whenever you have a good, portable C compiler on each system that runs your program, is to translate the bytecodes into C and then compile the C into binary native code. If you wait until the first use of a method or class, and then perform this as an "invisible" optimization, it gains an additional speedup over the approach outlined previously, without the Java programmer needing to know about it.

Of course, this does limit you to systems with a C compiler, but there are extremely good, freely available C compilers for the Mac and most other platforms. In theory, your Java code might be able to travel with its own C compiler, or know where to pull one from the Net as needed, for each new computer and operating system it faced. (Because this violates some of the rules of normal Java code movement over the Net, though, it should be used sparingly.)

A similar approach is to use Natural Intelligence's soon-to-be-released Roaster Pro software, which enables you to compile your Java applications (but not applets) straight to native code for the Mac or for Windows. This eliminates the intermediate steps of translating to C and then compiling the C native code—unfortunately, it also eliminates the possiblilty of end users compiling your code for their platform.

You'd probably take this approach if, for example, you're using Java to write a server that lives only on *your* computer. It might be appropriate to use Java for its flexibility in writing and maintaining the server (and for its capability of dynamically linking new Java code on the fly), and then to run Roaster Pro to translate the basic server itself entirely into native code. You'd link the Java run-time environment into that code so that your server remains a fully capable Java program, but it's now an extremely fast one.

NOTE   Unfortunately, as of the current release, just-in-time compilation, `java2c` tools, and Roaster Pro are still under construction. Stay tuned to http://www.Roaster.com for more information about new developments.

The Bytecodes Themselves

Let's look at a (progressively less and less) detailed description of each class of bytecodes.

NOTE

Remember that if you open a compiled .class bytecode file directly with Roaster, it will disassemble the bytecodes and display the instructions for each method in the file in a readable form, using the instruction names below. An excellent way to gain a better understanding of Java bytecodes is to use Roaster to look through some of the .class files for the examples in this book, using the descriptions below to figure out what each instruction is doing.

For each bytecode, some brief text describes its function, and a textual "picture" of the stack, both before and after the bytecode has been executed, is shown. This text picture will look like the following:

```
..., value1, value2 => ..., value3
```

This means that the bytecode expects two operands—value1 and value2—to be on the top of the stack, pops them both off the stack, operates on them to produce value3, and pushes value3 back onto the top of the stack. You should read each stack from right to left, with the rightmost value being the top of the stack. The ... is read as "the rest of the stack below," which is irrelevant to the current bytecode. All operands on the stack are 32 bits wide.

Because most bytecodes take their arguments from the stack and place their results back there, the brief text descriptions that follow only say something about the source or destination of values if they are *not* on the stack. For example, the description Load integer from local variable. means that the integer is loaded onto the stack, and Integer add. intends its integers to be taken from—and the result returned to—the stack.

Bytecodes that don't affect control-flow simply move the pc onto the next bytecode that follows in sequence. Those that do affect the pc say so explicitly. Whenever you see byte1, byte2, and so forth, it refers to the first byte, second byte, and so on that follow the opcode byte itself. After such a bytecode is executed, the pc automatically advances over these operand bytes to start the next bytecode in sequence.

NOTE

The next few sections are in "reference manual style," presenting each bytecode separately in all its (often redundant) detail. Later sections begin to collapse and coalesce this verbose style into something shorter and more readable. The verbose form is shown at first because the online reference manuals will look more like it, and because it drives home the point that each bytecode "function" comes in many, nearly identical bytecodes, one for each primitive type in Java.

Pushing Constants onto the Stack

```
bipush        ... => ..., value
```

Push one-byte signed integer. byte1 is interpreted as a signed 8-bit value. This value is expanded to an int and pushed onto the operand stack.

```
sipush        ... => ..., value
```

Push two-byte signed integer. byte1 and byte2 are assembled into a signed 16-bit value. This value is expanded to an int and pushed onto the operand stack.

```
ldc1          ... => ..., item
```

Push item from constant pool. byte1 is used as an unsigned 8-bit index into the constant pool of the current class. The item at that index is resolved and pushed onto the stack.

```
ldc2          ... => ..., item
```

Push item from constant pool. byte1 and byte2 are used to construct an unsigned 16-bit index into the constant pool of the current class. The item at that index is resolved and pushed onto the stack.

```
ldc2w         ... => ..., constant-word1, constant-word2
```

Push long or double from constant pool. byte1 and byte2 are used to construct an unsigned 16-bit index into the constant pool of the current class. The two-word constant at that index is resolved and pushed onto the stack.

```
aconst_null   ... => ..., null
```

Push the null object reference onto the stack.

```
iconst_m1     ... => ..., -1
```

Push the int -1 onto the stack.

```
iconst_<I>    ... => ..., <I>
```

Push the int <I> onto the stack. There are six of these bytecodes, one for each of the integers 0–5: iconst_0, iconst_1, iconst_2, iconst_3, iconst_4, and iconst_5.

```
lconst_<L>    ... => ..., <L>-word1, <L>-word2
```

Push the long <L> onto the stack. There are two of these bytecodes, one for each of the integers 0 and 1: lconst_0, and lconst_1.

```
fconst_<F>    ... => ..., <F>
```

Push the `float` `<F>` onto the stack. There are three of these bytecodes, one for each of the integers 0–2: `fconst_0`, `fconst_1`, and `fconst_2`.

```
dconst_<D>     ... => ..., <D>-word1, <D>-word2
```

Push the `double` `<D>` onto the stack. There are two of these bytecodes, one for each of the integers 0 and 1: `dconst_0`, and `dconst_1`.

Loading Local Variables onto the Stack

```
iload          ... => ..., value
```

Load `int` from local variable. Local variable `byte1` in the current Java frame must contain an `int`. The `value` of that variable is pushed onto the operand stack.

```
iload_<I>      ... => ..., value
```

Load `int` from local variable. Local variable `<I>` in the current Java frame must contain an `int`. The `value` of that variable is pushed onto the operand stack. There are four of these bytecodes, one for each of the integers 0–3: `iload_0`, `iload_1`, `iload_2`, and `iload_3`.

```
lload          ... => ..., value-word1, value-word2
```

Load `long` from local variable. Local variables `byte1` and `byte1 + 1` in the current Java frame must together contain a long integer. The values contained in those variables are pushed onto the operand stack.

```
lload_<L>      ... => ..., value-word1, value-word2
```

Load `long` from local variable. Local variables `<L>` and `<L> + 1` in the current Java frame must together contain a long integer. The value contained in those variables is pushed onto the operand stack. There are four of these bytecodes, one for each of the integers 0–3: `lload_0`, `lload_1`, `lload_2`, and `lload_3`.

```
fload          ... => ..., value
```

Load `float` from local variable. Local variable `byte1` in the current Java frame must contain a single precision floating-point number. The `value` of that variable is pushed onto the operand stack.

```
fload_<F>      ... => ..., value
```

Load `float` from local variable. Local variable `<F>` in the current Java frame must contain a single precision floating-point number. The value of that variable is pushed onto the operand stack. There are four of these bytecodes, one for each of the integers 0–3: `fload_0`, `fload_1`, `fload_2`, and `fload_3`.

```
dload          ... => ..., value-word1, value-word2
```

Load `double` from local variable. Local variables `byte1` and `byte1 + 1` in the current Java frame must together contain a double precision floating-point number. The value contained in those variables is pushed onto the operand stack.

```
dload_<D>      ... => ..., value-word1, value-word2
```

Load `double` from local variable. Local variables `<D>` and `<D> + 1` in the current Java frame together must contain a double precision floating-point number. The value contained in those variables is pushed onto the operand stack. There are four of these bytecodes, one for each of the integers 0–3: `dload_0`, `dload1`, `dload_2`, and `dload_3`.

```
aload          ... => ..., value
```

Load object reference from local variable. Local variable `byte1` in the current Java frame must contain a return address or reference to an object or array. The value of that variable is pushed onto the operand stack.

```
aload_<A>      ... => ..., value
```

Load object reference from local variable. Local variable `<A>` in the current Java frame must contain a return address or reference to an object. The array value of that variable is pushed onto the operand stack. There are four of these bytecodes, one for each of the integers 0–3: `aload_0`, `aload_1`, `aload_2`, and `aload_3`.

Storing Stack Values into Local Variables

```
istore         ..., value => ...
```

Store `int` into local variable. `value` must be an `int`. Local variable `byte1` in the current Java frame is set to `value`.

```
istore_<I>     ..., value => ...
```

Store `int` into local variable. `value` must be an `int`. Local variable `<I>` in the current Java frame is set to `value`. There are four of these bytecodes, one for each of the integers 0–3: `istore_0`, `istore_1`, `istore_2`, and `istore_3`.

```
lstore         ..., value-word1, value-word2 => ...
```

Store `long` into local variable. `value` must be a long integer. Local variables `byte1` and `byte1 + 1` in the current Java frame are set to `value`.

```
lstore_<L>      ..., value-word1, value-word2 => ...
```

Store long into local variable. value must be a long integer. Local variables <L> and <L> + 1 in the current Java frame are set to value. There are four of these bytecodes, one for each of the integers 0–3: lstore_0, lstore_1, lstore_2, and lstore_3.

```
fstore          ..., value                 => ...
```

Store float into local variable. value must be a single precision floating-point number. Local variables byte1 and byte1 + 1 in the current Java frame are set to value.

```
fstore_<F>      ..., value                 => ...
```

Store float into local variable. value must be a single precision floating-point number. Local variables <F> and <F> + 1 in the current Java frame are set to value. There are four of these bytecodes, one for each of the integers 0–3: fstore_0, fstore_1, fstore_2, and fstore_3.

```
dstore          ..., value-word1, value-word2 => ...
```

Store double into local variable. value must be a double precision floating-point number. Local variables byte1 and byte1 + 1 in the current Java frame are set to value.

```
dstore_<D>      ..., value-word1, value-word2 => ...
```

Store double into local variable. value must be a double precision floating-point number. Local variables <D> and <D> + 1 in the current Java frame are set to value. There are four of these bytecodes, one for each of the integers 0–3: dstore_0, dstore_1, dstore_2, and dstore_3.

```
astore          ..., handle => ...
```

Store object reference into local variable. handle must be a return address or a reference to an object. Local variable byte1 in the current Java frame is set to value.

```
astore_<A>      ..., handle => ...
```

Store object reference into local variable. handle must be a return address or a reference to an object. Local variable <A> in the current Java frame is set to value. There are four of these bytecodes, one for each of the integers 0–3: astore_0, astore_1, astore_2, and astore_3.

```
iinc            -no change-
```

Increment local variable by constant. Local variable byte1 in the current Java frame must contain an int. Its value is incremented by the value byte2, where byte2 is treated as a signed 8-bit quantity.

Managing Arrays

```
newarray        ..., size => result
```

Allocate new array. size must be an int. It represents the number of elements in the new array. byte1 is an internal code that indicates the type of array to allocate. Possible values for byte1 are as follows: T_BOOLEAN (4), T_CHAR (5), T_FLOAT (6), T_DOUBLE (7), T_BYTE (8), T_SHORT (9), T_INT (10), and T_LONG (11).

An attempt is made to allocate a new array of the indicated type, capable of holding size elements. This will be the result. If size is less than zero, a NegativeArraySizeException is thrown. If there is not enough memory to allocate the array, an OutOfMemoryError is thrown. All elements of the array are initialized to their default values.

```
anewarray       ..., size => result
```

Allocate new array of objects. size must be an int. It represents the number of elements in the new array. byte1 and byte2 are used to construct an index into the constant pool of the current class. The item at that index is resolved. The resulting entry must be a class.

An attempt is made to allocate a new array of the indicated class type, capable of holding size elements. This will be the result. If size is less than zero, a NegativeArraySizeException is thrown. If there is not enough memory to allocate the array, an OutOfMemoryError is thrown. All elements of the array are initialized to null.

NOTE   anewarray is used to create a single dimension of an array of objects. For example, the request new Thread[7] generates the following bytecodes:

```
bipush 7
anewarray <Class "java.lang.Thread">
```

anewarray can also be used to create the outermost dimension of a multidimensional array. For example, the array declaration new int[6][] generates this:

```
bipush 6
anewarray <Class "[I">
```

(See the section "Method Signatures" for more information on strings such as [I.)

```
multianewarray  ..., size1 size2...sizeN => result
```

Allocate a new multidimensional array. Each size<I> must be an int. Each represents the number of elements in a dimension of the array. byte1 and byte2 are used to construct an index into the constant pool of the current class. The item at that index is resolved. The resulting entry must be an array class of one or more dimensions.

byte3 is a positive integer representing the number of dimensions being created. It must be less than or equal to the number of dimensions of the array class. byte3 is also the number of elements that are popped off the stack. All must be ints greater than or equal to zero. These are used as the sizes of the dimensions. An attempt is made to allocate a new array of the indicated class type, capable of holding size<1> * size<2> * ... * <sizeN> elements. This will be the result. If any of the size<I> arguments on the stack is less than zero, a NegativeArraySizeException is thrown. If there is not enough memory to allocate the array, an OutOfMemoryError is thrown.

NOTE

new int[6][3][] generates these bytecodes:

```
bipush 6

bipush 3

multianewarray <Class "[[[I"> 2
```

It's more efficient to use newarray or anewarray when creating arrays of single dimension.

arraylength   ..., array => ..., length

Get length of array. array must be a reference to an array object. The length of the array is determined and replaces array on the top of the stack. If array is null, a NullPointerException is thrown.

```
iaload             ..., array, index => ..., value
laload             ..., array, index => ..., value-word1, value-word2
faload             ..., array, index => ..., value
daload             ..., array, index => ..., value-word1, value-word2
aaload             ..., array, index => ..., value
baload             ..., array, index => ..., value
caload             ..., array, index => ..., value
saload             ..., array, index => ..., value
```

Load <type> from array. array must be an array of <type>s. index must be an int. The <type> value at position number index in array is retrieved and pushed onto the top of the stack. If array is null, a NullPointerException is thrown. If index is not within the bounds of array, an ArrayIndexOutOfBoundsException is thrown. <type> is, in turn, int, long, float, double, object reference, byte, char, and short. <type>s long and double have two word values, as you've seen in previous load bytecodes.

```
iastore            ..., array, index, value => ...
lastore            ..., array, index, value-word1, value-word2 => ...
fastore            ..., array, index, value => ...
dastore            ..., array, index, value-word1, value-word2 => ...
aastore            ..., array, index, value => ...
bastore            ..., array, index, value => ...
castore            ..., array, index, value => ...
sastore            ..., array, index, value => ...
```

Store into <type> array. array must be an array of <type>s, index must be an integer, and value a <type>. The <type> value is stored at position index in array. If array is null, a NullPointerException is thrown. If index is not within the bounds of array, an ArrayIndexOutOfBounds Exception is thrown. <type> is, in turn, int, long, float, double, object reference, byte, char, and short. <type>s long and double have two word values, as you've seen in previous store bytecodes.

Stack Operations

```
nop          -no change-
```

Do nothing.

```
pop          ..., any => ...
```

Pop the top word from the stack.

```
pop2         ..., any2, any1 => ...
```

Pop the top two words from the stack.

```
dup          ..., any => ..., any, any
```

Duplicate the top word on the stack.

```
dup2         ..., any2, any1 => ..., any2, any1, any2,any1
```

Duplicate the top two words on the stack.

```
dup_x1       ..., any2, any1 => ..., any1, any2,any1
```

Duplicate the top word on the stack and insert the copy two words down in the stack.

```
dup2_x1      ..., any3, any2, any1 => ..., any2, any1, any3,any2,any1
```

Duplicate the top two words on the stack and insert the copies two words down in the stack.

```
dup_x2       ..., any3, any2, any1 => ..., any1, any3,any2,any1
```

Duplicate the top word on the stack and insert the copy three words down in the stack.

```
dup2_x2    ..., any4, any3, any2, any1 => ..., any2, any1, any4,any3,any2,any1
```

Duplicate the top two words on the stack and insert the copies three words down in the stack.

```
swap       ..., any2, any1 => ..., any1, any2
```

Swap the top two elements on the stack.

Arithmetic Operations

```
iadd       ..., v1, v2 => ..., result
ladd       ..., v1-word1, v1-word2, v2-word1, v2-word2 => ..., r-word1, r-word2
fadd       ..., v1, v2 => ..., result
dadd       ..., v1-word1, v1-word2, v2-word1, v2-word2 => ..., r-word1, r-word2
```

v1 and v2 must be <type>s. The vs are added and are replaced on the stack by their <type> sum. <type> is, in turn, int, long, float, and double.

```
isub       ..., v1, v2 => ..., result
lsub       ..., v1-word1, v1-word2, v2-word1, v2-word2 => ..., r-word1, r-word2
fsub       ..., v1, v2 => ..., result
dsub       ..., v1-word1, v1-word2, v2-word1, v2-word2 => ..., r-word1, r-word2
```

v1 and v2 must be <type>s. v2 is subtracted from v1, and both vs are replaced on the stack by their <type> difference. <type> is, in turn, int, long, float, and double.

```
imul       ..., v1, v2 => ..., result
lmul       ..., v1-word1, v1-word2, v2-word1, v2-word2 => ..., r-word1, r-word2
fmul       ..., v1, v2 => ..., result
dmul       ..., v1-word1, v1-word2, v2-word1, v2-word2 => ..., r-word1, r-word2
```

v1 and v2 must be <type>s. Both vs are replaced on the stack by their <type> product. <type> is, in turn, int, long, float, and double.

```
idiv       ..., v1, v2 => ..., result
ldiv       ..., v1-word1, v1-word2, v2-word1, v2-word2 => ..., r-word1, r-word2
fdiv       ..., v1, v2 => ..., result
ddiv       ..., v1-word1, v1-word2, v2-word1, v2-word2 => ..., r-word1, r-word2
```

v1 and v2 must be <type>s. v2 is divided by v1, and both vs are replaced on the stack by their <type> quotient. An attempt to divide by zero results in an ArithmeticException being thrown. <type> is, in turn, int, long, float, and double.

```
irem        ..., v1, v2 => ..., result
lrem        ..., v1-word1, v1-word2, v2-word1, v2-word2 => ..., r-word1, r-word2
frem        ..., v1, v2 => ..., result
drem        ..., v1-word1, v1-word2, v2-word1, v2-word2 => ..., r-word1, r-word2
```

v1 and v2 must be <type>s. v2 is divided by v1, and both vs are replaced on the stack by their <type> remainder. An attempt to divide by zero results in an ArithmeticException being thrown. <type> is, in turn, int, long, float, and double.

```
ineg        ..., value => ..., result
lneg        ..., value-word1, value-word2 => ..., result-word1, result-word2
fneg        ..., value => ..., result
dneg        ..., value-word1, value-word2 => ..., result-word1, result-word2
```

value must be a <type>. It is replaced on the stack by its arithmetic negation. <type> is, in turn, int, long, float, and double.

NOTE

> Now that you're familiar with the look of the bytecodes, the summaries that follow will become shorter and shorter (for space reasons). You can always get any desired level of detail from the full virtual machine specification at http://www.sun.com or http://www.javasoft.com.

Logical Operations

```
ishl        ..., v1, v2 => ..., result
lshl        ..., v1-word1, v1-word2, v2 => ..., r-word1, r-word2
ishr        ..., v1, v2 => ..., result
lshr        ..., v1-word1, v1-word2, v2 => ..., r-word1, r-word2
iushr       ..., v1, v2 => ..., result
lushr       ..., v1-word1, v1-word2, v2-word1, v2-word2 => ..., r-word1, r-word2
```

For types int and long: arithmetic shift-left, shift-right, and logical shift-right.

```
iand        ..., v1, v2 => ..., result
land        ..., v1-word1, v1-word2, v2-word1, v2-word2 => ..., r-word1, r-word2
ior         ..., v1, v2 => ..., result
```

```
lor        ..., v1-word1, v1-word2, v2-word1, v2-word2 => ..., r-word1, r-word2
ixor       ..., v1, v2 => ..., result
lxor       ..., v1-word1, v1-word2, v2-word1, v2-word2 => ..., r-word1, r-word2
```

For types int and long: bitwise AND, OR, and XOR.

Conversion Operations

```
i2l        ..., value => ..., result-word1, result-word2
i2f        ..., value => ..., result
i2d        ..., value => ..., result-word1, result-word2
l2i        ..., value-word1, value-word2 => ..., result
l2f        ..., value-word1, value-word2 => ..., result
l2d        ..., value-word1, value-word2 => ..., result-word1, result-word2
f2i        ..., value => ..., result
f2l        ..., value => ..., result-word1, result-word2
f2d        ..., value => ..., result-word1, result-word2
d2i        ..., value-word1, value-word2 => ..., result
d2l        ..., value-word1, value-word2 => ..., result-word1, result-word2
d2f        ..., value-word1, value-word2 => ..., result

int2byte   ..., value => ..., result
int2char   ..., value => ..., result
int2short  ..., value => ..., result
```

These bytecodes convert from a value of type <lhs> to a result of type <rhs>. <lhs> and <rhs> can be any of i, l, f, and d, which represent int, long, float, and double, respectively. The final three bytecodes have types that are self-explanatory.

Transfer of Control

```
ifeq       ..., value => ...
ifne       ..., value => ...
iflt       ..., value => ...
ifgt       ..., value => ...
ifle       ..., value => ...
ifge       ..., value => ...

if_icmpeq  ..., value1, value2 => ...
if_icmpne  ..., value1, value2 => ...
if_icmplt  ..., value1, value2 => ...
if_icmpgt  ..., value1, value2 => ...
if_icmple  ..., value1, value2 => ...
if_icmpge  ..., value1, value2 => ...
```

```
ifnull      ..., value => ...
ifnonnull   ..., value => ...
```

When value `<rel>` 0 is true in the first set of bytecodes, value1 `<rel>` value2 is true in the second set, or value is null (or not null) in the third, byte1 and byte2 are used to construct a signed 16-bit offset. Execution proceeds at that offset from the pc. Otherwise, execution proceeds at the bytecode following. `<rel>` is one of eq, ne, lt, gt, le, and ge, which represent equal, not equal, less than, greater than, less than or equal, and greater than or equal, respectively.

```
lcmp        ..., v1-word1, v1-word2, v2-word1, v2-word2 => ..., result

fcmpl       ..., v1, v2 => ..., result
dcmpl       ..., v1-word1, v1-word2, v2-word1, v2-word2 => ..., result

fcmpg       ..., v1, v2 => ..., result
dcmpg       ..., v1-word1, v1-word2, v2-word1, v2-word2 => ..., result
```

v1 and v2 must be long, float, or double. They are both popped from the stack and compared. If v1 is greater than v2, the int value 1 is pushed onto the stack. If v1 is equal to v2, 0 is pushed onto the stack. If v1 is less than v2, -1 is pushed onto the stack. For floating-point, if either v1 or v2 is NaN, -1 is pushed onto the stack for the first pair of bytecodes, +1 for the second pair.

```
if_acmpeq   ..., value1, value2 => ...
if_acmpne   ..., value1, value2 => ...
```

Branch if object references are equal/not equal. value1 and value2 must be references to objects. They are both popped from the stack. If value1 is equal/not equal to value2, byte1 and byte2 are used to construct a signed 16-bit offset. Execution proceeds at that offset from the pc. Otherwise, execution proceeds at the bytecode following.

```
goto        -no change-
goto_w      -no change-
```

Branch always. byte1 and byte2 (plus byte3 and byte4 for goto_w) are used to construct a signed 16-bit (32-bit) offset. Execution proceeds at that offset from the pc.

```
jsr         ... => ..., return-address
jsr-w       ... => ..., return-address
```

Jump subroutine. The address of the bytecode immediately following the jsr is pushed onto the stack. byte1 and byte2 (plus byte3 and byte4 for goto_w) are used to

construct a signed 16-bit (32-bit) offset. Execution proceeds at that offset from the
pc.

```
ret        -no change-
ret2_w     -no change-
```

Return from subroutine. Local variable byte1 (plus byte2 are assembled into a 16-bit
index for ret_w) in the current Java frame must contain a return address. The contents of that local variable are written into the pc.

NOTE

jsr pushes the address onto the stack, and ret gets it out of a local variable. This
asymmetry is intentional. The jsr and ret bytecodes are used in the implementation
of Java's finally keyword.

Method Return

```
return     ... => [empty]
```

Return (void) from method. All values on the operand stack are discarded. The interpreter then returns control to its caller.

```
ireturn    ..., value => [empty]
lreturn    ..., value-word1, value-word2 => [empty]
freturn    ..., value => [empty]
dreturn    ..., value-word1, value-word2 => [empty]
areturn    ..., value => [empty]
```

Return <type> from method. value must be a <type>. The value is pushed onto the
stack of the previous execution environment. Any other values on the operand stack
are discarded. The interpreter then returns control to its caller. <type> is, in turn, int,
long, float, double, and object reference.

NOTE

The stack behavior of the "return" bytecodes may be confusing to anyone expecting
the Java operand stack to be just like the C stack. Java's operand stack actually consists of a number of discontiguous segments, each corresponding to a method call. A
return bytecode empties the Java operand stack segment corresponding to the frame
of the returning call, but does not affect the segment of any parent calls.

Table Jumping

```
tableswitch  ..., index => ...
```

tableswitch is a variable-length bytecode. Immediately after the tableswitch opcode,
zero to three 0 bytes are inserted as padding so that the next byte begins at an

address that is a multiple of four. After the padding are a series of signed 4-byte quantities: default-offset, low, high, and then (high - low + 1) further signed 4-byte offsets. These offsets are treated as a 0-based jump table.

The index must be an int. If index is less than low or index is greater than high, default-offset is added to the pc. Otherwise, the (index - low)'th element of the jump table is extracted and added to the pc.

```
lookupswitch   ..., key => ...
```

lookupswitch is a variable-length bytecode. Immediately after the lookupswitch op-code, zero to three 0 bytes are inserted as padding so that the next byte begins at an address that is a multiple of four. Immediately after the padding is a series of pairs of signed 4-byte quantities. The first pair is special; it contains the default-offset and the number of pairs that follow. Each subsequent pair consists of a match and an offset.

The key on the stack must be an int. This key is compared to each of the matches. If it is equal to one of them, the corresponding offset is added to the pc. If the key does not match any of the matches, the default-offset is added to the pc.

Manipulating Object Fields

```
putfield       ..., handle, value => ...
putfield       ..., handle, value-word1, value-word2 => ...
```

Set field in object. byte1 and byte2 are used to construct an index into the constant pool of the current class. The constant pool item is a field reference to a class name and a field name. The item is resolved to a field block pointer containing the field's width and offset (both in bytes).

The field, offset from the start of the instance and pointed to by handle, will be set to the value on the top of the stack. The first stack picture is for 32-bit, and the second for 64-bit wide fields. This bytecode handles both. If handle is null, a NullPointerException is thrown. If the specified field is a static field, an IncompatibleClassChangeError is thrown.

```
getfield       ..., handle => ..., value
getfield       ..., handle => ..., value-word1, value-word2
```

Fetch field from object. byte1 and byte2 are used to construct an index into the con-stant pool of the current class. The constant pool item will be a field reference to a class name and a field name. The item is resolved to a field block pointer containing the field's width and offset (both in bytes).

handle must be a reference to an object. The value at offset into the object referenced by handle replaces handle on the top of the stack. The first stack picture is for 32-bit, and the second for 64-bit wide fields. This bytecode handles both. If the specified field is a static field, an IncompatibleClassChangeError is thrown.

```
putstatic     ..., value => ...
putstatic     ..., value-word1, value-word2 => ...
```

Set static field in class. byte1 and byte2 are used to construct an index into the constant pool of the current class. The constant pool item will be a field reference to a static field of a class. That field will be set to have the value on the top of the stack. The first stack picture is for 32-bit, and the second for 64-bit wide fields. This bytecode handles both. If the specified field is not a static field, an IncompatibleClassChangeError is thrown.

```
getstatic     ..., => ..., value_
getstatic     ..., => ..., value-word1, value-word2
```

Get static field from class. byte1 and byte2 are used to construct an index into the constant pool of the current class. The constant pool item will be a field reference to a static field of a class. The value of that field is placed on the top of the stack. The first stack picture is for 32-bit, and the second for 64-bit wide fields. This bytecode handles both. If the specified field is not a static field, an IncompatibleClassChangeError is thrown.

Method Invocation

```
invokevirtual     ..., handle, [arg1, arg2, ...]], ... => ...
```

Invoke instance method based on runtime. The operand stack must contain a reference to an object and some number of arguments. byte1 and byte2 are used to construct an index into the constant pool of the current class. The item at that index in the constant pool contains the complete method signature. A pointer to the object's method table is retrieved from the object reference. The method signature is looked up in the method table. The method signature is guaranteed to exactly match one of the method signatures in the table.

The result of the lookup is an index into the method table of the named class that's used to look in the method table of the object's runtime type, where a pointer to the method block for the matched method is found. The method block indicates the type of method (native, synchronized, and so on) and the number of arguments (nargs) expected on the operand stack.

If the method is marked synchronized, the monitor associated with handle is entered.

The base of the local variables array for the new Java stack frame is set to point to handle on the stack, making handle and the supplied arguments (arg1, arg2, ...) the first nargs local variables of the new frame. The total number of local variables used by the method is determined, and the execution environment of the new frame is pushed after leaving sufficient room for the locals. The base of the operand stack for this method invocation is set to the first word after the execution environment. Finally, execution continues with the first bytecode of the matched method.

If handle is null, a NullPointerException is thrown. If during the method invocation a stack overflow is detected, a StackOverflowError is thrown.

```
invokenonvirtual   ..., handle, [arg1, arg2, ...]] ... => ...
```

Invoke instance method based on compile-time type. The operand stack must contain a reference (handle) to an object and some number of arguments. byte1 and byte2 are used to construct an index into the constant pool of the current class. The item at that index in the constant pool contains the complete method signature and class. The method signature is looked up in the method table of the class indicated. The method signature is guaranteed to exactly match one of the method signatures in the table.

The result of the lookup is a method block. The method block indicates the type of method (native, synchronized, and so on) and the number of arguments (nargs) expected on the operand stack. (The last three paragraphs are identical to the previous bytecode.)

```
invokestatic      ..., , [arg1, arg2, ...]] ... => ...
```

Invoke class (static) method. The operand stack must contain some number of arguments. byte1 and byte2 are used to construct an index into the constant pool of the current class. The item at that index in the constant pool contains the complete method signature and class. The method signature is looked up in the method table of the class indicated. The method signature is guaranteed to match one of the method signatures in the class's method table exactly.

The result of the lookup is a method block. The method block indicates the type of method (native, synchronized, and so on) and the number of arguments (nargs) expected on the operand stack.

If the method is marked synchronized, the monitor associated with the class is entered. (The last two paragraphs are identical to those in invokevirtual, except that no NullPointerException can be thrown.)

```
invokeinterface   ..., handle, [arg1, arg2, ...] => ...
```

Invoke interface method. The operand stack must contain a reference (`handle`) to an object and some number of arguments. `byte1` and `byte2` are used to construct an index into the constant pool of the current class. The item at that index in the constant pool contains the complete method signature. A pointer to the object's method table is retrieved from the object reference. The method signature is looked up in the method table. The method signature is guaranteed to exactly match one of the method signatures in the table.

The result of the lookup is a method block. The method block indicates the type of method (`native`, `synchronized`, and so on) but, unlike the other "invoke" bytecodes, the number of available arguments (`nargs`) is taken from `byte3`; `byte4` is reserved for future use. (The last three paragraphs are identical to those in `invokevirtual`.)

Exception Handling

```
athrow              ..., handle => [undefined]
```

Throw exception. `handle` must be a handle to an exception object. That exception, which must be a subclass of `Throwable`, is thrown. The current Java stack frame is searched for the most recent `catch` clause that handles the exception. If a matching "catch-list" entry is found, the `pc` is reset to the address indicated by the catch-list pointer, and execution continues there.

If no appropriate `catch` clause is found in the current stack frame, that frame is popped and the exception is rethrown, starting the process all over again in the parent frame. If `handle` is `null`, then a `NullPointerException` is thrown instead.

Miscellaneous Object Operations

```
new                 ... => ..., handle
```

Create new object. `byte1` and `byte2` are used to construct an index into the constant pool of the current class. The item at that index should be a class name that can be resolved to a class pointer, class. A new instance of that class is then created and a reference (`handle`) for the instance is placed on the top of the stack.

```
checkcast           ..., handle => ..., [handle¦...]
```

Make sure object is of given type. `handle` must be a reference to an object. `byte1` and `byte2` are used to construct an index into the constant pool of the current class. The string at that index of the constant pool is presumed to be a class name that can be resolved to a class pointer, class.

`checkcast` determines whether `handle` can be cast to a reference to an object of that class. (A `null` `handle` can be cast to any class.) If `handle` can be legally cast, execution proceeds at the next bytecode, and the handle for `handle` remains on the stack. If not, a `ClassCastException` is thrown.

```
instanceof          ..., handle => ..., result
```

Determine whether object is of given type. `handle` must be a reference to an object. `byte1` and `byte2` are used to construct an index into the constant pool of the current class. The string at that index of the constant pool is presumed to be a class name that can be resolved to a class pointer, class.

If `handle` is `null`, the `result` is (`false`). Otherwise, `instanceof` determines whether `handle` can be cast to a reference to an object of that class. The `result` is `1` (`true`) if it can, and `0` (`false`) otherwise.

Monitors

```
monitorenter        ..., handle => ...
```

Enter monitored region of code. `handle` must be a reference to an object. The interpreter attempts to obtain exclusive access via a lock mechanism to `handle`. If another thread already has `handle` locked, the current thread waits until the `handle` is unlocked. If the current thread already has `handle` locked, execution continues normally. If `handle` has no lock on it, this bytecode obtains an exclusive lock.

```
monitorexit         ..., handle => ...
```

Exit monitored region of code. `handle` must be a reference to an object. The lock on `handle` is released. If this is the last lock that this thread has on that `handle` (one thread is allowed to have multiple locks on a single `handle`), other threads that are waiting for `handle` are allowed to proceed. (A `null` in either bytecode throws `NullPointerException`.)

Debugging

```
breakpoint          -no change-
```

Call breakpoint handler. The breakpoint bytecode is used to overwrite a bytecode to force control temporarily back to the debugger prior to the effect of the overwritten bytecode. The original bytecode's operands (if any) are not overwritten, and the original bytecode is restored when the breakpoint bytecode is removed.

The _quick Bytecodes

The following discussion, straight out of the Java virtual machine documentation, shows you an example of the cleverness mentioned earlier that's needed to make a bytecode interpreter fast:

The following set of pseudo-bytecodes, suffixed by _quick, are all variants of standard Java bytecodes. They are used by the runtime to improve the execution speed of the byte-code interpreter. They aren't officially part of the virtual machine specification and are invisible outside a Java virtual machine implementation. However, inside that implementation they have proven to be an effective optimization.

First, you should know that javac *still generates only non-_quick bytecodes. Second, all bytecodes that have a _quick variant reference the constant pool. When _quick optimization is turned on, each non-_quick bytecode (that has a _quick variant) resolves the specified item in the constant pool, signals an error if the item in the constant pool could not be resolved for some reason, turns itself into the _quick variant of itself, and then performs its intended operation.*

This is identical to the actions of the non-_quick bytecode, except for the step of overwriting itself with its _quick variant. The _quick variant of a bytecode assumes that the item in the constant pool has already been resolved, and that this resolution did not produce any errors. It simply performs the intended operation on the resolved item.

Thus, as your bytecodes are being interpreted, they are automatically getting faster and faster! Here are all the _quick variants in the current Java runtime:

```
ldc1_quick
ldc2_quick
ldc2w_quick

anewarray_quick
multinewarray_quick

putfield_quick
putfield2_quick
getfield_quick
getfield2_quick
putstatic_quick
putstatic2_quick
getstatic_quick
getstatic2_quick

invokevirtual_quick
invokevirtualobject_quick
invokenonvirtual_quick
invokestatic_quick
invokeinterface_quick

new_quick
checkcast_quick
instanceof_quick
```

If you'd like to go back in today's lesson and look at what each of these does, you can find the name of the original bytecode on which a _quick variant is based by simply removing the _quick from its name. The bytecodes putstatic, getstatic, putfield, and getfield have two _quick variants each, one for each stack picture in their original descriptions. invokevirtual has two variants: one for objects and one for arrays to do fast lookups in java.lang.Object.

NOTE

One last note on the _quick optimization, regarding the unusual handling of the constant pool (for detail fanatics only):

When a class is read in, an array constant_pool[] of size nconstants is created and assigned to a field in the class. constant_pool[0] is set to point to a dynamically allocated array that indicates which fields in the constant_pool have already been resolved. constant_pool[1] through constant_pool[nconstants - 1] are set to point at the "type" field that corresponds to this constant item.

When a bytecode is executed that references the constant pool, an index is generated, and constant_pool[0] is checked to see whether the index has already been resolved. If so, the value of constant_pool[index] is returned. If not, the value of constant_pool[index] is resolved to be the actual pointer or data, and overwrites whatever value was already in constant_pool[index].

The .class File Format

You won't be given the entire .class file format here, only a taste of what it's like. (You can read all about it in Sun's release documentation.) It's mentioned here because it is one of the parts of Java that needs to be specified carefully if all Java implementations are to be compatible with one another, and if Java bytes are expected to travel across arbitrary networks—to and from arbitrary computers and operating systems—and yet arrive safely.

The rest of this section paraphrases the latest (alpha) release of the .class documentation.

.class files are used to hold the compiled versions of both Java classes and Java interfaces. Compliant Java interpreters must be capable of dealing with all .class files that conform to the following specifications.

A Java .class file consists of a stream of 8-bit bytes. All 16-bit and 32-bit quantities are constructed by reading in two or four 8-bit bytes, respectively. The bytes are joined together in big-endian order. (Use java.io.DataInput and java.io.DataOutput to read and write class files.)

The .class file format is presented below as a series of C-struct-like structures. However, unlike a C struct, there is no padding or alignment between pieces of the structure, each field of the structure may be of variable size, and an array may be of variable size (in this case, some field prior to the array gives the array's dimension). The types u1, u2, and u4 represent an unsigned one-, two-, or four-byte quantity, respectively.

Attributes are used at several different places in the .class format. All attributes have the following format:

```
GenericAttribute_info {
    u2 attribute_name;
    u4 attribute_length;
    u1 info[attribute_length];
}
```

The attribute_name is a 16-bit index into the class's constant pool; the value of constant_pool[attribute_name] is a string giving the name of the attribute. The field attribute_length gives the length of the subsequent information in bytes. This length does not include the four bytes needed to store attribute_name and attribute_length. In the following text, whenever an attribute is required, names of all the attributes that are currently understood are listed. In the future, more attributes will be added. Class file readers are expected to skip over and ignore the information in any attributes that they do not understand.

The following pseudo-structure gives a top-level description of the format of a class file:

```
ClassFile {
    u4   magic;
    u2   minor_version;
    u2   major_version;
    u2   constant_pool_count;
    cp_info         constant_pool[constant_pool_count - 1];
    u2   access_flags;
    u2   this_class;
    u2   super_class;
    u2   interfaces_count;
    u2   interfaces[interfaces_count];
    u2   fields_count;
    field_info      fields[fields_count];
    u2   methods_count;
    method_info     methods[methods_count];
```

```
    u2  attributes_count;
    attribute_info  attributes[attribute_count];
}
```

Here's one of the smaller structures used:

```
method_info {
    u2  access_flags;
    u2  name_index;
    u2  signature_index;
    u2  attributes_count;
    attribute_info  attributes[attribute_count];
}
```

Finally, here's a sample of one of the later structures in the .class file description:

```
Code_attribute {
    u2  attribute_name_index;
    u2  attribute_length;
    u1  max_stack;
    u1  max_locals;
    u2  code_length;
    u1  code[code_length];
    u2  exception_table_length;
    {   u2_    start_pc;
        u2_    end_pc;
        u2_    handler_pc;
        u2_    catch_type;
    }   exception_table[exception_table_length];
    u2  attributes_count;
    attribute_info  attributes[attribute_count];
}
```

None of this is meant to be completely comprehensible (though you might be able to guess what a lot of the structure members are for), but just suggestive of the sort of structures that live inside .class files. Because the compiler and run-time sources are available, you can always begin with them if you actually have to read or write .class files yourself. Thus, you don't need to have a deep understanding of the details, even in that case.

Method Signatures

Because method signatures are used in .class files, now is an appropriate time to explore them in the detail promised on earlier days.

NEW TERM   A *signature* is a string representing the type of a method, field, or array.

A field signature represents the value of an argument to a method or the value of a variable and is a series of bytes in the following grammar:

```
<field signature> := <field_type>
<field type>      := <base_type> ¦ <object_type> ¦ <array_type>
<base_type>       := B ¦ C ¦ D ¦ F ¦ I ¦ J ¦ S ¦ Z
<object_type>     := L <full.ClassName> ;
<array_type>      := [ <optional_size> <field_type>
<optional_size>   := [0-9]*
```

Here are the meanings of the base types: B (byte), C (char), D (double), F (float), I (int), J (long), S (short), and Z (boolean).

A return-type signature represents the return value from a method and is a series of bytes in the following grammar:

```
<return signature>    := <field type> ¦ V
```

The character V (void) indicates that the method returns no value. Otherwise, the signature indicates the type of the return value. An argument signature represents an argument passed to a method:

```
<argument signature>  := <field type>
```

Finally, a method signature represents the arguments that the method expects, and the value that it returns:

```
<method_signature>    := (<arguments signature>) <return signature>
<arguments signature> := <argument signature>*
```

Let's try out the new rules: a method called complexMethod() in the class my.package.name.ComplexClass takes three arguments—a long, a boolean, and a two-dimensional array of shorts—and returns this. Then, (JZ[[S)Lmy.package.name.ComplexClass; is its method signature.

A method signature is often prefixed by the name of the method, or by its full package (using an underscore in the place of dots) and its class name followed by a slash / and the name of the method, to form a *complete method signature*. Now, at last, you have the full story! Thus, the following:

my_package_name_ComplexClass/complexMethod(JZ[[S)Lmy.package.name.ComplexClass;

… is the full, complete method signature of method complexMethod(). (Whew!)

The Garbage Collector

Decades ago, programmers in both the Lisp and the Smalltalk communities realized how extremely valuable it is to be able to ignore memory deallocation. They realized that, although allocation is fundamental, deallocation is forced on the programmer by the laziness of the system—*it* should be able to figure out what is no longer useful, and get rid of it. In relative obscurity, these pioneering programmers developed a whole series of garbage collectors to perform this job, each getting more sophisticated and efficient as the years went by. Finally, now that the mainstream programming community has begun to recognize the value of this automated technique, Java can become the first really widespread application of the technology those pioneers developed.

The Problem

Imagine that you're a programmer in a C-like language (probably not too difficult for you, because these languages are the dominant ones right now). Each time you create something—anything—*dynamically* in such a language, you are completely responsible for tracking the life of this object throughout your program and deciding when it will be safe to deallocate it. This can be quite a difficult (sometimes impossible) task, because any of the other libraries or methods you've called might have "squirreled away" a pointer to the object, unbeknownst to you. When it becomes impossible to know, you simply choose *never* to deallocate the object, or choose to wait until every library and method call involved has completed—which usually means "never deallocate."

The uneasy feeling you get when writing such code is a natural, healthy response to what is inherently an unsafe and unreliable style of programming. If you have tremendous discipline—and so does everyone who writes every library and method you call—you can, in principle, survive this responsibility without too many mishaps. But aren't you human? Aren't they? There must be some small slips in this perfect discipline. What's worse, such errors are virtually undetectable, as anyone who has tried to hunt down a stray pointer problem in C will tell you. What about the thousands of programmers who don't have that sort of discipline?

Another way to ask this question is, Why should any programmers be forced to have this discipline, when it is entirely possible for the system to remove this heavy burden from their shoulders?

Software engineering estimates have recently shown that for every 55 lines of production C-like code in the world, there is one bug. This means that your electric razor has about 80 bugs, and your TV, 400. Soon they will have even more, because the size of this kind of embedded computer software is growing exponentially. When you begin to think of how much C-like code is in your car's engine, it should give you pause.

Many of these errors are due to the misuse of pointers, by misunderstanding or by accident, and to the early, incorrect freeing of allocated objects in memory. Java addresses both of these—the former, by eliminating explicit pointers from the Java language altogether and the latter, by including, in every Java system, a garbage collector that solves the problem.

The Solution

Imagine a run-time system that tracks each object you create, notices when the last reference to it has vanished, and frees the object for you. How could such a thing actually work?

One brute-force approach, tried early in the days of garbage collecting, is to attach a reference counter to every object. When the object is created, the counter is set to 1. Each time a new reference to the object is made, the counter is incremented, and each time such a reference disappears, the counter is decremented. Because all such references are controlled by the language—as variables and assignments, for example—the compiler can tell whenever an object reference might be created or destroyed, just as it does in handling the scoping of local variables, and thus it can assist with this task. The system itself "holds onto" a set of root objects that are considered too important to be freed. The class Object is one example of such a V.I.P. object (V.I.O.?). Finally, all that's needed is to test, after each decrement, whether the counter has hit 0. If it has, the object is freed.

If you think carefully about this approach, you can soon convince yourself that it is definitely correct when it decides to free anything. It is so simple that you can immediately tell that it will work. The low-level hacker in you might also feel that if it's *that* simple, it's probably not fast enough to run at the lowest level of the system—and you'd be right.

Think about all the stack frames, local variables, method arguments, return values, and local variables created in the course of even a few hundred milliseconds of a program's life. For each of these tiny, nano-steps in the program, an extra increment—at best—or decrement, test, and deallocation—at worst—will be added to the running time of the program. In fact, the first garbage collectors were slow enough that many predicted they could never be used at all!

Luckily, a whole generation of smart programmers has invented a big bag of tricks to solve these overhead problems. One trick is to introduce special "transient object" areas that don't need to be reference counted. The best of these generational scavenging garbage collectors today can take less than three percent of the total time of your program—a remarkable feat if you realize that many other language features, such as loop overheads, can be as large or larger!

There are other problems with garbage collection. If you are constantly freeing and reclaiming space in a program, won't the heap of objects soon become fragmented, with small holes everywhere and no room to create new, large objects? Because the programmer is now free from the chains of manual deallocation, won't they create even more objects than usual?

What's worse, there is another way that this simple reference counting scheme is inefficient, in space rather than time. If a long chain of object references eventually comes full circle, back to the starting object, each object's reference count remains at least 1 *forever*. None of these objects will ever be freed!

Together, these problems imply that a good garbage collector must, every once in a while, step back to compact or to clean up wasted memory.

NEW TERM

Compaction occurs when a garbage collector steps back and reorganizes memory, eliminating the holes created by fragmentation. Compacting memory is simply a matter of repositioning objects one by one into a new, compact grouping that places them all in a row, leaving all the free memory in the heap in one big piece.

Cleaning up the circular garbage still lying around after reference counting is called *marking and sweeping*. A mark-and-sweep of memory involves first marking every root object in the system and then following all the object references inside those objects to new objects to mark, and so on, recursively. Then, when you have no more references to follow, you "sweep away" all the unmarked objects, and compact memory as before.

The good news is that this solves the space problems you were having. The bad news is that when the garbage collector "steps back" and does these operations, a non-trivial amount of time passes during which your program is unable to run—all its objects are being marked, swept, rearranged, and so forth, in what seems like an uninterruptible procedure. Your first hint to a solution is the word "seems."

Garbage collecting can actually be done a little at a time, between or in parallel with normal program execution, thus dividing up the large time needed to "step back" into numerous so-small-you-don't-notice-them chunks of time that happen between the cracks. (Of course, years of smart thinking went into the abstruse algorithms that make all this possible!)

One final problem that might worry you a little has to do with these object references. Aren't these "pointers" scattered throughout your program and not just buried in objects? Even if they're only in objects, don't they have to be changed whenever the object they point to is moved by these procedures? The answer to both of these questions is a resounding *yes*, and overcoming them is the final hurdle to making an efficient garbage collector.

There are really only two choices. The first, brute force, assumes that all the memory containing object references needs to be searched on a regular basis, and whenever the object references found by this search match objects that have moved, the old reference is changed. This assumes that there are "hard" pointers in the heap's memory—ones that point directly to other objects. By introducing various kinds of "soft" pointers, including pointers that are like forwarding addresses, the algorithm improves greatly. Although these brute-force approaches sound slow, it turns out that modern computers can do them fast enough to be useful.

NOTE
You might wonder how the brute-force techniques identify object references. In early systems, references were specially tagged with a "pointer bit," so they could be unambiguously located. Now, so-called conservative garbage collectors simply assume that if it looks like an object reference, it is—at least for the purposes of the mark-and-sweep. Later, when actually trying to update it, they can find out whether it really is an object reference.

The final approach to handling object references, and the one Java currently uses, is also one of the very first ones tried. It involves using 100 percent "soft" pointers. An object reference is actually a handle, sometimes call an "OOP," to the real pointer, and a large object table exists to map these handles into the actual object reference. Although this does introduce extra overhead on almost every object reference (some of which can be eliminated by clever tricks, as you might guess), it's not too high a price to pay for this incredibly valuable level of indirection.

This indirection allows the garbage collector, for example, to mark, sweep, move, or examine one object at a time. Each object can be independently moved "out from under" a running Java program by changing only the object table entries. This not only allows the "step back" phase to happen in the tiniest steps, but it makes a garbage collector that runs literally in parallel with your program much easier to write. This is what the Java garbage collector does.

WARNING

You need to be very careful about garbage collection when you're doing critical, real-time programs—but how often will your Java code be flying a commercial airliner in real time, anyway?

Java's Parallel Garbage Collector

Java applies almost all these advanced techniques to give you a fast, efficient, parallel garbage collector. Running in a separate thread, it cleans up the Java environment of almost all trash (it is conservative), silently and in the background, is efficient in both space and time, and never steps back for more than an unnoticeably small amount of time. You should never need to know it's there.

By the way, if you want to force a full mark-and-sweep garbage collection to happen soon, you can do so simply by calling the System.gc() method. You might want to do this if you just freed up a majority of the heap's memory in circular garbage, and want it all taken away quickly. You might also call this whenever you're idle, as a hint to the system about when it would be best to come and collect the garbage. This "meta knowledge" is rarely needed by the system, however.

Ideally, you'll never notice the garbage collector, and all those decades of programmers beating their brains out on your behalf will simply let you sleep better at night—and what's wrong with that?

The Security Story

Speaking of sleeping well at night, if you haven't stepped back yet and said, "You mean Java programs will be running rampant on the Internet!?!" you better do so now, for it is a legitimate concern. In fact, it is one of the major technical stumbling blocks (the other stumbling blocks being mostly social and economic) to achieving the dream of ubiquity and code sharing mentioned earlier in today's lesson.

NOTE

The current Developer Release of Roaster does not implement all of the run-time bytecode verification checks found in the Java Virtual Machine specifications. According to Natural Intelligence, this is a high priority and will certainly be added to future versions. Remember that the Roaster Applet Runner is not a Web browser; if you only run applets you've compiled yourself (with javac) or applets you know were compiled by a "safe" compiler, you will avoid the potential problems the Java bytecode verifier is intended to circumvent.

Why You Should Worry

Any powerful, flexible technology can be abused. As the Net becomes mainstream and widespread, it, too, will be abused. Already, there have been many blips on the security radar screens of those of us who worry about such things, warning that (at least until today) not enough attention has been paid by the computer industry (or the media) to solving some of the problems that this new world brings with it. One of the benefits of solving security once and for all will be a flowering unseen before in the virtual communities of the Net; whole new economies based on people's attention and creativity will spring to life, rapidly transforming our world in new and positive ways.

The downside to all this new technology is that we (or someone!) must worry long and hard about how to make the playgrounds of the future safe for our children, and for us. Fortunately, Java is a big part of the answer.

Why You Might Not Have to Worry

What gives me any confidence that the Java language and environment will be *safe*, that it will solve the technically daunting and extremely thorny problems inherent in any good form of security, especially for networks?

One simple reason is the history of the people, and the company, that created Java. Many of them are the very smart programmers referred to throughout the book who helped pioneer many of the ideas that make Java great and who have worked hard over the decades to make techniques such as garbage collection a mainstream reality. They are technically capable of tackling and solving the hard problems that need to be solved. In particular, from discussions with Chuck McManis, one of Java's security gurus, I have confidence that he has thought through these hard problems deeply, and that he knows what needs to be done.

Sun Microsystems, the company, has been pushing networks as the central theme of all its software for more than a decade. Sun has the engineers and the commitment needed to solve these hard problems, because these same problems are at the very center of both its future business and its vision of the future, in which networking is the center of everything—and global networks are nearly useless without good security. Just this year, Sun has advanced the state of the art in easy-to-use Internet security with its new SunScreen products, and it has assigned Whitfield Diffie to oversee them. Yes, *the* Whitfield Diffie, the man who discovered the underlying ideas on which essentially *all* interesting forms of modern encryption are based.

Enough "deep background." What does the Java environment provide *right now* that helps us feel secure?

Java's Security Model

Java protects you against potential "nasty" Java code via a series of interlocking defenses that together form an imposing barrier to any and all such attacks.

WARNING

> Of course, no one can protect you from your own ignorance or carelessness. If you're the kind of person who blindly downloads binary executables from your Internet browser and runs them, you need read no further! You are already in more danger than Java will ever pose.
>
> As a user of this powerful new medium, the Internet, you should educate yourself to the possible threats this new and exciting world entails. In particular, downloading "auto running macros" or reading email with "executable attachments" is just as much a threat as downloading binaries from the Net and running them.
>
> Java does not introduce any new dangers here, but by being the first mainstream use of executable and mobile code on the Net, it is responsible for making people suddenly aware of the dangers that have always been there. Java is already, as you will soon see, much less dangerous than any of these common activities on the Net, and can be made safer still over time. Most of these other (dangerous) activities can never be made safe. So please, do not do them!
>
> A good rule of thumb on the Net is Don't download anything that you plan to execute (or that will be automatically executed for you) except from someone (or some company) you know well and with whom you've had positive, personal experience. If you don't care about losing all the data on your hard drive, or about your privacy, you can do anything you like, but for most of us, this rule should be law.
>
> Fortunately, Java enables you to relax that law. You can run Java applets from anyone, anywhere, in complete safety.

Java's powerful security mechanisms act at four different levels of the system architecture. First, the Java language itself was designed to be safe, and the Java compiler ensures that source code doesn't violate these safety rules. Second, all bytecodes executed by the runtime are screened to be sure that they also obey these rules. (This layer guards against having an altered compiler produce code that violates the safety rules.) Third, the class loader ensures that classes don't violate name space or access restrictions when they are loaded into the system. Finally, API-specific security prevents applets from doing destructive things. This final layer depends on the security and integrity guarantees from the other three layers.

Let's now examine each of these layers in turn.

The Language and the Compiler

The Java language and its compiler are the first line of defense. Java was designed to be a safe language.

Most other C-like languages have facilities to control access to "objects," but also have ways to "forge" access to objects (or to parts of objects), usually by (mis)using pointers. This introduces two fatal security flaws to any system built on these languages. One is that no object can protect itself from outside modification, duplication, or "spoofing" (others pretending to be that object). Another is that a language with powerful pointers is more likely to have serious bugs that compromise security. These pointer bugs, where a "runaway pointer" starts modifying some other object's memory, were responsible for most of the public (and not-so-public) security problems on the Internet this past decade.

Java eliminates these threats in one stroke by eliminating pointers from the language altogether. There are still pointers of a kind—object references—but these are carefully controlled to be safe: they are unforgeable, and all casts are checked for legality before being allowed. In addition, powerful new array facilities in Java not only help to offset the loss of pointers, but also add additional safety by strictly enforcing array bounds, catching more bugs for the programmer (bugs that, in other languages, might lead to unexpected and, thus, bad-guy-exploitable problems).

The language definition, and the compilers that enforce it, create a powerful barrier to any "nasty" Java programmer.

Because an overwhelming majority of the "Net-savvy" software on the Internet may soon be written in Java, its safe language definition and compilers help to guarantee that most of this software has a solid, secure base. With fewer bugs, Net software will be more predictable—a property that thwarts attacks.

Verifying the Bytecodes

What if that "nasty" programmer gets a little more determined, and rewrites the Java compiler to suit his nefarious purposes? The Java runtime, getting the lion's share of its bytecodes from the Net, can never tell whether those bytecodes were generated by a "trustworthy" compiler. Therefore, it must *verify* that they meet all the safety requirements.

Before running any bytecodes, the runtime subjects them to a rigorous series of tests—varying in complexity from simple format checks all the way to running a theorem prover—to make certain that the bytecodes are playing by the rules. These tests verify that the bytecodes do not forge pointers, violate access restrictions, access objects as other than what they are (InputStreams are always used as InputStreams, and never as anything else), call methods with inappropriate argument values or types, nor overflow the stack.

Consider the following Java code:

```java
public class VectorTest {
    public int  array[];

    public int  sum() {
        int[]  localArray = array;
        int    sum        = 0;

        for (int  i = localArray.length;  —i >= 0;  )
            sum += localArray[i];
        return sum;
    }
}
```

If you compile this code and open the resulting .class file with Roaster, you will see a set of bytecode instructions listed for the sum() class. Below are those instructions as Roaster will display them, along with a description of what each does:

0x0000:	aload_0	Load this
0x0001:	getfield Vector Test.array <int[ ]>	Load array
0x0004:	astore_1	Store in localArray
0x0005:	iconst_0	Load 0
0x0006:	istore_2	Store in sum
0x0007:	aload_1	Load localArray
0x0008:	arraylength	Gets its length
0x0009:	istore_3	Store in i
0x000A:	goto 0x0013	Jump to line 0x0013
0x000D:	iload_2	Load sum
0x000E:	aload_1	Load localArray
0x000F:	iload_3	Load i
0x0010:	iaload	Load localArray[i]
0x0011:	iadd	Add sum
0x0012:	istore_2	Store in sum

0x0013:	iinc 3, 255	Subtract 1 from i
0x0016:	iload_3	Load i
0x0017:	ifge 0x000D if i>=0	Repeat from 0x000D
0x001A:	iload_2	Load sum
0x001B:	ireturn	Return it

NOTE

The excellent examples and descriptions in this section of the book are paraphrased from the tremendously informative security paper in the alpha Java release. I'd encourage you to read the latest version of this document if you want to follow the ongoing Java security story.

Extra Type Information and Requirements

Java bytecodes encode more type information than strictly is necessary for the interpreter. Even though, for example, the aload and iload opcodes do exactly the same thing, aload is always used to load an object reference and iload is used to load an integer. Some bytecodes (such as getfield) include a symbol table reference—and that symbol table has *even more* type information. This extra type information enables the run-time system to guarantee that Java objects and data aren't illegally manipulated.

Conceptually, before and after each bytecode is executed, every slot in the stack and every local variable has some type. This collection of type information—all the slots and local variables—is called the *type state* of the execution environment. An important requirement of the Java type state is that it must be determinable statically by induction—that is, before any program code is executed. As a result, as the run-time systems read bytecodes, each is required to have the following inductive property: given only the type state before the execution of the bytecode, the type state afterward must be fully determined.

Given "straight-line" bytecodes (no branches), and starting with a known stack state, the state of each slot in the stack is therefore always known. For example, starting with an empty stack:

iload_1   Load integer variable. Stack type state is I.

iconst 5   Load integer constant. Stack type state is II.

iadd   Add two integers, producing an integer. Stack type state is I.

NOTE   Smalltalk and PostScript bytecodes do not have this restriction. Their more dynamic type behavior does create additional flexibility in those systems, but Java needs to provide a secure execution environment. It must therefore know all types *at all times*, in order to guarantee a certain level of security.

Another requirement made by the Java runtime is that when a set of bytecodes can take more than one path to arrive at the same point, all such paths must arrive there with exactly the same type state. This is a strict requirement, and implies, for example, that compilers cannot generate bytecodes that load all the elements of an array onto the stack. (Because each time through such a loop the stack's type state changes, the start of the loop—"the same point" in multiple paths—would have more than one type state, which is not allowed.)

The Verifier

Bytecodes are checked for compliance with all these requirements, using the extra type information in a .class file, by a part of the run-time called the *verifier*. It examines each bytecode in turn, constructing the full type state as it goes, and verifies that all the types of parameters, arguments, and results are correct. Thus, the verifier acts as a gatekeeper to your run-time environment, letting in only those bytecodes that pass muster.

WARNING   The verifier is *the crucial piece* of Java's security, and it depends on your having a correctly implemented (no bugs, intentional or otherwise) run-time system. You should be careful when downloading or buying new versions of the Java run-time environment. Eventually, Sun will implement validation suites for runtimes, compilers, and so forth to be sure that they are safe and correct. In the meantime, *caveat emptor*! Your runtime is the base on which all the rest of Java's security is built, so make sure it is a good, solid, secure base.

When bytecodes have passed the verifier, they are guaranteed not to:

☐ Cause any operand stack under- or overflows

☐ Use parameter, argument, or return types incorrectly

☐ Illegally convert data from one type to another (from an integer to a pointer, for example)

☐ Access any object's fields illegally (that is, the verifier checks that the rules for public, private, package, and protected are obeyed)

As an added bonus, because the interpreter can now count on all these guarantees, it can run much faster than before. All the required checks for safety have been done up front, so it can run at full throttle. In addition, object references can now be treated as capabilities, because they are unforgeable—capabilities enable, for example, advanced security models for file I/O and authentication to be safely built on top of Java.

NOTE

Because you can now trust that a private variable really is private, and that no byte-code can perform some magic with casts to extract information from it (such as your credit card number), many of the security problems that might arise in other, less safe environments simply vanish! These guarantees also make erecting barriers against destructive applets possible, and easier. Because the Java system doesn't have to worry about "nasty" bytecodes, it can get on with creating the other levels of security it wants to provide to you.

The Class Loader

The class loader is another kind of gatekeeper, albeit a higher-level one. The verifier was the security of last resort. The class loader is the security of first resort.

When a new class is loaded into the system, it must come from one of several different "realms." In the current release, there are three possible realms: your local computer, the firewall-guarded local network on which your computer is located, and the Internet (the global Net). Each of these realms is treated differently by the class loader.

NOTE

Actually, there can be as many realms as your desired level of security (or paranoia) requires. This is because the class loader is under your control. As a programmer, you can make your own class loader that implements your own peculiar brand of security. (This is a radical step: you may have to give the users of your program a whole bunch of classes—and they give you a whole lot of trust—to accomplish this.)

As a user, you can tell your Java-aware browser or Java system what realm of security (of the three) you'd like it to implement for you right now or from now on.

As a system administrator, Java has global security policies that you can set up to help guide your users to not "give away the store" (that is, set all their preferences to be unrestricted, promiscuous, "hurt me please!").

In particular, the class loader never allows a class from a "less protected" realm to replace a class from a more protected realm. The file system's I/O primitives, about which you should be *very* worried (and rightly so), are all defined in a local Java class, which means that they all live in the local-computer realm. Thus, no class from outside your computer (from either the supposedly trustworthy local network or from the Internet) can take the place of these classes and "spoof" Java code into using "nasty" versions of these primitives. In addition, classes in one realm cannot call upon the methods of classes in other realms, unless those classes have explicitly declared those methods public. This implies that classes from other than your local computer cannot even *see* the file system I/O methods, much less call them, unless you or the system wants them to.

In addition, every new applet loaded from the network is placed into a separate package-like namespace. This means that applets are protected even from each other! No applet can access another's methods (or variables) without its cooperation. Applets from inside the firewall can even be treated differently from those outside the firewall, if you like.

NOTE

Actually, it's all a little more complex than this. In the current release, an applet is in a package "namespace" along with any other applets from that *source*. This source, or origin, is most often a host (domain name) on the Internet. This special "sub-realm" is used extensively in the next section. Depending on where the source is located, outside the firewall (or inside), further restrictions may apply (or be removed entirely). This model is likely to be extended in future releases of Java, providing an even finer degree of control over which classes get to do what.

The class loader essentially partitions the world of Java classes into small, protected little groups, about which you can safely make assumptions that will *always* be true. This type of predictability is the key to well-behaved and secure programs.

You've now seen the full lifetime of a method. It starts as source code on some computer, is compiled into bytecodes on some (possibly different) computer, and can then travel (as a .class file) into any file system or network anywhere in the world. When you run an applet in a Java-aware browser (or download a class and run it by hand using java), the method's bytecodes are extracted from its .class file and carefully looked over by the verifier. After they are declared safe, the interpreter can execute them for you (or a code generator can generate native binary code for them using either the "just-in-time" compiler or java2c, and then run that native code directly).

At each stage, more and more security is added. The final level of that security is the Java class library itself, which has several carefully designed classes and APIs that add the final touches to the security of the system.

The Security Manager

SecurityManager is an abstract class that was recently added to the Java system to collect, in one place, all the security policy decisions that the system has to make as bytecodes run. You learned before that you can create your own class loader. In fact, you may not have to, because you can subclass SecurityManager to perform most of the same customizations.

An instance of some subclass of SecurityManager is always installed as the current security manager. It has complete control over which of a well-defined set of "dangerous" methods are allowed to be called by any given class. It takes the realms from the last section into account, the source (origin) of the class, and the type of the class (standalone or loaded by an applet). Each of these can be separately configured to have the effect you (the programmer) like on your Java system. For nonprogrammers, the system provides several levels of default security policies from which you can choose.

What is this "well-defined set" of methods that are protected? Also in this protected set are the methods that create and use network connections, both incoming and outgoing. The final members of the set are those methods that enable one thread to access, control, and manipulate other threads. (Of course, additional methods can be protected as well by creating a new subclass of SecurityManager that handles them.)

For both file and network access, the user of a Java-aware browser can choose between three realms (and one subrealm) of protection:

☐ *unrestricted* (enables applets to do anything)

☐ *firewall* (enables applets within the firewall to do anything)

☐ *source* (enables applets to do things only with their origin [Internet] host, or with other applets from there)

☐ *local* (disenables all file and network access)

For file access, the *source* subrealm is not meaningful, so it really has only three realms of protection. (As a programmer, of course, you have full access to the security manager and can set up your own peculiar criteria for granting and revoking privileges to your heart's content.)

For network access, you can imagine wanting many more realms. For example, you might specify different groups of trusted domains (companies), each of which is allowed added privileges when applets from that group are loaded. Some groups can be more trusted than others, and you might even allow groups to grow automatically by allowing existing members to recommend new members for admission. (The Java seal of approval?)

In any case, the possibilities are endless, as long as there is a secure way of recognizing the original creator of an applet.

You might think this problem has already been solved, because classes are tagged with their origin. In fact, the Java runtime goes far out of its way to be sure that that origin information is never lost—any executing method can be dynamically restricted by this information anywhere in the call chain. So why *isn't* this enough?

Because what you'd really like to be able to do is permanently "tag" an applet with its original creator (its true origin), and no matter where it has traveled, a browser could verify the integrity and authenticate the creator of that applet. Just because you don't know the company or individual that operates a particular server machine doesn't mean that you *want* to mistrust every applet stored on that machine. It's just that, currently, to be really safe, you *should* mistrust those applets.

If somehow those applets were irrevocably tagged with a digital signature by their creator, and that signature could also guarantee that the applet had not been tampered with, you'd be golden.

NOTE

> Luckily, Sun is planning to do exactly that for Java, as soon as export restrictions can be resolved.
>
> Here's a helpful hint of where the team would like to go, from the security documentation: "… a mechanism exists whereby public keys and cryptographic message digests can be securely attached to code fragments that not only identify who originated the code, but guarantee its integrity as well. This latter mechanism will be implemented in future releases."
>
> Look for these sorts of features in every release of Java; they will be a key part of the future of the Internet!

One final note about security. Despite the best efforts of the Java team, there is always a trade-off between useful functionality and absolute security. For example, Java applets can create windows, an extremely useful capability, but a "nasty" applet could use this to spoof the user into typing private password information, by showing a familiar program (or operating system) window and then asking an expected, legitimate-looking question in it. (The beta release of Java added a special banner to applet-created windows to solve this problem.)

Flexibility and security can't both be maximized. Thus far on the Net, people have chosen maximum flexibility, and have lived with the minimal security the Net now provides. Let's hope that Java can help tip the scales a bit, enabling much better security, while sacrificing only a minimal amount of the flexibility that has drawn so many to the Net.

Summary

Today, you learned about the grand vision that some of us have for Java, and about the exciting future it promises.

Under the hood, the inner workings of the virtual machine, the bytecode interpreter (and all its bytecodes), the garbage collector, the class loader, the verifier, the security manager, and the powerful security features of Java were all revealed.

You now know *almost* enough to write a Java run-time environment of your own—but luckily, you don't have to. You can simply use Roaster to enjoy the benefits of Java right away.

I hope that Java ends up opening new roads in your mind, as it has in mine.

Questions and Answers

Q I'm still a little unclear about why the Java language and compiler make the Net safer. Can't they just be "side-stepped" by nasty bytecodes?

A Yes, they can—but don't forget that the whole point of using a safe language and compiler was to make the Net *as a whole* safer as more Java code is written. An overwhelming majority of this Java code will be written by "honest" Java programmers, who will produce safe bytecodes. This makes the Net more predictable over time, and thus more secure.

Q I know you said that garbage collection is something I don't have to worry about, but what if I want (or need) to?

A So, you *are* planning to fly a plane with Java. Cool! For just such cases, there is a way to ask the Java runtime, during startup (java -noasyncgc), *not* to run garbage collection unless forced to, either by an explicit call (System.gc()) or by running out of memory. (This can be quite useful if you have multiple threads that are messing each other up and want to "get the gc thread out of the way" while testing them.) Don't forget that turning garbage collection off means that any object you create will live a *long, long time*. If you're in real time, you never want to "step back" for a full gc—so be sure to reuse objects often, and don't create too many of them!

Q I like the control above; is there anything else I can do to the garbage collector?

A You can also force the `finalize()` methods of any recently freed objects to be called immediately via `System.runFinalization()`. You might want to do this if you're about to ask for some resources that you suspect might still be tied up by objects that are "gone but not forgotten" (waiting for `finalize()`). This is even rarer than starting a gc by hand, but it's mentioned here for completeness.

Q What's the last word on Java?

A Java adds much more than it can ever take away. It has always done so for me, and now, I hope it will for you, as well.

The future of the Net is filled with as-yet-undreamt horizons, and the road is long and hard, but Java is a great traveling companion.

Language Summary

by Laura Lemay

This appendix contains a summary or quick reference for the Java language, as described in this book.

NOTE

This is not a grammar, nor is it a technical overview of the language itself. It's a quick reference to be used after you already know the basics of how the language works. If you need a technical description of the language, your best bet is to visit the Java Web site (http://java.sun.com) and download the actual specification, which includes a full BNF grammar.

Language keywords and symbols are shown in a monospace font. Arguments and other parts to be substituted are in *italic monospace*.

Optional parts are indicated by brackets (except in the array syntax section). If there are several options that are mutually exclusive, they are shown separated by pipes (¦) like this:

```
[ public ¦ private ¦ protected ] type varname
```

Reserved Words

The following words are reserved for use by the Java language itself (some of them are reserved but not currently used). You cannot use these terms to refer to classes, methods, or variable names:

abstract	do	implements	package	throw
boolean	double	import	private	throws
break	else	protected	transient	byte
extends	instanceof	public	try	case
final	int	finally	interface	return
void	catch	float	long	short
volatile	char	for	native	static
while	class	new	super	const
null	switch	continue	goto	synchronized
default	if	this		

Comments

```
/* this is a multiline comment */
// this is a single-line comment
/** Javadoc comment */
```

Literals

number	Type int
number[l ¦ L]	Type long
0x*hex*	Hex integer
0X*hex*	Hex integer
0*octal*	Octal integer
[*number*].*number*	Type double
number[f ¦ f]	Type float
number[d ¦ D]	Type double
[+ ¦ -] *number*	Signed

numberenumber	Exponent
numberEnumber	Exponent
'*character*'	Single character
"*characters*"	String
" "	Empty string
\b	Backspace
\t	Tab
\n	Line feed
\f	Form feed
\r	Carriage return
\"	Double quote
\'	Single quote
\\	Backslash
\uNNNN	Unicode escape (NNNN is hex)
true	Boolean
false	Boolean

Variable Declaration

[byte ¦ short ¦ int ¦ long] *varname*	Integers (pick one type)
[float ¦ double] *varname*	Floats (pick one type)
char *varname*	Characters
boolean *varname*	Boolean
classname varname	Class types
type *varname*, *varname*, *varname*	Multiple variables

The following options are available only for class and instance variables. Any of these options can be used with a variable declaration.

[static] *variableDeclaration*	Class variable
[final] *variableDeclaration*	Constants
[public ¦ private ¦ protected] *variableDeclaration*	Access control

Variable Assignment

`variable = value`	Assignment
`variable++`	Postfix Increment
`++variable`	Prefix Increment
`variable--`	Postfix Decrement
`--variable`	Prefix Decrement
`variable += value`	Add and assign
`variable -= value`	Subtract and assign
`variable *= value`	Multiply and assign
`variable /= value`	Divide and assign
`variable %= value`	Modulus and assign
`variable &= value`	AND and assign
`variable ¦= value`	OR and assign
`variable ^= value`	XOR and assign
`variable <<= value`	Left-shift and assign
`variable >>= value`	Right-shift and assign
`variable <<<= value`	Zero-fill right-shift and assign

Operators

`arg + arg`	Addition
`arg - arg`	Subtraction
`arg * arg`	Multiplication
`arg / arg`	Division
`arg % arg`	Modulus
`arg < arg`	Less than
`arg > arg`	Greater than
`arg ≤ arg`	Less than or equal to
`arg   arg`	Greater than or equal to
`arg == arg`	Equal
`arg != arg`	Not equal
`arg && arg`	Logical AND

arg ¦¦ *arg*	Logical OR
! *arg*	Logical NOT
arg & *arg*	AND
arg ¦ *arg*	OR
arg ^ *arg*	XOR
arg << *arg*	Left-shift
arg >> *arg*	Right-shift
arg >>> *arg*	Zero-fill right-shift
~ *arg*	Complement
(*type*)*thing*	Casting
arg instanceof class	Instance of
test ? *trueOp* : *falseOp*	Tenary (if) operator

Objects

new *class*();	Create new instance
new *class*(*arg,arg,arg...*)	New instance with parameters
object.variable	Instance variable
object.classvar	Class variable
Class.classvar	Class variable
object.method()	Instance method (no args)
object.method(*arg,arg,arg...*)	Instance method
object.classmethod()	Class method (no args)
object.classmethod(*arg,arg,arg...*)	Class method
Class.classmethod()	Class method (no args)
Class.classmethod(*arg,arg,arg...*)	Class method

Arrays

NOTE   The brackets in this section are parts of the array creation or access statements. They do not denote optional parts as they do in other parts of this appendix.

`type varname[]`	Array variable
`type[] varname`	Array variable
`new type[numElements]`	New array object
`array[index]`	Element access
`array.length`	Length of array

Loops and Conditionals

`if ( test) block`	Conditional
`else block`	Conditional with `else`

`switch (test) {`
`    case value : block`
`    case value : block`
`    ...`
`    default : block`
`}`
	switch (only with integer or char types)

`for (initializer,` `test, change ) block`	for loop
`while ( test ) block`	while loop
`do block` `while (test)`	do loop
`break [ label ]`	break from loop or `switch`
`continue [ label ]`	continue loops
`label:`	Labeled loops

Class Definitions

`class classname` *`block`*	Simple Class definition

Any of the following optional modifiers can be added to the class definition:

`[ final ] class` *`classname block`*	No subclasses
`[ abstract ] class` *`classname block`*	Cannot be instantiated
`[ public ] class` *`classname block`*	Accessible outside package
`class` *`classname`* `[ extends` *`Superclass`* `]` *`block`*	Define superclass
`class` *`classname`* `[ implements` *`interfaces`* `]` *`block`*	Implement one or more interfaces

Method and Constructor Definitions

The basic method looks like this, where *`returnType`* is a type name, a class name, or void.

`returnType methodName``()` *`block`*	Basic method
`returnType methodName``(`*`parameter, parameter, ...`*`)` *`block`*	Method with parameters

Method parameters look like this:

`type parameterName`

Method variations can include any of the following optional keywords:

`[ abstract ]` *`returnType methodName`*`()` *`block`*	Abstract method
`[ static ]` *`returnType methodName`*`()` *`block`*	Class method
`[ native ]` *`returnType methodName`*`()` *`block`*	Native method
`[ final ]` *`returnType methodName`*`()` *`block`*	final method

`[ synchronized ] `*`returnType`*`  `*`methodName`*`() `*`block`*	Thread lock before executing
`[ public ¦ private ¦  protected ] `*`returnType methodName`*`()`	Block access control

Constructors look like this:

`classname``() `*`block`*	basic constructor
`classname``(`*`parameter, parameter,  parameter...`*`) `*`block`*	constructor with parameters
`[ public ¦ private ¦  protected] `*`classname`*`()`*`block`*	Access control

In the method/constructor body, you can use these references and methods:

`this`	Refers to current object
`super`	Refers to superclass
`super.`*`methodName`*`()`	Call a superclass's method
`this(...)`	Calls class's constructor
`super(...)`	Calls superclass's constructor
`return [ `*`value`*` ]`	Returns a value

Packages, Interfaces, and Importing

`import `*`package.className`*	Imports specific class name
`import `*`package`*`.*`	Imports all classes in package
`package `*`packagename`*	Classes in this file belong to this package

`interface interfaceName [ extends anotherInterface ] block`

`[ public ] interface interfaceName block`

`[ abstract ] interface interfaceName block`

Exceptions and Guarding

`synchronized ( object ) block`	Waits for lock on *object*
`try block`	Guarded statements
`catch ( exception ) block`	Executed if *exception* is thrown
`[ finally block ]`	Always executed

`try block`
`[ catch ( exception ) block ]`
`finally block`
	Same as previous example (can use optional catch or finally, but not both)

Class Hierarchy Diagrams

by Charles L. Perkins

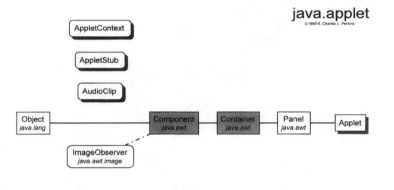

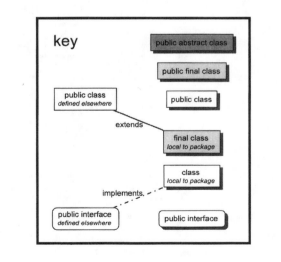

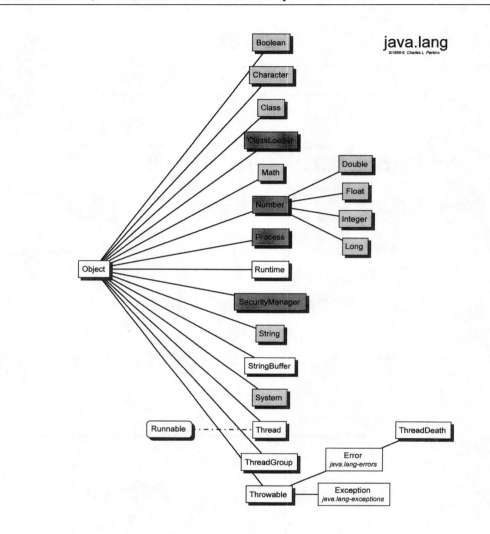

java.lang
©1995-6, Charles L. Perkins

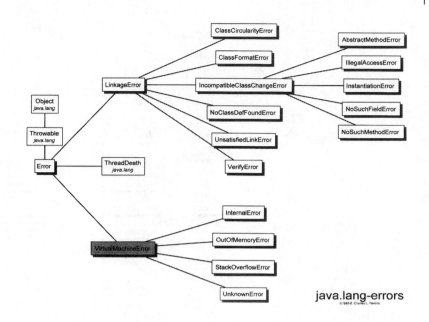

java.lang-errors

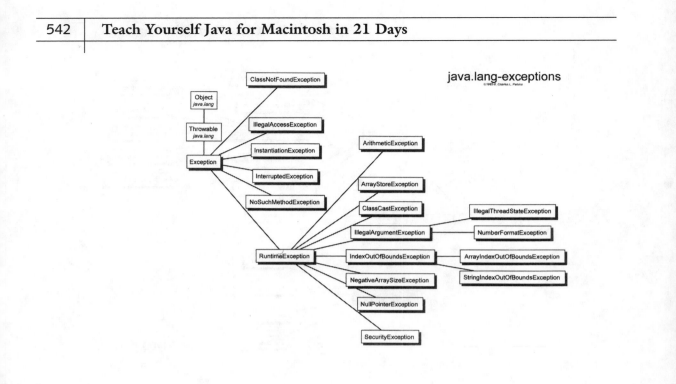

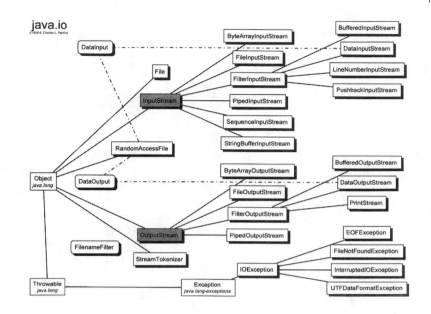

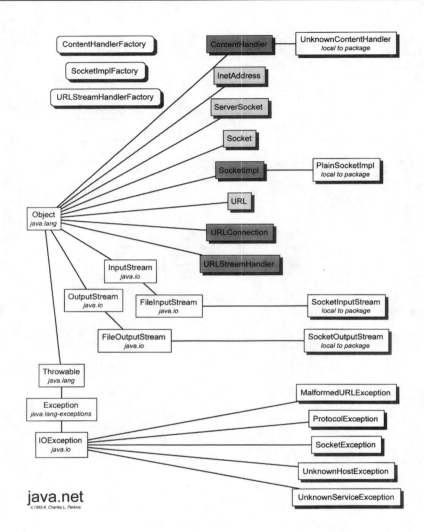

java.net

© 1995-6, Charles L. Perkins

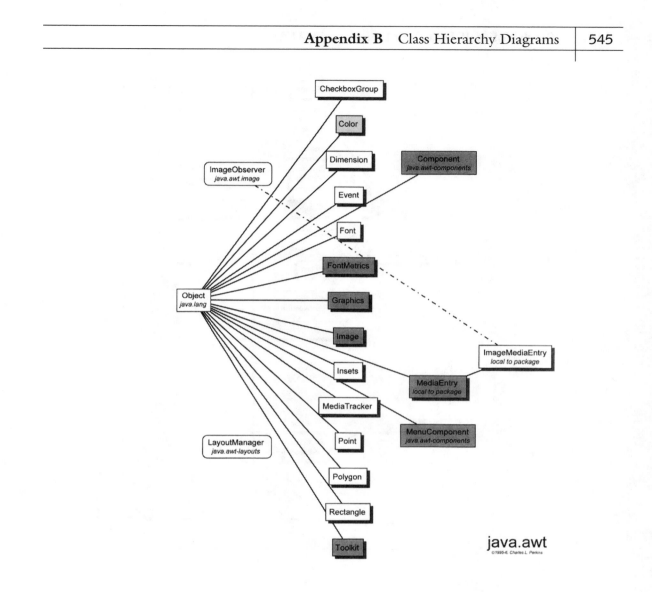

java.awt

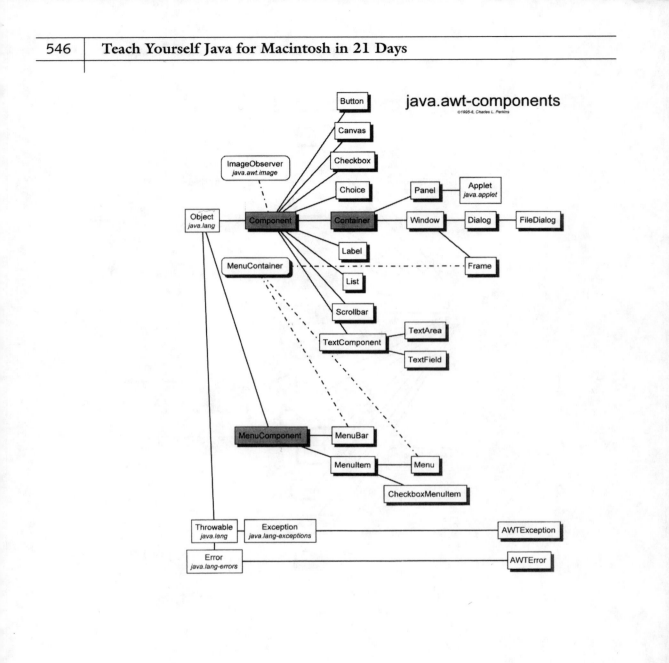

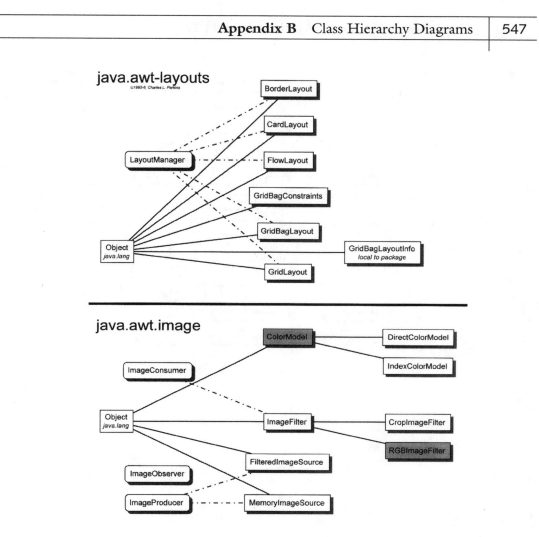

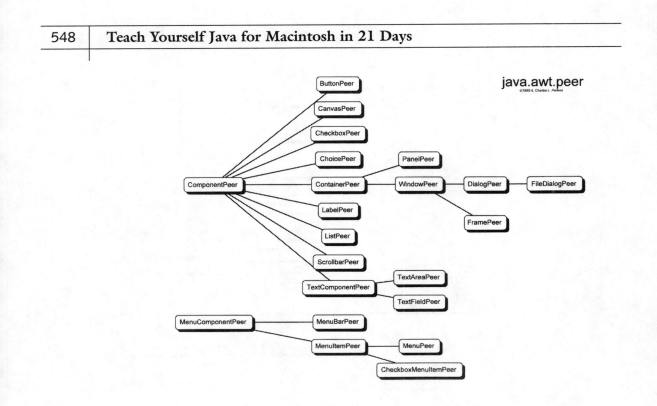

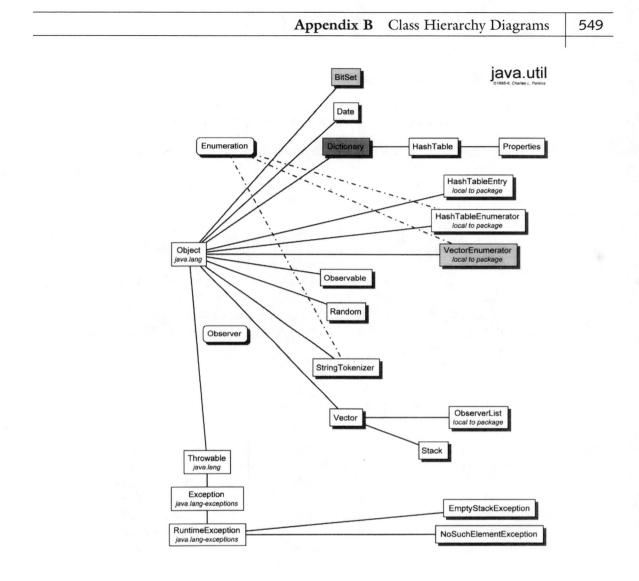

About These Diagrams

The diagrams in this appendix are class hierarchy diagrams for the package java and for all the subpackages recursively below it in the Java beta binary release.

Each page contains the class hierarchy for one package (or a subtree of a particularly large package) with all its interfaces included, and each class in this tree is shown attached to its superclasses, even if they are on another page. A detailed key is located on the first page of this appendix.

NOTE

Win32Process and UNIXProcess appear in their respective distributions of Java, but both implement (essentially) the same protocol as their common abstract superclass—Process—so only it was included. This means that are no platform-dependent classes in the diagrams. (Of course, each release actually has some such classes in its .class directories.) Several abstract classes have no subclasses in the documented library, but any concrete implementation of Java would define subclasses of them.

I supplemented the (incomplete) API documentation by looking through all the source files (below src/java) to find all the (missing) package classes and their relationships.

I've heard there are various programs that auto-lay out hierarchies for you, but I did these the old-fashioned way (in other words, I *earned* it, as J.H. used to say). One nice side effect is that these diagrams should be more readable than a computer would produce, though you will have to live with my aesthetic choices (sorry). I chose, for example, to attach lines through the center of each class node, something which I think looks and feels better overall (to me) but which on occasion can be a little confusing. Follow lines through the center of the classes (not at the corners, nor along any line not passing through the center) to connect the dots mentally.

The Java Class Library

by Laura Lemay

This appendix provides a general overview of the classes available in the standard Java packages (that is, the classes that are guaranteed to be available in any Java implementation). This appendix is intended for general reference; for more specific information about each class (its inheritance, variables, and methods), as well as the various exceptions for each package, see the API documentation from Sun at http://java.sun.com.

java.lang

The java.lang package contains the classes and interfaces that make up the core Java language.

Interfaces

Cloneable   Interface indicating that an object may be copied or cloned

Runnable   Methods for runnable objects (for example, applets that include threads)

Classes

Boolean	Object wrapper for boolean values
Character	Object wrapper for char values
Class	Run-time representations of classes
ClassLoader	Abstract behavior for handling loading of classes
Compiler	System class that gives access to the Java compiler
Double	Object wrapper for double values
Float	Object wrapper for float values
Integer	Object wrapper for int values
Long	Object wrapper for long values
Math	Utility class for math operations
Number	Superclass of all number classes (Integer, Float, and so on)
Object	Generic Object class, at top of inheritance hierarchy
Process	Processes such as those spawned using methods in the System class
Runtime	The Java run-time
SecurityManager	Abstract behavior for implementing security policies
String	Character strings
StringBuffer	Mutable strings
System	System-based behavior, provided in a platform-independent way
Thread	Methods for managing threads and classes that run in threads
ThreadDeath	Class of objects
ThreadGroup	A group of threads
Throwable	A superclass for errors and exceptions
UNIXProcess	Unix-specific processes
Win32Process	Windows-specific processes

java.util

The `java.util` package contains various utility classes and interfaces, including random numbers, system properties, and other useful utility classes.

Interfaces

Enumeration	Methods for enumerating sets of values
Observer	Methods for enabling classes to be observable by `Observable` objects

Classes

`BitSet`	A set of bits
`Date`	The current system date, as well as methods for generating and parsing dates
`Dictionary`	An abstract class that maps between keys and values (superclass of `HashTable`)
`Hashtable`	A hash table
`Observable`	An abstract class for observable objects
`Properties`	A hashtable that contains behavior for setting and retrieving persistent properties of the system or of a class
`Random`	Utilities for generating random numbers
`Stack`	A stack (a last-in-first-out queue)
`StringTokenizer`	Utilities for splitting strings into individual "tokens"
`Vector`	A growable array, similar to a linked list

java.io

The java.io package provides input and output classes and interfaces for streams and files.

Interfaces

DataInput	Methods for reading machine-independent input streams
DataOutput	Methods for writing machine-independent output streams
FilenameFilter	Methods for filtering file names

Classes

BufferedInputStream	A buffered input stream
BufferedOutputStream	A buffered output stream
ByteArrayInputStream	A byte array buffer for an input stream
ByteArrayOutputStream	A byte array buffer for an output stream
DataInputStream	Enables you to read primitive Java types (ints, chars, booleans, and so on) from a stream in a machine-independent way
DataOutputStream	Enables you to write primitive Java data types (ints, chars, booleans, and so on) to a stream in a machine-independent way
Class	Run-time representations of classes
File	Represents a file on the host's file system
FileDescriptor	Holds onto the Unix-like file descriptor of a file or socket
FileInputStream	An input stream from a file, constructed using a filename or descriptor
FileOutputStream	An output stream to a file, constructed using a file-name or descriptor
FilterInputStream	Abstract class that provides a filter for input streams (and for adding stream functionality such as buffers)

FilterOutputStream	Abstract class that provides a filter for output streams (and for adding stream functionality such as buffers)
InputStream	An abstract class presenting an input stream of bytes; the parent of all input streams in this package
LineNumberInputStream	An input stream that keeps track of line numbers
OutputStream	An abstract class representing an output stream of bytes; the parent of all output streams in this package
PipedInputStream	A piped input stream, which should be connected to a PipedOutputStream to be useful
PipedOutputStream	A piped output stream, which should be connected to a PipedInputStream to be useful
PrintStream	An output stream for printing
PushbackInputStream	An input stream with a 1-byte push back buffer
RandomAccessFile	A random-access input and output file that can be constructed from filenames, descriptors, or objects
SequenceInputStream	Converts a sequence of input streams into a single input steam
StreamTokenizer	Converts an input stream into a series of individual tokens
StringBufferInputStream	Use a string buffer as an input stream to a StringBuffer object

java.net

The java.net package contains classes and interfaces for performing network operations, such as sockets and URLs.

Interfaces

ContentHandlerFactory	Methods for creating ContentHandler objects
SocketImplFactory	Methods for creating socket implementations (instance of the SocketImpl class)
URLStreamHandlerFactory	Methods for creating URLStreamHandler objects

Classes

ContentHandler	A class that can read data from a URL connection and construct the appropriate local object, based on mime types
DatagramPacket	A datagram packet (UDP)
DatagramSocket	A datagram socket
InetAddress	An object representation of an Internet host (host name, IP address)
ServerSocket	An abstract server-side socket
Socket	An abstract socket
SocketImpl	An abstract class for specific socket implementations
URL	An object representation of a URL
URLConnection	A socket that can handle various Web-based protocols (http, ftp, and so on)
URLEncoder	Turns strings into X-WWW-form-URL coded format
URLStreamHandler	Abstract class for managing streams to object references by URLs

java.awt

The java.awt package contains the classes and interfaces that make up the Abstract Window Toolkit.

Interfaces

LayoutManager	Methods for laying out containers
MenuContainer	Methods for menu-related containers

Classes

BorderLayout	A layout manager for arranging items in border formation

Button	A UI pushbutton
Canvas	A canvas for drawing and performing other graphics operations
CardLayout	A layout manager for HyperCard-like metaphors
Checkbox	A checkbox
CheckboxGroup	A group of exclusive checkboxes (radio buttons)
CheckboxMenuItem	A toggle menu item
Choice	A popup menu of choices
Color	An abstract representation of a color
Component	The generic class for all UI components
Container	A component that can hold other components or containers
Dialog	A window for brief interactions with users
Dimension	Width and height
Event	An class representing events called by the system or generated by user input
FileDialog	A dialog for getting file names from the local file system
FlowLayout	A layout manager that lays out objects from left to right in rows
Font	An abstract representation of a font
FontMetrics	Information about a specific font's character shapes and height and width information
Frame	A top-level window with a title
Graphics	A representation of a graphics context and methods to draw and paint shapes and objects
GridBagConstraints	Constraints for components laid out using GridBagLayout
GridBagLayout	A layout manager that aligns components horizontally and vertically based on their values from GridBagConstraints
GridLayout	A layout manager with rows and columns; elements are added to each cell in the grid

Image	An abstract representation of a bitmap image
Insets	Distances from the outer border of the window to lay out components
Label	A text label for UI components
List	A scrolling list
MediaTracker	A way to keep track of the status of media objects being loaded over the net
Menu	A menu, which can contain menu items and is a container on a menu bar
MenuBar	A menu bar (container for menus)
MenuComponent	The superclass of all menu elements
MenuItem	An individual menu item
Panel	A container that is displayed
Point	x and y coordinates
Polygon	A set of points
Rectangle	x and y coordinates for the top corner, plus width and height
Scrollbar	A UI scrollbar object
TextArea	A multiline, scrollable, editable text field
TextComponent	The superclass of all editable text components
TextField	A fixed-size editable text field
Toolkit	Binds the abstract AWT classes to a platform-specific toolkit implementation
Window	A top-level window, and the superclass of the Frame and Dialog classes

java.awt.image

The java.awt.image package is a subpackage of the AWT that provides classes for managing bitmap images.

Interfaces

ImageConsumer	Methods for receiving image data filters through an ImageProducer
ImageObserver	Methods to keep track of the loading and construction of an image
ImageProducer	Methods to construct or filter image data

Classes

ColorModel	A class for managing color information for images
CropImageFilter	A filter for cropping images to a particular size
DirectColorModel	A specific color model for managing and translating pixel color values
FilteredImageSource	An ImageProducer that takes an image and an ImageFilter object and produces an image for an ImageConsumer
ImageFilter	A filter that takes image data from an ImageProducer, modifies it in some way, and hands it off to a ImageConsumer
IndexColorModel	A specific color model for managing and translating color values in a fixed-color map
MemoryImageSource	An image producer to construct an image by hand
PixelGrabber	An ImageConsumer that retrieves a subset of the pixels in an image
RGBImageFilter	A filter for modifying the RBG values of pixels in RGB images

java.awt.peer

The `java.awt.peer` package is a subpackage of AWT that contains abstract classes to link AWT to the code to display platform-specific interfaces elements (for example, Motif, Macintosh, Windows 95).

Interfaces

ButtonPeer	Peer for the Button class
CanvasPeer	Peer for the Canvas class
CheckboxMenuItemPeer	Peer for the CheckboxMenuItem class
CheckboxPeer	Peer for the Checkbox class
ChoicePeer	Peer for the Choice class
ComponentPeer	Peer for the Component class
ContainerPeer	Peer for the Container class
DialogPeer	Peer for the Dialog class

java.applet

The `java.applet` package provides applet-specific behavior.

Interfaces

AppletContext	Methods to refer to the applet's context
AppletStub	Methods for nonbrowser applet viewers
AudioClip	Methods for playing audio files

Classes

Applet	The base applet class

How Java Differs from C and C++

by Laura Lemay

This appendix contains a description of most of the major differences between C, C++, and the Java language. If you are a programmer familiar with either C or C++, you may want to review this appendix to catch some of the common mistakes and assumptions programmers make when using Java.

Pointers

Java does not have an explicit pointer type. Instead of pointers, all references to objects—including variable assignments, arguments passed into methods, and array elements—are accomplished by using implicit references. References and pointers are essentially the same thing except that you can't do pointer arithmetic on references (nor do you need to).

Reference semantics also enable structures such as linked lists to be created easily in Java without explicit pointers; merely create a linked list node with variables that point to the next and the previous node. Then, to insert items in the list, assign those variables to other node objects.

Arrays

Arrays in Java are first class objects, and references to arrays and their contents are accomplished through explicit references rather than via point arithmetic. Array boundaries are strictly enforced; attempting to read past the ends of an array is a compile or run-time error. As with other objects, passing an array to a method passes the original reference to that array, so changing the contents of that array reference changes the original array object.

Arrays of objects are arrays of references to objects, and are not automatically initialized to contain actual objects. Using the following Java code produces an array of type `MyObject` with 10 elements, but that array initially contains only nulls:

```
MyObject arrayofobjs[] = new MyObject[10];
```

You must now add actual `MyObject` objects to that array:

```
for (int i; i< arrayofobjs.length; i++) {
    arrayofobjs[i] = new MyObject();
```

Java does not support multidimensional arrays as in C and C++. In Java, you must create arrays that contain other arrays.

Strings

Strings in C and C++ are arrays of characters, terminated by a null character (`\0`). To operate on and manage strings, you treat them as you would any other arrays, with all the inherent difficulties of keeping track of pointer arithmetic and being careful not to stray off the end of the array.

Strings in Java are objects, and all methods that operate on strings can treat the string as a complete entity. Strings are not terminated by a null, nor can you accidentally overstep the end of a string (like arrays, string boundaries are strictly enforced).

Memory Management

All memory management in Java is automatic; memory is allocated automatically when an object is created, and a run-time garbage collector frees that memory when the object is no longer in use. C's `malloc()` and `free()` functions do not exist in Java.

To "force" an object to be freed, remove all references to that object (assign variables to null, remove the object from arrays, and so on). The next time the Java CG runs, that object is reclaimed.

Data Types

As mentioned in the early part of this book, all Java primitive data types (`char`, `int`, `long`, and so on) have consistent sizes and behavior across platforms and operating systems. There are no unsigned data types as in C and C++.

The boolean primitive data type can have two values: true or false. boolean is not an integer, nor can it be treated as one, although you can cast 0 or 1 (integers) to boolean types in Java.

Composite data types are accomplished in Java exclusively through the use of class definitions. The struct, union, and typedef keywords have all been removed in favor of classes.

Casting between data types is much more controlled in Java; automatic casting occurs only when there will be no loss of information. All other casts must be explicit. The primitive data types (int, float, long, char, boolean, and so on) cannot be cast to objects or vice versa; there are methods and special "wrapper" classes to convert values between objects and primitive types.

Operators

Operator precedence and association behaves as it does in C. Note, however, that the new keyword (for creating a new object) binds tighter than dot notation (.), which is different behavior from C++. In particular, note the following expression:

```
new foo().bar;
```

This expression operates as if it were written like this:

```
(new foo()).bar;
```

Operator overloading, as in C++, cannot be accomplished in Java.

The >>> operator produces an unsigned logical right shift (remember, there are no unsigned integer data types).

The + operator can be used to concatenate strings.

Control Flow

Although the if, while, for, and do statements in Java are syntactically the same as they are in C and C++, there is one significant difference. The test expression for each control flow construct must return an actual boolean value (true or false). In C and C++, the expression can return an integer.

Arguments

Java does not support mechanisms for variable-length argument lists to functions as in C and C++. All method definitions must have a specific number of arguments.

Command-line arguments in Java behave differently from those in C and C++. The first element in the argument vector (`argv[0]`) in C and C++ is the name of the program itself; in Java, that first argument is the first of the additional arguments. In other words, in Java, `argv[0]` is `argv[1]` in C and C++; there is no way to get hold of the actual name of the Java program.

Other Differences

The following other minor differences from C and C++ exist in Java:

☐ Java does not have a preprocessor, so it does not have `#defines` or macros. Constants can be created by declaring class and instance variables with the `final` keyword.

☐ Java does not have template classes as in C++.

☐ Java does not include C's `const` keyword or the capability to pass by `const` reference explicitly.

☐ Java is singly inherited, with multiple-inheritance features provided through interfaces.

☐ All functions are implemented as methods and tied to objects or classes.

☐ The `goto` keyword does not exist in Java (it's a reserved word, but currently unimplemented). You can, however, use labeled `breaks` and `continues` to break out of and continue executing loops.

Roaster and Regular Expressions

by Timothy Webster

"Regular expression" is a syntax used for specifying patterns of text characters. If you've ever used the Unix operating system or a language like Perl, you're probably familiar with regular expressions. If you've spent most of your time working within Mac applications, you may have never heard of regular expressions, or as our Unix-usin' cousins say, *regexps*. Don't worry—you were probably invited to a few parties that the Unix crew missed out on, and regular expressions aren't that hard to figure out.

The most important idea to latch onto is that a regular expression consists of symbols that stand for themselves—an "a" is an "a," and a "rose" is a "rose"—and metasymbols that stand for ideas—"." stands for "any character except the end of a line" and "[a-z]" stands for "any character between lowercase 'a' and lowercase 'z.'" Once you have an idea of how the metacharacters work, you're all set.

We'll use as an example my favorite paragraph from *Moby Dick:*

```
Were this world an endless plain, and by sailing eastward we could for ever reach
new distances, and discover sights more sweet and strange than any Cyclades or
Islands of King Solomon, then there were promise in the voyage. But in pursuit of
those far mysteries we dream of, or in tormented chase of that demon phantom that,
some time or another, swims before all human hearts; while chasing such over his
round globe, they either lead us on in barren mazes or midway leave us whelmed.
```

Roaster will recognize regular expressions as such only if the Regexp checkbox in the search window is checked. If you're experimenting here, it's best to check the Batch checkbox as well, so you can see at once all the matches for a given expression. *Don't* put your expressions between quotation marks—just type them into the Search field.

Here's a basic introduction to metacharacters:

. The "." character matches everything—letters, numbers, spaces—*except* end-of-line characters. For example, if we enter the expression "m.n", searching our paragraph matches "Solomon", "tormented", "demon", and "human". The characters need not be in the same word: "s.m" matches "some" and "sights more".

* The character "*" is an operator that means "match any number (including the number zero) of the preceding character, or group of characters." For example, " o.*f " matches all strings that start with " o", end with "f ", and don't break from one line to another. *The spaces are important!* In our text, " o.*f " matches eight strings, including "or islands of", "of, or in tormented chase of", and simply "of".

+ The character "+" works pretty much like "*", but it must find at least one instance of the preceding character. " o.+f " would find "or islands of" and "of, or in tormented chase of", but *not* "of".

? The "?" character matches the preceding character once, or not at all. For example, " any?" matches " an", " any", and " and".

[] The "[]" characters specify a set of characters to be matched. For example, [ab] specifies "the characther 'a' or the character 'b,'" and [a-z] specifies the characters "a" through "z." If we search our paragraph for " o[rf]", it returns "or" or "of".

^ The "^" character constrains your search to matches that occur at the beginnings of a line. For example, searching on "^an" in the paragraph above returns "another", but not "an", because all the instances of "an" are at the ends of lines.

$ The "$" character constrains the search to matches at the ends of lines. Searching on "or$" finds only the "or" at the end of line 4—not the "or" in "Cyclades or islands".

¦ The "¦" character means "or." Searching on "sweet¦strange" in our sample paragraph returns both "sweet" and "strange".

\ The "\" character is used to signify that the following metacharacter is to be interpreted literally—"\." matches ".", "\$" matches "$", etc.

NOTE

Roaster doesn't support some of the special operators that may be familiar to seasoned *grepistas,* such as \b (which matches the beginning or end of a word) and things like backreferences. A future version of Roaster may support these metacharacters.

Most significantly, Roaster doesn't support \w and \W, which signify "word" and "nonword" characters, but it doesn't differentiate between spaces and tabs, either. So, if you want to find a word that starts with "a," you need to enter " a.* ", rather than "\wa.*\w". This is unfortunate, as " a.* " finds all the space-terminated strings that start with a word that start with "a," rather than just the words that start with "a."

For the Latest Java™ News & Information, Visit Roaster on the Web

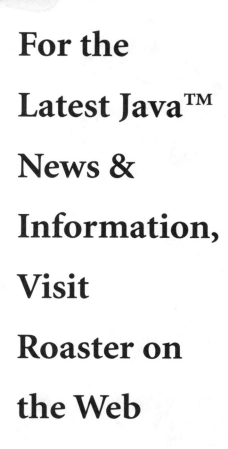

At www.roaster.com you can:

- subscribe to the Roaster-announce mailing list
- keep up to date on the latest Java news and information
- subscribe to the java-mac or java-win mailing lists
- check out applets that were created with Roaster

Stop by soon or send email to info@natural.com to find out all the latest answers to your questions about Roaster and Java.

Ni Natural Intelligence

www.roaster.com

Natural Intelligence

DragStrip™

The Ultimate Desktop Organizer

DragStrip 2.0 is the Ultimate Desktop Organizer for the Macintosh. Why? It's simple. DragStrip allows you to access your most frequently used files, folders, and applications, all with a click of your mouse. DragStrip also supports plug-in Additions that add functionality to DragStrip in the form of a CD-player, calendar, volume control, and much, much more!

The CD that comes with this book includes a full copy of DragStrip 1.0. We are confident that you will find DragStrip so useful that you will want to upgrade to the NEW DragStrip 2.0 as soon as possible.

Orders & Information FAX	800-999-4649 orders@natural.com info@natural.com 617-492-7425	Upgrade to DragStrip 2.0 for only **$19.95** (a $40.00 savings!)

Upgrade/Registration Form

Company

Name

Address

City _____ State

Zip _____ Phone (   )

Payment Method (check one)

☐ Visa ☐ MasterCard ☐ Discover ☐ American Express

Card # _____ Exp. Date

Signature

DragStrip 2.0 Upgrade	$19.95
Tax for MA orders 5%	
U.S. S&H	$5.00
Total	

Send to:
Natural Intelligence, Inc.
725 Concord Avenue
Cambridge, MA 02138-1052
617-876-4876
fax 617-492-7425
orders@natural.com
www.natural.com

THE MACMILLAN INFORMATION SUPERLIBRARY™

Free information and vast computer resources from the world's leading computer book publisher—online!

FIND THE BOOKS THAT ARE RIGHT FOR YOU!

A complete online catalog, plus sample chapters and tables of contents give you an in-depth look at *all* of our books, including hard-to-find titles. It's the best way to find the books you need!

● **STAY INFORMED** with the latest computer industry news through our online newsletter, press releases, and customized Information SuperLibrary Reports.

● **GET FAST ANSWERS** to your questions about MCP books and software.

● **VISIT** our online bookstore for the latest information and editions!

● **COMMUNICATE** with our expert authors through e-mail and conferences.

● **DOWNLOAD SOFTWARE** from the immense MCP library:
- Source code and files from MCP books
- The best shareware, freeware, and demos

● **DISCOVER HOT SPOTS** on other parts of the Internet.

● **WIN BOOKS** in ongoing contests and giveaways!

TO PLUG INTO MCP: ➤ WORLD WIDE WEB: **http://www.SuperLibrary.com**

FTP: ftp.mcp.com

REGISTRATION CARD

Teach Yourself Java for Macintosh in 21 Days

Hayden Books

Name _____ Title _____

Company_____Type of business _____

Address _____

City/State/ZIP _____

Have you used these types of books before? ☐ yes   ☐ no

If yes, which ones? _____

_____

How many computer books do you purchase each year? ☐ 1–5   ☐ 6 or more

How did you learn about this book? _____

☐ recommended by a friend   ☐ received ad in mail
☐ recommended by store personnel   ☐ read book review
☐ saw in catalog   ☐ saw on bookshelf

Where did you purchase this book? _____

Which applications do you currently use? _____

Which computer magazines do you subscribe to? _____

What trade shows do you attend? _____

Please number the top three factors that most influenced your decision for this book purchase.

☐ cover   ☐ price
☐ approach to content ☐ author's reputation
☐ logo   ☐ publisher's reputation
☐ layout/design   ☐ other _____

Would you like to be placed on our preferred mailing list? ☐ yes   ☐ no   e-mail address _____

☐ **I would like to see my name in print!** You may use my name and quote me in future Hayden products and promotions. My daytime phone number is _____

Comments _____

_____

_____

Hayden Books   Attn: Product Marketing ◆ 201 West 103rd Street ◆ Indianapolis, Indiana 46290 USA

Fax to **317-581-3576**   Visit our Web Page   **http://WWW.MCP.com/hayden/**

Fold Here

BUSINESS REPLY MAIL
FIRST-CLASS MAIL PERMIT NO. 9918 INDIANAPOLIS IN

POSTAGE WILL BE PAID BY THE ADDRESSEE

HAYDEN BOOKS
Attn: Product Marketing
201 W 103RD ST
INDIANAPOLIS IN 46290-9058

IMPORTANT: READ CAREFULLY BEFORE BREAKING THE SEAL AND OPEN-
ING THIS PACKAGE!

NATURAL INTELLIGENCE LICENSES THE ENCLOSED SOFTWARE TO YOU
ONLY UPON THE CONDITION THAT YOU ACCEPT ALL OF THE TERMS CON-
TAINED IN THIS LICENSE AGREEMENT. OPENING THE PACKAGE CONSTI-
TUTES YOUR ACCEPTANCE OF THESE TERMS. IF YOU DO NOT AGREE WITH
THIS LICENSE, DO NOT OPEN THE PACKAGE. PROMPTLY RETURN THE UN-
OPENED PACKAGE TO THE PLACE WHERE YOU OBTAINED IT AND YOUR
MONEY WILL BE REFUNDED.

License.

The software that accompanies this license, including the program(s) and electronic documentation (referred to collectively throughout this agreement as the "Software"), is the
property of Natural Intelligence, Inc. or its licensors and is protected by United States
copyright law and international copyright conventions. Natural Intelligence and its licensors retain all intellectual property rights including but not limited to patent, trademark,
copyright, and trade secret rights in the Software. You agree that the Software is confiden-
tial and is a trade secret of and is owned by Natural Intelligence, Inc. You agree to do nothing inconsistent with such ownership. While Natural Intelligence and its licensors continue
to own the Software, you will have certain rights to use the Software after your acceptance
of this license. Except as may be modified by a license addendum which accompanies this
license or an upgrade to the Software, your rights and obligations with respect to the use of
this Software are as follows:

You may

(1) use one copy of the Software on a single computer at any one time. This means that
you can use the Software at home, at work, or on another computer provided that only
you, the licensee, use the program and that you use only one copy at a time. You must
purchase a license for each additional user. Site licenses and multi-user licenses are available.
Please contact Natural Intelligence for further details.

(2) make one copy of the software for archival purposes, or copy the software onto the hard
disk of your computer and retain the original for archival purposes. All copies of the Software must contain all copyright and restrictive legends appearing in the original copy of the
Software in their entirety and must not be omitted, obscured or otherwise misrepresented.

(3) use the Software over a network, provided that you have a licensed copy of the Software for each user that can access the Software over that network and that each user is only using the Software from one computer at a time in accordance with (1) above; and

(4) after written notice to Natural Intelligence, transfer the Software on a permanent basis to another person or entity, provided that you retain no copies of the Software and the transferee agrees to the terms of this agreement. All of your rights to use the Software will revert back to Natural Intelligence upon the termination of this license.

Because the Software is a Natural Intelligence development environment product, you have a royalty-free right to include object code derived from the libraries in programs that you develop using the Software and you also have the right to use, distribute, and license such programs without payment of any further license fees, so long as a copyright notice sufficient to protect your copyright in the program is included in the graphic display of your programs and on the labels affixed to the media on which your program is distributed. (Example: "Copyright © 1996 [Licensee's Name]. All rights reserved.")

You may not

(1) copy the electronic documentation that accompanies the Software except as provided above;

(2) sublicense, rent, or lease the Software in whole or in part;

(3) reverse engineer, decompile, disassemble, modify, translate, make any attempt to discover the source code of the Software, or create derivative works from the Software; or

(4) use a previous version or copy of the Software after you have received a disk replacement set or an upgraded version as a replacement of the prior version unless specifically authorized to do so in an addendum to this agreement. The upgraded version constitutes a single product with the Software that you upgraded. You cannot allow or make both versions available for use by two different people at the same time, nor can the versions be transferred separately.

Limited Warranty

Macmillan Computer Publishing warrants that the physical media on which the Software is distributed will be free from defects in materials and workmanship for a period of 90 days from the date purchase. Macmillan Computer Publishing and Natural Intelligence, Inc.'s entire liability and your sole remedy will be a replacement of the defective media. To obtain a replacement you must return the entire package, including receipt, to the authorized dealer from whom it was purchased, or to Macmillan Computer Publishing, within the 90 day warranty period.

Natural Intelligence does not warrant that the Software will meet your requirements or that operation of the Software will be uninterrupted or that the Software will be error-free, or that the defects in the Software will be corrected. You expressly acknowledge and agree that use of the Software is at your sole risk. The Software is provided "AS IS" without warranty of any kind. Natural Intelligence does not warrant or make any representations regarding the use or the results of the use of the Software, including the documentation, in terms of their correctness, accuracy, reliability, or otherwise.

THE ABOVE WARRANTIES ARE EXCLUSIVE AND IN LIEU OF ALL OTHER WARRANTIES, WHETHER EXPRESS OR IMPLIED, INCLUDING THE IMPLIED WARRANTIES OF MERCHANTABILITY, FITNESS FOR A PARTICULAR PUR-POSE, AND NON-INFRINGEMENT. THIS WARRANTY GIVES YOU SPECIFIC LEGAL RIGHTS. YOU MAY HAVE OTHER RIGHTS, WHICH VARY FROM STATE TO STATE.

Disclaimer of Liability

IN NO EVENT WILL NATURAL INTELLIGENCE BE LIABLE TO YOU FOR ANY SPECIAL, CONSEQUENTIAL, INDIRECT, OR SIMILAR DAMAGES, INCLUDING ANY LOST PROFITS OR LOST DATA ARISING OUT OF THE USE OR INABILITY TO USE THE SOFTWARE, EVEN IF NATURAL INTELLIGENCE HAS BEEN AD-VISED OF THE POSSIBILITY OF SUCH DAMAGES. SOME STATES DO NOT AL-LOW THE LIMITATION OR EXCLUSION OF LIABILITY FOR INCIDENTAL OR CONSEQUENTIAL DAMAGES SO THE ABOVE LIMITATION MAY NOT APPLY TO YOU. IN NO CASE SHALL NATURAL INTELLIGENCE'S LIABILITY EXCEED THE PURCHASE PRICE OF THE SOFTWARE. The disclaimers and limitations set forth above will apply regardless of whether you accept the Software.

US Government Restricted Rights

RESTRICTED RIGHTS LEGEND. Use, duplication, or disclosure by the Government is subject to restrictions as set forth in subparagraph (c) (1) (ii) of the Rights in Technical Data and Computer Software clause at DFARS 252.227-7013 or subparagraphs (c) (1) and (2) of the Commercial Computer Software-Restricted Rights clause at 48 CFR 52.227-19, as applicable.

General

This agreement will be governed by the laws of the Commonwealth of Massachusetts. This agreement may only be modified by a license addendum that accompanies this license or an upgrade to the Software, or by a written document that has been signed by both you and an officer of Natural Intelligence. This license automatically terminates if the licensee violates any of the requirements of this license. You agree to abide by the rules, regulations, and restrictions for export established by the United States Government.

Should you have questions concerning this agreement, or if you desire to contact Natural Intelligence for any reason, please write: Roaster Customer Service, Natural Intelligence, Inc., 725 Concord Avenue., Cambridge MA 02138-1052 or by Internet to info@natural.com.

The Java Developer's Kit (JDK) from Sun Microsystems, Inc. is included in its entirety on the Roaster CD. Use of the JDK is subject to the terms and conditions of the Sun Microsystems' license and copyright information contained in the JDK folder contained herein. You must accept the Sun license in order to use the JDK. The JDK is required for running applets on your Macintosh.